MW01253071

Advances in Exercise and Health for People With Mobility Limitations

David Hollar
Editor

Advances in Exercise and Health for People With Mobility Limitations

Editor
David Hollar
Health Administration
Pfeiffer University
Misenheimer, NC, USA

ISBN 978-3-319-98451-3 ISBN 978-3-319-98452-0 (eBook)
https://doi.org/10.1007/978-3-319-98452-0

Library of Congress Control Number: 2018958911

This Springer imprint is published by the registered company Springer Nature Switzerland AG
The registered company address is: Gewerbestrasse 11, 6330 Cham, Switzerland

For our families

Preface

The purpose of this book is to provide public health, disability, and rehabilitation professionals/practitioners evidence-based science and advocacy perspectives with respect to health disparities faced by people with disabilities, especially people with mobility limitations, alternative methods of rehabilitation and exercise science for this population, assistive device technology, and improved access to health care, employment, and social participation. The book should be of interest to a broad audience, including but not limited to public health practitioners and educators, disability and rehabilitation researchers, clinicians and sports medicine practitioners, and disability advocates.

According to the National Institute on Disability, Independent Living, and Rehabilitation Research (NIDILRR), approximately 57 million Americans live with a disability. Disability severity and types vary considerably, such that each individual with a disability faces unique physical, social, and environmental barriers in order to enjoy quality of life and full participation in society. A large research literature shows that people with disabilities face substantial employment and health disparities compared to people without disabilities. People with mobility limitations often experience secondary conditions to compound their primary disability. Several studies have shown that people living with mobility limitations are significantly more likely to experience obesity and lack of access to physical exercise. Other studies have shown that access to proper physical examination facilities and equipment remains a substantial barrier in many clinics and hospitals despite the enactment of the Americans with Disabilities Act 25 years ago. Research on alternative exercise programs and new assistive device technologies offers promise to improve physical functioning and exercise for people with mobility limitations. Furthermore, increased focus on biopsychosocial over traditional medical models for disability will help policymakers and the public to recognize the complex, contextual issues (e.g., personal, social, environmental) that impact the lives of people with disabilities. Moreover, educating the public, health providers, educators, and other professionals on the need and variety of accommodations to improve exercise access plus opportunity continues to constitute both a challenge and an area of increased focus.

The book begins with Chap. 1, a personal testimony by Lee Groce, an individual living with a disability who has been successful, actively exercises, and advocates for increased access and the rights of people with disabilities. With Chap. 2, David Hollar provides an overview of both the United States and global prevalence of disability, which illustrates that most people know someone with a disability. In Chap. 3, Linda Haymes, Debra Cote, and Keith Storey outline a major emphasis of disability movements that is central to increasing exercise and access to health facilities: community integration.

Lynda Lahti Anderson, Sarah MapelLentz, and Sheryl Larson follow with Chap. 4, where they discuss the widespread health and other disparities faced by people living with disabilities. In Chap. 5, David Hollar covers the major aspects of musculoskeletal physiology that are pertinent to mobility limitations, rehabilitation, and the design of assistive device technologies to improve performance for people living with mobility limitations. Hollar continues with Chap. 6, which logically follows with an overview of major technological devices, especially focusing on the new exoskeletons and various limb prosthetics that are improving physical functioning and exercise opportunities that can impact anyone with or without disabilities.

With Chap. 7, Sherry Adams addresses exercise and physical therapeutic approaches to rehabilitation and the improvement of functioning for various types of disabilities. In Chap. 8, Nur Onvural discusses the economic aspects of assistive device technologies and how the growth of these technologies will impact the health-care industry while simultaneously benefitting consumers with disabilities. In Chap. 9, Meredith Gammons describe radiological and other imaging technologies that provide improved diagnostics for musculoskeletal physiology in rehabilitation and sports medicine.

Beginning with Chap. 10, Jennifer Lewis addresses major social, legal, and cultural barriers faced by people with disabilities to obtain equal access to education, employment, health and exercise, basic participation in society that is the primary focus of the modern disability movement. David Hollar follows with Chap. 11 with a perspective on social selectionist models of human behavior that create these barriers, and he posits research-based deficiencies in human thinking that might contribute to these barriers and too many false perceptions of disability.

Chapters 12, 13, and 14 by Katerina Ivanov and David Hollar deal with improved exercise and health access programs that can benefit people living with mobility limitations. Hollar's concluding Chaps. 13 and 14 focus on lifespan educational interventions starting from early ages that build sport and exercise self-concepts that can promote inclusive sports modifications and greater participation in physical fitness programs by people with disabilities.

The chapters are by no means conclusive in describing efforts towards improving exercise and health for people with mobility limitations and other disabilities. The convergence of technology, improved public attitudes, and effective policies to promote health and access for this population is gradually gaining momentum. We definitely need schools and institutions to promote health and exercise for this vast population of human diversity that can include any of us at any time.

Misenheimer, NC, USA David Hollar

Acknowledgments

I thank my wife, Paige, and daughter, Brooke, for their tremendous support during the writing of this book, plus colleagues Drs. Barnett Parker, Nur Onvural, Katerina Ivanov, Sherry Adams, Mr. Lee Groce, and the chapter authors. We thank Janet Kim, Acquisitions Editor at Springer, for encouraging and guiding this project.

Acknowledgments

Contents

About the Authors

Sherry Adams is an assistant professor at Pfeiffer University in Misenheimer, North Carolina. Her work has centered around traumatic brain injury (TBI)/concussion and the effect on respiration, somatosensory, somatomotor, and anxiety in animals and humans. She has found that animals have a disruption in the respiratory network evidenced by a period of apnea at the onset of a TBI. The animals also displayed disruption in somatosensory and somatomotor function chronically following the injuries. Anxiety is also enhanced in animals that have been exposed to a TBI. Her current research focuses on changes in respiratory function when athletes are exposed to a respiratory load similar to what they might experience during intensive play on the field. This respiratory load is applied during a submaximal exercise bout with physiological parameters and perception measurements recorded.

Lynda Lahti Anderson is a PhD candidate in rehabilitation science with a focus on supporting health and wellness for people with disabilities. Her research interests include health disparities, social determinants of health, and access to health care. Past research has included analyses of the National Health Interview survey, examining the health outcomes associated with care coordination for people with physical disabilities, and the development and testing of wellness programs for individuals with intellectual disabilities.

Debra L. Cote is an associate professor in the Department of Special Education at CSUF Fullerton. She is the co-teaching coordinator and fieldwork coordinator for the Special Education Department. Dr. Cote received her doctorate from the University of Nevada, Las Vegas. Her research interests include autism, positive behavior supports, cognitive behavioral supports, transition, evidence-based practices, and teacher preparation. Dr. Cote is associate director of the CSUF Center for Autism, Education Core, and faculty advisor to the CSUF Student Council for Exceptional Children. Dr. Cote served as far west region member for the national Division on Autism and Developmental Disabilities (2010–2016). She serves as past president to the Greater Orange County (OC) Council for Exceptional

Children (CEC) Chapter 188 and OC Chapter 188 Representative to the CA CEC Executive Committee. Dr. Cote serves on the Grandparents Autism Network Board of Directors.

Meredith Gammons is a registered radiologic technologist in the medical imaging modalities of radiography, mammography, computed tomography, magnetic resonance imaging, and bone densitometry by the American Registry of Radiologic Technologists. She is a graduate of the Pfeiffer University Master of Health Administration program. She has been employed in medical imaging for over 20 years as an imager in the settings of an academic medical center, multi-state not-for-profit integrated health-care system, and as community college clinical instructor. She is currently employed as a radiology clinical educator with Novant Health in Winston-Salem, NC.

Lee Groce is an independent entrepreneur with a disability. He graduated from Surry Community College with an applied science degree in electronics. Additionally, he is an active member of the American Radio Relay League (ARRL), where he earned the ARRL's highest level Amateur Extra License and communicates on worldwide radio on all licensed amateur radio bands and modes. Mr. Groce is active in his community, church, and YMCA.

Linda K. Haymes is an associate professor of special education in the Graduate School of Education at Touro University. She has over 25 years experience in special education as a teacher, researcher, and clinician. She is a board certified behavior analyst doctoral level and licensed psychologist in California and has maintained a practice focusing on supporting students with disabilities and their families. She received her PhD in psychology from Claremont Graduate University and her master's from University of Kansas in early childhood education and applied behavior analysis. Dr. Haymes has published research in *The Journal of Autism and Developmental Disabilities*, *Journal of Early Intervention*, *Behavioral Interventions*, *Education and Training in Autism and Developmental Disabilities*, *Developmental Neurorehabilitation*, and *Research and Practice for Persons with Severe Disabilities*. Most recently, Dr. Haymes and Dr. Keith Storey published the book *Case Studies in Applied Behavior Analysis for Students and Adults with Disabilities* from Charles C Thomas Publishing. Dr. Haymes has been a person with physical limitations and also the parent of a child with disability.

David Hollar is an associate professor of health administration at Pfeiffer University. He received his PhD in curriculum and teaching from the University of North Carolina at Greensboro, where he was awarded the graduate school's Outstanding Dissertation Award. He has BS and MS degrees in biology. He successfully completed postdoctoral research in community health at the NIDILRR-funded Rehabilitation Research and Training Center on Substance Abuse and Employment at Wright State University in Dayton, Ohio. In 2004, he wrote and supervised a University of Tennessee $2 million AHRQ grant-funded project to develop electronic health records for children with genetic or metabolic conditions. He also has a graduate certificate in public health entrepreneurship. His specialties include multivariate statistics, structural equation models, mathematical models, disability policy, and decision-making. He has numerous peer-reviewed publications on health risk factors, allostatic load, behavioral genetics, and disability policy, along with presentations at numerous national conferences. He edited and coauthored the *Handbook of Children with Special Health Care Needs* and *Epigenetics, the Environment, and Children's Health Across Lifespans*, both published by Springer in 2012 and 2016, respectively. He wrote *Trajectory Analysis in Health Care*, also published by Springer in 2017. He serves on the editorial board of the *Maternal and Child Health Journal*, he is a member of the American Public Health Association, and he volunteers with the Billy Graham Evangelistic Association Rapid Response Team. He and wife Paige have one daughter.

Katerina Ivanov who earned doctoral degree in business administration and Master of Science in mathematical finance, both from University of North Carolina at Charlotte, currently works as an assistant professor of healthcare, finance, and economics at Pfeiffer University, Department of Health Administration. She serves on board at American College of Healthcare Executives of the Triad in addition to being an active researcher with the main focus on Affordable Care Act and its implication for hospital performance and nursing care providers. Along with publications in peer-reviewed journals and as book chapters, she presented her works and chaired committee sessions at a variety of conferences, including Magna Teaching with Technology Conference 2018; American Public Health Association Annual Meeting 2017; Midwest Finance Association Annual Meetings 2014 and 2015; Eastern Finance Association Annual Meetings 2014, 2015, and 2016; Financial Management Association Annual Meeting 2014; and European Financial Management Association Annual Meeting 2016 in Basel.

Sheryl A. Larson is a principal investigator and research manager 3 at the University of Minnesota's Institute on Community Integration (ICI) where she has worked since 1988. Dr. Larson directs the national residential information systems project. She has had 49 federal, state, and local grant funded research, training, or technical assistance projects focused on people with intellectual or developmental disabilities. Her research topics have included Medicaid long-term supports and services; deinstitutionalization; Direct Support Professional and Supervisor recruitment, retention and training; disability statistics and demographics; access to health care; quality assurance and enhancement, and inclusive community-based supports for people with disabilities. She has also analyzed national and state datasets such as the National Health Interview Survey to examine service utilization, quality outcomes, and the direct support workforce. Dr. Larson has authored or coauthored 3 books, 29 book chapters, 51 peer-reviewed journal articles, and more than 100 technical reports and other products. She made more than 250 presentations at professional conferences, workshops, and seminars in nearly every US state and in Australia, Canada, France, and South Africa. Her research findings are used by state and federal governmental agencies in their policy activities and by the press.

Jennifer S. Lewis serves as the compliance coordinator for the University of Southern Mississippi (2015–present). Prior thereto, she served as a USM business analyst (2014–2015); a technical analyst TIAA-CREF (2014), learning administrator for Novant Health (2009–2014), and paralegal to T. Travis Medlock, former South Carolina Attorney General, (2001–2004).

In addition to holding a bachelor's in English, a certificate in paralegal studies and a master's in adult education and training, Ms. Lewis also holds a master's in healthcare administration (Pfeiffer University), a business administration certificate (University of Southern Mississippi/USM) and is working on her PhD in higher education (emphasis in Student Affairs from USM). She has coauthored an article in the *Journal of Disability Studies* and a chapter in the treatise *Epigenetics, the Environment and Children's Health Across Life Spans.* She has presented at several national conferences [WICHE Cooperative for Educational Technologies (WCET) and the Association of Specialized and Professional Accreditors (ASPA)-2016] and presented research at *Unite for Sight* Conference (Yale 2014).

She serves as USM Association of Office Professionals (USM AOP) President, Mississippi Educational Office Professionals (MAEOP) Secretary, MAEOP Higher Education Division Vice President, and Southeast Region of the National Association of Educational Office Professionals (NAEOP) Secretary.

Sarah MapelLentz is a researcher at the University of Minnesota's Institute on Community Integration. Her previous work has focused on the social determinants of health, as well as health and quality of life disparities experienced by children, youth, and adults with disabilities and their families. Her past research experience was in self-management during the transition period among youth with epilepsy and the quality of life outcomes experienced by youth with mobility limitations.

Nur Onvural is an associate professor of economics and finance at Pfeiffer University's Division of Applied Health Sciences and Division of Business. She holds a PhD in economics (1990), an MS in management (1986) both from North Carolina State University and a BS in chemical engineering (1981) from Middle East Technical University in Ankara, Turkey. Her research interests are in the areas of health economics, health-care finance focusing on health administration and health disparities as well as entrepreneurship and innovation in health care. Throughout her career, she held positions in the industry and academia. Before joining Pfeiffer University, she ran her own business while keeping adjunct faculty positions at North Carolina State University and Pfeiffer. She also worked at Blue Cross Blue Shield of NC, where she managed the design and implementation of cutting-edge health-care reimbursement projects for physicians and hospitals in a managed care environment and development of the electronic exchange capabilities between insurer and providers. She is a certified quality matters (QM) peer reviewer for online courses. In 2016, *Cary Magazine* awarded her as one of the five women of western Wake country for her contributions to the community as an educator and entrepreneur.

Keith Storey received his PhD from the University of Oregon. He is currently a clinical director at Juvo Autism and Behavioral Health in Oakland, California. After many years in higher education, he returned to a direct service role. Keith currently serves on the editorial boards of *Research and Practice for Persons with Severe Disabilities*, *Career Development for Exceptional Individuals*, *Journal of Vocational Rehabilitation*, *Journal of Positive Behavior Interventions*, and *Education and Training in Autism and Developmental Disabilities*. Keith previously served on the editorial boards of *Education and Treatment of Children*, *Vocational Evaluation and Career Assessment Professional Journal*, and *Exceptionality*. He has published the books *Positive Behavior Supports in Classrooms and Schools: Effective and Practical Strategies for Teachers and Other Service Providers*; *Case Studies in Applied Behavior Analysis for Students and Adults with Disabilities*; *Positive Behavior Supports for Adults with Disabilities in Employment, Community, and Residential Settings; Practical Strategies That Work*; *Systematic Instruction for Students and Adults with Disabilities*; *Walking Isn't Everything: An Account of the Life of Jean Denecke*; *The Road Ahead: Transition to Adult Life for Persons with Disabilities*; and *Functional Assessment and Program Development for Problem Behavior: A Practical Handbook.*

Chapter 1
A Testimony

Lee Groce

1.1 Early Years and School

I was born with a disability. I grew up in the 1960s and 1970s as a child. I was enrolled into a handicapped school at a young age where I was taught reading, writing, and arithmetic as well as physical therapy and speech therapy. I wore braces from my hips to my heels and later from below my knees to my heels. I started walking using parallel bars and other physical therapies. I was also introduced to various speech therapies.

I guess that my disability is about average. I have known people who have more severe problems than I do and some that are hardly noticeable. What I have learned is that all people have some type of problem; mine is just more noticeable than theirs.

We were taught a lot of what I would think was taught in grade school at the time. I enjoyed a lot of reading in our library with subjects that interested me. I realized that I had trouble walking, a little trouble with one arm, and a slight bit of speech problems.

I owe my walking and speech abilities that I have today to my wonderful therapists for my abilities. At the age of 12, I graduated from the school for children with disabilities, was then called "handicapped," and entered public school in the sixth grade. My new friends welcomed and accepted me into the school. I still had some trouble walking, so I had a friend assigned to help me with certain tasks.

There were fire drills and certain events during which we needed to exit the school quickly, so someone came up with a three-man carry. Some of the larger boys would interlock their hands; I would sit on their arms and be carried outside.

Like my previous school, the middle school teachers were friendly and supportive. I had some new challenges to meet and overcame them. My new classmates and

L. Groce (✉)
Yadkinville, NC, USA

D. Hollar (ed.), *Advances in Exercise and Health for People With Mobility Limitations*, https://doi.org/10.1007/978-3-319-98452-0_1

I learned a lot from each other. One thing that I enjoyed was our arm wrestling matches, where I am pretty good. I performed well academically with several favorite subjects.

1.2 Wrestling

Then we graduated to high school and were introduced to kids from other schools our age. It was an interesting experience. During my freshman year, the coach of the wrestling team asked me to be the team manager, and I accepted the position. I learned a lot from this experience. When we were at away matches, I would keep the wrestlers' personal property in a bag for which I was responsible. I never lost anything. I was in charge of various other tasks at home matches. This was an important responsibility, and I value the trust that the coach and my teammates placed in me. People with disabilities have no limitations when you see just what we can do.

During my high school freshman through senior years, my friends and I continued to arm wrestle. The more that I wrestled, the stronger I got. I was taking on all comers. I had big guys who were wrestlers, football players, etc. My record was pretty good, and during my senior year I retired as arm wrestling champion of our high school!

One day while the wrestlers were out running laps, I started working on the weights. I began bench-pressing more weight than I should have when I got into trouble. I only had a short time before I got tired, so I chose the only option I had to escape.

Rule: Never lift free weights without someone to spot you. This goes for everybody!

I was allowed to wrestle with the other wrestlers in practice but not in competition. I earned my letter jacket after 2 years of intramural competition.

1.3 Explaining Disability

During my freshman year, I had a tutor for one subject. She was several years ahead of me and was studying business. She also taught me a bit of shorthand that proved to be very helpful. I explained my disability when she asked about it. My sophomore classes went well, and I enjoyed driver's education and later got my driver's license.

One day after school, several of us were sitting in the lobby after school. There were five girls sitting on the benches with me. Some were waiting for rides home, and others had finished after-school tests. We enjoyed talking about television shows.

Some of the shows were humorous, such as the damsel-in-distress where one was tied up and attempted to escape. The girls talked about it then made a bet on who could get loose first. Two girls tied up the other three girls, and they began working on the rope. Two of the girls escaped in a few minutes, but one girl never did. One by one the other girls left. The last girl offered to take her home, but she wanted me to take her home, and I agreed to do so. Her wrists were tied securely behind her, and her ankles were tied about 6 inches apart. When we were ready to leave, I started to untie the knot, but she asked to remain that way. She began walking toward the door, so I picked up her purse and walked beside her. A teacher held the door for us. I helped her into my car and put her purse in the back seat. When I got into the driver's seat, she told me that she was beginning to understand what it was like to have a disability. I told her that not many people understand that and that it was not contagious. She smiled, "Do people really think that?" "Some people do," I replied.

Once home, her mother was baking cookies and offered us some. She served us on the deck outside. She asked if her daughter had been naughty, and I replied that she lost the bet on the game that they had played. We sat there drinking milk through straws, and I fed her cookies. She asked about having a disability and various other types of disabilities. She stood just over 5 feet tall and reminded me of one of Charlie's Angels! I appreciated and adored her for these efforts to understand my problem.

She asked me about another girl who was a mutual friend. I explained that this friend intrigued me by wearing her wristwatch on her ankle. She asked why, so I removed the rope from her wrists and ankles and asked her to stand up and cross her leg as if she were looking at a watch on her ankle, and she did! I told her that on my best day I could not do that. She smiled at me because she understood my interest.

These types of events were good examples where I could really describe my experience to others so that they could understand, and many did.

I used to play with a friend in our neighbor's front yard. Knowing that our games were good-natured and safe, her mother once gave me a wonderful complement: "He is her friend and protector; as long as she is with him, I know that she is safe." That was the proudest moment of my life!

After graduation I went to a community college. I enjoyed making new friends but lost track of part of my high school friends, something that often happens. During college, I kept active through various activities. I arm-wrestled a few times, but it was not a sport that was as popular there as it had been in high school. I earned my associate degree after 3 years of study.

1.4 Staying Active and Overcoming Misperceptions

Exercise is important to everyone and especially to those of us who have disabilities. Overcoming some mobility limitations, I have rode bicycles for as long as I can remember and met a lot of people along the way. In my late 30s, I had to have a surgery that ended my bicycle riding.

Some people like to help others, and I have had people take my arm or elbow to assist me in walking. I have watched other people get helped this way. What these people do not understand is that we have become used to our walk, and when they help they throw our balance off. My advice is to ask how you can help. Most people will ask when they need help. Like most people with disabilities, we are quite able and know best what the barriers are that we encounter.

I have dealt with people who think that the "physically handicapped" means that we are mentality handicapped or retarded, and this is not so. Nothing could be further from the truth.

I have been discriminated against by well-meaning, "educated" people like doctors and lawyers and people who don't understand that physically handicapped does not mean that we are mentally handicapped or disabled. Disability comes in all types, and everybody has some disability, however big or small. I (and my friends with disabilities) am far more able than some people think. The discrimination has even extended to one situation where I did nothing wrong but was unable to obtain legal assistance. The golden rule: do unto others as you would have them do unto you. In the United States, you are presumed to be innocent until you are proven guilty. Sadly, many "educated" people do not understand this, and I have lost close friends because of this and misunderstandings related to disability.

1.5 Ham Radio

I am an amateur "ham" radio operator and have earned the highest level of license available. I am also a volunteer examiner and have helped give amateur radio exams for decades now. Prior to getting my amateur radio license, I was a citizen's band radio operator talking to people locally. I am grateful for the teacher and friend who encouraged me to pursue this wonderful hobby.

With my ham radio license and my equipment, I can talk to people all over the world. I primarily use voice and telegraphy (Morse code) although there are several other modes of communication possible with computers. This further demonstrates just how far you can go with a "disability." There are no boundaries, except perhaps in other people's minds. But that can change.

1.6 Final Recommendations

I would like to make some suggestions for dealing with a physically handicapped person: Never assume anything! If you are in doubt, then ask. People with disabilities have the same wants, needs, and desires that everyone has. Treat us with respect. Respect and trust are earned, not given. Once they are gone, it is almost impossible to restore these values.

If a person with a disability is sitting down, then if possible sit down with them and make eye contact while talking with them. Be kind. Like children and adults, we do not like to be mistreated – the golden rule applies again.

Be patient. If you are with a person with a disability, walk beside them instead of in front of or behind them. If someone is working on something and being slow, let them finish what they are doing unless they ask you for help. Nothing makes me more angry than to have someone take something out of my hands and finish what I started to do.

If they have slurred speech, do not assume that they are drunk or mentally challenged. Too often, people jump to the wrong conclusions, usually because they have not bothered to evaluate and think through a situation. Get to know people and know where they are coming from. There is plenty of science that shows that people do not slow down enough to think things through correctly.

1.7 Moving Forward

There is a widely quoted proverb in various forms that goes: "Never judge someone unless you have walked a mile in their shoes," and I would bet that you have heard it too. The world has become full of rules and regulations that the people who put them there do not understand the full scope of their rules. Despite their good intentions, these organizations, the Internet, etc. have changed things from common sense to idiotic rules. Many of these rules put more barriers in the way of people with disabilities.

The negative attitudes of some people toward people with disabilities are in all parts of our world. Besides what I have mentioned earlier, I was once called for jury duty on an important trial, but after one attorney approved my selection, the other attorney attacked my character and reputation. As a result, I was not selected for the jury. Later, I needed help on another legal issue, but the attorney I asked for help completely belittled me. With respect to my disability, another person told me to "just live with it." Nobody should ever say those four words to another person, especially if they have a disability. We are more than able to do things that many people without disabilities cannot or will not do.

What a world it would be if people would stop being so serious about everything. Just loosen up and be able to laugh at yourself and the funny things that happen around us. The changes that have happened over the years have made people too self-centered and unwilling to see the good and beauty in other people. I think this situation is where so many of our society's problems come from and where we need to start paying more attention to each other.

As a person with many abilities, I have been successful. I have many friends, and I have overcome obstacles that have been needlessly placed in the way of people with disabilities. Sports, regular exercise, arm wrestling, ham radio, and spending time with family and friends keep me active. The important things for all people, including people with disabilities, are freedom and independence. I hope that others join us to respect and value the many things that each of us have to give the world. Thank you.

Chapter 2
The Demographics of Disability and Mobility Limitations

David Hollar

Abbreviations

ACS	American Community Survey
BMI	Body mass index
CDC	US Centers for Disease Control and Prevention
DHHS	US Department of Health and Human Services
GIS	Geographic Information Systems
HDL	High-density lipoprotein (cholesterol)
HPSA	Health Professional Shortage Area
HRSA	Health Resources Services Administration
ICD	International Classification of Diseases
ICDR	Interagency Committee on Disability Research
ICF	International Classification of Functioning, Disability and Health
IRT	Item response theory
LDL	Low-density lipoprotein (cholesterol)
LSVRSP	Longitudinal Study of Vocational Rehabilitation Services Programs
NELS	National Education Longitudinal Study of 1988–2000
NHANES	National Health and Nutrition Examination Survey
NIDILRR	National Institute on Disability, Independent Living, and Rehabilitation Services
NIH	National Institutes of Health
RSA	Rehabilitation Services Administration
SSDI	Social Security Disability Insurance
TBI	Traumatic brain injury
UN	United Nations
VR	Vocational rehabilitation
WHO	World Health Organization
YRBSS	Youth Risk Behavior Surveillance Survey

D. Hollar (✉)
Health Administration, Pfeiffer University, Misenheimer, NC, USA
e-mail: David.Hollar@pfeiffer.edu

D. Hollar (ed.), *Advances in Exercise and Health for People With Mobility Limitations*, https://doi.org/10.1007/978-3-319-98452-0_2

2.1 Introduction

The International Classification of Functioning, Disability, and Health (ICF; World Health Organization 2001) identifies hundreds of different body structures and functions plus related environmental and activities/participation factors to which any person could experience a range of few problems (i.e., zero functional barriers) to complete problems (i.e., nonactivity with 100% barriers), either acutely or chronically. This approach contradicts the typical broad categories of blindness/low vision, deafness/low hearing (or sensory disabilities), intellectual disabilities, developmental disabilities, and mobility limitations that generically and incorrectly/inappropriately label so many people with disabilities. Even the over 300 categories of disability in the Longitudinal Study of Vocational Rehabilitation Services Programs (LSVRSP) do not adequately address the experience of each person with a disability (Hollar et al. 2008). Disability represents a situation of varying degrees that is unique to each affected individual, and the ICF model serves to clarify the dynamic variation of this health and social phenomenon, as we here apply with respect to demographic variation.

Furthermore, the experience of disability is a fluid dynamic because every individual experiences some type of disability, acute and temporary or chronic, at some point in their lives. The ICF model fits well with this fact because it provides levels of functioning that complement traditional medical International Classification of Diseases 10 (ICD-10; World Health Organization 1990; http://www.who.int/classifications/icd/en/) and that can be utilized for any person with any health condition. Its extra advantage is the recognition that health conditions translate and are affected by factors well beyond simply body structures and functions (i.e., personal, social, environmental, institutional factors). The upshot is that this approach helps us to gain a much clearer of the unique experience of disability and ability for each individual so that we can provide better services to this population in addition to better health for everyone. This includes more innovative approaches to understanding the comprehensive epidemiology of health and functioning (Hollar 2017a).

2.2 Demographics of Disability in the United States

The National Institute on Disability, Independent Living, and Rehabilitation Research (NIDILRR 2017) estimates that approximately 57 million Americans (17.3%) are living with a disability. Working with the nationally representative National Education Longitudinal Study (NELS) 1988–2000 data on approximately 26,000 people who started high school in 1988, Hollar and Moore (2004) and Hollar (2005) identified 10.5% of the sample to have parent and student combined identification of disability, although the NELS data was limited by the exclusion of certain people with disabilities at the base-year data collection and although the sample was "freshened" with a small, subsample entry into the overall sample during the first follow-up data collection. Several US state Youth Risk Behavior Surveillance Surveys (YRBSS) estimated the population of youth with disabilities at between 15 and 30% (Hollar 2005). A similar range of estimates come from the Longitudinal Study of Vocational Rehabilitation Services Programs (LSVRSP; Hollar et al. 2007, 2008), although the LSVRSP is limited by missing data and several hundred general categories of disability. Of vocational rehabilitation (VR) participants, Hollar et al. (2007) estimated that about 10.8% LSVRSP participants and 14.0% of Rehabilitation Services Administration RSA-911 database participants have a co-occurring substance abuse condition. Based upon patient interview questions in the US Centers for Disease Control and Prevention (CDC) National Health and Nutrition Examination Survey (NHANES), approximately 26% of the 50% of participants older than age 20 who were measured on American Heart Association cardiac risk factors reported considerable difficulty with vision, hearing, physical/mental/emotional, lifting/carrying, or mobility tasks (Hollar 2013, Hollar and Lewis 2015).

Of the 52,195 people who were surveyed and clinically examined during the five consecutive 2-year data collection periods (i.e., approximately 10,000 people per 2-year data collection period: 2001–2002, 2003–2004, 2005–2006, 2007–2008, and 2009–2010) of NHANES, approximately 2.3% had substantial difficulty hearing (even with a hearing aid), 14% had vision-related disabilities, 4.6% had memory/cognitive disabilities, 1.5% had physical/mental/emotional disabilities, 10.7% reported substantial difficulty in mobility (e.g., walking up ten steps, lifting, and carrying), and 5.3% used assistive devices (Hollar 2013). Across this same 10-year Healthy People 2010 period, Hollar and Lewis (2015) identified approximately 60–65% of people living with mobility limitations as being female and 35–51% being members of ethnic minority groups, depending upon the 2-year data collection period. Likewise, 53–55% of people who use assistive devices were female, and 36–50% were ethnic minorities (Hollar and Lewis 2015).

Whereas NIDILRR (2017) estimated 57 million Americans who live with disabilities, Houtenville et al. (2013) examined American Community Survey (ACS) and other nationally representative data sources to estimate the number of people living with disabilities to be about 38,397,863, or 12.3% of the 2012 US total population of 312,538,222 people. Narrowing this total population to those people between the ages of 18 and 64 years (195,697,202 people), they estimated that 2.1% had a hearing disability, 1.8% had a vision disability, 4.3% had a cognitive disability, 5.2% had a mobility disability, and 3.6% had an independent living disability (Houtenville et al. 2013). The states of Virginia and Utah, respectively, had the highest and lowest prevalence rates at 19% and 9.2%. For ages 5–17, the prevalence rate was 5.4% nationwide, whereas for ages 65 and up, the prevalence rate (36.1%) was much higher due to cumulative and age-related disabilities (Houtenville et al. 2013).

Therefore, in the United States, roughly 5–10% of the population has a mobility limitation, which is one-third of all Americans with disabilities (15–17% of the population), based upon these fairly consistent and varied estimates. The demographic statistics demonstrate that many Americans, plus their families, are directly impacted by disability. All of our communities have the responsibility to provide safety nets and opportunities for people living with disabilities. These social constructs include recreational, exercise, health, nutrition, and employment opportunities to engage every person in normal social and work-related activities.

The wide variation on estimates of the numbers of people living with disabilities in the United States stems from very few or inconsistent questionnaire items for survey respondents to provide self-reports. The self-report aspect further complicates interpretation with respect to self-presentation bias as a threat to study internal validity (Crocker and Algina 1986; Messick 1988). The triangulation of multiple disability measures/sources in NELS (Hollar 2005; Hollar and Moore 2004) contributed to some credence on those estimates, even given the limitations on disability inclusion with the original study design. Still, nationally "representative" surveys have too few assessments for disability given the wide variation in levels of functioning that are unique to each individual. Therefore, estimates of disability continue to be unreliable given fewer than six disability indicator questions in most current and foreseen upcoming national surveys. The ambitious National Institutes of Health (NIH) All of Us study (https://allofus.nih.gov/) of approximately one million Americans is being planned for the next decade, roughly in conjunction with the ongoing US CDC Healthy People 2010, 2020, and 2030 (https://www.healthypeople.gov/2020/About-Healthy-People/Development-Healthy-People-2030) decadal estimates of national health trends that relies on national data sources such as NHANES. Hopefully, the All of Us study will use some type of disability matrix evaluation of functioning using the straightforward ICF coding format.

2.3 Global Estimates

The World Health Organization (2011, p. 30) estimated that 2.9% of the world's population lives with a severe disability, including approximately 10.2% of people older than 60 years of age, slightly higher for longer-lived females than for males. Across global regions, the percentage of severe disability ranged from a low of 2.6% in Latin America to a high of 3.2% in high-income countries. Combining moderate and severe disabilities, the World Health Organization (2011, p. 30) estimated 15.3% of the world's population, with 46.1% of those older than 60 years. These estimates ranged from a low of 14.0% for the Eastern Mediterranean countries to highs of 16.4% and 16.0% for Europe and Southeast Asia, respectively. The United Nations (2017) estimates that about 80% of people living with disabilities live in developing nations that have less health services and socioeconomic infrastructure.

Globally, the burden of disability is greatest in sub-Saharan Africa, where there is a preponderance of poverty, poor health conditions, and gradual containment of devastating HIV and malaria epidemics. The prevalence of disability is approximately 25–30% higher in Africa across ages compared to Europe and the Americas (World Health Organization 2011). The report places substantial emphasis on infectious diseases associated with disabilities, and Africa faces the emerging threat of antibiotic-resistant bacterial pathogens, much like many world regions.

Here, severe disability was defined for "conditions such as quadriplegia, severe depression, or blindness" (World Health Organization 2011, p. 29) using the "cannot perform this activity" ICF score. Moderate disability represented ICF scores of "some difficulty" or greater on a 0–100 scale, with 40 representing the threshold for moderate disability and 50 representing severe disability in the World Health Organization (2011, Technical Appendix C) item response theory (IRT) model.

Sampling various nations by age, the World Health Organization (2011) found that disability prevalence was higher for people less than 65 years of age in poorer nations compared to wealthier nations, even with increasingly older populations worldwide and trends for age-related disability. Consistent with higher prevalences of disability among the global poor, with people with disabilities being more than twice as likely to be unemployed compared to people without disabilities. This last finding also occurs in wealthier nations such as the United States (Houtenville et al. 2013). Thus, the trends for increased disability are associated with lower socioeconomic status, further accompanied by the correlating variables lack of access to healthcare, poor nutrition, and less exercise. These patterns occur not only between wealthier and poorer nations but also between wealthier and poor regions within nations. The World Health Organization (2011) further notes these trends exist despite relatively minor differences in immunization rates between most nations. They further note the recognized need for increased numbers of clinicians, health clinics, exercise facilities, and accommodations for people living with disabilities, who number close to one billion globally. With a rapidly expanding global population, the numbers of people living with disabilities will increase unless greater healthcare is provided to avoid preventable disabilities (e.g., genetic, injury-related, violence-related, infection-related). Likewise, there is a dramatic need for assistive devices, specialized healthcare and social supports, exercise, and nutrition to help people living with disabilities to improve their lives and to minimize the occurrence of secondary conditions.

In 2001, the United Nations (UN) Statistical Commission established an international panel of experts called the Washington Group on Disability Statistics. This panel uses the ICF functioning codes as a model for assessing disability in various national surveys worldwide. They utilize a core set of six questions (World Health Organization 2011, p. 26) that includes "Do you have difficulty…" for "seeing even with glasses, hearing even with a hearing aid, walking or climbing steps, remembering or concentrating, communicating (using one's own language), and self care activities." While generic in nature and not even approaching the full scope and complex patterns of disability and secondary conditions for each individual situation, the six questions provide researchers, clinicians, and policy makers a framework for evaluating the prevalence of disability.

Still, the use of the six questions has been sporadic such that we have only a patchwork collection of more accurate, less accurate, and inconsistent measures from country to country. The move to greater standardization and adoption of these six questions (and perhaps more) will be a long-term process. Even within the United States, the Interagency Committee on Disability Research (ICDR), a panel of disability research representatives from all major federal agencies, has advocated the use of the Washington Group six questions in all nationally representative surveys on health and health behaviors. To date, there has been increased but still incomplete adoption of these six disability questions, with pushback often coming from questionnaire compression due to large numbers of questionnaire items. US national surveys such as NHANES and NELS have been more successful at providing a stronger determination of disability prevalence, as described in the previous section.

With greater statistical tools, the use of Geographic Information Systems (GIS) offers further power to the analysis and determination of disability prevalence. Again here, the more substantial work has been done in the United States with extensive, county-level or zip code-level estimates of disability prevalence for small, political units. For instance, the County Health Rankings of 3221 US county units have been collected and posted annually in Excel format by the University of Wisconsin Population Health Institute (http://www.countyhealthrankings.org) with funding by the Robert Wood Johnson Foundation. These data are compiled from county health departments and from nationally representative surveys. The European Union and other national consortia that have large population health infrastructures are developing similar GIS-based data repositories. However, these systems rarely have disability data at the geographic level. Hollar (2017b) linked Social Security Disability Insurance (SSDI) data with the County Health Rankings to evaluate geospatial associations between disability prevalence and health outcomes, finding that US counties high in disability prevalence were more likely to have negative health outcomes as well as lower socioeconomic status, consistent with World Health Organization (2011) and other research studies showing this general association.

2.4 Rural Health

People living with disabilities, including mobility disabilities, are overrepresented in rural US populations. As a result, this population is at risk for higher morbidity, mortality, and secondary conditions due to lowered access to high-technology medical facilities and transportation and time issues for reaching adequate medical care on a regular or urgent care basis. This situation is further compounded by the lower socioeconomic conditions in many rural areas. The US Health Resources and Services Administration (HRSA 2018; see also US Department of Health and Human Services, DHHS 2017) has identified 7176 primary medical, 5866 dental, and 5042 mental health Health Professional Shortage Areas (HPSAs) spanning every US state and impacting overlapping populations of 84 million, 63 million, and 124 million people, respectively. The large mental health disparity is of particular concern given rising insurance costs, lack of treatment, and prevalence (Rowan et al. 2013). The breakdown of HPSAs is estimated to be 59% rural and 7% partially rural for both primary medical and dental HPSAs, and it is 53% rural and 9% partially rural for mental health HPSAs (Health Resources Services Administration 2018).

Rural health conditions are of major concern due to several studies showing increased despair and death rates for US rural populations (Case and Deaton 2015; Erwin 2017; Roux 2017; Stein et al. 2017). Isaacs and Schroeder (2004) correctly identified the large role of social and socioeconomic class in health disparities, with these healthcare access and treatment inequities largely correlating with race and education. The tendency of societies to organize populations around metropolitan areas of wealth and prosperity has been a trend for human societies for the past 10,000 years following the agricultural revolution, and it has accelerated with the late nineteenth century industrialization (currently occurring in many third world nations) and the late twentieth–/early twenty-first century technology revolution. Medical and other healthcare likewise has gravitated to the major university and industrial centers in cities, this process occurring in spite of several decades of attempts to attract primary caregivers and specialists to rural areas.

Case and Deaton (2015) discovered that mortality rates across race and ethnicity declined at about 2% per year from 1978 to 1998, consistent with other wealthy nations. However, American non-Hispanic Caucasian mortality began to increase by about 0.5% per year from 1999 to 2013. Much of this unexpected increase is occurring during middle age and is primarily attributable to increased suicides, drug overdoses, and alcohol-related disease.

Stein et al. (2017) extended this work, finding that mortality by cancer and cardiovascular disease significantly declined for all races and ethnicities, rural and urban, ages 35–54. However, while poisoning and suicide rates did increase across races for ages 25–34 and 55–64, poisoning and suicide were consistently and significantly higher across all age groups for Caucasians and especially so for rural and suburban Caucasians aged 25–44. Stein et al. (2017) attributed the increased Caucasian mortality in these non-urban areas to "despair" resulting from negatively changing socioeconomic changes in these areas.

These findings are consistent with geospatial regression analyses (Hollar 2017b) showing heightened morbidity, mortality, and disability in rural, low socioeconomic US counties. Nationally and globally, people with disabilities and their heightened risk for secondary conditions and poor health outcomes tend to live in poorer regions that do not have access to adequate health, exercise, nutrition, and other safety-net support mechanisms. There also is evidence that disability also is more strongly correlated with minority race and ethnicity, probably a correlate of lower socioeconomic status. This observation is not necessarily inconsistent with the findings of Case and Deaton (2015) or Stein et al. (2017). Both Erwin (2017) and Roux (2017) argued that while mortality rates are reversed for Caucasians and African Americans in the United States since 1999, African Americans still have higher overall mortality rates associated with socioeconomic and health disparities. All of these researchers are in agreement that greater public health attention needs to be placed on improved health infrastructures in rural American communities to address these health disparities in mortality rates for all races and disability-related conditions. Bor (2017) used a geospatial regression analysis of these trends to argue that the health disparities might have impacted voting patterns in the 2016 US presidential election. If true, the impact of public demand for improved health policies can occur via the engagement of people with disabilities and other underserved populations to vote in democratic societies.

Case and Deaton (2015) did observe that there were significant differences in activities of daily living (ADLs) such as standing and walking for non-Hispanic Caucasians from 1997–1999 (lower mean) to 2011–2013 (higher mean). These findings further support the association between rural poor health outcomes and heightened disabilities and secondary conditions in these communities. This is a phenomenon that occurs not only in the United States but also worldwide (Hosain et al. 2002).

2.5 Despair, Population, and Physiological Health

Stein et al. (2017) illustrated the plight of a dynamically changing economic environment and its detrimental effects on population health. For people with disabilities, Houtenville et al. (2013) found that 39.1% of people with disabilities in the United States are obese, compared to 24.5% of people without disabilities. Hollar (2013) found that 60% of people living with certain mobility limitations in NHANES were obese. Furthermore, Hollar and Lewis (2015) found that people with mobility limitations tended to have significantly increased heart disease risk and negative heart age differentials (i.e., hearts older than chronological age) compared to people without disabilities and people living with non-mobility disabilities.

Houtenville et al. (2013) also found that people with disabilities were significantly more likely to smoke than people without disabilities, although they were less inclined to engage in binge drinking. At least on this last point, people with disabilities might not resort to alcohol in response to the despair that was cited by Stein et al. (2017) and that has been discussed for people with disabilities, especially when associated with other negative environmental conditions.

Seeman et al. (2001, 2002, 2010) identified ten physiological thresholds (e.g., upper systolic and diastolic blood pressures, low high-density lipoprotein (HDL), and high low-density lipoprotein (LDL) cholesterol levels) as indicators of allostatic load, the body's "cumulative biological risk" from internal and external stressors. With respect to social supports, of particular note was their finding that people with fewer than three friends were significantly more likely to experience morbidity and mortality. Hollar (2013) found that people living with mobility limitations were significantly more likely to have fewer than three friends, compared to people without disabilities and people living with non-mobility limitations. Similarly, people living with mobility limitations were significantly more likely to exceed various allostatic thresholds, including systolic and diastolic blood pressures and body mass index (BMI) compared to people without disabilities. These findings likely also contribute to the significantly greater negative heart age differentials for people living with mobility limitations (Hollar and Lewis 2015).

Whereas the recent findings of increased drug overdose and suicide rates in rural America have not been directly examined for people with disabilities who live in rural areas, Heinemann, Corrigan, and Moore (2004) discussed increased risks for substance abuse among people living with traumatic brain injury (TBI). People with TBI and other traumatically acquired disabilities often experience lifelong pain that is not fully addressed by pain medications, hence sometimes leading to their use of illicit drugs. Hollar (2017b) did show geospatial patterns that associated counties with higher prevalence rates of disabilities with increased negative health outcomes plus lower socioeconomic conditions, including high rates of people who are physically inactive, who experience preventable hospital stays, higher percentage diabetics, increased injury death rates, and worse food environment indices. It is probable that these combinations of factors create negative overall environments that represent substantial barriers for the health and well-being of people with and without disabilities who live in low socioeconomic, rural areas.

The role of stress in personal and population health was established long ago by Selye's (1950) general adaptation syndrome and by Christian and Davis' (1956, 1964) studies of population collapse in response to stress. Allostatic load (Seeman et al. 2001, 2002) represents a further extension of this work, illustrating the close linkages between environmental stressors, mind, body, behaviors, and health outcomes. Kotas and Medzhitov (2015) provided an extensive summary of the relationships between the mind, stress, physiological balance or homeostasis, and immunity. The principal connections within exercise, mind, and stress are molecules called cytokines that balance pro- and anti-inflammatory responses by the immune system. In fact, these molecules are responsible for much of proper body functioning at multiple levels. Disturbances to health and mental well-being can disrupt this delicate balance. This concept has been little studied for people living with disabilities, but the research literature has generated the ICF biopsychosocial model that highlights many of these factors in relation to the health of people living with disabilities. For people living with and without disabilities, we should pay heed to the complex interplay between body systems and the external environment. Population demography and dynamics are but the most visible level of this process, which goes much deeper within every individual person and their unique health circumstances.

Therefore, the pervasiveness of disabilities across societies and the demonstrated connections with poor access to health, exercise, and nutrition warrant the need for intensified research, policy development, and knowledge translation into improved health and exercise entities to benefit this population. Societies cannot ignore this large population. Furthermore, our hubris should be controlled by the realization that each of us will have a disability, great or small, at some point in our lives.

2.6 The ICF and Its Role for Improved Demography and Health Policies

The International Classification of Functioning, Disability, and Health (ICF; World Health Organization 2001) divides health and ability/disability into several conceptual components: (a) body functions and structures, (b) activities and participation,

(c) environmental factors, and (d) personal factors. Within the many subcategories of variables across these four components, each variable or factor can be viewed from two perspectives: facilitators or barriers. Facilitators contribute to optimal health outcomes. Barriers block successful outcomes. Therefore, for each of the almost one billion people on earth with disabilities, we must optimize facilitators and minimize barriers.

The ICF codes for each condition (e.g., s120 – spinal cord and related structures) follow a 0–4 Likert-style ranking for both barriers and facilitators. The 0–4 first decimal qualifiers go from no impairment (0) through mild (1), moderate (2), severe (3), and complete (4), each of which covers a certain perceived percentage level of limitation with respect to the body structure, function, activity, or environmental variable. As such, s120.2 would be a mild (25–49%) spinal cord injury limitation. Conversely, facilitators are likewise numbered 0–4 with a positive sign. For s120.+2, we have a spinal cord injury with a moderate facilitator that contributes up to 49% assistance to the injury, perhaps representing a motorized wheelchair. Further secondary and tertiary decimal qualifiers specify affected regions and characteristics for body structures. For activities and participation, secondary and tertiary qualifiers reflect levels of functioning with and without assistance, respectively.

This ICF coding mechanism represents a coherent approach to evaluating and quantifying levels of functioning for any condition or situation related to disability or ability in general. As a result, the ICF represents a straightforward diagnostic and population health measurement tool for everyone. Its use would greatly enhance identification of levels of functioning and changes thereof for both patient and physician so that proper health interventions can be provided. Moreover, with widespread adoption of the ICF model, researchers, policy makers, and clinicians could have a better understanding of the distribution and types of disability worldwide. Ethically conducted, we could evaluate health intervention needs and target specific geographic areas where services and opportunities are limited.

The ICF embodies the current public health view of disability as a complex interaction between condition and environment. This replaces the traditional medical model of body structures with a comprehensive, biopsychosocial model of health and functioning for every person. The ICF has a health outcome emphasis in accordance with our strategic health objectives of improving human health, reducing morbidity and mortality, and expanding quality longevity. As with any condition and its correlating variables, it brings into play developmental and contextual considerations such as family, peer, and social supports plus personal behaviors.

Whereas the precise coding mechanism of the ICF can be too specific for population- and demographic-based statistics, an abbreviated use of the ICF measures in national surveys of health conditions and behaviors or public access to de-identified patient data can help researchers and other health professionals to improve population assessments of disability prevalence and needs for social safety net improvements. We recommend at least a cursory use of the ICF for levels of functioning in nationally representative surveys and population assessments of disability.

2.7 Next Steps

We now have rough estimates of the prevalence of disability worldwide, roughly 15–17% with variations in the types of disability based upon geographic and societally specific population health characteristics. This knowledge enables the US Centers for Disease Control and Prevention and the World Health Organization to work with national and international health programs to improve the lives of disabilities everywhere.

Most importantly, we have very little genuine information on the lives of people living with disabilities. Obviously, this can be more difficult data to obtain. Nevertheless, the voices of people with disabilities have been heard only on occasion. As researchers, we often see numbers, conditions, and variables in a statistical sense when the true lives of people with disabilities are far more meaningful. Therefore, the qualitative analysis of the lived experience of disability represents a population-based research component that offers a more valid picture of the needs for this population.

Furthermore, research studies and policy-making processes on disability, rehabilitation, exercise, and independent living rarely involve input from actual consumers of disability services. The inclusion of people with disabilities on advisory consumer boards has been a priority of many disability advocacy organizations and agencies such as NIDILRR. The insight and guidance of people with disabilities demonstrate that they are the ultimate authority in our efforts to improve health and functioning via exercise, health, and nutrition programming. Such qualitative measures will support stronger quantitative population health measures such as those collected with NHANES, further being expanded with genomic and improved clinical data.

2.8 Summary

In the United States, roughly 5–10% of the population has a mobility limitation, which is one-third of all Americans with disabilities (15–17% or 57 million people), based upon these fairly consistent and varied estimates. Globally, almost one billion people have some level of disability. These estimates ranged from a low of 14.0% for the Eastern Mediterranean countries to highs of 16.4% and 16.0% for Europe and Southeast Asia. Eighty percent of people living with disabilities live in developing nations that have less health services and socioeconomic infrastructure, a phenomenon that also is mirrored within both wealthy and poor nations across Health Professional Shortage Areas (HPSAs). The burden of disability is greatest in sub-Saharan Africa, where there is a preponderance of poverty and poor health conditions.

Improved data collection procedures are needed to better estimate the varied types of disability worldwide. Individual experiences of disability need documentation so that health researchers can place a genuine human face on the factors that impact so many people. The ultimate goal is to improve health, functioning, exercise, and quality of living for all people with and without disabilities.

References

Bor, J. (2017). Diverging life expectancies and voting patterns in the 2016 US presidential election. *American Journal of Public Health, 107*(10), 1560–1562.

Case, A., & Deaton, A. (2015). Rising morbidity and mortality in midlife among white non-Hispanic Americans in the 21st century. *Proceedings of the National Academy of Sciences USA, 112*(49), 15078–15083.

Christian, J. J., & Davis, D. E. (1956). The relationship between adrenal weight and population status of urban Norway rats. *Journal of Mammalogy, 37*(4), 475–486.

Christian, J. J., & Davis, D. E. (1964). Endocrines, behavior, and population. *Science, 146*(3651), 1550–1560.

Crocker, L., & Algina, J. (1986). *Introduction to classical and modern test theory*. Forth Worth: Harcourt Brace Jovanovich.

Department of Health and Human Services. (2017). Lists of designated primary medical care, mental health, and dental health professional shortage areas. *Federal Register, 82*(121), 28863–28864.

Erwin, P. C. (2017). Despair in the American heartland? A focus on rural health. *American Journal of Public Health, 107*(10), 1533–1534.

Health Resources Services Administration. (2018). *Designated health professional shortage areas statistics, first quarter of fiscal year 2018 designated HPSA quarterly summary as of December 31, 2017*. Washington, DC: Bureau of Health Workforce, Health Resources Services Administration, U.S. Department of Health and Human Services.

Heinemann, A. W., Corrigan, J. D., & Moore, D. (2004). Case management for traumatic brain injury survivors with alcohol problems. *Rehabilitation Psychology, 49*(2), 156–166.

Hollar, D. & Moore, D. (2004). Relationship of substance use by students with disabilities to long-term educational and social outcomes. Substance Use & Misuse, 39(6), 929–960.

Hollar, D.W. (2005). Risk Behaviors for Varying Categories of Disability in NELS:88. *Journal of School Health, 75*(9), 350–358.

Hollar, D. (2013). Cross-sectional patterns of allostatic load among persons with varying disabilities, NHANES: 2001–2010. *Disability and Health Journal, 6*, 177–187.

Hollar, D. (2017a). *Trajectory analysis in health care*. New York: Springer Nature http://www.springer.com/us/book/9783319596259.

Hollar, D. (2017b). Disability and health outcomes in geospatial analyses of Southeastern U.S. county health data. *Disability and Health Journal, 10*, 518–524.

Hollar, D., & Lewis, J. (2015). Heart age differentials and general cardiovascular risk profiles for persons with varying disabilities: NHANES 2001–2010. *Disability and Health Journal, 8*, 51–60. https://doi.org/10.1016/j.dhjo.2014.07.007.

Hollar, D., McAweeney, M., & Moore, D. (2007, October 16–17). *Factors that contribute to unsuccessful case closures among consumers of vocational rehabilitation services*. Alexandria: SARDI/NIDRR Rehabilitation Research and Training Center on Substance Use, Disability and Employment State of the Science Conference.

Hollar, D., McAweeney, M., & Moore, D. (2008). The relationship between substance use disorders and unsuccessful case closures in vocational rehabilitation agencies. *Journal of Applied Rehabilitation Counseling, 39*(2), 25–29.

Hosain, G. M., Atkinson, D., & Underwood, P. (2002). Impact of disability on quality of life of rural disabled people in Bangladesh. *Journal of Health, Population, and Nutrition, 20*(4), 297–305.

Houtenville, A., Brucker, D., Gould, P., Lauer, E., Santoro, J., Brennan-Curry, A., & Gianino, M. (2013). *2013 annual disability statistics compendium*. Durham: Disability Statistics & Demographics Rehabilitation Research and Training Center, Institute on Disability, University of New Hampshire.

Isaacs, S. L., & Schroeder, S. A. (2004). Class – The ignored determinant of the nation's health. *The New England Journal of Medicine, 351*(11), 1137–1141.

Kotas, M. E., & Medzhitov, R. (2015). Homeostasis, inflammation, and disease susceptibility. *Cell, 160*(5), 816–827.

Messick, S. (1988). Validity. In R. L. Linn (Ed.), *Educational measurement* (3rd ed.). New York: American Council on Education/Macmillan.

NIDILRR. (2017). NIDILRR Long Range Plan, 2018–2023. Washington, DC: Administration for Community Living, U.S. Department of Health and Human Services.

Roux, A. V. D. (2017). Despair as a cause of death: More complex than it first appears. *American Journal of Public Health, 107*(10), 1566–1567.

Rowan, K., McAlpine, D., & Blewett, L. (2013). Access and cost barriers to mental health care by insurance status, 1999 to 2010. *Health Affairs (Millwood), 32*(10), 1723–1730.

Seeman, T. E., McEwen, B. S., Rowe, J. W., & Singer, B. H. (2001). Allostatic load as a marker of cumulative biological risk: MacArthur studies of successful aging. *Proceedings of the National Academy of Sciences USA, 98*(8), 4770–4775.

Seeman, T. E., Singer, B. H., Ryff, C. D., Love, G. D., & Levy-Storms, L. (2002). Social relationships, gender, and allostatic load across two age cohorts. *Psychosomatic Medicine, 64*, 395–406.

Seeman, T., Epel, E., Gruenewald, T., Karlamangla, A., & McEwen, B. S. (2010). Socio-economic differentials in peripheral biology: Cumulative allostatic load. *Annals of the New York Academy of Sciences, 1186*, 223–239.

Selye, H. (1950). Stress and the general adaptation syndrome. *British Medical Journal, 1*(4667), 1382–1392.

Stein, E. M., Gennuso, K. P., Ugboaja, D. C., & Remington, P. L. (2017). The epidemic of despair among white Americans: Trends in the leading causes of premature death, 1999–2015. *American Journal of Public Health, 107*(10), 1541–1547.

United Nations. (2017). *United Nations enable: Fact sheet on persons with disabilities*. New York: Author.

World Health Organization. (1990). *The international classification of diseases, version 10*. Geneva: Author.

World Health Organization. (2001). *The international classification of functioning, disability and health*. Geneva: Author.

World Health Organization. (2011). *World report on disability*. Geneva: Author.

Chapter 3
Improving Community Integration and Participation

Linda K. Haymes, Debra L. Cote, and Keith Storey

Abbreviations

CDC	US Centers for Disease Control and Prevention
ICF	International Classification of Functioning, Disability and Health
SCI	Spinal cord injury
UDL	Universal Design for Learning

3.1 Introduction

Despite proven benefits of moderate physical activity upon health and psychological well-being, the majority of Americans do not engage in regular exercise (CDC 2015). Often cited barriers to exercise for the majority of adults are not enough time; lack of self-motivation; lack of self-management skills; fear of injury; no access to parks, sidewalks, or trails convenient to home or office; and lack of transportation to activities for children (Sallis et al. 1992; Sallis and Hovell 1990). For people with disabilities, exercise is of equal importance to prevent secondary conditions and promote health. The barriers for those with limited mobility include the usual ones cited for nondisabled as well as a list of additional barriers such as physical and attitudinal barriers like a negative social response to disabilities (Fine and Asch 1988). It is important for healthcare professionals to understand the relationship between barriers, benefits, and facilitators for leisure time physical activity (Williams et al. 2014).

L. K. Haymes (✉)
Graduate School of Education, Touro University California, Vallejo, CA, USA
e-mail: Linda.Haymes@tu.edu

D. L. Cote
Department of Special Education, Cal State Fullerton, Fullerton, CA, USA

K. Storey
Juvo Autism and Behavioral Health Services, Berkeley, CA, USA

D. Hollar (ed.), *Advances in Exercise and Health for People With Mobility Limitations*, https://doi.org/10.1007/978-3-319-98452-0_3

Exercise alone is important for improving quality-of-life measures and health promotion, but it is also a means to improve community inclusion and participation, which are critical for living well. Community integration and participation is essential for all people. Having access to choice and full range of opportunities in the community from social and civic participation to recreation and leisure is a component of quality of life. Community integration for those with limited mobility should occur across the lifespan. The community roles and activities for recreation, leisure, and exercise will vary depending on whether they are a child, youth, or adult and vary based upon interest and degree of limitation.

3.2 Benefits of Exercise, Leisure, and Recreation

3.2.1 Physical and Psychological

For people with disabilities, moderate- to high-level physical activity has been associated with many benefits including increased strength, mobility, endurance, weight control, increased immunity, and improved circulation (Bowden et al. 2008; Guttmann 1976; Jackson and Davis 1983; Kehn and Kroll 2009). Physical activity for those with disabilities includes reduced body fat (Cowell et al. 1986), greater HDL cholesterol (LaPorte et al. 1983), and reduced smoking (Shephard 1991). Curtis et al. (1986) found that disabled athletes had fewer physician visits and fewer medical complications.

Muraki et al. (2000) analyzed the psychological benefits of activity for males with spinal cord injuries (SCI) through categorizing the males into groups based on activity level. High active groups were defined as physical activity three or more times per week, middle active was once to twice per week, low active was once to three times per month, and inactive had no physical activity. The men were administered tests for depression and anxiety. Muraki et al. (2000) concluded that the males in the high active group had the lowest rating of depression and highest ratings of vigor. Similarly, Valliant et al. (1985) compared athletes and nonathletes with disabilities and found that the athletes reported higher self-esteem and more satisfaction with life and were in general better educated. Geron (1976) notes that people with mobility limitations engaged in sports demonstrated decreased rates of anxiety and depression.

3.2.2 Social

People engaged in inclusive community leisure programs have access to other people that are more reflective of the general society. Participation in competitive and recreational sports embeds people with disabilities into the greater community.

Sports can be a tool to the development of social skills (Stewart 1981). However, as noted by Bedini and Henderson (1994), women with disabilities who experienced more stigmatization and stereotyping from nondisabled peers were less satisfied with their leisure activities. In fact women with disabilities engage in less frequent physical activity than nondisabled women (Brown et al. 2005; Sharts-Hopko and Sullivan 2003). Thus it is imperative that women have access to leisure and physical activities that promote social acceptance. Bedini and Henderson (1994) suggested that it is up to leisure service providers to engage in "socially responsive initiatives" to make the environment more socially comfortable for females and males with disabilities. Social acceptance is a core factor in participation in integrated leisure activities for adults and youths with disabilities. Wilhite et al. (1999) noted that youth with mobility impairments had fewer negative reactions from peers without disabilities than youth with intellectual disabilities. As disheartening as that is, when there was more frequent contact between youths with disabilities and without disabilities with prior preparation for the youth without disabilities, accommodations were provided naturally, and the youths were seen as competent and of equal status; the inclusive participation was enhanced for all of the youths.

In general youth with disabilities participate in fewer social and recreational activities than their nondisabled peers (Solish et al. 2010). Additionally, it was determined that they more often engage in sedentary leisure activities such as watching television. There are many social and emotional benefits of engaging in leisure and recreational activities with peers (Cannella-Malone et al. 2016). Williams and Dattilo (1997) found that young adults with disabilities who participated in a leisure education program reported a more positive affect following the training program. In a study conducted by Jerome et al. (2007), adults with developmental disabilities increased the social interactions with typical peers following a leisure skills training intervention. Carter et al. (2013) explored methods for fostering friendships and noted that true friendships come from participation in shared interests and activities such as afterschool programs and community teams and recreation. The friendships that are developed are an important determinant of quality of life for people with and without disabilities. Friendships provide companionship, social support, and a buffer for handling stressful life events (Solish et al. 2010). Devine (2013) interviewed 16 undergraduate students with disabilities which centered upon access to an engagement in leisure time physical activities. Some of the themes that emerged from these interviews were right fit, quality of life, and connectedness. The students all emphasized that the physical activity had to be the right fit for their interests, energy level, and access. Most of the respondents stated their quality of life was enhanced through physical activity within the college community, but for some of the respondents, they were reminded of what they used to be able to do and now found difficult. Leisure time physical activity promoted social connectedness for the individuals. All noted the stress reduction benefits but also the development of friendships with other college students with and without disabilities. Some enjoyed showing those without disabilities just what they could do. Others reported that it gave them something to talk to peers about and provided confidence to try other things.

While there is research on the benefits of sports with a focus on athletes versus nonathletes, for the average person with mobility limitations, it is also about access to leisure and recreation integration and participation. Leisure can be considered a nonwork activity, and recreation similarly is an activity engaged for enjoyment. According to Anderson and Kress (2003), the personal benefits of leisure and recreation include management of stress, gain of life satisfaction, and participation in other aspects of life learned during leisure. Social benefits include building of communities; gaining access to relationships, friendships, and community development; and promoting diversity in the community.

3.3 Impact on Secondary Health Effects

Individuals with spinal cord injuries are at a higher risk for secondary health concerns (SHC) such as respiratory issues, obesity, and pressure ulcers. Secondary conditions from limitations in mobility include joint and muscle pain, sleep disturbances, weight problems, arthritis, circulatory problems, sexual dysfunction, isolation, and depression (Kinne et al. 2004). They are also at risk for chronic diseases and lower life expectancy (Wilroy and Knowlden 2016). Ravesloot et al. (2007) conducted an extensive analysis of secondary conditions for participants with mobility impairments participating in the Living Well with a Disability program. Those that participated in the Living Well program reported fewer limitations from secondary conditions. The US Department of Health and Human Services published guidelines for increasing physical activity with targets for individuals with disabilities. Under Healthy People 2020, they have guidelines to reduce barriers to health programs and increase physical activity (U.S. Department of Health and Human Services 2008). Van der Ploeg et al. (2004) promoted a conceptual model for a physically active lifestyle to prevent secondary health problems and improve everyday life functioning. The Active Lifestyle Rehabilitation Interventions in aging Spinal Cord injury (ALLRISC) is a multicenter multidisciplinary research program designed to research the impact of an active lifestyle upon the secondary health conditions of people aging with SCI (Van Der Woude et al. 2013).

3.4 Defining Community Integration and Participation for Adults and School-Aged Children

According to the International Classification of Functioning, Disability and Health (ICF), participation is involvement in a life situation. Activity limitations are difficulties an individual may have in executing activities. Participation restrictions are problems an individual may experience in involvement in life situations (ICF 2001, WHO). In defining participation in leisure, recreation, and sports, we are looking at more than just a life situation. Participation in leisure and physical activities is more closely related to quality of life than either level of impairment or functional performance. Therefore, participation outcomes are significant in their relationship to overall life satisfaction and quality of life of people with SCI.

Integration typically is defined as the person with the disability has access and opportunities to participate with nondisabled in settings with some adaptations and resources. Inclusion is the goal where inclusion is defined as participation alongside nondisabled peers, where there is a commitment to remove all barriers to the full participation of everyone as equally valued and unique individuals (Anderson and Kress 2003). When people with disabilities are not fully integrated into their community with able-bodied athletes, Shephard (1991) warns that we risk creating "ghettos" for disabled athletes. The impressive wheelchair marathon racer may aid in the perception of disabled athletes as competent, athletic, and valued. However, that same athlete can be seen with those attributes when competing with nondisabled athletes and participating in the same competition, albeit with some modifications and accommodations.

Social integration means that the person with disability is seen as having a value to society and to their community (Lemay 2006). Inclusion and social integration is influenced by social acceptance (Devine and Dattilo 2000). Longmore (1995) described the lack of social acceptance of people with disabilities in our society where the emphasis has been on remediation, cure, or correction of the functional aspects of the disability. Inclusion is possible when we drop stereotypes and treat people with disabilities as equal to those without disabilities. Disability is a socially constructed role defined by those that are nondisabled.

> Traditional rehabilitation a policy defined accommodations such as architectural modifications, adaptive devices (wheelchairs, optical readers) and services (sign-language interpreters) as special benefits to those who are fundamentally dependent. Disability-rights ideology redefined them as merely different modes of functioning, and not inherently inferior. (Longmore 1995)

Lemay (2006) lays out "roles of thumb" for achieving social integration that are relevant here for people with mobility limitations: (a) consider one person at a time within one setting, (b) ensure that the setting and role fit with preparations of partners in the setting, (c) choose smaller undermanned settings, and (d) seek the assistance of family members and friends.

Inclusion can enhance and lead to friendships and social support networks. These networks can be established through participation in athletics and leisure activities as well as through employment and school. Curtis et al. (1986) looked at the benefits of sports participation for people with spinal cord injuries (SCI) beyond social networks from the sports activities and the impact of sports participation upon health, vocational rehabilitation, and functional status. Wheelchair athletes had a higher functional status than nonathletes and had more hours of employment and education participation. However, employment and education differences were not at the significant level. Importantly, 72% of the SCI participated in sports at least one time per week; the sports included basketball, swimming, weight lifting, tennis, sailing, and pool/billiards. Only 28% were participating at the competitive level, and even the nonathletes showed an interest in participation in sports as a leisure time activity. Another important consideration was the involvement with sports did not limit vocational pursuits, thus providing access to communities through sports and through employment.

Inclusive leisure and recreation access for youths can lead to participation in recreational activities across the lifespan (Hoge et al. 1999). Inclusive recreational activities provide an outlet for people with disabilities to participate in activities of their choice, based upon interest and not restricted by availability of tailored programs. Exposure results in greater acceptance of people with varying levels of skill, needs, and backgrounds which benefits all participants (Schleien and Green 1992). When looking at integrated recreation, it is recreation services provided by the community for all people in the community as opposed to therapeutic recreation designed for those with disabilities.

3.5 Barriers to Community Integration and Participation and Methods for Addressing These Barriers

3.5.1 Physical

Researchers studied the physical benefits and positive impact of exercise for those with and without disabilities (Anderson and Kress 2003; Stroud et al. 2009). Potential physical benefits included increased strength/energy, sense of one's own accomplishment, improved muscle tone, psychological improvements, reduced health costs, decreased injuries, increased social interactions, and improved health (Lazarus 2016; Pfaffenbach 2016; Stroud et al. 2009). However, researchers identified physical barriers to exercise for persons with disabilities. They include (a) exhaustion from exercise, (b) poor facilities, (c) limited hours of operation, (d) worsening of symptoms, (e) health, (f) poor transportation, and (g) level of difficulty (Jaarsma et al. 2014; Stroud et al. 2009). Persons become frustrated when they cannot perform a sport, interact with healthcare professionals who know about their needs/disability, or want to exercise but have limited access to relevant activities (Devine 2012; Williams et al. 2014).

For some persons, in spite of knowing the physical benefits, environmental barriers prevent participation (e.g., lack of possibilities, lack of accessibility); however, facilitators (i.e., support to replace the barrier) can be put in place (Jaarsma et al. 2014). Cultural beliefs may place an undue burden on one's psychological health suggesting that a person's strength, able-bodiedness, or physical abilities is congruent with one's manliness (Kleiber and Hutchinson 1999). Thus, undue pressure can negatively impact the health of a person with disability (Williams et al. 2014). It is important to recognize the relationships these barriers play when promoting the possible positive results of physical activities for people with disabilities. When addressing physical barriers for persons with disabilities, collaboration with community organizations is key to increasing accessibility. Equally important is to provide staff with professional development on accommodations and methods for arranging equipment (Devine 2012; Wahman et al. 2006). Recreational programs and activities should fully integrate a person with disability (Schleien et al. 2009). Positive social connections (i.e., family, friends) are environmental facilitators that certainly influence the physical activity and health of people with disabilities (van der Ploeg et al. 2004).

3.5.2 Income and Economics

Interestingly, persons, whose income exceeded $50,000 annually, identified financial funding and time as barriers to their participation in exercise (Cowan et al. 2012). Persons with lowered annual incomes may find income/economics negatively impact their participation in recreational activities of choice. Stephens et al. (2012) found the economic costs associated with participating in recreational activities prohibitive for those with disabilities (e.g., specialized chairs, cost of travel/preparation, expensive equipment). Researchers assert people with disabilities experience both health and economic inequalities when compared to the general population (Drum et al. 2009). Equipment is often old or poorly maintained in recreational facilities that promote health; health promotion programs for persons with disabilities are at an economic disadvantage, as many do not meet the American with Disabilities Act of 1990 requirements (Drum et al. 2009).

Drum et al. (2009, p. 98) advocated that "Health promotion programs should be affordable to people with disabilities and their families or caregivers." They stressed keeping costs reasonable for participants since many are economically at a disadvantage. Despite the economic costs associated with recreational facilities (e.g., state run, local public), researchers recommend organizations to take the lead in providing facilities that are accessible and in funding specialized equipment (Stephens et al. 2012). Persons with disabilities, families/caregivers, program providers, service providers, administrators, staff, and policy makers can advocate for changes in local, state, and government funding of health programs and support bills that include funding for programs that target exercise, quality of life, and self-determination (Ravesloot et al. 2007). One suggestion (i.e., facilitator) to negate cost is for people with disabilities to access recreational activities that are free. Examples include (a) neighborhood walk, (b) exercise at the public park, (c) swimming, and/or (d) engaging with a friend in a physical activity (van der Ploeg et al. 2004).

3.5.3 Attitudinal

For someone whose life circumstance resulted in acquiring a disability, he/she requires a period of time to grieve and adapt mentally (i.e., attitudinal) to the fact that there are new limitations that previously never existed (van der Ploeg et al. 2004). This mental process could serve as an internal barrier. While there is an emphasis on community participation and integration, negative attitudes directed toward persons with physical disabilities can serve as significant external barriers (Shikako-Thomas et al. 2008). Sadly, literature has emerged showing lack of acceptance, bullying, unnecessary rules, and ignorance and bias in societal views, driving persons with disabilities to withdraw to segregated environments when engaging in physical activities (Mihaylov et al. 2004; Shikako-Thomas et al. 2008). Researchers have also found that parents identified their children's limited mobility as obstacles to their involvement in physical activities (Welsh et al. 2006). Additional obstacles included social and cultural attitudes, lowered socioeconomic status, and the educational level of caregivers (Shikako-Thomas et al. 2008). When family units are not united, it compounds the stress level, resulting in decreased levels of participation and community integration (Shikako-Thomas et al. 2008).

As we continue to recognize that participation and integration are essential to the well-being of a person with a disability, it is important that those individuals who deliver assistance display positive supportive attitudes and become advocates for policy change (Wahman et al. 2006; Shikako-Thomas et al. 2008). Stephens et al. (2012) suggested a multidisciplinary approach be used to support people with disabilities. Included in the approach would be methods to increase a person's self-determination and confidence (i.e., goal setting, cognitive behavioral strategies, learning new information). People with physical disabilities often benefit from associating with someone with the same impairment who can serve as a role model, as the relationship may encourage a positive shift in one's attitude (Wahman et al. 2006). According to Devine and Dattilo (2000), recreational settings can/do promote persons with disabilities perceived social acceptance and satisfaction as a consequence of the friendships that develop between those with and without disabilities. Surely, a person's self-efficacy is enhanced when those with and without disabilities engage in recreation, leisure, and sports activities together (van der Ploeg et al. 2004).

3.5.4 Administrative

While the emphasis has been on providing inclusive recreational activities to people with disabilities, the types of appropriate administrative supports are varied. Parents expressed that policy makers and administrators failed to provide recreational access and accommodations to people with disabilities, resulting in lost trust (Schleien et al. 2014) . Noteworthy was one policy maker's comment that funds were limited since access to community activities was problematic for a few persons with disabilities, while other issues predominated concerns of the general population (Schleien et al. 2014). These barriers imply there is a need for organizational changes to be made in the way that recreational inclusive practices are provided for people with disabilities (Schleien and Miller 2010).

Critical for the success of inclusive recreation activities is the hiring of licensed qualified staff and programming specialists to support people with disabilities and to work with families (Schleien and Miller 2010). Recreational providers should collect data with an understanding that data (a) drive decisions, (b) indicate what practices should be implemented, and (c) reveal what practices should be maintained and/or what reforms should be made to the current model (Miller et al. 2009). Administrators, agencies, and recreational organizations must work to bridge relationships with families fully respectful of the knowledge that parents have of their children and what supports are needed for accessing recreational facilities (Schleien et al. 2014).

3.5.5 Skills for People with Disabilities (PWD)

Some people with disabilities struggle psychologically (i.e., mental health issues) and socially, thus creating barriers in the community (Stumbo et al. 2015). Others (such as those who are deaf, hard of hearing, have sensory issues, or have an intellectual disability) may have difficulty in communication (Drum et al. 2009). As a result, some researchers have focused on the severity (i.e., mild, moderate, severe) of impairment (e.g., use of a wheelchair, assistive technology device), skill level, education, primary disability, and participation in physical activities (Froehlich-Grobe et al. 2008). Other researchers found a person's participation in a physical activity is not so much about the disability and other factors, but more importantly, the interactions within the environment influence (e.g., increase, decrease) capacity (Drum et al. 2009; Gray et al. 2006).

For those who struggle with mental health issues, facilitators include environments that stress choice and provide rich social interactions and opportunities for inclusive recreation activities (Stumbo et al. 2015). This involves active engagement with needed supports that encourage an individual's interdependence and independence while impacting the community at large (Stumbo et al. 2015). It is important to examine the role of parents in teaching specific skills that would increase a child's participation in recreational activities (Wuang et al. 2013). Wuang et al. (2013) stressed that skills need to be valuable and applicable to the daily lives of people with disabilities plus fit the routines of their environments. Setting goals for specific skills (e.g., strength training, jumping jacks, running) can be mutually established by the person and family; recreational activities should be appropriate to the culture and dynamics of the individual/family, consistent with norms, values, and significance (Wuang et al. 2013). Communication barriers might be overcome with large font, legible and simple text, pictures, alternative methods of communication, or accessible documents/formats to encourage and facilitate an individual's physical activity (Drum et al. 2009). It is important to note that interactions are fluid as people experience changes due to age, technology (e.g., something inaccessible becomes accessible), preference, or community accessibility (Gray et al. 2006).

3.5.6 *Skills for Professionals in Recreation Settings*

Data suggest professionals in inclusive recreational settings may be unaware of the needs and supports required for people with disabilities and that professionals may fail to demonstrate appropriate sensitivity or to offer desirable choices (Devine and Kotowski 1999). For example, professionals may expect a person with a disability to participate in an activity without choice. However, a person's participation does not mean his/her choice was intentional or autonomous (Seekins et al. 2012). Professionals who are skillful look for signs that the person with a disability had a choice in the context (e.g., available of facility, type of equipment, assistance from others) and form of participation (Seekins et al. 2012; van der Ploeg et al. 2004).

Professionals who work in recreational settings and support people with disabilities must address both personal (e.g., age, gender, health, injury, disease, mental attitude, race) and environmental factors (e.g., transportation, family, friends, social network), as they are important to the health of the individuals and influence their ability to successfully participate (van der Ploeg et al. 2004). Those who support people with disabilities should know the ability levels of the person they are working with and be aware of the existing supports in place (e.g., family, friends, community providers) (Stumbo et al. 2015). Jaarsma et al. (2014) suggested that professionals present possible barriers prior to participation in a sport, as the knowledge better prepares a person with a disability should obstacles occur. Of equal importance is to design programs that are individualized, culturally relevant, and specifically targeted to a person's age and disability (Jaarsma et al. 2014). Graham et al. (2009) emphasized the importance of professionals coaching parents/caregivers in an effort to increase the person's quality of relationships and involvement. However, for this to happen, it seems the person with a disability, professionals, parents, and the social influences must work together to increase skill levels and participation in valued recreational activities within the community.

3.6 Improving Community Integration and Participation

3.6.1 *Evidence-Based Programs and Best Practices*

Scientifically based research results in replicable and applicable findings from empirical research that used appropriate methods to generate persuasive, empirical conclusions. The use of the best available research results (evidence) allows service providers, as well as decision-makers (recreational administrators), to make informed decisions based upon empirical evidence. The National Autism Center's National Standards Report (2009) stated that evidence-based practice involves the integration of research findings with (a) professional judgment and data-based clinical decision-making, (b) values and preferences of families, and (c) assessing and improving the capacity of the system to implement the intervention with a high degree of accuracy. This report is very useful as it provides guidelines for evaluating whether or not an intervention is an evidence-based practice or not.

3.6.2 Universal Design

The National Universal Design for Learning Task Force (2011) defines UDL as

> a framework that provides all students equal opportunities to learn [by encouraging] teachers to design flexible curricula that meets the needs of all learners.

The advantage to using Universal Design for Learning strategies is that doing so creates access for all participants to the recreational environment curriculum, eliminates barriers to learning, and provides alternatives for methods of instruction, delivery of instruction materials, and participant responses (Lieberman et al. 2008). Sherlock-Shangraw (2013) recommends analyzing Universal Design for Learning into three categories. These are multiple means of representation (to how content is delivered to recreational participants such as telling, modeling, providing written instructions), multiple means of action and expression (how learners demonstrate skill level such as explaining to a peer or demonstrating skill), and multiple means of engagement (varying the ways in which individuals participate in activities such as providing opportunities for group as well as individual involvement).

3.6.3 Accommodations and Modifications

Making changes or modifications to instruction and supports can be a key component of recreational services. It is not always necessary that the individual do the recreational activity in exactly the same way as others or to the same criterion. The terms accommodations and modifications are often used interchangeably, but they represent two different changes. Accommodations provide different ways for individuals to take in (access) information or to display their knowledge or skill in the recreational setting. These changes do not alter or lower the standards or expectations for a task. Accommodations do not substantially change the instructional level, the content, or the performance criteria for the individual. Using a chair in a stretching class would represent an accommodation in a recreational setting.

Modifications are changes in the delivery, content, or completion level of tasks. They result in changing or lowering expectations and create a different standard for some individuals. Modifications do change the expected performance level for an individual. Having a basketball player being able to dribble, stop, and then dribble again without a foul being called (when other players are not) is an example of a modification.

3.6.4 Behavioral Intervention Strategies

Goal Setting

Goal setting involves the individual setting specific recreational goals he or she will meet and the specific reinforcement he or she will receive for meeting that goal (Lassman et al. 1999). It is important to have a goal that is realistic, achievable, and requires effort on the part of the individual. It is recommended that the goal/contract includes:

1. A task or activity the individual plans to learn or the behavior that they will engage in.
2. Specified activities and/or specific behaviors the person will engage in (defined and positively worded).
3. The degree of proficiency the individual will attain.
4. How the person will demonstrate that the learning has occurred.
5. What are the time dimensions for the goal.
6. How the goal will be measured and evaluated.
7. The role and responsibilities for each person.
8. A written contract that is signed by all parties involved.
9. Short-term goals should be initially used for quick reinforcement.
10. The goal intervention ties into self-management strategies.

Creating Routines

In order to increase physical activity and/or participation in recreational activities, the use of routines can often be very important. Routines facilitate participation if it is part of a daily routine such as meeting a group of friends for early morning walks, playing basketball after work, or joining a workout group at the recreational center. The use of self-management strategies can help the individual to establish and follow through on routines for recreation. The routines that are created can reflect the "new normal" of life following the acquisition of a disability, but also these should reflect the individual's lifestyle, routines, and choices prior to an injury. If the person was active, non-active, competitive, and areas of interest need to be reflected and taken into consideration when developing routines.

Self-Management

Self-management broadly refers to specific procedures used by an individual to influence his/her own behavior. Self-management procedures are effective because in part that they create independent performance and reduce the need for support from others during recreational activities. Self-management strategies can involve contracts, antecedent cue regulation, self-monitoring, self-evaluation, self-recruited feedback, and self-reinforcement. It is recommended that self-management strategies be an integral part of recreational support staff's instructional "tool kit." It is also important to carefully assess the person's learning needs, preferences, and the recreational environment before developing a self-management strategy to determine the appropriateness of a particular strategy.

Motivation

Every person has factors that motivate him or her to participate in recreational activities. Kerstin et al. (2006) found that for individuals with spinal cord injuries, there were a variety of motives for pursuing physical activity such as independence, improving health, physical appearance, becoming a role model for others, becoming part of a social network, and being needed. Motivation factors will match to the individual and their lifestyle but can be explored through education and mentoring.

Self-Determination

Self-determination can perhaps simply be defined as having control in one's life and as empowerment and control over one's life such as where and with whom to recreate. While the concept is simple, the implementation can be complex (Wehmeyer 1999). Self-determination involves choosing and then acting on the basis of those choices (Wehmeyer et al. 2002).

Person-Centered Planning

Person-centered planning encourages a positive view of the future based on strengths and preferences rather than focusing on eliminating deficits that the person may have. Person-centered planning consists of four components: (1) a personal profile that promotes a positive view of the individual, (2) a positive vision of the future, (3) action steps leading to the attainment of the desirable future lifestyle, and (4) any necessary changes to the current support system (Storey and Miner 2017).

Role of Choice

Choice making is perhaps the central element of self-determination. Promoting choice making has become an important focus of recreational services for people with disabilities and is a basic component in service delivery. The more opportunities an individual has to make meaningful choices, the more control he/she will experience in his/her life. However, as Agran et al. (2010) and Storey (2005) have noted, many people with disabilities are restricted to limited or meaningless choices in their lives.

3.7 Systematic Instructional Methodologies

By systematic instruction we mean instructional procedures that involve antecedent and consequence manipulations, frequent assistance to the learner (e.g., cues), correction procedures, and direct and ongoing measurement that is designed to increase specific skills (e.g., behaviors) for the learner. We would also like to emphasize here that systematic instruction is "evidence-based" and there is an extensive empirical base for the effectiveness of these procedures for teaching new skills (Iovannone et al. 2003).

The purpose of instruction is to develop competence for individuals (Gold 1980). This competence may be thought of as recreational skills or behaviors that the person can perform in specific circumstances. People may learn skills in a variety of ways, but for many individuals with disabilities, they will only learn skills with systematic instruction. Independence, competent performance, and social integration are all based upon having skills necessary to be competent in specific situations such as being a member of a club, playing on a sports team, or taking an aerobics class. Participation and integration in recreational settings are all based upon individuals having the skills necessary to be competent in specific situations (e.g., participating in workout group, going to a movie, etc.). For many individuals, such competence is not acquired incidentally. In other words, the emphasis of instruction must be to develop competence to function successfully in recreational settings. Systematic instruction provides evidence-based methods to teach those skills (Storey and Miner 2017).

3.7.1 Partial Participation

Partial participation means that individuals who might not have or be able to acquire all of the skills needed to completely participate in activities are still capable of partially participating in the activity (Baumgart et al. 1982; Ferguson and Baumgart 1991). In other words, partial participation means that everyone can be involved, even if they can't do all of the task or activity. Partial participation helps individuals to go beyond more than just being present in a situation and can increase their "membership."

Baumgart et al. (1982) stated that partial participation requires the consideration of adaptations that enhance the performance of existing skills, compensate for missing skills that will not likely be acquired, and allowing for the acquisition and utilization of alternative skills. There are four types of individualized adaptations:

Utilizing/Creating Materials and Devices

These adaptations refer to portable objects, equipment, or materials that enhance or allow partial participation. For example, for an individual that cannot hit a pitched ball when playing softball, hitting a ball off of a batting tee would allow that individual to participate.

Utilizing Personal Assistance

This refers to cues or supervisory assistance provided by another person. For example, an individual could have someone help them swing a bat at a pitched ball or push their chair around the bases.

Adapting Skills Sequences

This involves using a sequence that is different from that used by most individuals without disabilities. Most players put on their fielding glove by holding it in the air and sliding their opposite hand into the glove. A different sequence would be a player putting the glove on the bench and holding it down with one hand and sliding their opposite hand into the glove.

Adapting Rules

Rules are prescribed guidelines, procedures, or customs for engaging in activities. An example of adapting rules is provided by Bernabe and Block (1994) who helped to include a 12-year-old female with moderate/severe disabilities in a softball league. One adaptation that was made for her was that if she caught a ball on a bounce when fielding that, it was considered a "catch," and the batter was out.

A possible misuse of partial participation is where it is too easy to decide that an individual cannot add new skills and that they are then only allowed to partially participate in activities. Ferguson and Baumgart (1991) also stress the importance of achieving active instead of passive partial participation. This involves increasing opportunities for individuals to practice their recreational skills multiple times in a situation or to partially participate at different times during a day.

3.8 Summary

Improving community integration and participation in recreational, physical fitness, and sports is important for the physical and mental health of individuals with limited mobility. People with disabilities experience barriers to full integration in their community with able-bodied friends, teammates, and athletes. These barriers can be addressed with consideration of facilitators and evidence-based practices.

References

Agran, M., Storey, K., & Krupp, M. (2010). Choosing and choice making are not the same: Asking "what do you want for lunch?" is not self-determination. *Journal of Vocational Rehabilitation, 33*, 77–88.

Anderson, L., & Kress, C. B. (2003). *Inclusion: Including people with disabilities in parks and recreation opportunities*. State College: Venture.

Baumgart, D., Brown, L., Pumpian, I., Nisbet, J., Ford, A., Sweet, M., Messina, R., & Schroeder, J. (1982). Principle of partial participation and individualized adaptations in educational programs for severely handicapped students. *Journal of the Association for the Severely Handicapped, 7*, 17–27.

Bedini, L. A., & Henderson, K. A. (1994). Women with disabilities and the challenges to leisure service providers. *Journal of Park & Recreation Administration, 12*(1), 17–34.

Bernabe, E. A., & Block, M. E. (1994). Modifying rules of a regular girls softball league to facilitate the inclusion of a child with severe disabilities. *Journal of the Association for Persons with Severe Handicaps, 19*, 24–31.

Bowden, M. G., Hannold, E. M., Nair, P. M., Fuller, L. B., & Behrman, A. L. (2008). Beyond gait speed: A case report of a multidimensional approach to locomotor rehabilitation outcomes in incomplete spinal cord injury. *Journal of Neurologic Physical Therapy, 32*(3), 129–138.

Brown, D. R., Yore, M. M., Ham, S. A., & Macera, C. A. (2005). Physical activity among adults > or = 50 yr with and without disabilities, BRFSS 2001. *Medicine & Science in Sports & Exercise, 37*(4), 620–629, 610p.

Cannella-Malone, H. I., Miller, O., Schaefer, J., Jimenez, E., Page, E. J., & Sabielny, L. M. (2016). Using video prompting to teach leisure skills to students with significant disabilities. *Exceptional Children, 82*(4), 463–478. https://doi.org/10.1177/0014402915598778

Carter, E. W., Asmus, J., & Moss, C. K. (2013). Fostering friendships: Supporting relationships among youth with and without developmental disabilities. *Prevention Researcher, 20*(2), 14–17, 14p.

Centers for Disease Control and Prevention. (2015). *Physical activity and health: A report of the Surgeon General*. Atlanta: U.S. Department of Health and Human Services.

Cowan, R. E., Nash, M. S., & Anderson-Erisman, K. (2012). Perceived exercise barriers and odds of exercise participation among persons with SCI living in high-income households. *The Spinal Cord Injury Rehabilitation, 18*(2), 126–127.

Cowell, L. L., Squires, W. G., & Raven, P. B. (1986). Benefits of aerobic exercise for the paraplegic: A brief review. *Medical Science Sports and Exercise, 18*, 501–508.

Curtis, K. A., McClanahan, S., Hall, K. M., Dillon, D., & Brown, K. F. (1986). Health, vocational, and functional status in spinal cord injured athletes and nonathletes. *Archives of Physical Medicine and Rehabilitation, 67*(12), 862–865.

Devine, M. A. (2012). A nationwide look at inclusion: Gains and gaps. *Journal of Parks and Recreation Administration, 30*(2), 1–18.

Devine, M. A. (2013). Group member or outsider: Perceptions of undergraduates with disabilities on leisure time physical activity. *Journal of Postsecondary Education and Disability, 26*(2), 119–133.

Devine, M. A., & Dattilo, J. (2000). Social acceptance and leisure lifestyles of people with disabilities. *Therapeutic Recreation Journal, 34*(4), 306–322.

Devine, M. A., & Kotowski, L. (1999). Inclusive leisure services: Results of a national survey of park and recreation departments. *Journal of Park and Recreation Administration, 17*(4), 65–83.

Drum, C. E., Peterson, J. J., Culley, C., Krahn, G., Heller, T., McCubbin, J., et al. (2009). Guidelines and criteria for the implementation of community-based health promotion programs for individuals with disabilities. *Critical Issues and Trends: Underserved Populations, 24*, 93–101.

Ferguson, D. L., & Baumgart, D. (1991). Partial participation revisited. *Journal of the Association for Persons with Severe Handicaps, 16*, 218–227.

Fine, M., & Asch, A. (1988). Disability beyond stigma: Social interaction, discrimination, and activism. *Journal of Social Issues, 44*(1), 3–21. https://doi.org/10.1111/j.1540-4560.1988.tb02045.x

Froehlich-Grobe, K., Figoni, S. F., Thompson, C., & White, G. W. (2008). Exploring the health of women with mobility impairments. *Women & Health, 48*, 21–41.

Geron, E. (1976). Differences between sport form and physical fitness from a psychological point of view. *International Journal of Sport Psychology, 7*, 133–142.

Gold, M. W. (1980). *Did I say that? Articles and commentary on the try another way system*. Champaign: Research Press.

Graham, F., Rodger, S., & Ziviani, J. (2009). Coaching parents to enable children's participation: An approach for working with parents and their children. *Australian Occupational Therapy Journal, 56*, 16–23.

Gray, D. B., Hollingsworth, H. H., Stark, S. L., & Morgan, K. L. (2006). Participation survey/mobility: Psychometric properties of a measure of participation for people with mobility impairments and limitations. *Archives of Physical Medicine and Rehabilitation, 87*, 189–197.

Guttmann, L. (1976). Significance of sport in rehabilitation of spinal paraplegics and tetraplegics. *Journal of the American Medical Association, 236*(2), 195–197.

Hoge, G., Dattilo, J., & Williams, R. (1999). Effects of leisure education on perceived freedom in leisure of adolescents with mental retardation. *Therapeutic Recreation Journal, 33*(4), 320–332.

Iovannone, R., Dunlap, G., Huber, H., & Kincaid, D. (2003). Effective educational practices for students with autism spectrum disorders. *Focus on Autism and Other Developmental Disabilities, 18*, 150–165.

Jaarsma, E. A., Dijkstra, P. U., Geertzen, J. H., & Dekker, R. (2014). Barriers to and facilitators of sports participation for persons with physical disabilities: A systematic review. *Scandinavian Journal of Medicine & Science in Sports, 24*, 871–881.

Jackson, R. W., & Davis, G. M. (1983). The value of sports and recreation for the physically disabled. *The Orthopedic Clinics of North America, 14*(2), 301–315.

Jerome, J., Frantino, E. P., & Sturmey, P. (2007). The effects of errorless learning and backward chaining on the acquisition of internet skills in adults with developmental disabilities. *Journal of Applied Behavior Anaylsis, 40*(1), 185–189.

Kehn, M., & Kroll, T. (2009). Staying physically active after spinal cord injury: A qualitative exploration of barriers and facilitators to exercise participation. *BMC Public Health, 9*, 168–178.

Kerstin, W., Gabriele, B., & Richard, L. (2006). What promotes physical activity after spinal cord injury? An interview study from a patient perspective. *Disability and Rehabilitation, 28*(8), 481–488.

Kinne, S., Patrick, D. L., & Doyle, D. L. (2004). Prevalence of secondary conditions among people with disabilities. *American Journal of Public Health, 94*(3), 443–445.

Kleiber, D. A., & Hutchinson, S. L. (1999). Heroic masculinity in the recovery from spinal cord injury. In A. Sparkes & M. Silvennoinen (Eds.), *Talking bodies: Men's narratives of the body and sport* (pp. 135–155). Jyvaskyla: SoPhi University of Jyvaskyla.

LaPorte, R. E., Brenes, G., Dearwater, S., Murphy, M. A., Cauley, J. A., Dietrick, R., & Robertson, R. (1983). HDL cholesterol across a spectrum of physical activity from quadriplegia to marathon running. *Lancet (London, England), 1*(8335), 1212–1213.

Lassman, K. A., Jolivette, K., & Wehby, J. H. (1999). "My teacher said I did good work today!": Using collaborative behavioral contracting. *Teaching Exceptional Children, 31*, 12–18.

Lazarus, M. (2016). Wellness in the workplace. *Behavioral Health News, 3*(2), 1–14.

Lemay, R. (2006). Social role valorization insights into the social integration conundrum. *Mental Retardation, 44*(1), 1–12, 12p.

Lieberman, L. J., Lytle, R. K., & Clarcq, J. A. (2008). Getting it right from the start: Employing the universal design for learning approach to your curriculum. *The Journal of Physical Education, Recreation and Dance, 79*, 32–39.

Longmore, P. K. (1995). *The second phase: From disability rights to disability culture*. Retrieved 25 June 2016, from http://www.independentliving.org/docs3/longm95.html

Mihaylov, S., Jarvis, S. N., Colver, A., & Beresford, B. (2004). Identification and description of environmental factors that influence participation of children with cerebral palsy. *Developmental Medicine and Child Neurology, 46*, 299–304.

Miller, K. D., Schleien, S. J., & Lausier, J. (2009). Search for best practices in inclusive recreation: Programmatic findings. *Therapeutic Recreation Journal, 43*, 27–41.

Muraki, S., Tsunawake, N., Hiramatsu, S., & Yamasaki, M. (2000). The effect of frequency and mode of sports activity on the psychological status in tetraplegics and paraplegics. *Spinal Cord, 38*(5), 309.

National Autism Center. (2009). *Evidenced-based practice & autism in the schools*. Randolph: National Autism Center.

National Center on Universal Design for Learning. (2011). *UDL Taskforce*. Retrieved 20 Aug 2016, from http://www.udlcenter.org/aboutudl

Pfaffenbach, R. J. (2016). Health education class in the workplace. *Behavioral Health News, 3*(2), 21–22.

Ravesloot, C. H., Seekins, T., Cahill, T., Lindgren, S., Nary, D. E., & White, G. (2007). Health promotion for people with disabilities: Development and evaluation of the living well with a disability program. *Health Education Research, 22*(4), 522–531. https://doi.org/10.1093/her/cyl114.

Sallis, J. F., & Hovell, M. F. (1990). Determinants of exercise behavior (Determinants de la pratique de l'activite physique). *Exercise & Sport Sciences Reviews, 18*, 307–330.

Sallis, J. F., Alcaraz, J. E., McKenzie, T. L., Hovell, M. F., Kolody, B., & Nader, P. R. (1992). Parental behavior in relation to physical activity and fitness in 9-year-old children. *American Journal of Diseases of Children, 146*(4), 1383–1388.

Schleien, S. J., & Green, F. P. (1992). Three approaches for integrating persons with disabilities into community recreation. *Journal of Park & Recreation Administration, 10*(2), 51–66.

Schleien, S. J., & Miller, K. D. (2010). Diffusion of innovation: A roadmap for inclusive community recreation services. *Research & Practice for Persons with Severe Disabilities, 35*, 93–101.

Schleien, S. J., Miller, K. D., & Shea, M. (2009). Searching for best practices in inclusive recreation: Preliminary findings. *Journal of Park and Recreation Administration, 27*(1), 17–34.

Schleien, S. J., Miller, K. D., Walton, G., & Pruett, S. (2014). Parent perspectives of barriers to child participation in recreational activities. *Therapeutic Recreation Journal, 48*(1), 61–73.

Seekins, T., Shunkamolah, W., Bertsche, M., Cowart, C., Summers, J. A., Reichard, A., et al. (2012). A systematic scoping review of measures of participation in disability and rehabilitation research: A preliminary report of findings. *Disability and Health Journal, 5*, 224–232.

Sharts-Hopko, N. C., & Sullivan, M. P. (2003). Obesity as a confounding health factor among women with mobility impairment. *Journal of the American Academy of Nurse Practitioners, 15*(10), 438–443, 436p.. https://doi.org/10.1111/j.1745-7599.2003.tb00329.x.

Shephard, R. J. (1991). Benefits of sport and physical activity for the disabled: implications for the individual and for society. *Scandinavian Journal of Rehabilitation Medicine, 23*(2), 51–59.

Sherlock-Shangraw, R. (2013). Creating inclusive youth sport environments with the universal design for learning. *The Journal of Physical Education, Recreation and Dance, 84*, 40–46.

Shikako-Thomas, K., Majnemer, A., Law, M., & Lach, L. (2008). Determinants of participation in leisure activities in children and youth with cerebral palsy: Systematic review. *Physical & Occupational Therapy in Pediatrics, 28*(2), 155–169.

Solish, A., Perry, A., & Minnes, P. (2010). Participation of children with and without disabilities in social, recreational and leisure activities. *Journal of Applied Research in Intellectual Disabilities, 23*(3), 226–236.

Stephens, C., Neil, R., & Smith, P. (2012). The perceived benefits and barriers of sport in spinal cord injured individuals: A qualitative study. *Disability & Rehabilitation, 34*(24), 2016–2070.

Stewart, N. (1981). Value of sport in rehabilitation of the physically disabled. *Canadian Journal of Applied Sports Sciences, 6*, 166–167.

Storey, K. (2005). Informed choice: The catch-22 of self-determination. *Research and Practice for Persons with Severe Disabilities, 30*, 232–234.
Storey, K., & Miner, C. (2017). Systematic instruction of functional skills for students and adults with disabilities (2nd ed.). Springfield: Charles C. Thomas Publisher.
Stroud, N., Minahan, C., & Sabapathy, S. (2009). The perceived benefits and barriers to exercise participation in persons with multiple sclerosis. *Disability and Rehabilitation, 31*(26), 2216–2222.
Stumbo, N. J., Wilder, A., Zahl, M., DeVries, D., Pegg, S., et al. (2015). Community Integration: Showcasing the evidence for therapeutic recreation services. *Therapeutic Recreation Journal, 49*(1), 35–60.
U.S. Department of Health and Human Services. (2008). Healthy people 2020. Health and disability. Retrieved 15 June 2016, from https://www.healthypeople.gov/2020/topics-objectives/topic/disability-and-health
Valliant, P. M., Bezzubyk, I., Daley, L., & Asu, M. E. (1985). Psychological impact of sport on disabled athletes. *Psychological Reports, 56*(3), 923–929.
Van der Ploeg, H. P., Van der Beek, A. J., Van der Woude, L. H. V., & Van Mechelen, W. (2004). Physical activity for people with a disability: A conceptual model. *Sports Medicine, 34*(10), 639–649.
Van Der Woude, L. H. V., De Groot, S., Postema, K., Bussmann, J. B. J., Janssen, T. W. J., & Post, M. W. M. (2013). Active LifestyLe Rehabilitation Interventions in aging Spinal Cord injury (ALLRISC): A multicentre research program. *Disability & Rehabilitation, 35*(13), 1097–1103.
Wahman, K., Biguet, G., & Levi, R. (2006). What promotes physical activity after spinal cord injury? An interview study from a parent perspective. *Disability and Rehabilitation, 28*(8), 481–488.
Wehmeyer, M. (1999). A functional model of self-determination: Describing development and implementing instruction. *Focus on Autism and Other Developmental Disabilities, 14*, 53–62.
Wehmeyer, M. L., Lance, G. D., & Bashinski, S. (2002). Promoting access to the general curriculum for students with mental retardation: A multi-level model. *Education and Training in Mental Retardation and Developmental Disabilities, 37*, 223–234.
Welsh, B., Jarvis, S., Hammal, D., & Colver, A. (2006). How might districts identify local barriers to participation for children with cerebral palsy? *Public Health, 120*, 167–175.
Wilhite, B., Devine, M. A., & Goldenberg, L. (1999). Perceptions of youth with and without disabilities: Implications for inclusive leisure programs and services. *Therapeutic Recreation Journal, 33*, 15–28.
Williams, T. L., & Dattilo, J. (1997). Effects of leisure education on self-determination, social interaction, and positive affect of young adults with mental retardation. *Therapeutic Recreation Journal, 31*(4), 244–258.
Williams, T. L., Smith, B., & Papathomas, A. (2014). The barriers, benefits and facilitators of leisure time physical activity among people with spinal cord injury: A meta-synthesis of qualitative findings. *Health Psychology Review, 8*(4), 404–425. https://doi.org/10.1080/17437199.2014.898406.
Wilroy, J., & Knowlden, A. (2016). Systematic review of theory-based interventions aimed at increasing physical activity in individuals with spinal cord injury. *American Journal of Health Education, 47*(3), 163–175. https://doi.org/10.1080/19325037.2016.1158673.
World Health Organization. (2001). *International classification of functioning, disability and health*. Retrieved 25 June 2016, from http://www.who.int/classifications/icf/en/
Wuang, Y. P., Ho, G. S., & Su, C. Y. (2013). Occupational therapy home program for children with intellectual disabilities: A randomized controlled trial. *Research in Developmental Disabilities, 34*, 528–537.

Chapter 4
Physical Disability and Health Disparities

Lynda Lahti Anderson, Sarah MapelLentz, and Sheryl A. Larson

Abbreviations

NHIS	National Health Interview Survey
NCI	National Core Indicators
BRFSS	Behavioral Risk Factor Surveillance System
SES	Socioeconomic status

4.1 Introduction

Healthy People 2020 describes the nation's health goals for the coming decade. One of the overarching goals is to eliminate health disparities. The Office of Disease Prevention and Health Promotion (ODPHP) (2014) defines health disparities as:

> A particular type of health difference that is closely linked with social, economic, and/or environmental disadvantage. Health disparities adversely affect groups of people who have systematically experienced greater obstacles to health based on their racial or ethnic group; religion; socioeconomic status; gender; age; mental health; cognitive, sensory, or physical disability; sexual orientation or gender identity; geographic location; or other characteristics historically linked to discrimination or exclusion. (Disparities section, paragraph 4)

Determinants of health play a powerful role in health disparities. Determinants of health include individual behavior and genetics as well as environmental factors such as socioeconomic status, literacy, poverty, discrimination, and public policy (ODPHP 2014). Disparities often stem from a lack of access to resources needed by members of a group to manage risk stemming from biology or other factors (Warnecke et al. 2008). Health disparities may also result from an accumulation of experiences that lead to poor health (Krahn and Fox 2014). Population-level health determinants such as poverty, educational levels, gender, and race/ethnicity affect health outcomes independently from individual risk factors (Warnecke et al. 2008).

L. L. Anderson (✉) · S. MapelLentz · S. A. Larson
University of Minnesota, Minneapolis, MN, USA
e-mail: lla@umn.edu

D. Hollar (ed.), *Advances in Exercise and Health for People With Mobility Limitations*, https://doi.org/10.1007/978-3-319-98452-0_4

While people with disabilities also experience health disparities due to poverty or discrimination, disability is a risk factor for health disparities in and of itself (Krahn and Fox 2014). As a group, people with disabilities are much more likely to experience chronic conditions and at an earlier age than individuals without disabilities (Krahn et al. 2015). However, their needs are often not considered or accommodated in population-based efforts to address public health concerns such as smoking or obesity (Krahn et al. 2015). Thirty adults with spinal cord injuries, cerebral palsy, or multiple sclerosis reported that lack of access to healthcare affected their lives in five areas. Those areas included social (strained relationships, limitations in social role, and participation), psychological (depression, frustration, stress, and feeling devalued as a person), physical (deterioration in health and increased activity limitations), economic (financial strain due to missed work/inability to work, additional healthcare expenses), and loss of independence (Neri and Kroll 2003).

4.2 Prevalence of Physical Disabilities

Estimates of the prevalence of physical disabilities in the United States vary depending on the date of the estimate, the source, and the operational definition of disability. In the 2015 National Health Interview Survey, an estimated 15.2% of adults reported it was very difficult or not possible to walk a quarter of a mile; climb up ten steps without resting; stand for 2 h; sit for 2 h; stoop, bend, or kneel; reach overhead; grasp or handle small objects; lift or carry 10 pounds; or push or pull large objects (Blackwell and Villarroel 2015). The proportion with one or more of these limitations increased from 5.4% among adults 18–44 years to 48.0% among adults 75 years or older.

In the 2014 American Community Survey (ACS), an estimated 12.3% of people had one or more of six types of disabilities (hearing, vision, cognitive, ambulatory, self-care, and independent living). An estimated 7.0% of people ages 5 years or older had ambulatory disabilities (see Table 4.1; United States Census Bureau 2017).

Physical disabilities may be acquired (e.g., spinal cord injury) or congenital (e.g., cerebral palsy). Common causes of acquired disabilities include spinal cord injuries (SCI), traumatic brain injuries (TBI), back pain, osteoarthritis (OA), rheumatoid arthritis (RA), multiple sclerosis (MS), stroke, and limb loss (Ma et al. 2014). The prevalence of disability among people with these conditions varies depending on the severity of the condition. Strokes are the leading cause of long-term disability in the United States with 2.8% of the population having a long-term disability related to stroke (Ma et al. 2014). Estimates of the prevalence of back pain range from 5 to 22% for adults. Based on the Survey of Program Participation (SIPP), 7.6 million adults were estimated to have back pain as the primary cause of their disability (Ma et al. 2014).

Relatively few adults (0.6%) report rheumatoid arthritis as their primary cause of disabilities (Ma et al. 2014). However, as many as 21.6% of adults report having

Table 4.1 Disability prevalence in the 2014 American Community Survey

Disability type	Definition	Ages (years)	% with disability
Hearing	Deaf or serious difficulty hearing	All	3.5
Vision	Blind or serious difficulty seeing even with glasses	All	2.2
Cognitive	Difficulty remembering, concentrating, or making decisions because of a physical, mental, or emotional problem	5+	4.9
Ambulatory	Serious difficulty walking or climbing stairs	5+	7.0
Self-care	Difficulty bathing or dressing	5+	2.7
Independent living	Difficulty doing errands such as shopping alone because of a physical, mental, or emotional problem	18+	2.7
Any	One or more of the six types of disabilities	All	12.3

Source: U.S. Census Bureau (2017), 2010–2014 American Community Survey 5-Year Estimates

osteoarthritis, with 8.6 million identifying it as the primary cause of their disability. In addition, an estimated 400,000 people with multiple sclerosis and between 238,000 and 337,000 adults with a spinal cord injury have a physical disability (Ma et al. 2014).

Limb loss affects approximately two million individuals in the United States (Ma et al. 2014). Diabetes is a risk factor for limb loss and for several other potentially disabling conditions such as cardiovascular disease, stroke, peripheral vascular disease, renal disease, peripheral neuropathy, and retinopathy (Wong et al. 2013). People with diabetes were 1.71 times more likely to have mobility limitations, 1.92 times more likely to have limitations in activities of daily living, and 1.65 times more likely to have limitations in instrumental activities of daily living (Wong et al. 2013).

Developmental disabilities often associated with physical disabilities include spina bifida and cerebral palsy. In the United States, the birth prevalence of spina bifida is 2 per 10,000 live births, a decline since the introduction of folic acid fortified foods (Au et al. 2010). An estimated 166,000 people had spina bifida. The birth prevalence of cerebral palsy is 2.11 per 1000 live births (Oskoui et al. 2013). An estimated 734,000 adults and children have cerebral palsy.

4.3 Health Disparities for People with Disabilities

People with disabilities are more likely than the general population to report fair or poor health. Physical disability is sometimes associated with a chronic condition such as diabetes. However, individuals with physical disabilities are also at greater risk for a number of health disparities stemming from lack of access to medical resources (Havercamp et al. 2004; Chevarley et al. 2006; Nosek et al. 2006; Iezzoni 2011; Reichard et al. 2001; Mahmoudi and Meade 2015). People with disabilities are more likely to rate their health as poor compared to those without a disability (National Healthcare Disparities Report 2015).

Havercamp et al. (2004) compared the health outcomes of people with no disabilities and people with disabilities in North Carolina using the 2001 North Carolina Behavioral Risk Factor Surveillance System (BRFSS) to health outcomes for a group of adults with intellectual or developmental disabilities (IDD) using the 2001 National Core Indicators (NCI). Adults with IDD in the NCI experienced greater health disparities than people with or without disability in the BRFSS. On the BRFSS, people with disabilities were more likely than those without disabilities to have chronic conditions such as hypertension, cardiovascular disease, arthritis, diabetes, and chronic pain and were less likely to have exercised in the previous month or to have seen a dentist or had their teeth cleaned in the prior 5 years.

In the 2001–2005 National Health Interview Surveys, people with disabilities were more likely to smoke or to be obese and less likely to be physically active, all factors associated with increased risk of heart disease and certain cancers (Iezzoni 2011). Despite the presence of these risk factors, they were less likely to report that their healthcare providers had discussed issues such as smoking history during office visits.

The 2006 Medical Expenditure Panel Survey (MEPS) data show the same pattern of lack of access and poorer health outcomes. After controlling for age, sex, race, income, education level, health insurance status, and obesity status, people with disabilities had higher rates of arthritis, asthma, cardiovascular disease, diabetes, hypertension, high cholesterol, and stroke than people without disabilities (Reichard et al. 2011). Medical expenses for people with disabilities ($10,288 per year) were 4.3 times higher than for people without disabilities (Reichard et al. 2011).

The 2002 through 2011 MEPS data showed that people with disabilities are more likely to have unmet medical (75%), dental (57%), and prescription medication needs (85%) than people without disabilities (Mahmoudi and Meade 2015). Being female, lacking insurance, and being at or near the poverty level also increased the risk of having unmet medical needs.

Some subgroups such as women or those from underserved populations such as people of color experience higher rates of poor health outcomes (Chevarley et al. 2006; Nosek et al. 2006; Iezzoni 2011). In the 1994–1995 National Health Interview Disability Supplement, women with one or more functional limitations were more likely to report fair to poor health (Chevarley et al. 2006). They also reported greater prevalence of smoking, hypertension, being overweight, and having mental health problems. Women with functional limitations were also more likely to report not having had a Pap smear. Women with three or more functional limitations reported less access to general healthcare, dental care, mammograms, prescription medications, or eyeglasses (Chevalry et al. 2006). Other researchers have also reported that women with disabilities were more likely to die from breast cancer and less likely to report having mammograms or Pap tests (Iezzoni 2011). Women with more significant movement impairments were least likely to have had these screenings (Iezzoni 2011).

In a survey of 443 of women with physical disabilities (due to SCI, stroke, MS, polio, or other conditions) from diverse race and ethnic backgrounds, participants reported an average of 14.6 secondary conditions (range 1–42), of which an average of 5.7 was significant or chronic (range 0–20; Nosek et al. 2006). Three-quarters of the sample reported being overweight or obese. Other common conditions included pain, fatigue, visual impairments, weakness, circulatory problems, sleep problems, spasticity, blood pressure problems, and memory impairments.

Failure to recognize people with disabilities as an underserved population or to address their health needs is costly to both the individual and to society. Poor health outcomes may lead to increased functional limitations and further disability. Lack of access to medical care increases the risk of deterioration or development of additional chronic conditions. Having a disability is a risk factor for acquiring a chronic condition (Dixon-Ibarra and Horner-Johnson 2014). In the 2006–2012 NHIS, people with disabilities had increased odds of having cardiovascular disease (adjusted odds ratio (AOR) = 2.92), cancer (AOR = 1.61), diabetes (AOR = 2.57), obesity (AOR = 1.81), and hypertension (AOR = 2.18; Dixon-Ibarra and Horner-Johnson 2014).

Multiple chronic conditions complicate care and increase the burden for the individual and for the healthcare system. Among people dually eligible for Medicaid and Medicare, 53% of those ages 18–64 years had multiple chronic conditions, as did 73.5% of those 65 and older (Fox and Reichard 2013). Multiple chronic conditions are also associated with increased financial burdens. For example, one study found that having more chronic conditions was linearly associated with higher out-of-pocket expenses (Hwang et al. 2001). Individuals with three or more conditions had out-of-pocket healthcare expenses averaging $1334 compared to an overall average of $427. A similar relationship was reported in the 2009 MEPS sample of whom 18.3% had two to three chronic conditions and 7% had four or more. People with four or more chronic conditions were more likely to have had a hospital stay (27.7%) or emergency department visit (29.7%) than people with no chronic conditions (5.3% and 11.1%, respectively; Machlin and Soni 2013). People with multiple chronic conditions also took more prescription medications and had more ambulatory care visits. Average annual medical expenses were $2367 for people with no chronic conditions compared to $8478 for people with two or three chronic conditions and $16,257 for people with four or more chronic conditions (Machlin and Soni 2013). Addressing the causes of health disparities may help reduce medical expenditures for individuals and the healthcare system.

4.4 Health Disparity Models

4.4.1 The Stress Process Model

Pearlin's stress process model (1989) describes the causal mechanism of social inequalities on health outcomes and health disparities. Physical, mental, and general health are influenced by the extent to which social and personal resources mediate stress exposure experienced by individuals (Pearlin 1989; Turner 2009). Social resources include concepts such as social connections, while personal resources include concepts such as mattering (the extent to which an individual believes they are important to others) or mastery. For example, in a study of depression in 967 adults with physical disabilities, the effect of life events and chronic stress was mediated by social support and mastery (Turner and Noh 1988).

4.4.2 Center for Interdisciplinary Health Disparities Research (CIHDR) Model

The CIHDR model is a health promotion model for addressing health disparities in particular populations. This model, developed at the University of Chicago's Center for Interdisciplinary Health Disparities Research, describes distal (upstream) factors such as socioeconomic status and stigma, intermediate factors such as social relationships and physical context, and proximal (downstream) factors such as individual risk behaviors and previous illnesses that contribute to disparate health outcomes (Gehlert et al. 2008). It highlights the importance of upstream (distal) factors that may influence an individual's health status even at the cellular level. For example, a study of why more black women die of breast cancer than white women even though more white women are diagnosed with the disease found that cellular changes associated with increased levels of stress explained differences in mortality rates. A similar association was found in rat models. This model acknowledges that while downstream factors such as access to appropriate healthcare and access to transportation affect health outcomes, upstream socio-environmental factors such as stigma and poverty can have serious, deleterious consequences on cell function and may trigger health disparities (Gehlert et al. 2008). It posits that upstream factors such as poverty need to be addressed as part of public health interventions (Gehlert et al. 2008).

Both the stress process model and CIHDR model offer insight into the determinants of health disparities among people with disabilities as well as potential interventions. Understanding upstream causes of health disparities as well as potential mediators on an individual and societal level can inform models for effective interventions.

4.5 Downstream Causes of Health Disparities

Individuals with disabilities experience proximal (downstream) in addition to distal (upstream) causes of health disparities. Downstream causes include extrinsic or intrinsic factors that inherently overlap and frequently mutually reinforce one another. Similar to a feedback loop, individual causes of health disparities can have a net negative, positive, or neutral (balancing) impact on the health outcomes of an individual with a physical disability (Diez Roux 2011). For example, if an individual has a physical disability that significantly impairs functional capacity (intrinsic factor) which in turn limits employment options, the individual is likely to have lower income-earning potential than if able-bodied (extrinsic factor). This lower income-earning potential in turn makes transportation (extrinsic factor) to provider appointments more difficult than if financial resources were readily available. In this way, the intrinsic and extrinsic factors that cause health disparities are closely related.

4.5.1 Health Behavior

Individual health behaviors such as exercising regularly and eating a balanced diet are key intrinsic factors contributing to health disparities. Defined as "an action taken by a person to maintain, attain, or regain good health and to prevent illness," health behaviors reflect a person's health beliefs (Anderson et al. 2002). While externally influenced, health behaviors directly affect health outcomes. For example, if an individual with a disability believes that he is able to lose weight through healthy eating and activity, he is more likely to select healthy foods and to maintain a regime of regular physical activity. However, individuals with physical disabilities face stigmatized challenges as they try to actuate healthy living in accord with their positive health beliefs. Presumptions are made that those with physical disabilities cannot be physically active or chose healthy foods (Seburg et al. 2015).

The lack of positive health beliefs contributes to poorer health outcomes. For example, a person with a family history of coronary heart disease who habitually eats high-cholesterol foods is more likely to develop atherosclerosis than one who routinely eats heart-healthy foods. Similarly, an individual who tends toward inactivity is more likely to become overweight, leading to an increased risk of developing several types of cancer (National Cancer Institute 2017).

Individuals with physical disabilities face unique challenges, heavily rooted in external factors, to actualize positive health behaviors (Rimmer et al. 2008). For example, a relatively inactive individual in a wheelchair has less potential to become active than a fully able-bodied counterpart if the area in which he lives lacks accessible recreational areas. Given this, it is not surprising that rates of obesity among a study sample of adults with physical disabilities were nearly 40% as compared to approximately 24% among those without a physical disability (Reichard et al. 2011). Similarly high cholesterol levels, a condition correlated with unhealthy dietary intake, were found in over two-thirds of the sample of individuals with physical disabilities but in less than 20% of those without physical disabilities (Reichard et al. 2011). Stroke rates were twice as high, and high blood pressure (correlated with higher weight status) was four times more common in those with a physical disability compared to those without (Reichard et al. 2011). Each of these physical states correlates with underlying health behaviors and is a consequence of specific health behaviors. Higher rates of obesity-related health conditions among those with physical disabilities may be attributable to a lack of individual positive health beliefs or to a lack of accessible recreational exercise facilities or areas or both. Evidence and sound policy suggests that increasing the availability of accessible active areas for those with physical disabilities may have a positive impact on health beliefs and may increase healthy activity levels (Rimmer et al. 2005).

4.5.2 Accessibility of Healthcare

Barriers to healthcare accessibility include extrinsic factors that create health disparities in direct and indirect manners. Individuals with physical disabilities experience multiple barriers to accessing care such as medical provider biases and capacities, difficulty arranging accessible transportation, lack of physically accessible healthcare environments, or lack of affordable healthcare.

4.6 Provider Knowledge, Skills, and Abilities

The standard Western perception of healthcare views disability from the medical model, which considers disability to be any impairment that interferes with performance rather than a variant of human experience that requires physical adaptation to enable participation (Sharby et al. 2015). Medical providers in the United States are often educated to view disability as a negative health outcome that requires intervention to cure the impairment (Sharby et al. 2015). In this view, the negative impact of disability is considered to reside solely in the patient. The role of the medical provider is to fix the disability to the degree possible to improve the patient's quality of life. While this model enables amelioration of impairment when possible, it creates implicit provider biases and ignores social determinants of health outcomes described in the stress process model and CIHDR model. When viewed through the medical model, disability is seen as a tragedy. Social and integrative models, on the other hand, describe disability as part of normal variation within diverse communities (WHO 2002). Social and integrative models encourage medical providers to view physical disability not as an absolute impairment to a high quality of life but instead as an event of diversity unique to the individual patient. This view enables providers to recognize desired levels of participation, and not functional capacity, as the desired goal of treatment (Roush and Sharby 2011).

A conceptualization of physical disability as a patient deficit makes effective provider-patient communication difficult particularly when the patient does not view their physical disability as an impairment (Sharby et al. 2015). While a patient may request a consultation to discuss an acute illness, reproductive health, or another non-disability-specific topic, their requests may be overshadowed by a provider's preoccupation with fixing the patient's impairment. Both subtle biases and overt emphasis on a patient's disability cause ineffective provider-patient communication, causing people with physical disabilities to feel they have been unheard with regard to their self-perceived needs and to feel devalued and disrespected (Iezzoni 2006).

Provider communication style affects how individuals with disabilities experience healthcare encounters and can cause individuals to feel more or less willing to return for follow-up care or seek preventative services. A 2015 review of a decade's worth of literature on barriers to care for individuals with disabilities reported that individuals with disabilities frequently perceive providers as either not interested in or insensitive to their unique needs (Sharby et al. 2015).

Other barriers are created by specific in-clinic routine exams and treatment practices that convey a sense of disrespect to patients with disabilities. The National Healthcare Disparities Report noted that disability severity and patient satisfaction are inversely related. Those with disabilities are ten times more likely to report low satisfaction with their healthcare (2010, 2015). Individuals with more complex limitations were more likely to report a provider-patient encounter over the past 12 months during which the provider had not listened carefully to them, failed to explain things in an understandable manner, did not spend adequate time with them listening to their concerns, and did not show respect for their statements (Sharby et al. 2015). In one qualitative study, a woman with a disability described that during a radiographic procedure, masking tape was used to secure her arm to a table when the provided Velcro straps proved inadequate (Yee 2014).

Professionals and medical students acknowledge their lack of training in how to appropriately and effectively interact with or treat individuals with disabilities (Iezzoni et al. 2005). For example, medical students admitted to negative views of patients with disabilities (Iezzoni et al. 2005). In an analysis of medical student's clinical skills, students were less proficient in interpersonal and physical examination skills with patients with disabilities as compared to interactions and examinations of those without (Brown et al. 2010).

While physical disability is an intrinsic cause of health disparities, lack of access to preventative care at pivotal life points is a contributing external factor. Individuals with disabilities are offered fewer preventative measures such as flu vaccinations, gynecological examinations, or mammograms (Sharby et al. 2015). This lack of emphasis on preventive healthcare is seen across the lifespan for those with disabilities. A 2013 study analyzed the relationship between mobility status and likelihood of discussion of health-related behaviors with a primary care provider among a sample of youth and young adults ages 16–24 years (Seburg et al. 2015). Compared to their non-mobility-restricted counterparts, youth and young adults with mobility limitations were less likely to report discussions with their providers on important, health-impacting topics like substance abuse, and sexual and reproductive health, but were more likely to discuss healthy eating, weight, and physical activity.

4.7 Transportation

The lack of transportation options for getting to and from medical appointments is often a healthcare access barrier for people with physical disabilities. Being able to drive or having a caregiver who is able to provide transportation is associated with increased likelihood of visits to healthcare providers (Lishner et al. 1996; Arcury et al. 2005a, b).

For individuals in areas with poor public transportation, travel to and from medical appointments is particularly challenging (Peacock et al. 2015). The individual might have to travel long distances between home and a fixed route stop or between a fixed route stop and an appointment location. Public transportation may also run less frequently, which may require leaving home much sooner than would be necessary if door-to-door transportation was available. People with disabilites in rural areas report even greater difficulties finding transportation to access healthcare due to increased distances to reach a provider or limited or no availability of accessible transportation (Iezzoni et al. 2006).

Even in areas with frequent and reliable public transport, challenges include difficulties caused by harsh weather conditions or poorly maintained sidewalks or roads. Although significant advances have been made that enable personal transportation (curb ramps and cutouts for wheelchair access; street lights with audible and visual pedestrian crosswalk signals for those with low vision or who are hard of hearing; automatic door opening entryways), improvements are still needed (Peacock et al. 2015). Residents in rural areas often have fewer choices of medical providers, poorer access to specialty care, and less access to expensive technologies near where they live. They often travel greater distances to receive care and as a result have fewer healthcare visits (Arcury et al. 2005a, b).

When a provider's appointment schedule falls behind, patients who rely upon public transportation may miss their ride home. Taxis are infrequently equipped to transport individuals with certain assistive equipment, including wheelchairs. An appointment that might take a non-disabled counterpart a couple hours can easily occupy the entire day for an individual with a disability who is reliant on public transportation.

When considered through a "transportation equity" lens (analysis of which services and activities are considered basic, alongside the quality of the services considered adequate to satisfy basic access needs; Rawls 1971), the transportation burden experienced disproportionately by those with disabilities, as well as those with limited incomes, creates an unjustified access inequity.

4.8 Physically Accessible Environments

While more than 25 years have passed since the Americans with Disabilities Act was signed into law, many healthcare environments are still not fully accessible. Barriers to physical accessibility include but are not limited to:

- Lack of parking to accommodate people using a wheelchair lift
- Building and office entrances with steps or doors that are difficult to open
- Waiting rooms, exam rooms, and hallways that are too small or too narrow to navigate with assistive equipment

- Chairs, wheelchairs, exam tables, scales, and imaging equipment that are not adjustable or do not accommodate people of various sizes or those needing positioning assistance
- Lack of equipment to assist with transfers to and from exam tables
- Lack of appropriately trained staff and providers or specific specialists such as sign language interpreters

4.9 Upstream Causes of Health Disparities

Individuals with physical disabilities also experience external, or upstream, causes of health disparities such as socioeconomic factors and barriers related to the interaction between internal and external causes of health disparities.

4.9.1 Socioeconomic Factors

Socioeconomic status (SES) directly and indirectly affects the health of all vulnerable populations, particularly individuals with physical disabilities. Socioeconomic status, commonly conceptualized as the social standing or class of an individual or group, is frequently considered the most fundamental cause of health disparities (Link and Phelan 1995). Level of education, income, and occupation are distinct components of socioeconomic status that influence multiple health outcomes (Adler and Newman 2002). However, each component also influences the others. For example, lower educational attainment is correlated with fewer occupational prospects, which is in turn correlated with lower income-earning potential (Fry 2013).

Compared to those without physical disabilities, individuals with physical disabilities are less likely to graduate from high school (Reichard et al. 2011). Lower educational attainment is both a causal and a compounding factor within the socioeconomic status construct. Taken alone, lower educational attainment causes a decrease in the measure of one's socioeconomic status, which in turn increases likelihood of health disparities compared to those with higher educational attainment (Link and Phelan 1995). Because lower academic attainment decreases individual employment options and income-earning potential, its impact compounds the income and occupation components of socioeconomic status, which then further lower one's socioeconomic status and increase the likelihood of poor health outcomes (Reichard et al. 2011).

Cumulatively, policies that result in low educational attainment for individuals with disabilities create negative health disparities. People age 16 to 64 years with a disability who are interested in employment are more than twice as likely to be unemployed as those in the same age group without a disability (Bureau of Labor

2018). Youth and young adults with disabilities also experience large educational outcome disparities relative to youth without disabilities. While nearly half of youth with disabilities enroll in college, only 15% graduate (Bureau of Labor Statistics 2018). Roughly, a quarter of adults with disabilities are employed, compared to nearly two-thirds of those without disabilities (Bureau of Labor Statistics 2018). Many adults with physical disabilities rely on Social Security, Medicare, and/or Medicaid to supplement their income or to access healthcare. However, these programs have eligibility income limits, effectively diminishing earning capacity of enrollees. Individuals with disabilities utilize more healthcare resources (Yee 2011), are more likely to become dependent on public support programs, experience increased personal or familial healthcare costs, and spend a great deal of time and attention managing the healthcare system that would otherwise be devoted to employment or family obligations. Many adults with disabilities live in poverty, while children with disabilities disproportionately live in homes with lower than average incomes.

SES influences health outcomes in other direct and indirect ways, including the ability to access quality healthcare, level of exposure to environmental toxins, and exposure to stress (Diez Roux and Mair 2010). Neighborhoods also influence health inequities indirectly. People with disabilities are more likely to experience poverty and often have less access to safe public spaces, transportation, recreation, healthy foods, and social connections, factors associated with conditions such as hypertension, diabetes, and obesity (Diez Roux and Mair 2010). Higher incomes are correlated with lower likelihood of disease and premature death (National Center for Health Statistics 2012). At all income levels, people with more financial resources are healthier than people with fewer financial resources (Braveman et al. 2010). The relationship between "income and health is a gradient: connected step-wise at every level of the economic ladder" (Wolf et al. 2015).

Among subpopulations of individuals with disabilities, those from racial and ethnic minorities experience the greatest health disparities attributable to lower socioeconomic status. While blacks and Hispanics experience higher rates of disease than non-Hispanic whites, health disparities within each racial and ethnic group are magnified by income and disability status (Dubay & Lebrun 2012). Those low-income minorities with physical disabilities face a "double burden," with increased health disparities attributable to prejudice, discrimination, economic barriers, and barriers to adequate healthcare access (US Dept. of Health and Human Services 2011; National Center for Health Statistics 2016).

Stigma is closely related to socioeconomic status and can reduce attainment of higher socioeconomic status. Stigma is an important social determinant for health outcomes (Hatzenbuehler et al. 2013). Stigma is "the co-occurrence of labeling, stereotyping, separation, status loss, and discrimination in a context in which power is exercised." Stigma is a significant stressor for many marginalized populations and conveys social disadvantages. Stigma negatively affects the availability of resources, social relationships, and psychological and behavioral responses and induces stress that can lead to adverse health outcomes (Hatzenbuehler et al. 2013).

4.10 Addressing Health Disparities

4.10.1 Access to Care

One strategy states are pursuing to improve the costly, uncoordinated, and, consequently, ineffective care received by persons with disabilities is managed healthcare which can increase access to care coordination for enrollees. Enrollment in a managed care program has been shown to improve clinical outcomes, provide greater access to health and long-term care services, increase consumer satisfaction, and decrease the use of expensive healthcare services for individuals with physical disabilities (Palsbo et al. 2006; Surpin 2007; Quinn et al. 1999; Palsbo 2004).

The Affordable Care Act (ACA) of 2010 addressed many healthcare access barriers by mandating minimum criteria for ensuring the accessibility of medical equipment be established, including exam tables and chairs, weight scales, mammography equipment, and other equipment used in healthcare facilities (Iezzoni 2011; Krahn et al. 2015). However, adoption of these standards is voluntary. Ongoing advocacy is needed to encourage healthcare facilities to comply with the standards. Efforts to repeal all or some aspects of the ACA may limit the effect of these provisions.

4.10.2 Policy Interventions

Research is needed to evaluate the effectiveness of policies implemented to address health inequities and to examine the scalability of multidisciplinary community-based interventions (Koh et al. 2010).

Krahn et al. (2015) described four changes to the healthcare and public health infrastructure needed to ameliorate healthcare disparities for people with disabilities. The first is to ensure access to healthcare and human services by enforcing Americans with Disability Act and Affordable Healthcare Act. This change might include, for example, ensuring that screening equipment such as mammogram machines or exam tables in clinics were accessible to people with disabilities (Drum et al. 2005).

The second change is to improve data about the health of people with disabilities in order to inform evidence-based decision-making about healthcare policies and practices (Krahn et al. 2015; Rimmer 2011). An example of change in this area would be inclusion of items in all national healthcare survey programs using a standard definition to identify people with disabilities and to compare their outcomes to those of other people surveyed (Drum et al. 2005).

The third change is to improve training of the health and human service workforce regarding the needs of people with disabilities (Krahn et al. 2015). This would include providing training to improve the effectiveness of communication between providers and people with disabilities by encouraging providers not to make assumptions about what an individual may want but to instead ask the person directly about their condition, symptoms, and healthcare goals and needs (Sharby et al. 2015). It would also include instructing students in healthcare professions about the life experiences of people with disability to combat negative attitudes and inaccurate assumptions (Sharby et al. 2015). When asked students express a desire to deepen their understanding of how to effectively interact with and treat people with disabilities (Iezzoni et al. 2005).

The fourth change is to include people with disabilities in the development and delivery of public health programs and services and as a key target audience for public health initiatives (Krahn et al. 2015). Despite increased prevalence of behaviors that increase risk for chronic conditions (e.g., smoking; Agaku et al. 2014), public health efforts aimed at changing health risk behavior in the general population seldom consider the needs of people with disabilities and do little to make public health campaigns accessible or people with disabilities.

4.11 Addressing Upstream Determinants

Addressing upstream determinants of health disparities such as poverty, stigma, and access requires comprehensive structural changes in the healthcare system.

4.11.1 Poverty

Poverty limits access to appropriate healthcare and other resources and can be a source of ongoing stress, which increases the risk for developing chronic conditions. Poverty increases one's exposure to environmental risk factors. Addressing chronic un- and underemployment of people with disabilities will require the combined efforts of federal and state agencies and private employers.

While Medicaid buy-in programs such as Ticket to Work and Work Incentives Improvement Act of 1999 (TWWIIA) (P.L. 106–179) encourage people with disabilities using public benefit programs to work, current estimates reflect lower workforce participation rates (18.% vs. 65.7%) and higher unemployment rates (9.2% vs. 4.2%) for people with disabilities than for the general population (Bureau of Labor 2018). In a study of 810 working-age Kansans with disabilities, participants reported being discouraged from working by federal policies and by their medical professionals (Hall et al. 2013).

States need to be encouraged to take advantage of federal policies that promote employment (and ultimately reduce costs) for people with disabilities, educate people with disabilities about employment options that allow them to maintain access to healthcare coverage, and educate employers about employing individuals with disabilities. States that opted to expand eligibility for Medicaid-funded healthcare under the ACA have higher employment rates for people with disabilities than states that did not (38% versus 31.9%; Hall et al. 2017). In Medicaid expansion states, recipients can seek employment and increase their earnings while maintaining healthcare coverage (Hall et al. 2017).

Employers should be encouraged to employ people with disabilities. In a survey of 132 human resource managers, participants were more likely to consider hiring a person with a physical disability if they felt knowledgeable about the ADA and job accommodations and if the employer included disability in diversity programs (Chan et al. 2010).

4.11.2 Future Directions

Further research is needed into the role of stigma and chronic stress and their association with health disparities in people with physical disabilities. Research on the factors that mediate upstream factors related to health disparities (e.g., social support) is also needed. People with disabilities should be included in medical research on biological factors associated with health disparities and on the effectiveness of public health interventions to reduce those disparities. Continued research is also needed on the impact of Medicaid expansion and other provisions of provisions in the ACA on employment of people with physical disabilities and on health disparities.

4.12 Conclusion

Individuals with physical disabilities experience a number of health disparities including higher rates of chronic conditions and poor health outcomes. Policy interventions that improve access to care and provider training are needed to address the health disparities experienced by people with physical disabilities. Effective interventions to reduce those disparities will only be effective when they recognize people with disabilities as an underserved population and incorporate health disparities models that recognize the biological effects of upstream social determinants of health.

References

Adler, N. E., & Newman, K. (2002). Socioeconomic disparities in health: Pathways and policies. *Health Affairs, 21*(2), 60–76.

Agaku, I. T., King, B. A., Dube, S. R., & Centers for Disease Control and Prevention (CDC). (2014). Current cigarette smoking among adults – United States, 2005–2012. *MMWR Morbidity and Mortality Weekly Report, 63*(2), 29–34.

Anderson, D. M., Anderson, L. E., & Glanze, W. (2002). *Mosby's medical dictionary (Vol. 26, no. 43, p. 1866)*. St. Louis, MO, Mosby.
Arcury, T. A., Gesler, W. M., Preisser, J. S., Sherman, J., Spencer, J., & Perin, J. (2005a). The effects of geography and spatial behavior on health care utilization among the residents of a rural region. *Health Services Research, 40*(1), 135–156.
Arcury, T. A., Preisser, J. S., Gesler, W. M., & Powers, J. M. (2005b). Access to transportation and health care utilization in a rural region. *Journal of Rural Health, 21*(1), 31–38.
Au, K. S., Ashley-Koch, A., & Northrup, H. (2010). Epidemiologic and genetic aspects of spina bifida and other neural tube defects. *Developmental Disabilities Research Reviews, 16*(1), 6–15.
Blackwell, D. L., & Villarroel, M. A. (2015). Tables of summary health statistics for U.S. adults. *2015 National Health Interview Survey*. National Center for Health Statistics. Available from: http://www.cdc.gov/nchs/nhis/SHS/tables.htm
Braveman, P., Cubbin, C., Egerter, S., Williams, D., & Pamuk, E. (2010). Socioeconomic disparities in health in the United States: What the patterns tell us. *American Journal of Public Health, 100*(1), 186–196.
Brown, R. S., Graham, C. L., Richeson, N., Wu, J., & McDermott, S. (2010). Evaluation of medical student performance on objective structured clinical exams with standardized patients with and without disabilities. *Academic Medicine., 85*(11), 1766–1771.
Bureau of Labor Statistics. (2017). Employment status of the civilian population by sex, age, and disability status, not seasonally adjusted. *Data retrieval: Labor force statistics (CPS)*. Washington, DC: US Department of Labor. https://www.bls.gov/webapps/legacy/cpsatab6.htm
Bureau of Labor (2018), *Persons with a disability: Labor force characteristics summary*. Retrieved 21 August 2018 from https://www.bls.gov/news.release/disabl.nr0.htm.
Chan, F., Strauser, D., Maher, P., Lee, E. J., Jones, R., & Johnson, E. T. (2010). Demand-side factors related to employment of people with disabilities: A survey of employers in the Midwest region of the United States. *Journal of Occupational Rehabilitation, 20*(4), 412–419.
Chevarley, F. M., et al. (2006). Health, preventive health care, and health care access among women with disabilities in the 1994–1995 National Health Interview Survey, supplement on disability. *Women's Health Issues, 16*(6), 297–312.
Diez Roux, A. V. (2011). Complex systems thinking and current impasses in health disparities research. *American Journal of Public Health, 101*(9), 1627–1634.
Diez Roux, A. V., & Mair, C. (2010). Neighborhoods and health. *Annals of the New York Academy of Sciences, 1186*(1), 125–145.
Dixon-Ibarra, A., & Horner-Johnson, W. (2014). Peer reviewed: Disability status as an antecedent to chronic conditions: National Health Interview Survey, 2006–2012. *Preventing Chronic Disease*, *11*, E15 pp.
Drum, C. E., Krahn, G., Culley, C., & Hammond, L. (2005). Recognizing and responding to the health disparities of people with disabilities. *Californian Journal of Health Promotion, 3*(3), 29–42.
Dubay, L. C., & Lebrun, L. A. (2012). Health, behavior, and health care disparities: Disentangling the effects of income and race in the United States. *International Journal of Health Services, 42*(4), 607–625.
Fox, M. H., & Reichard, A. (2013). Disability, health, and multiple chronic conditions among people eligible for both medicare and medicaid, 2005–2010. *Preventing Chronic Disease*, *10*, E157 pp.
Fry, R. (2013).*The growing economic clout of the college educated*. Washington, DC: PEW Research Center. Available at http://www.pewresearch.org/fact-tank/2013/09/24/the-growing-economic-clout-of-the-college-educated/. Accessed 4 June 2017.
Gehlert, S., Sohmer, D., Sacks, T., Mininger, C., McClintock, M., & Olopade, O. (2008). Targeting health disparities: A model linking upstream determinants to downstream interventions. *Health Affairs, 27*(2), 339–349.
Hall, J. P., Kurth, N. K., & Hunt, S. L. (2013). Employment as a health determinant for working-age, dually-eligible people with disabilities. *Disability and Health Journal, 6*(2), 100–106.

Hall, J. P., Shartzer, A., Kurth, N. K., & Thomas, K. C. (2017). Effect of medicaid expansion on workforce participation for people with disabilities. American Journal of Public Health, 107(2), 262–264.

Hatzenbuehler, M. L., Phelan, J. C., & Link, B. G. (2013). Stigma as a fundamental cause of population health inequalities. *American Journal of Public Health, 103*(5), 813–821.

Havercamp, S. M., Scandlin, D., & Roth, M. (2004). Health disparities among adults with developmental disabilities, adults with other disabilities, and adults not reporting disability in North Carolina. *Public Health Reports, 119*(4), 418–426.

Hwang, W., Weller, W., Ireys, H., & Anderson, G. (2001). Out-of-pocket medical spending for care of chronic conditions. *Health Affairs, 20*(6), 267–278.

Iezzoni, L. I. (2006). Make no assumptions: Communication between persons with disabilities and clinicians. *Assistive Technology, 18*(2), 212–219.

Iezzoni, L. I. (2011). Eliminating health and health care disparities among the growing population of people with disabilities. *Health Affairs, 30*(10), 1947–1954.

Iezzoni, L. I., Ramanan, R. A., & Drew, R. E. (2005). Teaching medical students about communicating with patients who have sensory or physical disabilities. *Disabilities Studies Quarterly, 25*(1). http://dsq-sds.org/article/view/527/704.

Koh, H. K., Oppenheimer, S. C., Massin-Short, S. B., Emmons, K. M., Geller, A. C., & Viswanath, K. (2010). Translating research evidence into practice to reduce health disparities: A social determinants approach. *American Journal of Public Health, 100*(S1), S72–S80.

Krahn, G. L., & Fox, M. H. (2014). Health disparities of adults with intellectual disabilities: What do we know? What do we do? *Journal of Applied Research in Intellectual Disabilities, 27*, 431–446.

Krahn, G. L., Walker, D. K., & Correa-De-Araujo, R. (2015). Persons with disabilities as an unrecognized health disparity population. *American Journal of Public Health, 105*(S2), S198–S206.

Link, B. G., & Phelan, J. (1995). Social conditions as fundamental causes of disease. *Journal of health and social behavior (Extra Issue)*, 80–94.

Lishner, D. M., Levine, P., & Patrick, D. (1996). Access to primary health care among persons with disabilities in rural areas: A summary of the literature. *Journal of Rural Health, 12*(1), 45–53.

Ma, V. Y., Chan, L., & Carruthers, K. J. (2014). Incidence, prevalence, costs, and impact on disability of common conditions requiring rehabilitation in the United States: Stroke, spinal cord injury, traumatic brain injury, multiple sclerosis, osteoarthritis, rheumatoid arthritis, limb loss, and back pain. *Archives of Physical Medicine and Rehabilitation, 95*(5), 986–995.

Machlin, S. R., & Soni, A. (2013). Peer reviewed: Health care expenditures for adults with multiple treated chronic conditions: Estimates from the medical expenditure panel survey, 2009. *Preventing Chronic Disease*, 10.

Mahmoudi, E., & Meade, M. A. (2015). Disparities in access to health care among adults with physical disabilities: Analysis of a representative national sample for a ten-year period. *Disability and Health Journal, 8*(2), 182–190.

National Cancer Institute. (2017). *Obesity and cancer*. Retrieved 6 June 2017, from https://www.cancer.gov/about-cancer/causes-prevention/risk/obesity/obesity-fact-sheet

National Center for Health Statistics. (2012). Health, United States, 2011: With Special Feature on Socioeconomic Status and Health. Hyattsville, MD: US Department of Health and Human Services, Centers for Disease Control and Prevention, National Center for Health Statistics. Retrieved 21 August 2018. http://www.cdc.gov/nchs/data/hus/hus11.pdf.

National Center for Health Statistics (US). (2016). Health, United States, 2015: with special feature on racial and ethnic health disparities. Retrieved 21 August 2018 from https://www.cdc.gov/nchs/data/hus/hus15.pdf

National Healthcare Disparities Report 2010. (2011). AHRQ publication number 11-0005. Rockville: U.S. Department of Health and Human Services, Agency for Healthcare research and quality.

2015 National Healthcare Quality and Disparities Report and 5th Anniversary Update on the National Quality Strategy. (2016). AHRQ publication number 16-0015. Rockville: U.S. Department of Health and Human Services, Agency for Healthcare research and quality.

Neri, M. T., & Kroll, T. (2003). Understanding the consequences of access barriers to health care: Experiences of adults with disabilities. *Disability and Rehabilitation, 25*(2), 85–96.

Nosek, M. A., Hughes, R. B., Petersen, N. J., Taylor, H. B., Robinson-Whelen, S., Byrne, M., & Morgan, R. (2006). Secondary conditions in a community-based sample of women with physical disabilities over a 1-year period. *Archives of Physical Medicine and Rehabilitation, 87*(3), 320–327.

Office of Disease Prevention and Health Promotion. (2014). *Healthy people 2020: Disparities*. Washington, DC: US Department of Health and Human Services. Retrieved 5 Feb 2015, from http://www.healthypeople.gov/2020/about/foundation-health-measures/Disparities

Oskoui, M., Coutinho, F., Dykeman, J., Jetté, N., & Pringsheim, T. (2013). An update on the prevalence of cerebral palsy: A systematic review and meta-analysis. *Developmental Medicine & Child Neurology, 55*(6), 509–519.

Palsbo, S. (2004). Medicaid payment for telerehabilitation. *Archives of Physical Medicine and Rehabilitation, 85*(7), 1188–1191.

Palsbo, S. E., Mastal, M. F., & O'Donnell, L. T. (2006). Disability care coordination organizations: Improving health and function in people with disabilities. *Lippincott's Case Management, 11*, 255–264.

Peacock, G., Iezzoni, L., & Harkin, T. (2015). Health care for Americans with disabilities – 25 years after the ADA. *New England Journal of Medicine, 3*, 373–893.

Pearlin, L. I. (1989). The sociological study of stress. *Journal of Health and Social Behavior, 30*, 241–256.

Quinn, J., Prybylo, M., & Pannone, P. (1999). Community care management across the continuum: Study results from a Medicare health maintenance plan. *Care Management Journals, 1*(4), 223–231.

Rawls, J. (1971). *A theory of justice*. Cambridge,MA: Harvard University Press.

Reichard, A., Turnbull, H. R., & Turnbull, A. P. (2001). Perspectives of dentists, families, and case managers on dental care for individuals with developmental disabilities in Kansas. *Mental Retardation, 39*(4), 268–285.

Reichard, A., Stolzle, H., & Fox, M. H. (2011). Health disparities among adults with physical disabilities or cognitive limitations compared to individuals with no disabilities in the United States. *Disability and Health Journal, 4*(2), 59–67.

Rimmer, J. H., Riley, B., Wang, E., & Rauworth, A. (2005). Accessibility of health clubs for people with mobility disabilities and visual impairments. *American Journal of Public Health, 95*(11), 2022–2028.

Rimmer, J. H., Wang, E., & Smith, D. (2008). Barriers associated with exercise and community access for individuals with stroke. *Journal of rehabilitation research & development, 45*(2).

Rimmer, J. H. (2011). Building a future in disability and public health. *Disability and Health Journal, 4*(1), 6–11.

Roush, S. E., & Sharby, N. (2011). Disability reconsidered: The paradox of physical therapy. *Physical Therapy, 91*(12), 1715–1727.

Seburg, E. M., McMorris, B. J., Garwick, A. W., & Scal, P. B. (2015). Disability and discussions of health-related behaviors between youth and health care providers. *Journal of Adolescent Health, 57*(1), 81–86.

Sharby, N., Matire, K., & Iversen, M. (2015). Decreasing health disparities for people with disabilities through improved communication strategies and awareness. *International Journal of Environmental Research and Public Health, 12*(3), 3301–3316.

Surpin, R. (2007). Independence care system: A disability care coordination organization in New York City. *Journal of Ambulatory Care Management, 30*(1), 52–63.

Turner, R. J. (2009). Understanding health disparities: The promise of the stress process model. In *Advances in the conceptualization of the stress process* (pp. 3–21). New York: Springer Verlag.

Turner, R. J., & Noh, S. (1988). Physical disability and depression: A longitudinal analysis. *Journal of Health and Social Behavior, 29*(1), 23–37.

U.S. Census Bureau. (2017). S1810 disability characteristics. 2010–2014 *American Community Survey 5-year estimates*. Downloaded 13 June 2017 from: https://factfinder.census.gov/faces/tableservices/jsf/pages/productview.xhtml?src=CF

US Department of Health and Human Services. (2011). Advisory Committee on Minority Health. Assuring Health Equity for Minority Persons with Disabilities: A Statement of Principles and Recommendations. Retrieved 21 August 2018 from https://minorityhealth.hhs.gov/assets/pdf/checked/1/acmhhealthdisparitiesreport.pdf

Warnecke, R. B., Oh, A., Breen, N., Gehlert, S., Paskett, E., Tucker, K. L., & Hiatt, R. A. (2008). Approaching health disparities from a population perspective: The National Institutes of Health Centers for Population Health and Health Disparities. *American Journal of Public Health, 98*(9), 1608–1615.

Wolf, S., Aron, L., Dubay, L., Simon, S.M., Zimmerman, E., & Lux, K.X. (2015). How are income and wealth linked to health and longevity? Center on Society and Health. Retrieved 21 August 2018. https://societyhealth.vcu.edu/media/society-health/pdf/IHIBrief1.pdf

Wong, E., Backholer, K., Gearon, E., Harding, J., Freak-Poli, R., Stevenson, C., & Peeters, A. (2013). Diabetes and risk of physical disability in adults: A systematic review and meta-analysis. *The Lancet Diabetes & Endocrinology, 1*(2), 106–114.

World Health Organization. (2002). *Toward a common language for functioning, disability and health*. http://www.who.int/classifications/icf/icfbeginnersguide.pdf

Yee, S. (2011). *Health and health care disparities among people with disabilities*. Disability rights education and defense fund. Downloaded from: https://dredf.org/healthcare/Health-and-Health-Care-Disparities-Among-People-with-Disabilities.pdf. Accessed 5 June 2017.

Yee, S (2014). Health and Health Care Disparities among People with Disabilities. Retrieved 21 August 2018. http://dredf.org/healthcare/Health-and-Health-Care-Disparities-Among-People-with-Disabilities.pdf.

Chapter 5
Musculoskeletal Physiology, Disability, and Exercise

David Hollar

Abbreviations

BMP	Bone morphogenetic proteins
BRU	Bone remodeling unit
CD	Cluster of differentiation (many types of immune cell membrane glycoproteins)
CNTF	Ciliary neurotrophic factor
CRP	C-reactive protein
FAM5C	Family with sequence similarity 5, member C myokine
FGF	Fibroblast growth factor
GDF	Growth differentiation factor
HLA	Human leukocyte antigen
HPA	Hypothalamic-pituitary-adrenal axis
ICF	International Classification of Functioning, Disability and Health
IFN	Interferon
IGF	Insulin-like growth factor
IL	Interleukin
MCP	Monocyte chemoattractant protein
MHC	Major histocompatibility complex
MIP	Macrophage inflammatory protein
MMP	Matrix metalloproteinase
NAP	Nucleosome assembly protein
NMES	Neuromuscular electrical stimulation
PTH	Parathyroid hormone
RANTES	Regulated on activation, normal T cell expressed and secreted
SCI	Spinal cord injury
SMAD	Signaling molecule for TGF-beta receptor molecules
TBI	Traumatic brain injury
TGF	Transforming growth factor

D. Hollar (✉)
Health Administration, Pfeiffer University, Misenheimer, NC, USA
e-mail: David.Hollar@pfeiffer.edu

D. Hollar (ed.), *Advances in Exercise and Health for People With Mobility Limitations*, https://doi.org/10.1007/978-3-319-98452-0_5

Th1	Cell-mediated (pro-inflammatory) immunity
Th2	Humoral- or antibody-mediated immunity
TNF	Tumor necrosis factor
Wnt	Wingless integration proto-oncogene

5.1 Introduction: Ecological Systems Analysis in Health

The physiological environment represents a system consisting of systems with vast complexities. Our biology is a natural extension of the living environments that are all about us. Each of us inherits an incredibly elaborate and unique genome that undergoes an even more complex series of genetic regulatory and epigenetic controls that interact with external environmental forces to produce differing levels of ability or disability. Disability merely refers to limitations and barriers to functioning within a given environment. In one environment, functioning is limited, hence a disability, further compounded by societal attitudes and lack of supports. In another environment, functioning is not limited, further advanced by positive societal attitudes and supports.

The analysis of physiological systems mirrors ecological analyses of complex environments, as the events within living organisms are just as intricate and myriad as the interactions between the individuals comprising hundreds of millions of species that compose the many ecosystems of planet earth. Naturalists describe the wonder of these environments and emphasize just how little we understand of the positive environmental contributions made by many of these species, even as they face endangered status and extinction in many instances. Efforts are made to save these species through relocation to protected areas or by habitat protections and environmental modifications. The common feature here is the alteration/modification of environments to accommodate disabilities or, from our perspective, abilities that are in an unaccommodating environment. This represents the essence of ecological system analysis, interactions of molecules, differentiated cells, and tissues just as there are intra- and interspecies interactions at multiple layers of ecosystems.

Before moving to physiological systems that impact exercise and health, we conclude this analogy with several pertinent examples. Leopold (1949) lamented the loss of wildlife and natural environments in the face of progress, as many people pursue progress and have little use for the simple things such as a flock of migrating Canadian geese, a book pigeon, or a stand of birch. Using the months and seasons of the year, the past 150 years of human settlement on the American Great Plains, tree rings, and past geological epochs, he wove an intriguing appreciation for the quality of nature and its benefits to us when we conserve it and take only what is needed. Along similar lines, Wilson (2016) stressed the importance of setting aside land and water ecosystems comprising approximately half of the earth's surface to slow down and halt the biosphere's "sixth major extinction" event.

Leopold (1949) and Wilson (2016) made the case for preserving environments, just as researchers, advocates, and policy makers for people with disabilities seek to modify environments, both natural and human-made. The ultimate goal is to create accommodating human-made environments and to create technologies that enable people living with mobility and sensory limitations plus other disabilities to move and to enjoy the natural world as well. Therefore, the preservation of the natural world includes our capabilities to make all life sustainable, whether it is a species endangered by human activity or a person who "does not fit in" from the false perspectives of society.

5.2 The Holistic Approach to Disability and Health

The American Osteopathic Association's House of Delegates' *Four Tenets of Osteopathic Medicine* (www.osteopathic.org) maintains four central principles: (a) the body is integrated "body, mind, and spirit,"; (b) the body relies on feedback for "self-regulation"; (c) body "structures relate to function" and vice versa; and (d) "rational treatment" relies on these preceding three principles. These principles are consistent with the World Health Organization's (2001) International Classification of Functioning, Disability and Health (ICF), a biopsychosocial model that stresses the integrated roles of body structures, body functions, environment, social supports and attitudes, and activities and participation related to any disabling condition, however major or minor. The osteopathic medicine principles and the ICF represent a welcome, holistic approach to understanding systems that goes well beyond the traditional medical models of treating structures and functions alone.

The biopsychosocial approach to health and medicine is hardly new. The founder of osteopathic medicine, Andrew Taylor Still, MD, developed the "whole patient" concept and the four osteopathic principles, during the late 1800s. However, it has only been since the advances in molecular medicine, the growth of osteopathic schools during the early twenty-first century, and extensive public health programming that the holistic, biopsychosocial approach has regained an emphasis in patient care and the prevention of poor health conditions.

We know that disability is impacted well beyond mere body structures and physiology. The following sections focus primarily on physiology in relation to ability and disability, bearing in mind that these processes are essential with respect to the development of accommodations and assistive device technologies, plus general health practices, exercise, and nutrition that can drive improved health and functioning.

5.3 Challenges of Form and Function

The mathematician René Thom (1972) described fundamental problems of morphogenesis as "successions of forms," and he attempted to model these processes in cellular and organismal development. Human development from conception through early infancy, adolescence, adult development, and physiological decline with age represents a continuous process with specific inflection points (leading to greater stability or instability) in various aspects of physical functioning. Some major physical functioning events include the neurological, bone, and muscle growth and coordination between the muscle and bone that leads to upright walking around 1 year of age. Certainly this event varies in timing depending upon a variety of individualized conditions, but the age of occurrence generally occurs along a Gaussian curve around specific time points in early development.

The occurrence of disability in the musculoskeletal system may occur early due to inherited genetic conditions or birth defects (e.g., spina bifida) related to combinations of factors such as low maternal folic acid nutrition, genetics, etc. Disabilities related to childhood overweight and obesity conditions also can alter normal muscular and bone development due to poor nutrition and lack of outdoor recreation as primary causes. Santos et al. (2017) stressed that for long-term musculoskeletal health, physical activity must begin at prepubertal ages given that bone density peaks during the late 20s and early 30s, followed by gradual decline that is more steep for women who have lower bone densities.

Injuries represent a substantial contribution to the burden of disability at all ages. With respect to the neuromuscular system, such injuries can occur at any age but can include brain damage from shaken baby syndrome, appendicular fractures, and spinal injuries, plus knee and ankle injuries, the latter becoming more prevalent with increased skeletal ossification during adolescence. Of particular but often overlooked note is the Gompertz curve (Ricklefs and Finch 1995), which shows that the greatest increase in the probability of dying across the life span occurs between ages 14 and 24 (doubling for females, quadrupling for males), much of the morbidity and mortality being due to accidents and violence. This difficult period of life is well noted in public discourse, but it has been poorly researched as a major transition point with respect to the onset of acquired disability. Many accidents across the life span are needless, usually due to unexpected factors but also sometimes due to poor decision-making, overexertion, lack of protective equipment, mechanical/device failures and entropy, and other conditions such as aging, just to mention a few.

There are at least 1.7 million new incidences of traumatic brain injury (TBI) each year in the United States, with a long-term TBI disability prevalence rate of at least 3.2 million people (Ma et al. 2014; Waxweiler et al. 1995). The World Health Organization estimates a minimum of ten million new cases of TBI annually, with higher incidence rates in sub-Saharan Africa (150–170 cases per 100,000 total population) compared to a global incidence rate of 106 cases per 100,000 total population (Hyder et al. 2007). Lee et al. (2014) estimated the global incidence of spinal cord injury (SCI) at about 180,000 (i.e., 2.3 cases per 100,000 total population), albeit with the highest incidence rate (4.0) in North America. The incidence of new, traumatic spinal cord injuries in the United States has remained steady at about 5.3–5.4 cases per 100,000 total population (Jain et al. 2015). Many of these cases likely are due to higher motor vehicle usage and corresponding collisions in North America, although it is probable that rates in other global regions might be higher due to greater difficulties and underreporting collected data.

Therefore, bone and muscle receive the brunt of injuries that substantially impact mobility for people, with millions affected each year. Thom's (1972) succession of forms represents a mathematical model of biological organization, but we use it here to illustrate the physiological complexities and challenges for improving health and functioning. The challenges include addressing not just the overall physical aspects of exercise, basic functioning, and overall performance but also the genetic and molecular aspects associated with these conditions. The ecological system complex illustrates as well as we can how to attack the biological barriers that are unique to each person living with a disability.

Secondary conditions represent a major issue confronted by people living with mobility limitations, especially for spinal cord and traumatic brain injuries due to chronic pain and lack of access to exercise and adequate neurorehabilitation. Sun et al. (2016) emphasized that severe neurological injury that impacts mobility has long-term, deleterious inflammatory effects across multiple organ systems, including the heart, lungs, liver, and kidneys, sometimes with life-threatening impacts on health. Infection also is a major risk due to neuroinflammatory effects across the body, in these cases usually involving pro-inflammatory cytokines that will be described below. Besides the morphogenesis of forms, Thom (1972) outlined several basic "catastrophes" that occur when systems collapse, a concept of central concern to physical functioning as well as to environmental supports, both of which need to be maintained and reinforced to help people with disabilities.

5.4 Bone

Within vertebrate animal skeletons, bone is a living tissue with bone cells called osteocytes secreting a tough extracellular matrix that principally consists of calcium phosphate crystals (i.e., hydroxyapatite). The construction of bone is facilitated by specialized cells called osteoblasts that are activated by the thyroid hormone calcitonin, whereas the breakdown of bone matrix is facilitated by parathyroid hormone (PTH). The construction and breakdown of bone are antiparallel, antagonistic processes that continuously are occurring throughout the skeletal system depending upon overall and localized physiological conditions (Hollar 2000). These conditions can include thyroid/parathyroid hormone levels, thymic hormone activity, immune system leukocyte and cytokine levels, and especially blood serum levels of the minerals calcium and phosphorus plus the fat-soluble vitamins A, D, E, and K (Arron and Choi 2000; Cyster 1999; Dustin and Chan 2000; Gravallese 2003; Eriksen et al. 1994; Hollar 2000, 2017a; Powell 2005; Werlen et al. 2003). Furthermore, nutritional supplementation of folic acid helps with skeletal development and the prevention of various birth defects such as spina bifida by promoting erythrocyte production in the red bone marrow as well as DNA purine and pyrimidine nucleotide biosynthesis in cells.

Human bones consist of two principal types: (a) higher-density cortical bone, making up approximately 80% of the skeleton, mostly in movement-related long bone shafts of the arms and legs, and (b) lower-density spongy or cancellous (also called trabecular) bone that makes up the remaining 20% in more protective areas such as the vertebrae, the pelvic bones, the ribs, and even the ends of the arm and leg long bones (Eriksen et al. 1994). Both types of bone are involved in movement, as the ribs with elastic cartilage to the sternum are pulled by intercostal muscles to increase and decrease the chest cavity for inhalation and exhalation, respectively. Likewise, the pelvic bones articulate with the respective femurs to support the body and to enable walking.

Whereas the developing child inside the mother's uterus has a skeleton composed mostly of cartilage, some bone development does occur prior to birth. Nevertheless, the human skeleton remains over 70% cartilage at birth, thus requiring substantial nutritive support via breastfeeding to obtain the human-specific vitamins A, D, E, and K, folic acid, calcium, phosphate, and immune system antibodies and cytokines to stimulate musculoskeletal, brain, and other organ system development. Even so, cartilage remains an essential connection between bones to enable slight movements as well as lubrication and shock absorption at critical joints as individuals grow and develop throughout life. Of particular note, knee and ankle joints as well as sternum to collarbone articulations remain heavily cartilaginous into late adolescence. However, decreasing knee and ankle cartilage in late adolescence predicates an onset of injuries to those joints in athletics and work, situations that tend to be worse with age.

Exercise and nutrition help to maintain the integrity of bone and the flexibility of joints throughout life. This situation represents a major challenge for people living with mobility limitations, as many do not have access to exercise facilities or to facilities that have modified assistive exercise equipment. The result is a high percentage (e.g., over 50–60%) of people with mobility limitations who are severely overweight or obese (Hollar 2013). Furthermore, women have approximately 30% less bone density than men, especially in the scaffolding support of cancellous spongy bone at the ends of the long bones. Consequently, women are at heightened risk of serious bone fractures as they age, leading to falls and additional injuries, accelerating after menopause with the reduced estrogen production that contributes to bone and muscular development. Of course, both women and men vary genetically in their susceptibility to such cancellous bone loss with age. Nevertheless, individuals, especially women, need to supplement their diets with folic acid, calcium, phosphate, and fat-soluble vitamins A, D, E, and K as they age. It is emphasized that such dietary supplementation, coupled with exercise, should start at an early age, even the late 20s because bone loss can gradually start early in life without showing visible effects until too late to reverse later in life. The situation is more urgent for women and other vulnerable people living with mobility limitations due to inequitable access to exercise and good nutrition.

In bone remodeling, Eriksen, Axelrod, and Melsen (1994) report that the total bone volume in a typical adult human skeleton is approximately 1.75×10^6 mm^3 and that the cumulative bone remodeling unit (BRU) through this massive volume is roughly 400 mm long and 200 mm wide. The BRU consists of a sequence of osteoclasts tunneling through and breaking down bone, followed by reabsorption of the mineralized matrix and cellular components by the bloodstream and subsequent invasion by osteoblasts to rebuild the bone. This cyclic process occurs continuously throughout bone tissue in tens of thousands of circular Haversian units with concentrically arranged cell networks secreting bone matrix with a capillary blood supply to each unit. Therefore, bone remodeling is an extremely dynamic process that is sensitive to slight changes in many factors. Decreased serum calcium levels would lead to greater bone breakdown, whereas too much calcium would lead to increased bone formation, coupled with a multitude of other calcium-triggered cellular events. Injuries, thyroid gland disorders, and other conditions can lead to wide swings in the balance of the cumulative BRU and overall bone health. Consequently, age, diet, and exercise play critical roles in maintaining this balance.

The intricate roles of cell-to-cell signaling and immune system functioning have been underestimated in bone and overall tissue functioning (Cyster 1999; Hollar 2017a; Powell 2005). Furthermore, these researchers stress the ecological systems approach to understanding physiology. Nutrition and exercise drive neuroendocrine functioning, which triggers complex cascades of cellular enzymes and biochemical pathways that regulate DNA transcription, the activation or suppression of gene expression, and that regulate other aspects of cell and tissue development. Another overlooked aspect of bone and muscle cell functioning is the energy-generating mitochondrion, of which several hundred exist in each bone cell and up to several thousand exist in muscle cells (Hollar 2017b; Romanello et al. 2010).

Among the extensive intercellular biochemical pathways that are involved in osteocyte growth, bone matrix secretion, and osteoblast/osteoclast differentiation and control of bone growth are myokines. Myokines are a type of cytokine protein (see cytokines discussed below) that regulate glucose metabolism, blood vessel vascularization, and bone growth (Kaji 2016). Cytokines are prominently involved in pro- and anti-inflammatory immune responses, as described below, although we will focus on a few of numerous myokines in this section. Myokines include transforming growth factor beta (TGF-β), bone morphogenetic proteins (BMPs), fibroblast growth factor 2 (FGF-2), myostatin, matrix metalloproteinase 2 (MMP-2), and interleukins 6, 7, and 15, among others (Kaji 2016). The various members of the extensive TGF-β myokine family plus myostatin play a major role in muscle growth as described below.

Myokines including MMP-2, interleukins 7 and 15 (IL-7 and IL-15), FGF-2, osteoglycin, follistatin, osteonectin, irisin, insulin-like growth factor 1 (IGF-1), and FAM5C are released from the muscle and promote bone growth (Kaji 2016). In contrast, the muscle-released myokines TGF-β, myostatin, activin, ciliary neurotrophic factor (CNTF), monocyte chemoattractant protein 1 (MCP-1), Il-6, and others inhibit bone growth (Kaji 2016). Myostatin likewise inhibits muscular growth via TGF-β-stimulated pathways, as described below. The complex interaction between these regulatory proteins and the control of cellular processes in both osteocytes and other bone cells as well as in myocytes and other specialized muscle tissue cells illustrates the close developmental relationship between muscle and bone. This is further elaborated by the roles of many of these specialized cytokine molecules throughout the body in virtually every tissue. Therefore, a major emphasis here is that health, exercise, and nutrition for people living with and without disabilities transcend every molecular aspect of being at every level in one's body at all times throughout life. The careful balance between activating and inactivating gene regulatory proteins and biochemical pathways can be altered in so many different ways by how we take care of our bodies. While the body is extraordinarily resilient to change for most of life until age-related entropy takes hold, even unpredictable environmental and social factors can disrupt the tenuous balance of these control molecules within our hundreds of trillions of cells, including muscle and bone (Besedovsky and Del Rey 1996; Cohen 2002; Hotamisligil 2006; Joyce and Pollard 2009; Richards et al. 2013; Sun et al. 2016; Turnbull and Rivier 1999; Zhang et al. 2010).

Kaji (2016) pays particular focus on the myokine irisin, which is produced by muscle tissue in response to exercise and the mechanical stimulation of the muscle. In turn, irisin stimulates biochemical pathways (e.g., Wnt/β-catenin) in mesenchymal stem cells to differentiate into osteoblasts for the construction of bone, plus it stimulates the differentiation of brown fat adipose tissue. These two critical cellular formations are critical not only for bone growth but also healthy aging, since brown fat is associated with lowered inflammation and cellular production of free radicals (Franceshi and Campisi 2014). Irisin simultaneously reduces insulin resistance and blocks monocytes from differentiating into bone-destroying osteocytes (Kaji 2016).

Therefore, physical health and functioning operates at multiple physiological layers from molecule to organelle to cell to tissue to body structure and functioning for the entire organism. Because of these molecular pathways and the central role of the myokines such as irisin, exercise is essential to muscle and bone development as well as to all of health. This fact demonstrates why exercise, activity, and good nutrition are even more critical for people living with mobility limitations. This population needs assistive motion devices and access to usable exercise equipment at health facilities in order to obtain needed exercise for health and the prevention of secondary conditions that can arise from stroke, spinal cord injury, traumatic brain injury, genetic diseases on muscle and bone, and other injuries and infections that damage muscle, bone, and the nervous system.

5.5 Muscle

For exercise, primary focus is placed upon the approximately 600 or so antagonistically arranged skeletal muscles that overlay and interconnect the bones as well as protecting the internal muscles of the abdominal cavity. Additionally, the single cardiac muscle is similar in structure, albeit with interconnected cytoplasm between myocytes to enhance electrochemical messaging and mitochondrial energy transmission that lead to reliable, consistent heartbeats for billions of times during a person's life span. Furthermore, the third muscle type, smooth muscle, consists of tens of thousands of muscles that layer the skin, organs, every hair follicle, and the tens of thousands of miles of blood vessels throughout the body.

All muscles respond to physical activity, the skeletal muscles and the heart more directly with the buildup of new muscle and maintenance of strong tone for continued contractility. The smooth muscle response to exercise is much more subtle. For instance, the degree of relaxation of smooth muscle surrounding arteries can be measured using the diastolic blood pressure, the blood pressure in a person's arteries in between heartbeats when the heart is relaxed. Nevertheless, even during heart relaxation, the arterial smooth muscle layers constrict and relax to a degree that forces the blood out to the trillions of body cells. A healthy diastolic pressure should not be too high (overconstriction or forcing due to blockage and/or physiological stress), nor should it be too low (excessive relaxation with suboptimal blood forcing). A standard healthy diastolic blood pressure range should be approximately 50–90 mmHg for an adult, depending upon other physiological considerations.

In skeletal muscle, hundreds of thousands of long muscle fibers/cells, each sometimes on the order of a few cm, overlay and connect to form a muscle such as the deltoid or trapezius. Within each fiber, repeating blocks of actin and myosin protein filaments are arranged parallel to each other to enable contractility. When a stimulating, ion channel electrical impulse moves down the axon of a motor neuron to the myofiber, chemical neurotransmitters and ions trigger a depolarization of the myofiber membrane to allow an influx of calcium. This influx of calcium coordinates with adenosine triphosphate recycled from the myocyte mitochondria and the protein troponin to swivel the actin and myosin filaments together all along the skeletal muscle myofibers, leading to shortening of the muscle. Upon inhibition of stimulatory neurotransmitters and the motor neuron, the process reverses and the filaments relax, with the cumulative effects across thousands of myofibers causing the muscle to shorten/relax. Most muscle systems are antagonistic so that the contraction of one muscle will move a body structure in one direction, whereas the paired muscle contraction will move the body structure in the opposite direction (e.g., think of the biceps and triceps brachii). This simplistic neurotransmission and protein contraction model is simplistic, but it addresses most of the factors that are involved in muscle contraction. Still, the gene regulatory and additional enzyme regulatory machinery is even more fascinating and complex.

Dr. Se-Jin Lee's research team at Johns Hopkins University has demonstrated that the protein myostatin binds to a receptor on muscle cells to inhibit further muscle growth, increasingly so for older people and for people who suffer from certain inherited or acute musculoskeletal diseases, including cachexia (Zimmers et al. 2002). Myostatin, also called growth differentiation factor 8 (GDF-8), is one of the many direct and indirect gene regulatory enzymes of the extensive TGF-β (transforming growth factor beta) system or family. By itself, TGF-beta binds to cell membrane receptors that trigger a cascade of enzymatic reactions, most notably involving various SMAD enzymes that maintain cells in a stable G1 cell cycle stage. However, acidic conditions such as hypoxia with elevated carbon dioxide levels can cause TGF-beta to overexpress, leading to cell proliferation and immune cell suppression that together lead to cancer. Consistent with TGF-beta's growth arrest role, myostatin inhibits muscle cell growth. Lee et al. (2005) constructed modified myostatin receptors that would not bind to myostatin as well as competitive inhibitors of myostatin that block myostatin receptors on cell membranes so that the cascade of growth arrest signals would not occur, thereby increased both muscular and skeletal mass in animal tests. Such molecular modifications are beginning to show similar positive results for people participating in early clinical trial tests of these pharmaceuticals. Furthermore, Bloch et al. (2014) noted that neuromuscular electrical stimulation (NMES), an effective muscular rehabilitation procedure, seems to promote myostatin (GDF-8) and another TGF-beta molecule GDF-15, thereby suggesting caution that NMES could damage muscles.

The cardiac myocytes are quite elaborate with their interconnected cytoplasms and especially with their voluminous, numerous mitochondria for energy transduction. Myocytes may contain up to 7000 mitochondria per cell, albeit shared along the extensive endoplasmic reticulum that spans across the many connected myocytes. Smooth muscle cells are more independent but structured with more of a wavelike shape to overlap with companion smooth muscle cells connected via structural glycoprotein connections that hold the tissue together. This arrangement environmentally is more important for the layered squeezing of vessels and organs as with blood flow and digestion, respectively.

As discussed earlier with bone, exercise and nutrition positively activate the common molecular pathways of muscle and bone development while inhibiting the breakdown of these tissues. The availability of alternative exercises and especially modified assistive mobility plus exercise equipment stimulate growth and proper functioning for every muscle type, even if the muscle tissue has been damaged or is atrophied from lack of use or from other conditions or disease processes. Moreover, these common molecular pathways extend to neurological and other body tissue functioning, such that exercise benefits every cell and tissue across the body.

5.6 The ICF, Exercise, and Musculoskeletal Physiology

ICF codes related to bone and muscle include s710-s799, structures that are related to movement, and s410-499, structures of the cardiovascular, immunological, and respiratory systems (World Health Organization 2001). For functioning, the codes include b730-b749 for muscle power, tone, and endurance functions; b750-b799 for muscle gait patterns in walking, reflexes, and control over these functions; and b410-b429 plus b440-b449 for cardiothoracic functioning. Activities and participation codes include d410-d429 for “changing and maintaining body position”; d430-d449 for moving, lifting, and carrying items; d450-d469 for walking and/or moving with/without assistive devices; d470-d499 for using transportation for movement; d510-d599 for taking care of oneself; and d630-d649 for performance of household tasks, among many other relevant codes (e.g., obtaining employment). Ultimately, the musculature enablement of movement translates into practically every type of functioning for every purpose in one’s life.

As discussed elsewhere in this book, people living with mobility limitations are at increased risk for obesity (Hollar 2013) and for having a negative heart age differential (i.e., heart age that is "older" than chronological age, according to an American Heart Association algorithm; Hollar and Lewis 2015). Rimmer, Schiller, and Chen (2012) observed that people living with neuromuscular disabilities tend to have deconditioning related to their primary and secondary conditions that place them at increased risk for additional health problems if they attempt exercise. They recommended a light, progressive buildup exercise regimen, a practical guideline that is applicable even to people without disabilities who have had no or limited exercise experience.

5.7 Neuroendocrine and Immune Function: Linking Everything

Neural, endocrine, and immune functions are linked together by the overlapping cell types and chemical neurotransmitters/hormones that directly and indirectly (via cell membrane receptor cascades) control gene regulation within cells across the body. Of particular note are the cytokines, molecules that are involved in gene and other molecular regulation within cells, particularly with respect to stress responses and immune function. Turnbull and Rivier (1999) identified six principal types of cytokines:

1. Pro-inflammatory cytokines, including interleukins IL-1α, IL-1β, IL-8, and IL-9 that promote inflammation in tissues, particularly with immune attacks on foreign antigens (see also Dinarello 2000).
2. Anti-inflammatory cytokines, including interleukins IL-1ra, Il-4, IL-10, and IL13 that reduce inflammation during healing processes (see also Opal and DePalo 2000).
3. Tumor necrosis factors TNF-α and TNF-β that destroy tumor cells.
4. Interferons IFN-α, IFN-β, and IFN-γ that inhibit virus replication within infected cells.
5. Chemokines such as IL-8, NAP-1, MIP-1α MIP-1β, and RANTES that attract macrophages and other leukocytes to infected sites.
6. Hematopoietins IL-6, IL-11, CNTF, and others that stimulate both B lymphocytes for infection response, immune "memory," as well as neuron survival.

These molecules illustrate the ecological systems approach to understanding functioning in relationship to body structure physiology down to the cellular and molecular levels. Disruption of these molecular pathways can lead to further neural, muscular, and bone disorders, as well as uncontrolled sepsis, a major cause of mortality for people with severe disabilities as well as for older adults and infants. Physiological stressors impact multiple organ systems, relationships that were mapped very accurately by Selye (1950) with his stress general adaptation syndrome. As a visionary, Hans Selye (1950) mapped physiological correlates of stress that impacted health and disease, specifically identifying the adrenal cortex and its production of glucocorticoid steroid hormones to downregulate the immune system. It was only much later when Besedovsky and Del Rey (1996), Turnbull and Rivier (1999), and others more thoroughly elucidated the positive and negative feedback mechanisms between the adrenal gland, pituitary, thymus, and nervous system and the hypothalamic-pituitary-adrenal (HPA) axis that also involves not only endocrine hormones but also a staggering array of cellular cytokine (and myokine) protein messengers that are produced by tissues throughout the body.

A substantial body of research has demonstrated that stress and poor physiological health conditions, both counteracted by exercise and nutrition, can trigger cellular and tissue disruptions of normal chemical cytokine levels that lead to atrophy, mitochondrial energy-producing disruption within cells, cellular transformations of cells into cancer, and microbial opportunism coupled with immune system dysfunction leading to life-threatening sepsis (Ademowo et al. 2017; Besedovsky and Del Rey 1996; Cohen 2002; Hotamisligil 2006; Joyce and Pollard 2009; Richards et al. 2013; Sun et al. 2016; Turnbull and Rivier 1999; Zhang et al. 2010). Sun et al. (2016) stressed cytokine balance as an important therapeutic target to prevent secondary conditions in people living with spinal cord and traumatic brain injuries.

Leukocytes differentiate from stem cells located in the red marrow of flat bones via the feedback of hormonal signaling mechanisms. Dendritic cells formed in the bone marrow accumulate antigens and mature through the influence of exposed pathogens, T lymphocytes, and pro-inflammatory cytokines such as TNF-alpha, interleukin-1-alpha (IL-1α), interleukin 1-beta (IL-1β), interleukin 8 (IL-8), and interleukin 9 (IL-9). The dendritic cells migrate to lymphoid organs such as the spleen and lymph nodes where they complete maturation, a process that involves intracellular increases in intracellular major histocompatibility complex or human leukocyte antigen (MHC/HLA) type II glycoproteins and their movement to the cellular membrane surface; increased chemokines (i.e., CD54, CD58, CD80, CD86, CD40, CD25, CD83), interleukin 12, and the protein p55; as well as decreased protein actin cables. Anti-inflammatory cytokines such as interleukin 10 can delay the maturation of dendritic cells (Banchereau and Steinman 1998; Cyster 1999; Dorshkind and Horseman 2000; Sternberg 1997).

Within the lymphoid tissues, dendritic cells, and other maturing leukocytes, including thymocytes in the thymus, there is positive selection for thymocytes having low-affinity T cell receptors that do not strongly bind MHC I or II "self" peptides, thus not having the tendency to reject "self" somatic cells. Thymocytes with high-affinity T cell receptors are likely to reject self MHC antigens, receive no survival signal, and undergo apoptosis (Werlen et al. 2003). Surviving thymocytes, dendritic cells, macrophages, and other antigen-presenting cells present endogenous antigens to $CD8^+$ cytotoxic T cells or exogenous antigens to $CD4^+$ helper T cells, thereby triggering an immune cascade. Furthermore, interleukin 12 stimulates T helper cells to develop into inflammatory interferon-gamma (IFN-γ)-producing Th1 cells and then to activated natural killer cells (via Th1 cell-mediated immunity), whereas interleukins 4, 10, and 13 (plus virally produced mimics of interleukin 10) induce T helper cells to stimulate Th2 (humoral- or antibody-mediated immunity) immunoglobulin production and clonal selection of B lymphocytes as "memory cells" directed at a specific antigen (Cyster 1999; Dorshkind and Horseman 2000; Sternberg 1997; Werlen et al. 2003). Interleukin 1 interacts closely with TNF and IFN-γ to promote inflammation (Dinarello 2000).

The emergent fact from these psychoneuroimmunity studies (Besedovsky and Del Rey 1996) is that exercise, nutrition, and positive well-being promote immune system function that fights disease and contains cancer, that promotes muscle and skeletal growth, and that enables healthy aging. Stem cells in bone marrow of flat bones differentiate into red blood cells as well as leukocytes that are involved in all aspects of immunity. Hormones and cytokines from the nervous and endocrine systems plus other tissues play important regulatory roles for the differentiation of these cells. Nerves innervate muscle to trigger the contraction of muscles to move bones at joints. All body systems are connected via feedback mechanisms, further driving a clear argument that exercise has profound, holistic positive benefits to every cell, tissue, and organ of the body.

5.8 Applications to Exercise Equipment and Facilities

Rimmer, Schiller, and Chen (2012) demonstrated the need for careful exercise preparation and structured protocols to guide exercise and health for people living with mobility limitations. The National Center for Health, Physical Activity, and Disability (NCHPAD; www.nchpad.org) provides multiple guidebooks for effective exercise. Rosenberg et al. (2011) further argued the need for substantial research to improve exercise programs and the most effective disability-specific physiological measures to promote these programs.

Francis et al. (2017a, b) demonstrated that a 12-week exercise program with nutritional supplements can improve muscle mass for older women. This finding is particularly important given greater risk for declines in bone mineral density among women. For people living with spinal cord injury, Krassioukov et al. (2009) noted that orthostatic hypotension is common and that supervised exercise can help to reduce the effects of this secondary condition. Likewise, Huang et al. (2013) found that people living with SCI tend to have heightened risk for arterial stiffening coupled with vascular resistance, further implicating the importance of exercise to counteract these negative conditions.

Furthermore, C-reactive protein (CRP), an indicator of cardiovascular problems as well as inflammation), is increased for people living with SCI. Morse et al. (2008) found that high CRP is associated with obesity and reduced activity, both of which are higher for people living with mobility limitations and with lack of exercise opportunities. Exercise programs can reverse these trends.

Lastly, exercise and nutrition promote improved quality of life self-perceptions as well as body self-image, both of which are important for psychological well-being and motivation to participate in society, even with the barriers faced by lack of acceptance in some areas (Hammell 2004; Luongo and Pazzaglia 2016). Selye's (1950) psychoneuroimmune model clearly resonates with these findings as well as with the overall interconnections between mindfulness, exercise, nutrition, and health. To date, few efforts have been made to bring these concepts into rehabilitation for people living with mobility limitations, even more compounded by their lack of access to adequate, accessible exercise equipment and facilities. Organizations such as NCHPAD as well as Special Olympics (www.specialolympics.org) have attempted to promote health and exercise opportunities for people living with disabilities, but much progress must be made for full inclusion of people with disabilities in sports and other healthy activities.

5.9 Summary: Ecological Models, Physiology, and Health

The human body behaves as a complex, interconnected system of over 100 trillion cells that have differentiated to form varying cell types, tissues, and structures, beginning from very early embryonic development. The complex changes in genetic and epigenetic regulation lead to amazing cooperativity and functioning at the overall organismic level that most of us take for granted. For physical activity related to mobility limitations, the principal body structures of concern are the skeleton and joints, skeletal muscles that move the skeleton, and cardiac muscle that delivers oxygenated blood to all body tissues via tens of thousands of miles of blood vessels, all of which is surrounded by smooth muscle.

These body systems connect and move the entire body. Yet it is the microscopic molecular cytokines and myokines that further connect the cellular metabolism of these critical movement body systems but also the immune, neural, and endocrine control centers of the body. Disruption of these biochemical pathways can lead to muscle and skeletal atrophy as well as disease and other secondary conditions. Therefore, not only do we need to provide accessible exercise equipment and facilities for people living with mobility limitations, we must provide nutrition and mindfulness wellness programs for overall holistic health. Exercise programs should be structured with preconditioning activities for a smooth transition to regular, buildup exercise routines.

The organization of the body emphasizes a system perspective at the microscopic and macroscopic levels, as exercise, nutrition, and psychological well-being all impact multiple levels of body function. Moreover, the interactions of these levels can be synergistic as well as antagonistic, invoking an ecological systems perspective that mirrors the interactions between species in the natural world. As with any system, balance is critical, and changes of morphology and form must be carefully maintained.

People living with mobility limitations and other disabilities need to be active and involved in inclusive environments, the latter of which depend upon the willingness of each society to provide reasonable accommodations and respect for people with disabilities. There needs to be constructive guidance from health and rehabilitation professionals to guide each individual's unique exercise program and to follow up with meaningful progress in each program. Currently, many people living with mobility limitations are overweight or obese due to the effects of their primary disability plus secondary disabilities that develop but even more so from not having equal access to exercise and nutrition. Every person needs exercise, and no disability precludes them from this basic life need. Other chapters in this book address the various technologies and exercise equipment that are available to help all people achieve good health and physical performance.

References

Ademowo, O. S., Dias, H. K. I., Burton, D. G. A., & Griffiths, H. R. (2017). Lipid (per) oxidation in mitochondria: An emerging target in the ageing process? *Biogerontology, 18*, 859–879.

Arron, J. R., & Choi, Y. (2000). Bone versus immune system. *Nature, 408*, 535–536.

Banchereau, J., & Steinman, R. M. (1998). Dendritic cells and the control of immunity. *Nature, 392*, 245–252.

Besedovsky, H. O., & Del Rey, A. (1996). Immune-neuro-endocrine interactions: Facts and hypotheses. *Endocrine Reviews, 17*(1), 64–102.

Bloch, S. A. A., Syburrah, T., Rosendahl, U., Kemp, P. R., Griffiths, M. J. D., & Polkey, M. I. (2014). A paradoxical rise in rectus femoris myotatin (GDF-8) and GDF-15 in response to neuromuscular electrical stimulation in critical care. *Thorax, 69*(Suppl 2), A74.

Cohen, J. (2002). The immunopathogenesis of sepsis. *Nature, 420*, 885–891.

Cyster, J. G. (1999). Chemokines and cell migration in secondary lymphoid organs. *Science, 286*, 2098–2102.

Dinarello, C. A. (2000). Proinflammatory cytokines. *Chest, 118*(2), 503–508.

Dorshkind, K., & Horseman, N. D. (2000). The roles of prolactin, growth hormone, insulin-like growth factor I, and thyroid hormones in lymphocyte development and function: Insights from genetic models of hormone and hormone receptor deficiency. *Endocrine Reviews, 21*(3), 292–312.

Dustin, M. L., & Chan, A. C. (2000). Signaling takes shape in the immune system. *Cell, 103*, 283–294.

Eriksen, E. F., Axelrod, D. W., & Melsen, F. (1994). *Bone histomorphometry*. New York: Raven Press.

Franceschi, C., & Campisi, J. (2014). Chronic inflammation (inflammaging) and its potential contribution to age-associated diseases. *The Journals of Gerontology Series A: Biological Sciences & Medical Sciences, 69*(Suppl 1), S4–S9. https://doi.org/10.1093/gerona/glu057.

Francis, P., Lyons, M., Piasecki, M., McPhee, J., Hind, K., & Jakeman, P. (2017a). Measurement of muscle health in aging. *Biogerontology, 18*, 901–911.

Francis, P., McCormack, W., Toomey, C., Norton, C., Saunders, J., Kerin, E., Lyons, M., & Jakeman, P. (2017b). Twelve weeks' progressive resistance training combined with protein supplementation beyond habitual intakes increases upper leg lean tissue mass, muscle strength and extended gait speed in healthy older women. *Biogerontology, 18*, 881–891.

Gravallese, E. M. (2003). Osteopontin: A bridge between bone and the immune system. *The Journal of Clinical Investigation, 112*(2), 147–149.

Hammell, K. W. (2004). Exploring quality of life following high spinal cord injury: A review and critique. *Spinal Cord, 42*(9), 491–502.

Hollar, D. W. (2000). Bone changes and disorders. In P. Roberts (Ed.), *Aging* (pp. 105–109). Pasadena: Salem Press.

Hollar, D. (2013). Cross-sectional patterns of allostatic load among persons with varying disabilities, NHANES: 2001–2010. *Disability and Health Journal, 6*, 177–187.

Hollar, D. (2017a). Understanding the evolutionary historical background behind the trajectories in human health and disease. In D. Hollar (Ed.), *Trajectory analysis in health care*. New York: Springer.

Hollar, D. (2017b). Biomarkers of chondriome topology and function: Implications for the extension of healthy aging. *Biogerontology, 18*, 201. https://doi.org/10.1007/s10522-016-9673-5.

Hollar, D., & Lewis, J. (2015). Heart age differentials and general cardiovascular risk profiles for persons with varying disabilities: NHANES 2001–2010. *Disability and Health Journal, 8*, 51–60.

Hotamisligil, G. S. (2006). Inflammation and metabolic disorders. *Nature, 444*, 860–867.

Huang, S. C., May-Kuen, W. A., Lien, H. Y., Fuk-Tan, T. S., Fu, T. C., Lin, Y., & Wang, J. S. (2013). Systematic vascular resistance is increased and associated with accelerated arterial stiffening change in patients with chronic cervical spinal cord injury. *European Journal of Physical Rehabilitation Medicine, 49*(1), 41–49.

Hyder, A. A., Wunderlich, C. A., Puvanachandra, P., Gururai, G., & Kobusingye, O. C. (2007). The impact of traumatic brain injuries: A global perspective. *NeuroRehabilitation, 22*(5), 341–353.

Jain, N. B., Ayers, G. D., Peterson, E. N., Harris, M. B., Morse, L., O'Connor, K. C., & Garshick, E. (2015). Traumatic spinal cord injury in the United States, 1993–2012. *JAMA, 313*(22), 2236–2243.

Joyce, J. A., & Pollard, J. W. (2009). Microenvironmental regulation of metastasis. *Nature Reviews Cancer, 9*(4), 239–252.

Kaji, H. (2016). Effects of myokines on bone. *BoneKEy Reports, 5*, 826. https://doi.org/10.1038/bonekey.2016.48.

Krassioukov, A., Eng, J. J., Warburton, E. R., Teasell, R., & The SCIRE Research Team. (2009). A systematic review of the management of orthostatic hypotension following spinal cord injury. *Archives of Physical Medicine and Rehabilitation, 90*(5), 876–885.

Lee, S.-J., Reed, L. A., Davies, M. V., Girgenrath, S., Goad, M. E. P., Tomkinson, K. N., Wright, J. F., Barker, C., Ehrmantraut, G., Holmstrom, J., Trowell, B., Gertz, B., Jiang, M.-S., Sebald, S. M., Matzuk, M., Li, E., Liang, L.-F., Quattlebaum, E., Stotish, R. L., & Wolfman, N. M. (2005). Regulation of muscle growth by multiple ligands signaling through activin type II receptors. *Proceedings of the National Academy of Sciences USA, 102*(50), 18117–18122.

Lee, B. B., Cripps, R. A., Fitzharris, M., & Wing, P. C. (2014). The global map for traumatic spinal cord injury epidemiology: Update 2011, global incidence rate. *Spinal Cord, 52*(2), 110–116.

Leopold, A. (1949). *A sand county almanac*. New York: Oxford University Press.

Luongo, M. A., & Pazzaglia, M. (2016). Commentary: Body image distortion and exposure to extreme body types: Contingent adaptation and cross adaptation for self and other. *Frontiers in Human Neuroscience, 10*, 526. https://doi.org/10.3389/fnhum.2016.00526.

Ma, V. Y., Chan, L., & Carruthers, K. J. (2014). The incidence, prevalence, costs and impact on disability of common conditions requiring rehabilitation in the US: Stroke, spinal cord injury, traumatic brain injury, multiple sclerosis, osteoarthritis, rheumatoid arthritis, limb loss, and back pain. *Archives of Physical Medicine and Rehabilitation, 95*(5), 986–995, e1. https://doi.org/10.1016/j.apmr.2013.10.032.

Morse, L. R., Stolzmann, K., Nguyen, H. P., Jain, N. B., Zayac, C., Gagnon, D. R., Tun, C. G., & Garshick, E. (2008). Association between mobility mode and C-reactive protein levels in men with chronic spinal cord injury. *Archives of Physical Medicine and Rehabilitation, 89*(4), 726–731.

Opal, S. M., & DePalo, V. A. (2000). Anti-inflammatory cytokines. *Chest, 117*(4), 1162–1172.

Powell, K. (2005). Stem cell niches: It's the ecology, stupid! *Nature, 435*, 268–270.

Richards, D. M., Hettinger, J., & Feuerer, M. (2013). Monocytes and macrophages in cancer: Development and functions. *Cancer Microenvironment, 6*, 179–191.

Ricklefs, R. E., & Finch, C. E. (1995). *Aging : A natural history*. New York: Scientific American Library.

Rimmer, J. H., Schiller, W., & Chen, M.-D. (2012). Effects of disability-associated low energy expenditure deconditioning syndrome. *Exercise and Sport Sciences Reviews, 40*(1), 22–29.

Romanello, V., Gguadagnin, E., Gomes, L., Roder, I., Sandri, C., Petersen, Y., Milan, G., Masiero, E., Del Piccolo, P., Foretz, M., Scorrano, L., Rudolf, R., & Sandri, M. (2010). Mitochondrial fission and remodeling contributes to muscle atrophy. *EMBO Journal, 29*(10), 1774–1785.

Rosenberg, D. E., Bombardier, C. H., Hoffman, J. M., & Belza, B. (2011). Physical activity among persons aging with mobility disabilities: Shaping a research agenda. *Journal of Aging Research, 2011*, 708510. https://doi.org/10.4061/2011/708510.

Santos, L., Elliott-Sale, K. J., & Sale, C. (2017). Exercise and bone health across the lifespan. *Biogerontology, 18*, 931–946.

Selye, H. (1950). Stress and the general adaptation syndrome. *British Medical Journal, 1*, 1383–1391.

Sternberg, E. M. (1997). Neural-immune interactions in health and disease. *The Journal of Clinical Investigation, 100*(11), 2641–2647.

Sun, X., Jones, Z. B., Chen, X.-M., Zhou, L., So, K.-F., & Ren, Y. (2016). Multiple organ dysfunction and systemic inflammation after spinal cord injury: A complex relationship. *Journal of Neuroinflammation, 13*, 260. https://doi.org/10.1186/s12974-016-0736-y.

Thom, R. (1972). *Structural stability and morphogenesis*. New York: W.A. Benjamin.

Turnbull, A. V., & Rivier, C. L. (1999). Regulation of the hypothalamic-pituitary-adrenal axis by cytokines: Actions and mechanisms of action. *Physiological Reviews, 79*(1), 1–71.

Waxweiler, R. J., Thurman, D., Sniezek, J., Sosin, D., & O'Neil, J. (1995). Monitoring the impact of traumatic brain injury – A review and update. *Journal of Neurotrauma, 12*(4), 509–516.

Werlen, G., Hausmann, B., Naeher, D., & Palmer, E. (2003). Signaling life and death in the thymus: Timing is everything. *Science, 299*, 1859–1863.

Wilson, E. O. (2016). *Half-earth: Our planet's fight for life*. New York: Liveright/W.W. Norton & Company.

World Health Organization. (2001). *The international classification of functioning, disability and health*. Geneva: Author.

Zhang, Q., Raoof, M., Chen, Y., Sumi, Y., Sursal, T., Junger, W., Brohi, K., Itagaki, K., & Hauser, C. J. (2010). Circulating mitochondrial DAMPs cause inflammatory responses to injury. *Nature, 464*, 104–108.

Zimmers, T. A., Davies, M. V., Koniaris, L. G., Haynes, P., Esquela, A. F., Tomkinson, K. N., McPherron, A. C., Wolfman, N. M., & Lee, S.-J. (2002). Induction of cachexia in mice by systemically administered myostatin. *Science, 296*, 1486–1488.

Chapter 6
Prototypes for Assistive Innovation

David Hollar

Acronymns

ADA	Americans with Disabilities Act
ADL	Activity of daily living
ANSI	American National Standards Institute
CE	Conformité Européene
EMG	Electromyographic (impulse)
FDA	US Food and Drug Administration
FES	Functional electrical stimulation
FNS	Functional neuromuscular stimulation
HCI	Human-computer interaction (or interface)
iBOT	Powered wheelchair that uses gyroscopes to balance and climb steps/terrain
IADL	Instrumental activity of daily living
ICF	International Classification of Functioning, Disability and Health
IMS	Inertial measurement system
ISO	International Organization for Standardization
LDS	Local dynamic stability
MOD	Mechatronic Orthotic Design
NCHPAD	National Center for Health, Physical Activity, and Disability
NIDILRR	National Institute on Disability, Independent Living, and Rehabilitation Research
RERC	Rehabilitation Engineering Research Center
RESNA	Rehabilitation Engineering Society of North America
RRTC	Rehabilitation Research and Training Center
RSP	Running-specific prosthesis
SCI	Spinal cord injury
TBI	Traumatic brain injury

D. Hollar (✉)
Health Administration, Pfeiffer University, Misenheimer, NC, USA
e-mail: David.Hollar@pfeiffer.edu

D. Hollar (ed.), *Advances in Exercise and Health for People With Mobility Limitations*, https://doi.org/10.1007/978-3-319-98452-0_6

6.1 Introduction: The Concept of Universal Exercise Access

The major advances in the development of assistive technology for people with disabilities have included rehabilitation research and engineering programs that are located at universities across the United States. Many of these programs receive federal funding from the National Institute on Disability, Independent Living, and Rehabilitation Research (NIDILRR). NIDILRR, a division of the US Department of Health and Human Services, periodically offers peer-reviewed grant competitions for 5-year Rehabilitation Engineering Research Centers (i.e., RERCs) and Rehabilitation Research and Training Centers (RRTCs) as well as annual competitions for research and development projects. All centers and projects have the twin goals of supporting the NIDILRR Long-Range Plan and the Rehabilitation Act of 1973 (Public Law 93–112, 87 Statute 344, 29 U.S.C. § 701) to promote research that advances the health, civil rights, community integration, and independent living for people with disabilities. NIDILRR-funded research projects at universities and rehabilitation hospitals across the United States are working to advance the technologies to support people living with mobility limitations and other disabilities.

The major areas of technological development for assistive devices include the following foci:

1. Wheelchairs that are specifically tailored to each user's unique needs, specific terrains and surfaces, and motion functions (e.g., specific sports)
2. Prostheses of varying capacities that replace upper or lower limbs
3. Advanced gait mechanisms and orthotics for people who can walk but face difficulties due to physiological barriers, anatomical anomalies, and/or terrain
4. Battery-operated exoskeleton devices for people living with spinal cord injury so that they can walk and experience mobility for performing daily tasks beyond the limitations of wheelchairs
5. Sensory-assisted technologies with eye motion and voice computer applications to perform tasks that may be limited by combinations of upper limb disabilities and/or vocal limitations brought about by traumatic brain injury (TBI), spinal cord injury (SCI), birth defects, or other events

These areas represent the foci of this chapter and the major research areas for rehabilitation assistive device technologies, although other areas exist as well. The principle of universal access derives from the well-developed and advocated architectural principles of universal design for buildings, transportation, and other structure access for people with disabilities (see Chap. 1 and https://www.cdc.gov/ncbddd/disabilityandhealth/disability-strategies.html). These principles promote independent living and community integration for people with disabilities in accordance with the Americans with Disabilities Act (ADA) and the Rehabilitation Act of 1973 and its amendments.

6.2 Advances in Technology

Technological developments have been driven by advances in the understanding of human performance, human factors, the mechanics of moving bodies, computer advances and miniaturization, human-computer interaction, and energy source (i.e., battery) maximization. Besides important issues involved in assessing the best, most appropriate, and economical assistive device, providers must work with consumers to plan the appropriate human factors and ergonomics mapping that best evaluates the consumers' environment, which also promotes product research and continuous process improvement (Fuhrer et al. 2003; Lenker and Paquet 2003). One of the most influential tools is the International Classification of Functioning, Disability and Health (ICF; World Health Organization 2000).

With all of these efforts, the objective is to maximize functioning in a variety of environments. Just as a biker will switch from a racing bicycle to a trail/mountain bike for off-road use or as an astronaut uses a highly complicated spacesuit that can withstand the near vacuum of outer space plus certain levels of cosmic radiation, we modify devices and machines to improve our access and functioning in diverse environments. The individual who lives with mobility limitations needs exercise and desires to participate in the environment. The environment extends beyond the workplace and city to natural environments that are even less accessible. Nevertheless, people have a natural affinity for the outdoors, for recreation, and for the living world (Wilson 1988). While often neglected, there is growing research that demonstrates the positive benefits of nature and the outdoors on human health (Hartig et al. 2014). Thus, we focus on devices to maximize functioning for people living with mobility limitations.

6.3 Wheelchairs

The standard tool for many people who live with mobility limitations is the wheelchair, a machine based upon the simple principle of placing a chair on wheels, with the wheels appropriately engineered for balance around the user/machine center of mass, smooth movement over relatively smooth surfaces, and the dual capacities for independent operation by the user or by a caregiver. There is historical evidence of at least some variation of the wheelchair being used by ancient cultures, including China, although the first specific development of wheelchairs to address mobility disabilities did not occur until a few 100 years ago (Woods and Watson 2004). Herbert Everest and Harry Jennings patented the first practical wheelchair during the 1930s, a model that has remained mostly intact for wheelchair design to the present day. The Everest/Jennings model was widely adopted by hospitals and ultimately for individual use at home and in public. Individual use models that are lower cost and lightweight structurally meet durability standards (e.g., Rehabilitation Engineering Society of North America – RESNA) that are comparable to heavy duty hospital wheelchairs (Gebrosky et al. 2013). Individual use wheelchairs are widely available from major retail and pharmaceutical stores.

Cooper et al. (2008) reported that wheelchairs represent approximately 1% of Medicare spending and are a $1.3 billion dollar industry in the United States with 170 wheelchair manufacturing companies. Regardless, they argue the need for advancements in wheelchair technologies and reduced costs to provide greater access and options for different environments and unique, individual situations.

A variety of rehabilitation hospitals and research centers (e.g., Craig Hospital, Denver, Colorado; Shepherd Center, Atlanta, Georgia; National Center for Health, Physical Activity, and Disability – NCHPAD; Shriners Hospitals for Children) have developed and provide to users many different wheelchair styles that are adapted for specific environments. For example, there are wheelchair designs for different Paralympic sports, including basketball, softball, soccer/football, rugby, and hunting/fishing. For direct contact competition, wheelchairs often have angled wheels and accessories for appropriate ball handling. For outdoor environments with rough terrain, wheelchairs may have modified tread on the wheels or even caterpillar tracking treads for electric wheelchairs that can maneuver over extremely rough terrain. Hunting and fishing wheelchairs also can include mounts for fly-fishing or for bow/rifle firing. Handcycles represent a synthesis of bicycles and wheelchairs for effective exercise.

With these modifications, we move to electric wheelchairs and even more advanced robotic/smart wheelchairs (Woods and Watson 2010). Electric wheelchairs, including scooters, provide motorized motion without the requirement of hand propulsion of the wheels. The iBOT is a motorized power chair that uses balance and spatial orientation for motion over difficult terrain, most notably its capacity to climb stairs. With the addition of a user-interactive computer system, the iBOT and similar power wheelchairs can be transformed into even more effective smart wheelchairs (Woods and Watson 2003). Such smart power wheelchairs are under continuous development and receive considerable investment from federal grant agencies (e.g., National Institute on Disability, Independent Living, and Rehabilitation Research – NIDILRR) and major transportation technologies that invest considerable research and development funding for customer accommodation needs.

Among the major obstacles to widespread use of smart wheelchairs is cost. Current research is focused on these more advanced technology wheelchairs so that they are more economical and will be covered by Medicare, Medicaid, and other insurance providers. With advances in neuroscience and computer interface, some experimentation with brain implants and virtual reality applications may make wheelchairs more easily operable over even greater physical obstacles and terrain, although such efforts are in the early stages and also face cost issues for widespread distribution (Pazzaglia and Molinari 2016). However, some preliminary studies question the added benefit of these more advanced wheelchair modifications (Harrand and Bannigan 2014; Simpson et al. 2008). Regardless of this debate, people with disabilities and disability researchers will continue to innovate with new ideas to advance capabilities of wheelchairs and other mobility devices.

Given the long history of wheelchair development and use, substantial research continues to further advance this technology. Much of this work focuses on the biomechanics of wheelchair use to optimize performance, to reduce physical stress, and to promote the health of the individual wheelchair user. Goosey-Tolfrey (2010) examined Paralympic training methods in Great Britain for wheelchair basketball, racing, rugby, and tennis. The research found that wheelchair biomechanics needs to be assessed at the individual level to promote optimum performance.

Faupin et al. (2013) examined synchronous versus asynchronous propulsion of wheelchairs among wheelchair basketball players. They found that synchronous propulsion was more efficient in terms of velocity and wheelchair performance during sprints. Nevertheless, asynchronous propulsion was superior for user applications of hand-to-rim forcing during sprints. Bergamini et al. (2015) recommended biomechanic evaluations of wheelchair athletes to reduce injury risk and to maximize performance. Munaretto et al. (2013) collected kinematic data on a wheelchair user, finding through data-based simulations that upper extremity injuries can occur due to excess mechanical load based upon type of use, forcing, seating position during locomotion, and other individual factors.

The individualized approach to the analysis of assistive devices can be further augmented by how these devices work well or contribute to additional physical problems due to the altered biophysical environment. For people living with spinal cord injury and long-term standard wheelchair use, Asheghan et al. (2016) found heightened risk for carpel tunnel syndrome as a secondary condition due to wrist motions. Findings such as these illustrate the need for more comprehensive biophysical studies as well as the further development of smart, robotic wheelchairs. At the same time, standard wheelchairs enable physical activity and upper body exercise. The risk for carpel tunnel syndrome and other secondary conditions can be prevented by careful exercise physiological and human factors assessments of functional form in wheelchair and other assistive device usage. Jain et al. (2010) observed that people living with spinal cord injury (SCI) are prone to shoulder pain, even with standard, manually prepared wheelchairs and with motorized wheelchairs. Assistive technologies offer advantages to the user, but they can contribute to injury if improperly used. Biomechanical assessments are important to improve human performance with assistive devices while minimizing risks. Russell et al. (2015) demonstrated that modified wheelchair usage with considerations for body position, propulsion, and reaction forces can reduce shoulder and other upper extremity injuries.

An expert trainer can identify potential form/pattern problems and train the user on biomechanic adjustments to reduce risk. Similarly for wheelchairs and certain prosthetics, the issue of pressure ulcers can be prevented by proper supports and repositioning activities exercise to avoid these sedentary risks. Requejo et al. (2015) argued that these evaluations need to be applied to age-related disability, as older adults who use wheelchairs are at increased risk to experience pain and mobility limitations. They strongly recommended individually based ergonomic assessments to reduce these risks as wheelchair user's age.

6.4 Prostheses

Artificial limbs, or prostheses, represent a major type of assistive technology for people living with mobility limitations. Prosthetics include artificial hands, feet, digits for either hands or feet, forearms and complete arms, and lower legs and full legs. Obviously, the greater area affected, the more substantial difficulty in producing and providing a functional device with few barriers. Prosthetics often are used for aesthetic purposes to hide the limb loss. However, device innovation is improving the functionality of these devices so that there are prosthetics with increasing capabilities that offer the user improved functioning and the performance of many desired activities of daily living (ADLs) and instrumental activities of daily living (IADLS) independently, a major goal of our efforts to improve devices for functioning and exercise. Even novel prosthetics such as running blades utilize innovative designs that are based upon physical principles, not on appearance, in order to provide superior mobility to users. Thus, the opportunities for innovation should incorporate aesthetic comparability to the affected limb as much as possible and as needed by the individual while simultaneously aiming for high functioning and unique designs.

Prosthetic limbs are needed for a variety of conditions, ranging from congenital birth defects to diabetic foot/limb neuropathic limb loss to cancer to limb loss from accidents/warfare. Aging-related loss of functioning can represent an additional factor. Recent historical events and global health as well as aging demographic trends have increased the need for prosthetics. Wounded warriors and civilians affected by the worldwide use of land mines and other explosives numbered over 8600 (42% children of the 78% civilian victims) in 2016, a sharp increase over previous years and likely a conservative estimate (International Campaign to Ban Landmines 2017). Furthermore, they have documented approximately 110,000 victims (approximately 80,000 surviving) since 1999.

Currently in the United States, approximately 1.6 million people live with limb loss, with an expected increase to 3.6 million by the year 2050, albeit with projected trends of decreased loss related to diabetes and peripheral neuropathy and projected increased loss due to dysvascular amputations (Varma et al. 2014). The projected increase may be attributable to many factors, most notably the long-term effects of diabetic and nondiabetic health declines related to the obesity epidemic and lack of exercise as well as other health conditions (e.g., aging, drug use/abuse). Also in the United States, Barmparas et al. (2010) found that limb and digit losses occurred primarily from motor vehicle accidents (51%) and equipment/machinery accidents (19.4%), with pedestrians and motorcyclists experiencing a greater degree of lower limb amputations.

Transplantation of organs for limb loss has improved and remains one option for treatment, although the primary limitations are the lack of organ/limb donors and HLA tissue matching to reduce transplant immune rejections. As a result, the number of limb transplants has remained very low, especially so for allogeneic transplants compared to autologous (self) digit transplants. Weissenbacher et al.

(2014) estimated slightly over 100 single or double hand transplants since 1998. Weissenbacher et al. (2014) followed up five hand transplant recipients for 8–14 years, finding that all of them experienced at least one tissue rejection event, although every event was successfully treated. Hand transplant recipients demonstrated increased sensory and grip strength functionalities during the years following the transplant, although one patient showed a slight decline in grip strength. Ziegler-Graham et al. (2008, see also Flaubert et al. 2017) reported over 41,000 cases of above-the wrist limb lost in the United States during 2005. Durban et al. (2015) reported a successful above-the-knee reimplantation of a severed leg for a child with few long-term complications at 24 years postsurgery. Despite these demonstrated successes, limb transplantation remains a complex, extremely limited procedure that requires regular monitoring and follow-up procedures. For the foreseeable future in the absence or limited (ethically) development of self-cloned tissues and organs, prosthetic devices remain the best assistive device for limb loss.

Flaubert et al. (2017) described four principal types of prosthetic devices:

1. Passive
2. Body-powered
3. Externally powered
4. Hybrid

These four prosthetic types have progressively increasing functionality for the user. All of them attach to a joint or remaining limb or partial limb. The passive prosthetic device provides only cosmetic/aesthetic replacement of the lost limb and has no functionality. The body-powered prosthetic device is moved along with another body part via some type of anchoring device, usually a strap and/or harness to position and manually operated cables to move the prosthesis in a limited fashion.

The externally powered prosthetic device receives an energy supply for motion from a battery connected to a small motor within the device that is coupled with neurological sensors linked to several of the user's antagonistic muscles for the affected region of the body. For example, the two primary antagonistic muscles for lifting versus extending the forearm are the upper arm biceps brachii and the triceps brachii, respectively. A prosthetic forearm would contain a motor for movement with a battery supply and sensors driven by contraction of the appropriate upper arm muscle.

Lower limb prosthetic devices operate on similar principles. Windrich et al. (2016) described advantages and disadvantages of 21 lower limb prostheses, 3 of which were being marketed. Lower limb devices may be for the entire leg (above the knee), lower leg and/or ankle, or combined knee-lower leg-ankle units. Some models provide a prosthesis that enables passive motion that is consistent with the attached limb/limb portion. Overwhelmingly, the newer models utilize external power (motor and battery) and are driven by electromyographic (EMG) muscle sensors, as described with the upper limb prosthetics. A few models utilized either pneumatic (i.e., air pressure forcing) or hydraulic mechanisms, although these devices have been problematic compared to the EMG models. Experiments with the EMG stimulation have focused on echo or resonance control by matching the prosthetic limb motion with the corresponding gait of the healthy leg. Alternatively, gait modeling can be recorded into the small computer for EMG signaling of prosthetic leg motion. Both approaches require computer control within the device and have required considerable work given the greater parameters involved for walking upright compared to upper limb motions.

With respect to prosthetic devices, many individuals receive surgery with titanium rods and other implantable bone replacement or joint support devices. Such implantable structures are prosthetic in their own right, but they generally operate efficiently with an intact limb such that substantial ranges of motion and functionality are maintained, thereby reducing disability. Nevertheless, implantable devices may limit certain types of physical activity such as high-impact sports and walking or running over rough terrain. Additionally, secondary conditions such as obesity or other conditions can be limiting factors. With respect to lower leg rods, aging can be a factor, as the rods have a given length and can cause pain with weakened muscle and slightly reduced stature as part of the aging process.

Returning to true prosthetic devices and specifically lower limbs, running blades have been popular with Paralympic runners. Running blades, termed running-specific prostheses (RSPs), are carbon-fiber passive devices that attach to the unaffected portion of the limb and enable the user to run using the force of their thigh muscles and the elastic spring-mass physical properties of the RSP and its shape. Beck et al. (2016) evaluated 55 different RSP models for running performance by female and male transtibial amputees working on treadmills. They found that manufacturer RSP models significantly differed in product stiffness relative to muscle stiffness. Most interestingly, they found that athletes could increase or decrease the stiffness during running by changing the angle of their RSP. Overall, the RSPs provided running performance approaching that of a nondisabled athlete, although biological ankles return over twice the power of the RSPs (Beck et al. 2016). Further advances with RSP technology look promising for people living with lower limb amputations to engage in running for health and for competition.

Hybrid prosthetic systems involve a mixture of body- and externally powered movement. Such devices may have less range of motion compared to the purely external power prosthetics, although the hybrid devices can be less expensive. Many such devices are available from various manufacturers, and more are in testing and development. Both Flaubert et al. (2017) and Windrich et al. (2016) provide a strong discussion of major researchers and distributors for externally powered prosthetic limbs, both upper and lower body in nature. The Amputee Coalition (www.amputee-coalition.org) provides numerous resources to assist people who are living with limb loss.

Motion sensors typically involve electromyographic (EMG) impulse inputs to the motor that drives the externally powered prosthetic device. Resnik et al. (2017) tested the new DEKA arm with patients having brachial plexus injury and who wanted to shift from a passive upper limb device. The DEKA device provides transhumeral and shoulder configurations, plus it operates with an array of inertial measurement unit (IMU) commands for ERG sensory control of the unit's motions. Participants demonstrated significant improvement in writing, grasping, opening cans, and other ADLs/IADLs, and they reported high satisfaction with the device along with a desire to ultimately have such a device for personal use.

Caputo and Collins (2014) addressed one critical issue involved with lower limb prostheses: increased required energy exertion leading to overall physical fatigue and damage to the remaining limb, upper limb joints, and muscle tissue. This is particularly a problem for ankle-foot prostheses. They modified such a prosthesis with an emulator, a device that can vary joint torque and angle. They measured variations on these two parameters for non amputee participants walking on a treadmill to effectively test and reduce the push-off work exerted by the ankle-foot prosthesis during each step. They discovered that these exertion/work reductions primarily helped lower metabolic rate involved with leg swing and that further biomechanics research needs to be conducted to better understand the dynamics of walking with prosthetic lower limbs (Caputo and Collins 2014).

These findings clearly show that a substantial body of work remains to be conducted to more completely understand the biomechanics of walking and the translation of this research into more precise, maneuverable prosthetic limbs that more realistically reproduce the movements of healthy limbs with minimal effort, fewer secondary effects on the body, and, hopefully, low cost for widespread distribution. Flaubert et al. (2017) and Caputo and Collins (2014) stressed this need as well as the synergy of robotics and human-computer interfaces (e.g., artificial intelligence applications) to continue device innovation. As described above, there are variations in the technologies such that the type of exercise to improve health will be different for each situation (e.g., wheelchairs for TBI, SCI, and lower limb loss versus lower limb prosthetics for lower limb loss alone). Quite succinctly, there is more work to be done!

6.5 Gait/Orthotics

Related to Caputo and Collins' (2014) gait work for walking with lower limb prosthetic devices, we move to the closely related orthotics, which also play an important role in the gait walking research that is so important for efficient walking with assistive devices. Many people experience foot, ankle, or lower leg injuries that require orthopedic shoes. Additionally, people who are overweight, diabetic, or aging are more likely to require additional foot support for walking, a basic task essential to health and wellness. The most critical feature of orthopedic shoe and foot orthotic design is individualized tailoring for the shoe to enable balance, comfort, and reduced energy expenditure for walking. Availability, access, and individual design represent some of the major barriers in this area, as too many providers of foot orthotics provide a "one size fits all" approach when an individualized, universal design approach is needed.

Terrier et al. (2013) examined gait and balance for study participants recovering from foot and ankle injuries at a rehabilitation clinic. Participant walking gait using orthopedic shoes or ankle boots was measured with piezoelectric skin sensors to evaluate local dynamic stability (LDS). The researchers found that the use of orthopedic shoes significantly stabilized walking gait and reduced walking–/injury-related pain. LDS is particularly important for prevention of falls with people recovering from ankle injuries, lower limb neuropathy, and older adults (Reynard et al. 2014).

Riskowski et al. (2011) reviewed studies of orthopedic shoe and orthotic interventions. Rigorous research studies are limited, but the researchers found that properly designed orthotics represent a preventative approach to foot health, walking, and exercise, especially for aging populations and the associated increased risk for mobility limitations. They cited 24% of adults who experience some type of foot ailment, often including arthritis, and these ailments increase with age. The expansion of orthotic foot supports can benefit from crossover exercise science and athletic training research so that a wider range of people with and without disabilities can benefit.

Orthotic insoles have been researched to maintain balance for people living with multiple sclerosis, lower limb neuropathy, and foot-ankle injuries. Dixon et al. (2014) found that insoles did not significantly benefit balance, but they do improve walking gait. For people living with diabetic foot neuropathy, Paton et al. (2016) found that memory fitting insoles maintained balance and improve pressure velocity, but they identified a need for the development of offloading insoles that offer both performance and balance while addressing the potential complications of diabetic foot ulcers. Shin et al. (2016) likewise found that full and partial insoles both improved anterior-posterior and medial-lateral balance while stabilizing the walking velocity of participants.

Few studies have addressed the individualized design of orthopedic shoes, ankle boots, and orthotic insoles. Infrared pressure contact assessments of foot support have become more widespread in the footwear industry. Furthermore, competitive athletic footwear involves the construction of each shoe that is specific to the athlete's feet. Advances in footwear technology should similarly move in this direction for people who face balance and walking stability issues. These issues indicate another strong opportunity area for further research and innovation for assistive footwear. One particular low-cost opportunity is the use of adaptive manufacturing, better known as 3D printing, for novice entrepreneurs and people with disabilities to design and produce functioning orthotics with a wide variety of 3D-printable resins that have become available, even with hobbyist 3D printers.

Effective walking gait assessments represent a central component for evaluating orthopedic shoes and foot orthotics. Kluge et al. (2017) described the validity of inertial measurement system (IMS) in the evaluation of gait movements. Sensors can be applied to study participants in order to measure posture, balance (e.g., LDS), specific motions, velocity, musculoskeletal exertion, and lower limb pressure per unit area of foot contact. Typically, participants walk or run over a flat surface, although treadmills or elliptical stepping devices usually are used to control for speed and ramp angle across participants. Kluge et al. (2017) found that IMS gait assessment systems are accurate and exhibit high test-retest reliability. Other exercise researchers combine such assessments with VO_2 max and other measures of biophysical stress and metabolism. Gait analysis has also played a central role in the analysis of lower limb prosthetic devices.

6.6 Exoskeletons

One of the most exciting, but still limited, types of advanced assistive device is the exoskeleton, a battery or corded electronic robot that fits around the torso and legs to physically support the body and uses muscular sensors to drive lower limb movements. The device is designed for people living with severe spinal cord injuries, including thoracic 4 vertebra (T4) injuries and below on the spinal column, although home use currently is limited for less severe spinal injuries. The marketed exoskeletons require extensive training for the user in order to operate independently. In the United States, FDA restrictions (US Code of Federal Regulations Title 21, Volume 8, Part 890 – Physical Medicine Devices) require the user to have a fully trained companion to assist the user with the robotic suit. In the European Union, no such restriction exists.

The primary exoskeleton robots on the market include the following products:

1. The Indego™ (www.indego.com), manufactured by Parker Hannifin, a technology company spin-off from device invention and development at Vanderbilt University's Center for Intelligent Mechatronics
2. The ReWalk™ (www.rewalk.com), invented by Amit Goffer in Israel and marketed by Argo Medical Technologies, Ltd.
3. The Ekso™ (www.eksobionics.com), invented and marketed by Ekso Bionics, a technology spin-off company of the University of California at Berkeley Robotics and Human Engineering Laboratory.
4. The Hybrid Assistive Limb (HAL 5™; www.cyberdyne.jp), invented and marketed by Professor Yoshiyuki Sankai of Japan's Tsukuba University and the company Cyberdyne
5. Fortis™ (www.lockheedmartin.com), invented and marketed by the aerospace corporation Lockheed Martin, initially for industrial workers but now available for people with disabilities

Other companies (e.g., U.S. Bionics, Panasonic) are developing exoskeleton models as well, but four of the above companies (ReWalk, Ekso, Cyberdyne, Lockheed Martin) have consolidated the majority of the exoskeleton market share, with 272 exoskeletons being sold during 2015, approximately 54% going to health-care rehabilitation, about half of all sales in the United States, and a 2015 global market value of US $25 million (Grand View Research 2016). Note that the majority of the roughly 140 exoskeletons that were sold in health care likely went to rehabilitation centers and hospitals for patient/user training. As of 2017, individual exoskeleton units cost around US $90,000, a cost that is prohibitive to most people living with disabilities but a cost that will decline as market demand increases and other companies market competitive exoskeleton alternatives. ReWalk and Indego were the first exoskeleton models to obtain FDA approval for personalized use beyond the rehabilitation clinic.

Grand View Research (2016) projects that the exoskeleton market will grow from the 2015 value of US $25 million to US $1.6 billion by 2025 with more products entering the market, growth of the global aging population to nearly two billion people, increasing spinal cord injuries, and substantial market growth/demand in Japan and China. All five of the above, highlighted exoskeleton companies have secured approval for product sales by the US Food and Drug Administration (FDA) and the European Union Conformité Européene (CE) product approval.

A typical exoskeleton consists of three measurable components for the lower abdomen, thigh, and lower leg. The parts are interchangeable and can be outfitted based upon the user's physical parameters up to certain limits, depending upon the manufacturer. Battery life is generally around 4 h, but batteries can be exchanged quickly and recharged within short time frames. Exoskeleton composition includes carbon fiber, plastic, and some metal, and the technology has advanced to lightweight models less than 30 pounds. The technology also is moving away from backpacks in order to remove weight. The exoskeleton moves via sensors located throughout the leg attachments that provide balance information to a small computer that sends signals to motors that usually are located in the unit hip and knee joints. The user can provide commands via a wireless remote.

Exoskeleton movement is slow for most users and often requires the use of canes for forward motion support. As stated earlier, the United States requires training for the user plus a companion individual to assist the user. With the rapid expansion of robotic exoskeleton use in rehabilitation settings and now even for personal use, various standards organizations such as the International Organization for Standardization (ISO) and ASTM International are developing guidelines for exoskeleton development, ergonomics, training, and use.

Fritz et al. (2017) evaluated the Ekso, Indego, ReWalk, and Rex Bionics exoskeleton models, finding that all of these models currently are inadequate for personalized use and independent living outside of rehabilitation training centers. They argued that the exoskeletons had balance and upper extremity support problems, plus they require substantial companion support. They recommended improved designs, the continued use of lightweight materials, and better collaboration between actual consumers/users of the devices, physicians, nurses, rehabilitation professionals, and design engineers.

Several manufacturers, including Ekso, are developing exoskeleton models that have differential left-right functioning for stroke victims (i.e., one body side affected). Exoskeleton research and development has been impressive, so the technology should steadily improve the maneuverability and independence of the user. Grand View Research (2016) cites the exoskeleton as one of the top technologies for development during the next 10 years. A search of the US Patent and Trademark Office (www.uspto.gov) for "full-body robotic exoskeleton" yielded approximately 250 matches, a number that likely will substantially increase during the next decade.

Onose et al. (2016) provide a thorough discussion of design issues for further technological development. As with other studies, balance for the exoskeleton itself is one of the major limitations. Of particular importance, Onose et al. (2016) emphasized several physiological features, including exoskeleton designs that reduce muscle spasticity and contractures, promote lower limb circulation for the avoidance of edema and more serious secondary conditions, and reduction of risks for lower limb fractures due to unit mechanical stress. They provided several Mechatronic Orthotic Design (MOD) illustrations to highlight specific engineering needs/opportunities.

The implications for full-body or other accessory robotic exoskeletons to health and exercise are considerable. Actual bipedal locomotion with robotic assistance might not necessarily promote widespread lower limb muscular contraction, but it can reduce atrophy, promote muscular activity with undamaged muscle tissue that otherwise might not receive necessary activity, promote neural activity, and promote circulation as well as cardiovascular functioning. Certainly, the exoskeletons likely will create unexpected side effects in conjunction with each person's particular injury such that regular physiological functioning will be necessary to prevent overexertion and the development of secondary conditions. Such scenarios plus substantial consumer input need to be considered during the development of these devices. Improvements on robotic exoskeletons potentially could open up this particular assistive device as an important contributor to improved physical activity for people living with SCI and stroke, providing them with renewed vigor, quality of life, command of environmental terrains, and neuromuscular activity that counteracts atrophy and related detrimental secondary events that severely impact this population.

Kolakowsky-Hayner et al. (2013) provided one of the early studies on the Ekso device. They studied motion and physiological characteristics of five male and two female participants, all of whom had an SCI of T1 or below. Over approximately 400 h in the device, about half of which was spent walking, the study participants tended to improve walking and speed with increased training time. Suit-up time ranged from 10 to 30 min. Kolakowsky-Hayner et al. (2013) recommended companion assistance during operation, including an overhead tether, and that the device should be used in rehabilitation settings. These findings are consistent with more recent studies described above on the limitations of current devices, particularly for personalized use.

Whereas current robotic exoskeletons use functional electrical stimulation (FES), Chang et al. (2017) experimented with an exoskeleton that uses functional neuromuscular stimulation (FNS). This latter approach would be a novel advance in the technology by involving the activity of nerves and muscles in the affected limbs, thereby promoting more natural driving of the exoskeleton with fewer manual, wireless commands. This FNS model does include battery-powered assistance to support limited muscle power in activities such as standing up, maintaining standing position with balance, and stepping with balance maintenance as well. The researchers tested the model with three people living with paraplegia, yielding positive results and yielding additional ideas for incorporation of foot plantar flexion and other capabilities.

Miller et al. (2016) performed a meta-analysis of 14 comprehensive research studies involving 111 people with SCI who used either the ReWalk, Ekso, or Indego exoskeletons in rehabilitation training. Strong positive results were consistent across all studies, including only 4.4% of participants experiencing falls during training, 76% being able to move in the unit without physical assistance, and 61% experiencing improved bowel regularity following training. The studies indicated only mild exertion requirements on participants during the training sessions. From this perspective, robotic exoskeletons seem to be highly beneficial to users when proper training methods and user needs are addressed. One curious note from the Miller et al. (2016) analysis was the high prevalence of males (over 80%) in these studies. As research progresses, differential male/female physiology with respect to bony density, musculature, and metabolism should be considered during the testing of robotic exoskeletons, particularly with respect to age and longitudinal use as well.

6.7 Other Robotics

Besides the "full-body," walking robotic exoskeletons, limb-specific robotic exoskeletons are more widely available on the market and are undergoing similar technological advancements for users. Powered upper limb robotic exoskeletons are being tested to assist people living with SCI and stroke to perform upper limb coordination and tasks such as grasping objects (Jarrassé et al. 2014). Pirondini et al. (2016) experimented with a lightweight robotic arm (ALEX™) on healthy subjects and demonstrated comparable EMG activity for various monitored upper limb muscles (as compared to sensors placed on nonusers) while performing a variety of tasks.

For all limb injuries, one of the major rehabilitation issues that confronts the development of robotic exoskeletons and other prosthetic devices is muscle spasticity in response to muscle and nerve damage as well as muscle atrophy. In a randomized control trial for upper arm strength activities among rehabilitation patients using robotic upper limb exoskeletons, Calabrò et al. (2017) demonstrated that applying muscle vibration antagonist action on the affected limbs significantly reduced spasticity during robotic motion activities. Consequently, combinations of physical principles and physical therapy should be incorporated with the most effective use of robotic exoskeletons and prosthetic assistive devices.

Beekhuis et al. (2013) described a self-aligning robotic arm accessory that uses sensors to monitor muscle forcing, torque, and other parameters as well as for adjusting direction of motion. The device is simple to place on the forearm and coordinates smoothly with the wrist and elbow joints, another issue with many limb prosthetic devices. Their proof of concept design is consistent with current state-of-the-art upper limb robotic exoskeletons.

Lower limb robotic orthoses are available for people who have greater leg movement but who have leg injuries or muscle deterioration due to aging or disease. Much of the research on these devices is focusing on gait mechanisms to improve walking, balance, and reproduction of natural gait patterns following injury. As with the full-body robotic exoskeletons, user training is important, but much research remains to be conducted to optimize the functionality of these orthoses (Hussain 2014; Maggioni et al. 2016). Computer simulations of gait patterns assist lower limb prosthetic design by matching natural patterns, and even animal models (e.g., horses), to improve user functionality and satisfaction with walking lower limb robotic prosthetic devices (Meyer et al. 2016).

6.8 Sensory Devices

While not directly pertinent to exercise and health at this time, a number of important sensory technologies exist that enable people with TBI or SCI-related speech, sight, hearing, or upper arm mobility to perform ADLs and IADLs that indirectly relate to activities and participation that are essential for good health and positive psychological well-being. Most of these devices are computer-based systems that enable simple commands to write, speak, and command household and office operations.

For writing on a computer, researchers have used virtual reality and human-computer interaction (HCI) technologies for the development of head-mounted laser and other electronic devices to link to a command screen on a computer. Pereira et al. (2009) described the use of a video camera and a hat/cap-mounted target that aligns so that the user can move and operate an on-screen cursor to manipulate a command screen. More recent developments have included cameras that detect and track eye movements, thereby moving the computer screen cursor to the appropriate commands (Lopez-Basterretxea et al. 2015). Such devices have been demonstrated to be highly reliable with error levels under 5% (Zhan et al. 2016). These devices work particularly well for people who cannot speak and/or use hands/arms for manipulating computers. However, the devices are expensive, but increased use and demand has reduced the costs to a certain degree. As with each of these technologies, our goals are not just to improve and provide them to people living with disabilities, but also to make the devices practical and affordable.

Voice-control technologies are widely advertised for the general population. For people with limited mobility, voice commands can be used with voice recognition software programs on computers for writing as well as for devices that activate/inactivate lights and other electronic appliances. One major issue with voice recognition is altered speech patterns due to speech disabilities or damage to cerebral vocalization centers from stroke, TBI, or SCI. Researchers have developed databases of altered speech patterns that can be accessed by special voice recognition programs and algorithms that utilize maximum likelihood regression analysis to match intended speech to appropriate computerized actions (Mustafa et al. 2014).

Therefore, continuing advances in technology and the interfacing of multiple technologies enable improved assistive devices that can address single or multiple sensory or motility disabilities. These developments illustrate a commitment by rehabilitation professionals, engineers, and other scientists to realistically troubleshoot basic functional problems and to yield efficient solutions to these barriers. As one example, the motor vehicle industry has provided people with limited hand, arm, and leg mobility alternative vehicle control technologies, now computer-driven, that enable them to demonstrate driving proficiency and to independently drive motor vehicles (Lane and Benoit 2011; Rapport et al. 2008). Major rehabilitation centers provide people with stroke, SCI, TBI, and other mobility limitations a variety of these many technologies to provide them with the best support mechanisms to optimally participate in society and to live independently, consistent with the objectives of the Rehabilitation Act of 1973 and its amendments plus other legislation and policy advocacy to enhance the lives of all people who live with disabilities.

6.9 Exercise Guides

The National Center for Health, Physical Activity, and Disability (NCHPAD; www.nchpad.org) is a NIDILRR-funded research and rehabilitation center that promotes physical activity for people living with mobility limitations. It provides a number of exercise guides for people with various conditions such as limb loss, paraplegia, tetraplegia (i.e., quadriplegia), spinal cord injury, cerebral palsy, and multiple sclerosis.

For limb loss, the NCHPAD guide recommends weighted cuffs that will match the prosthetic device. Strength exercises for the upper body include bicep curls, shoulder lateral and front raise, standing bent over shoulder fly, standing shoulder press, standing bent over row, and pectoral fly. The standing exercises can be seated for those individuals with lower limb loss or low functioning. For lower body workouts, weighted cuffs can be used with seated leg extensions, hip flexion, hip abduction, torso lateral bends, and lying abdominal crunches. Other exercise guidelines, including recommended consultations with rehabilitation fitness trainers, are provided.

For spinal cord injuries, exercises are coordinated with the level of injury, an important issue to consider with trained exercise physiologists to guide proper exercise regimens that minimize the risk of further injuries or secondary conditions. For T1-T6 thoracic spinal injuries, possible exercises recommended by NCHPAD include seated elastic resistance exercises such as rhomboid rowing, reverse fly, chest press, internal rotations, rotator cuff, deltoid shoulder presses, lateral and front raise, biceps curls, and triceps flexion. Again, the emphasis for T1-T6 injuries is elastic resistance exercises. For lower thoracic into lumbar spinal area injuries, seated and lying abdominal crunch, leg lifts, curls, and thigh adduction/abduction exercises can be performed.

For people living with tetraplegia, individual levels of functioning determine the appropriate level of physical exercise. As with all conditions, physician and rehabilitation exercise physiologist consultations are essential, and supervision/

assistance should be available during exercise. NCHPAD recommends weighted wrist cuffs and elastic resistance training for upper body exercises that are similar to the exercises described for spinal cord injury. Similar training approaches are provided for people living with paraplegia.

People living with multiple sclerosis or other disabilities that enable more mobility can perform standing, lying, and seated stretching exercises, appropriate lifting of weights, and elastic resistance as recommended by their physician and exercise trainer. People living with cerebral palsy can perform controlled weights, elastic training, and seated stationary exercise bicycling.

Public health policymakers, providers, and exercise center operators need to realize the added importance of exercise for the health, independence, and positive outlook of people living with mobility limitations. The coordination of an individual's specific physical needs, assistance devices, accessibility to suitable exercise equipment, and social/community supports can easily promote everybody's health, with no exceptions.

6.10 Challenges and Opportunities

Across this wide span of accessory devices, the user has little or some degree of motion and functionality. If we incorporate the degrees of barriers for functioning in each instance, exercise physiologists can work with each person to identify appropriate exercise devices, activities, and venues to perform needed daily and weekly exercise regimens. Therefore, the assistive devices provide a support mechanism to assist each person with a given mobility disability. It is still up to health and exercise professionals, family, friends, and other peers to be there to help each person achieve their physical activity goals with independence and confidence. That means that we still remove the social and environmental barriers that might present a barrier to the individual living with a disability as well as the assistive device that they are using.

With any of these devices and advancing motion technologies, a critical emphasis must be placed upon the individual. Each person is unique and faces their own array of facilitators and barriers for movement and exercise. Therefore, the process of rehabilitation involves a variety of community and professional supports to evaluate and continuously monitor the technology user's needs. This is part of any persons's standard annual health and wellness checkups plus follow-up evaluations for specific conditions. However, for everyone, unique personal, environmental, social, and condition-specific considerations must be weighed together over the life course of development to maximize health, wellness, and opportunities. Continued research on novel technologies, human factors, and ergonomic analysis of how these advances best work with individual needs, and, most importantly, consumer input, are needed to drive improved health and exercise opportunities for people with disabilities.

6.11 Summary

Advances in assistive technologies for people living with mobility limitations and other disabilities have been dramatic. Nevertheless, we remain in the early stages of this movement as scientists and rehabilitation engineers try to better model and understand the varied physical conditions that are unique to each individual, design of appropriate devices, and matching these devices for optimal use without generating secondary conditions, many of which could be as serious as the primary disability. Furthermore, the expense involved in many innovative technologies poses another dimension to the problem of access, including whether or not insurance companies, Medicaid, and/or disability insurance cover the devices. The last point on insurance is particularly problematic with new experimental devices.

Most of the more advanced technologies (e.g., robotic prostheses and exoskeletons) remain limited to rehabilitation centers due to costs, the complexity of operating the experimental devices, lengthy training times, and extensive need for support mechanisms. For people with disabilities to achieve independent living with these technologies, considerably more innovation, experiment, support, and distribution channels need to be developed to provide efficient, safe products at reasonable cost and that can be widely distributed. Policy experts, legislators, and business leaders can play an important role in driving public and private supports for these much needed efforts. We have only just started getting these assistive innovations to a small percentage of the population of 57 million Americans living with disabilities, and the availability is even lower for people with disabilities in much of the rest of the world.

The prospect for exercise and health looks promising, particularly with advanced wheelchairs and robotic devices that can promote movement and neuromuscular/skeletal actions that stimulate these organs and reduce their risks for atrophy. The kinematic aspects of these innovations cannot be understated. While nerves and muscles may be severely limited, any stimulation is beneficial and translatable across organ systems. Visionaries discuss the enhancement and even tissue cloning replacement of damaged organs, but these potential advances remain even further away. We currently need to provide artificial sources that can manipulate and enhance physical functioning for exercise and independent living.

References

Asheghan, M., Hollisaz, M. T., Taheri, T., Kazemi, H., & Aghda, A. K. (2016). The prevalence of carpel tunnel syndrome among long-term manual wheelchair users with spinal cord injury: A cross-sectional study. *The Journal of Spinal Cord Medicine, 39*(3), 265–271.

Barmparas, G., Inaba, K., Teixeira, P. G., Dubose, J. J., Criscuoli, M., Talving, P., Plurad, D., Green, D., & Demetriades, D. (2010). Epidemiology of post-traumatic limb amputation: A National Trauma Databank analysis. *The American Surgeon, 76*(11), 1214–1222.

Beck, O. N., Taboga, P., & Grabowski, A. M. (2016). Characterizing the mechanical properties of running-specific prostheses. *PLoS One, 11*(12), e0168298. https://doi.org/10.1371/journal.pone.0168298.

Beekhuis, J. H., Westerveld, A. J., van der Kooij, H., & Stienen, A. H. A. (2013, June 24–26). *Design of a self-aligning 3-DOF actuated exoskeleton for diagnosis and training of wrist and forearm after stroke*. Proceedings of the 2013 IEEE international conference on rehabilitation robotics, Seattle, WA.

Bergamini, E., Morelli, F., Marchetti, F., Vannozzi, G., Polidori, L., Paradisi, F., Traballesi, M., Cappozzo, A., & Delussu, A. S. (2015). Wheelchair propulsion biomechanics in junior basketball players: A method for the evaluation of the efficacy of a specific training program. *BioMed Research International, 2015*, 275965. https://doi.org/10.1155/2015/275965.

Calabrò, R. S., Naro, A., Russo, M., Milardi, D., Leo, A., Filoni, S., Trinchera, A., & Bramanti, P. (2017). Is two better than one? Muscle vibration plus robotic rehabilitation to improve upper limb spasticity and function: A pilot randomized controlled trial. *PLoS One, 12*(10), e0185936. https://doi.org/10.1371/journal.pone.0185936.

Caputo, J. M., & Collins, S. H. (2014). Prosthetic ankle push-off work reduces metabolic rate but not collision work in non-amputee walking. *Scientific Reports, 4*, 7213. https://doi.org/10.1038/srep07213.

Chang, S. R., Nandor, M. J., Li, L., Kobetic, R., Foglyano, K. M., Schnellenberger, J. R., Audu, M. L., Pinault, G., Quinn, R. D., & Triolo, R. J. (2017). A muscle-driven approach to restore stepping with an exoskeleton for individuals with paraplegia. *Journal of NeuroEngineering and Rehabilitation, 14*, 48. https://doi.org/10.1186/s12984-017-0258-6.

Cooper, R. A., Cooper, R., & Boninger, M. L. (2008). Trends and issues in wheelchair technologies. *Assistive Technology, 20*(2), 61–72.

Dixon, J., Hatton, A. L., Robinson, J., Gamesby-Iyayi, H., Hodgson, D., Rome, K., Warnett, R., & Martin, D. J. (2014). Effect of textured insoles on balance and gait in people with multiple sclerosis: An exploratory trail. *Physiotherapy, 100*(2), 142–149.

Durban, C. M. C., Lee, S.-Y., & Lim, H.-C. (2015). Above-the-knee replantation in a child: A case report with a 24-year follow-up. *Strategies in Trauma and Limb Reconstruction, 10*, 189–193.

Faupin, A., Borel, B., Meyer, C., Gorce, P., & Watelain, E. (2013). Effects of synchronous versus asynchronous mode of propulsion on wheelchair basketball sprinting. *Disability and Rehabilitation Assistive Technology, 8*(6), 496–501.

Flaubert, J.L., Spicer, C.M., & Jette, A.M. (eds.), National Academies of Sciences, Engineering, and Medicine; Health and Medicine Division; Board on Health Care Services; Committee on the Use of Selected Assistive Products and Technologies in Eliminating or Reducing the Effects of Impairments. (2017). The promise of assistive technology to enhance activity and work participation. Washington, DC: National Academies Press.

Fritz, H., Patzer, D., & Galen, S. S. (2017). Robotic exoskeletons for reengaging in everyday activities: Promises, pitfalls, and opportunities. *Disability and Rehabilitation*, 1–4. https://doi.org/10.1080/09638288.2017.1398786.

Fuhrer, M. J., Jutai, J. W., Scherer, M. J., & DeRuyter, F. (2003). A framework for the conceptual modeling of assistive technology device outcomes. *Disability and Rehabilitation, 25*(22), 1243–1251.

Gebrosky, B., Pearlman, J., Cooper, R. A., Cooper, R., & Kelleher, A. (2013). Evaluation of lightweight wheelchairs using ANSI/RESNA testing standards. *Journal of Rehabilitation Research and Development, 50*(10), 1373–1389.

Goosey-Tolfrey, V. (2010). Supporting the paralympic athlete: Focus on wheeled sports. *Disability and Rehabilitation, 32*(26), 2237–2243.

Grand View Research. (2016). Exoskeleton market revenue and volume analysis by type (mobile, stationary), by technology (drive system [pneumatic actuator, hydraulic actuator, electric servo, electric actuator, fully mechanical, shape memory alloy actuator, fuel cell]), by end-user (healthcare, military, industrial), and segment forecasts to 2025. San Francisco: Grand View Research, Inc. https://www.grandviewresearch.com/industry-analysis/exoskeleton-market. Accessed 3 Jan 2018.

Harrand, J., & Bannigan, K. (2014). Do tilt-in-space wheelchairs increase occupational engagement: A critical literature review. *Disability and Rehabilitation Assistive Technology, 11*, 3–12.

Hartig, T., Mitchell, R., de Vries, S., & Frumkin, H. (2014). Nature and health. *Annual Review of Public Health, 35*, 207–228.

Hussain, S. (2014). State-of-the-art robotic gait rehabilitation orthoses: Design and control aspects. *NeuroRehabilitation, 35*(4), 701–709.

International Campaign to Ban Landmines – Cluster Munition Coalition. (2017). *Landmine monitor 2015*. Geneva: Author.

Jain, N. B., Higgins, L. D., Katz, J. N., & Garshick, E. (2010). Association of shoulder pain with the use of mobility devices in persons with chronic spinal cord injury. *Physical Medicine and Rehabilitation, 2*(10), 896–900.

Jarrassé, N., Proietti, T., Crocher, V., Robertson, J., Sahbani, A., Morel, G., & Roby-Brami, A. (2014). Robotic exoskeletons: A perspective for the rehabilitation of arm coordination in stroke patients. *Frontiers in Human Neuroscience, 8*, 947. https://doi.org/10.3389/fnhum.2014.00947.

Kluge, F., Gaβner, H., Hannink, J., Pasluosta, C., Klucken, J., & Eskofier, B. M. (2017). Towards mobile gait analysis: Concurrent validity and test-retest reliability of an inertial measurement system for the assessment of spatio-temporal gait parameters. *Sensors, 17*(7), e1522. https://doi.org/10.3390/s17071522.

Kolakowsky-Hayner, S. A., Crew, J., Moran, S., & Shah, A. (2013). Safety and feasibility of using the Ekso™ bionic exoskeleton to aid ambulation after spinal cord injury. *Journal of Spine, S4*, 003. https://doi.org/10.4172/2165-7939.S4-003.

Lane, A. K., & Benoit, D. (2011). Driving, brain injury and assistive technology. *NeuroRehabilitation, 28*(3), 221–229.

Lenker, J. A., & Paquet, V. L. (2003). A review of conceptual models for assistive technology outcomes research and practice. *Assistive Technology, 15*(1), 1–15. https://doi.org/10.1080/10400435.2003.10131885.

Lopez-Basterretxea, A., Mendez-Zorrilla, A., & Garcia-Zapirain, B. (2015). Eye/head tracking technology to improve HCI with iPad applications. *Sensors, 15*(2), 2244–2264.

Maggioni, S., Melendez-Calderon, A., van Asseldonk, E., Klamroth-Marganska, V., Lünenburger, L., Riener, R., & van der Kooij, H. (2016). Robot-aided assessment of lower extremity functions: A review. *Journal of Neuroengineering and Rehabilitation, 13*, 72. https://doi.org/10.1186/s12984-016-0180-3.

Meyer, A. J., Eskinazi, I., Jackson, J. N., Rao, A. V., Patten, C., & Fregly, B. J. (2016). Muscle synergies facilitate computational prediction of subject-specific walking motions. *Frontiers in Bioengineering and Biotechnology, 4*, 77. https://doi.org/10.3389/fbioe.2016.00077.

Miller, L. E., Zimmerman, A. K., & Herbert, W. G. (2016). Clinical effectiveness and safety of powered exoskeleton-assisted walking in patients with spinal cord injury: Systematic review with meta-analysis. *Medical Devices: Evidence and Research, 9*, 455–466.

Munaretto, J. M., McNitt-Gray, J. L., Flashner, H., & Requejo, P. S. (2013). Reconfiguration of the upper extremity relative to the pushrim affects load distribution during wheelchair propulsion. *Medical Engineering Physics, 35*(8), 1141–1149.

Mustafa, M. B., Salim, S. S., Mohamed, N., Al-Qatab, B., & Siong, C. E. (2014). Severity-based adaptation with limited data for ASR to aid dysarthric speakers. *PLoS One, 9*(1), e86285. https://doi.org/10.1371/journal.pone.0086285.

Onose, G., Cârdei, V., Crăciunoiu, S. T., Avramescu, V., Opriş, I., Lebedev, M. A., & Constantinescu, M. V. (2016). Mechatronic wearable exoskeletons for bionic bipedal standing and walking: A new synthetic approach. *Frontiers in Neuroscience, 10*, 343. https://doi.org/10.3389/fnins.2016.00343.

Paton, J., Glasser, S., Collings, R., & Marsden, J. (2016). Getting the right balance: Insole design alters the static balance of people with diabetes and neuropathy. *Journal of Foot and Ankle Research, 5*(9), 40. https://doi.org/10.1186/s13047-016-0172-3.

Pazzaglia, M., & Molinari, M. (2016). The embodiment of assistive devices – from wheelchair to exoskeleton. *Physics Life Reviews, 16*, 163–175.

Pereira, C. A. M., Neto, R. B., Reynaldo, A. C., de Miranda Luzo, M. A., & Oliveira, R. P. (2009). Development and evaluation of a head-controlled human-computer interface with mouse-like functions for physically-disabled users. *Clinics, 64*(10), 975–981.

Pirondini, E., Coscia, M., Marcheschi, S., Roas, G., Salsedo, F., Frisoli, A., Bergamasco, M., & Micera, S. (2016). Evaluation of the effects of the Arm Light Exoskeleton on movement execution and muscle activities: A pilot study on healthy subjects. *Journal of NeuroEngineering and Rehabilitation, 13*, 9. https://doi.org/10.1186/s12984-016-0117-x.

Rapport, L. J., Bryer, R. C., & Hanks, R. A. (2008). Driving and community integration after traumatic brain injury. *Archives of Physical Medicine and Rehabilitation, 89*(5), 922–930.

Requejo, P. S., Furumasu, J., & Mulroy, S. J. (2015). Evidence-based strategies for preserving mobility for elderly and aging manual wheelchair users. *Topics in Geriatric Rehabilitation, 31*(1), 26–41.

Resnik, L., Fantini, C., Latlief, G., Phillips, S., Sasson, N., & Sepulveda, E. (2017). Use of the DEKA Arm for amputees with brachial plexus injury: A case series. *PLoS One, 12*(6), e0178642. https://doi.org/10.1371/journal.pone.0178642.

Reynard, F., Vuadens, P., Dériaz, O., & Terrier, P. (2014). Could local dynamic stability serve as an early predictor of falls in patients with moderate neurological gait disorders? A reliability and comparison study in healthy individuals and in patients with paresis of the lower extremities. *PLoS One, 9*(6), e100550. https://doi.org/10.1371/journal.pone.0100550.

Riskowski, J., Dufour, A. B., & Hannan, M. T. (2011). ArRthritis, foot pain & shoe wear: Current musculoskeletal research on feet. *Current Opinion in Rheumatology, 23*(2), 148–155.

Russell, I. M., Raina, S., Requejo, P. S., Wilcox, R. R., Mulroy, S., & McNitt-Gray, J. L. (2015). Modifications in wheelchair propulsion technique with speed. *Frontiers in Bioengineering and Biotechnology, 3*, 171. https://doi.org/10.3389/fbioe.2015.00171.

Shin, J. Y., Ryu, Y. U., & Yi, C. W. (2016). Effects of insoles contact on static balance. *Journal of Physical Therapy Science, 28*(4), 1241–1244.

Simpson, R. C., LoPresti, E. F., & Cooper, R. A. (2008). How many people would benefit from a smart wheelchair? *Journal of Rehabilitation Research and Development, 45*(1), 53–71.

Terrier, P., Luthi, F., & Dériaz, O. (2013). Do orthopaedic shoes improve local dynamic stability of gait? An observational study in patients with chronic foot and ankle injuries. *BMC Musculoskeletal Disorders, 14*, 94. https://doi.org/10.1186/1471-2474-14-94.

Varma, P., Stineman, M. G., & Dillingham, T. R. (2014). Epidemiology of limb loss. *Physical Medicine and Rehabilitation Clinics of North America, 25*(1), 1–8.

Weissenbacher, A., Hautz, T., Pierer, G., Ninkovic, M., Zelger, B. G., Zelger, B., Löscher, Rieger, M., Kumnig, M., Rumpold, G., Piza-Katzer, P., Bauer, T., Zimmermann, R., Gabl, M., Arora, R., Ninkovic, M., Margeiter, R., Brandacher, G., Schneeberger, S., & RTI-Group Innsbruck. (2014). Hand transplantation in its fourteenth year: The Innsbruck experience. *Vascularized Composite Allotransplantation, 1*(1–2), 11–21. https://doi.org/10.4161/23723505.2014.973798.

Wilson, E. O. (1988). *Biodiversity*. Washington, DC: National Academy of Sciences/Smithsonian Institution.

Windrich, M., Grimmer, M., Christ, O., Rinderknecht, S., & Beckerle, P. (2016). Active lower limb prosthetics, a systematic review of design issues and solutions. *BioMedical Engineering OnLine, 15*(Suppl 3), 140. https://doi.org/10.1186/s12938-016-0284-9.

Woods, B., & Watson, N. (2003). A short history of powered wheelchairs. *Assistive Technology, 15*(2), 164–180.

Woods, B., & Watson, N. (2004). The social and technological history of wheelchairs. *International Journal of Therapy and Rehabilitation, 11*(9), 407–410.

Woods, B., & Watson, N. (2010). A short history of powered wheelchairs. *Assistive Technology, 15*(2), 164–180.

World Health Organization. (2000). *The international classification of functioning, disability and health (ICF)*. Geneva: Author.

Zhan, Z., Zhang, L., Mei, H., & Fong, P. S. W. (2016). Online learners' reading ability detection based on eye-tracking sensors. *Sensors, 16*(9), 1457. https://doi.org/10.3390/s16091457.

Ziegler-Graham, K., MacKenzie, E. J., Ephraim, P. L., Travison, T. G., & Brookmeyer, R. (2008). Estimating the prevalence of limb loss in the United States: 2005 to 2050. *Archives of Physical Medicine and Rehabilitation, 89*(3), 422–429.

Chapter 7
Environmental Issues in Exercise Promotion

Sherry L. Adams

Abbreviations

ACA	Affordable Care Act
ADA	Americans with Disabilities Act
NIDILRR	National Institute on Disability, Independent Living and Rehabilitation Research
WHO	World Health Organization

7.1 Introduction

Health is defined as a state of physical, mental, and social well-being and not merely the absence of disease (Callahan 1973). The World Health Organization (WHO) goes further to identify that personal, social, economic, and environmental factors that determine the health condition of individuals and populations. These environmental factors have an impact on everyone, not just the disabled population. The impact can range from temperature or climate challenges to difficulty traversing city streets or rural settings. These environmental challenges impact able-bodied and people with disabilities in similar and also in very different ways.

Disability is a part of all human condition. The term disability encompasses impairments, activity limitations, and restriction in participation with any negative interaction between the individual and environmental/personal factors (Leonardi et al. 2006). Everyone will develop some type of impairment either temporary or permanent if they live long enough. Fortunately, there has been a shift in attitudes toward people with disabilities that recognize disability as a human rights issue. It is classified as a human rights issue because it is important that people with disabilities have equal access to health care, employment, education, and political participation (WHO World Report on Disability). Unfortunately, persons with disabilities

S. L. Adams (✉)
Pfeiffer University, Misenheimer, NC, USA
e-mail: Sherry.Adams@pfeiffer.edu

D. Hollar (ed.), *Advances in Exercise and Health for People With Mobility Limitations*, https://doi.org/10.1007/978-3-319-98452-0_7

may experience violence, abuse, prejudice, and disrespect due to their individual disability. Finally, the person may be subjected to involuntarily sterilization or confinement to an institution if that person is deemed legally incompetent (WHO World Report on Disability). Earlier in history (late 1800s and early 1900s), people with disabilities were sent to asylums in the United Kingdom, Australia, and the United States (Jackson 2018). The disabled population was not integrated, and they were both geographically and culturally removed from view (Wolfensburger 1969).

7.2 Models of Disability

In order to define impairment and provide strategies to meet needs of disabled people, models were devised. These models are made by people about other people and provide government and agencies attitudes, conceptions, and prejudices about disabled people and how this impacts this population. These models view disabled people as dependent upon society but also perceive the importance of this population in society. These models change as the society changes and continue to evolve leading to inclusiveness, empowerment, human rights, and integration.

7.2.1 Charity Model of Disability

The charity model of disability is also referred to as the tragedy model. This model classifies disabled people as victims of circumstances and is a common model where the nondisabled population feels pity for what are deemed as victims, the disabled individuals. This charity model of disability doesn't just include physical disabilities but also includes mentally disturbed, elderly, and what was deemed as defective children (Oliver 1990). This population was visibly removed from the population. This victimization of this population resulted in this removal from the population and the thought that the disabled people need cared for and are incapable of living a whole, independent life.

7.2.2 Medical Model for Disability

The medical model for disability used the classification of either a deficiency or a deviance compared to what was believed to be the normative state (Nankervis 2006). With this medical model, the person's impairment can be diagnosed, cured, or rehabilitated by medicine and/or interventions provided by medical professionals (Oliver 1998; Scotch 2000). This medical model resulted in the institutionalization of these individuals in the 1960s without regards to accessibility.

7.2.3 *Social Model for Disability*

Eventually in the 1980s, a social model was developed (Oliver 1983, 1998, 2013) which led to the thought process that disability is a result of barriers placed on the disabled individuals and not a particular impairment. It's these barriers that actually prevent inclusiveness and result in discrimination and oppression of people with disabilities (Sodar 2009). This resulted in recognizing that the built environment is an instrument for disability and resulted in putting greater emphasis on building inclusive environments.

7.3 Built Environment

In the 1960s, a Swedish social theorist emphasized the importance of social inclusion of people with disabilities within the community (Nirje 1994). It is vital to provide an appropriate built environment in order to be inclusive to a very diverse population. Although there is not one perfectly built environment, strides are being made in order to enhance and improve the built environment. It is expected by the year 2025 that Norway will have a contemporarily built environment that will be inclusive for accessibility (NMCE and SI 2016).

In 2006, the United National Convention on the Rights of Persons with Disabilities was enacted; however, not all accessibility needs are currently being met. Many barriers still exist including barriers to shopping, attending school/work, or recreational activities (Jackson 2018). People with disabilities are categorized by their primary disability (e.g., intellectual, autism, hearing impaired, wheel chair user, etc.) without any regard to other impairments that are typically experienced. These additional impairments also affect the environment in which these individuals interact. There is also a diversity problem, and US professors (Scotch and Shriner 1997) looked at the underrepresentation of disabled people in employment, education, and discrimination due to the environment.

Finally, the human rights model evolved due to a rights-based approach and this need for inclusiveness (Quinn et al. 2002). The 1980s were pivotal in the activism globally, but it was the United Nations human rights model in 2006 that increased the American Disabilities Act (ADA) rights to provide built environments for people with disabilities. This global activism is important to combat social exclusion due to unsuitable housing, problems with the pedestrian environment, and unusable public transportation due to lack of enforcement of legislation or misinterpretation of the legislation.

Even in the twenty-first century, there remains inaccessibility to the built environment. This remains a problem because disabled individuals are a heterogeneous group and there is only one built environment for this diverse population. It's imperative to understand the disability models but also crucial to include people with the disabilities when planning and developing these built environments due to this heterogeneity because one size does not fit all disabled people.

7.4 Built Environment and Economic Issues

This population is severely impacted by the amount and type of assistance they receive but more often than not do not receive the adequate assistance in order to live a full and productive life. This population is also at an increased risk of living in poverty that is associated with their disability. This sets the disabled individuals up for reduction in employment, lack of transport or access to transportation, and lack of resources to maintain their activities. There are oftentimes additional costs associated with being disabled stemming from medical care or assistive devices coupled with this increased risk for poverty that places the disabled person at greater detrimental hazards such as limited access to the proper medical treatment or care needed. This tendency to have higher costs and lower income results in potential food insecurity, inadequate housing, lack of safe water and sanitation which ultimately affects the disabled person's health, and an environmental hazard (Mitra et al. 2017; Beresford and Rhodes 2008; Loeb and Eide 2004; Eide and Loeb 2006; Eide and Jele 2011).

7.5 Built Environment and Health

The health of the disabled individual may be detrimentally impacted due to the built environment. The ADA was established in 1990 and health-care reform known as the Affordable Care Act (ACA) in October 2013 required every state to offer health insurance for individuals. The ADA provided access to build environments for people with disabilities. The health-care system in the United States is geared toward meeting the short-term needs or acute needs of individuals. People with disabilities often need long-term services and support to address their chronic health needs. These needs oftentimes include aiding with activities of daily living, taking medications, preparing meals, managing money, and obtaining employment and individual needs based on their specific disability. There may be multiple disabilities that impact these needs even more severely. Most of the long-term service expenses are provided out of pocket by the families and can range from $6000 to $16,000 annually depending on the disability (Mitra et al. 2017). There are only about 9% of the US population that have long-term care insurance, and Medicare only provides a limited amount of long-term care coverage (Mitra et al. 2017). Medicaid does provide long-term care coverage but primarily goes to fund institutional care. People who want to receive their coverage in community settings are not entitled to home or community-based services. This becomes a problem for people who have disabilities who are higher functioning but still need the additional medical care or services. Also, the problem with the ADA is that this regulatory act has resulted in a lack of fit because the disability population is heterogeneous and not homogeneous. There are around 40 million Americans in 2015 with a disability according to the US Census Bureau. This represents almost 13% of the civilian noninstitutionalized population. In order to be classified as a person with a disability, the person must have one of the six classifications: difficulty with hearing, vision, cognition, walking, or climbing stairs, and self-care and independent living (Pew Research, 2017). This population continues to grow and affects millions of people. The barriers of inclusiveness are as varied as the disabilities themselves.

Another barrier that institutions and organizations need to address is access to health-care services. There may be unintentional barriers placed upon someone with disabilities due to complicated booking systems to actually receive health care, problems with arriving early and/or staying all day (Miller et al. 2004). We have all experienced arriving at the health-care facility on time only to have to forfeit hours of your day waiting to be seen. This inconvenience may be exacerbated depending on the disability the individual may have. Funding may also be a deterrent, as reimbursement to providers doesn't account for additional time required for services for people with disabilities. Since reimbursement is typically a fixed amount, it might discourage providers from providing service (Smith 2000). Depending on the transportation needs and access to medical facilities that will provide services to disabled people may amplify this environmental barrier.

7.6 Environmental Barriers

There are five kinds of environmental barriers that people with disabilities face. These barriers include dependence on individuals, the disability of the individual, and other things that may affect the individual. The primary barriers include physical barriers, attitude barriers, assistance barriers, policy barriers, and work and school barriers (Hospital, Brainline).

7.6.1 Physical Barriers

Physical barriers can come from the natural environment or also from human-made changes within the natural environment. The natural environmental barriers can be as diverse as the terrain and climate to human-made changes including things such as walkways and other things built into the environment. Able-bodied people give little thought to these barriers, but it becomes a problem in people with disabilities when trying to navigate with a walker or a wheelchair. These barriers also vary depending on if the person with a disability lives in cities or in rural areas. Environmental barriers affect rural respondents more than their city-living counterparts (Visagie et al. 2017).

The United States has made significant strides in improving the lives of people with disabilities in regard to environmental barriers. Reasonable accommodation is ensured with the establishment of the American with Disabilities Act 19. A research agenda, "New Paradigm of Disability," was established by the National Institute on Disability, Independent Living, and Rehabilitation Research (NIDILRR) to help improve lives of people with disability. The Institute of Medicine has established disability as the basis of its research agenda, and they have placed importance on environmental barriers in people with disabilities as addressed in their report, Enabling America, 21. Also, there is a growing international interest in disability issues and the importance of environmental factors. This is not just a US problem but also a global problem. The United Nations (UN) has also focused attention on disability and established the Disability Year 25 and Disability Decade.

There are many different disabilities, but a group looked at barriers seen in people with spinal cord injuries and found there were five main barriers in this disabled population. These top barriers in descending order include environment, transportation, help at home, health care, and governmental policies (Whiteneck et al. 2004). Quality of life is likely adversely impacted as well due to the environmental factors; however, the authors did not perform a systematic review of that effect. The environment is a major barrier with people living with traumatic brain injury and includes physical barriers such as stairs, hills, roads, and buildings (Whiteneck et al. 2004). These physical barriers are more of a substantial problem in older adults than with younger adults but affects all populations to some degree (Brainline). The older population has problems with finding transportation either lack of transportation or limited access to transportation. There are also barriers in their surroundings that affect life such as poor lighting, too much noise, crowds, cold temperature, too much rain, steep hills, etc. (Brainline). Although these barriers were specifically addressed in people living with spinal cord injuries or traumatic brain injuries, they may have an effect on anyone living with a disability.

Providing adequate transportation can mitigate many of these environmental barriers. It is also important to design and layout buildings keeping in mind the needs to accommodate people with disabilities. The natural environment is not as easily manipulated or changed as temperature, terrain, and climate are more stationary or unadjustable. Lighting and noise can be managed or adjusted to help accommodate these individuals. Many of these adaptations can easily be made to improve the environment for individuals with disabilities.

The environment can create barriers for participation and inclusion. These barriers include things as simple as not having accessible building which could be lack of an elevator for someone with a walking disability or who is in a wheel chair. People living in poverty may not have access to drinkable water or sanitation, which provides an added barrier to someone with a disability. Policy changes need to be enacted to help improve conditions and provide proper buildings and building layouts, technology including Braille or hearing-impaired services, signage, and opportunities for people with disabilities.

Can disability be prevented? There are preventative measures that can be taken to help reduce the potential for disability. These measures include providing education and adequate nutrition, preventing diseases, providing safe water and sanitation, and improving safety on the roads and in the workplace (Caulfield et al. 2006). These preventative measures fall under the realm of public health and have three different prevention approaches. The first is primary prevention, which provides education to help promote health; an example would be educating people about HIV (Maart and Jelsma 2010). The secondary prevention detects a problem early on and provides a cure or reduces long-term effects; an example would be to provide screening for breast cancer in women with disabilities (McIlfatric et al. 2011). Finally, the tertiary prevention reduces disease-related complications; an example would be rehabilitation for someone with a musculoskeletal system impairment where they might receive physical or occupational therapy services (Atijosan et al. 2009).

7.6.2 Environmental Disability Caused by Inactive Lifestyle

Another interesting environmental disability is a deadly combination of inactive lifestyle and nutrition. This is not the typical disability that one thinks about when looking at environmental issues and the disabled individual. However, this is a growing problem as there has been an increase in obesity over the past couple of decades and it is related to the environment. You may be asking, "How is the environment to blame?" There is less space for people to engage in physical activity. Also, individuals are spending more time watching TV, surfing the Internet, and playing video games. In addition, many of our cities and rural areas are not conducive to walking or riding bikes to school or work. Food consumption also has an impact on this increase in the obesity epidemic. If we look at the current food consumption, people are eating out more often, the portion sizes are in greater proportion than they were just several decades ago, and there is increased consumption of sugary drinks and the size of these drinks compared to several decades ago (WHO). Also in specific regions where there is lower socioeconomic status, there is likely inadequate access to fresh foods including farm-raised meats, fruits, and vegetables. This limited access also plays a significant role in the increase in obesity in specific populations coupled with the lack of accessible parks and playgrounds, which compound this epidemic. This deadly combination of decrease in physical activity and increase in portion sizes has resulted in this environmental disability.

Why is this environmental disability a concern for the general population? As a result of this obesity epidemic, there is an impact to the health of people with disabilities that is far greater than the health of the general population. This is exacerbated as the person with a disability may be unable to walk or has limited walking ability. There may not be access to healthy foods due to proximity of a grocery store that sells healthy foods. This added layer of where to exercise and get healthy foods becomes even greater for people who have disabilities. This is problematic in the general, healthy population but is magnified when looking at people with disabilities.

7.6.3 Attitude as an Environmental Barrier

Another major problem is attitude toward people with disabilities. Challenging the negative attitudes that people may have and combatting negative language, stereotypes, and stigma are also very important (Thornicroft et al. 2007). Most people in the general public have a lack of understanding of disabilities and are unaware that the person can be successful if the appropriate or adequate environment is provided (Siperstein et al. 2003). Although people with medical disabilities face many challenges, there is an even greater discrimination seen toward people with mental disabilities. There are negative attitudes and treatment by the general population, discrimination by employers, taunting or teasing by schoolchildren, generalized bullying, and lack of support. These negative attitudes oftentimes result in low self-esteem and participation in people with disabilities (Thornicroft et al. 2007). Discrimination experienced regardless of the disability has an impact on quality of life of the individual and their families.

Disabilities are so varied that many people may not view some people who actually have disabilities as being disabled. A lot of these viewpoints are from the classic viewpoint that someone has to have a visible disability such as being wheelchair bound, being deaf, or being blind (Park et al. 2007). Disability can be a result of a traumatic experience and the person having post-traumatic stress disorder, which is oftentimes not exhibited outwardly. Children born with congenital diseases are also disabled and there is sometimes no outward sign of this. Other examples of disability would include severe arthritis or a person who has dementia. As many health conditions are visible, there are just as many that are invisible, and it's important to educate the general population that although you may not be able to outwardly see the disability, there may be one present. The disabled condition can be temporary, episodic, permanent, etc.; therefore, a person can be deemed disabled but can be temporarily disabled or permanently disabled (Australian Bureau of Statistics 2009).

7.6.4 Assistance as an Environmental Disability

Assistance and support are imperative for people with disabilities. If there is a lack of support system or services, the person with the disability and their families may become economically and socially excluded. Some examples of assistance include a sign language interpreter or an advocate for a person who has mental impairments such as dementia. Some overarching examples of assistance or support include assistance with self-care or household care provided by community support for independent living, residential support where there are group homes available to the persons with disabilities, respite services to give family and friends a break from the day-to-day caregiving roles, educational or employment support, communication support as referred to above with the sign language interpreter example, community access to day care centers, information and advice provided by advocates and professionals, and assistant animals such as trained dogs for visually impaired individuals (WHO World Report on Disability).

Support needs to change over the lifespan depending on what stage of the life cycle the person is currently in. The needs are very different from early childhood on into adulthood and will be exacerbated in the aged disabled population. Special education needs are warranted during childhood. Upon reaching adulthood, the person will likely need an advocate, perhaps residential support, and potentially even personal assistance will be required. During old age, the caregivers may need day care centers or home help and even palliative care depending on the stage of their life and state of health.

7.6.5 Barriers at School

Policy is also starting to shift toward community and educational inclusion. This new paradigm identifies social and physical barriers in disability (Barnes 1991 and McConachie 2006). Environmental barriers occur in both work and school environments. Typically funding is the biggest factor for these barriers for this population. When there is inadquate funding, employment of educators specialized in writing with disabled population is limited. There are also limitations to proper tools to facilitate learning for the disabled population. This population has a wide range of disabilities, and a one-size-fits-all approach does not work. Physical and material needs are obvious barriers. The barriers that are less obvious include the attitudes of the educators. The teachers and other students may perceive lack of ability of the disabled children to learn. This perception will become self-fulfilling and must be combatted against. The disabled student has to be in an inclusive environment in order to guarantee success. These preconceived ideas that the children are incapable of learning result in differences in interactions and treatments of the people with disabilities. This may be varied as well depending on the type of disability and the widely held beliefs of the peers and teacher.

In order to mitigate these preconceived ideas, programs and education for the educators are vital in changing this and bringing awareness that there is a capacity for learning in people with disabilities. Along with having adequate access to education, the student must actually be able to physically get to the school. Other impediments to learning in addition to attitudes may include transportation to the school, navigating the sidewalks and halls, or even being able to get into the classrooms. These are things that impede learning prior to arrival into the classroom. Therefore, modifications must be established in order for this population to be able to learn.

Once in the classroom, modifications may be needed for someone with a reading disability. Perhaps someone needs to read the questions to that individual. There may be another student who needs someone to take notes due to inability to take notes. These are just a few examples of modifications in order to maintain an inclusive environment. Although we can look at the environment and school as barriers, we also must not overlook the coordination and collaboration between the students, parents, and educators including the rest of faculty and administrators to enhance and improve the environment for learning for the disabled individual. Information needs to be provided as well as making the environment accessible by providing necessary modifications and having the cooperation and communication between the educators and the disabled students as well as with their families to provide a successful learning environment (United National Educational, Scientific and Cultural Organization 2008).

7.6.6 Employment Barriers

Even with the passage of the ADA, people with disabilities have lower employment rates than normal population, and this has remained unchanged (Gilbride et al. 2003). Employers do not realize this is an untapped workforce, but now education is helping change this (Brooke et al. 2000). Likely due to this lower employment rate, disabled people are three times more likely to live in poverty than the rest of the population and also more likely to drop out of high school (Krane and Hanson 2004). To add insult to injury, people with disabilities are less likely to have health-care coverage. Think of someone with severe disabilities who is at even a greater disadvantage. The culmination of lower employment rates, few high school graduates, and lack of health-care coverage results in the likelihood of remaining in lower socioeconomic groups.

Part of this employment problem is a result of lack of education and knowledge of employers. The employers likely have fear about hiring people with disabilities. The fears may be caused by the perceived financial loss due to accommodation costs; fear of increased supervision, which may result in loss of productivity with these employees; and fear of not being able to terminate the employee in case the employee does not work out. The fact remains that accommodations for disabled people rarely exceed $500 (McCary 2005). Research has found that even when employees are happy with their disabled employees, they rank satisfaction as lower due to these preconceived notions (Smith et al. 2004). This misconception about added expense without return on investment needs to be changed, and the only way that this will change is by education and employment of disabled individuals.

Employers need information and knowledge to help them reframe their thoughts about the disabled employees (Brooke et al. 2000). This is beginning to change with recognition of the value of this diverse population (McCary 2005). Research has found that employers that are willing to hire disabled individuals have very similar characteristics. These characteristics include a welcome environment for diversity and inclusiveness, also being able to job match by providing an internship, and if the person works out, then they can offer them a full-time position, dropping some of those requirements that aren't necessary such as requiring a driver's license. Finally, it's important to have support and involve both the employer and the disabled individuals so there is a positive employment outcome.

Education for these employers is crucial in changing these misconceptions. This is an easy fix and will mitigate the fears of hiring disabled individuals. Also, information regarding policy and funding is crucial in alleviating these fears. It's vital to ease transition of people with disabilities into positions of employment which will in turn result in increased autonomy. The diversity within this group ranges from disabilities of speech, hearing, sight, learning, mental, and physical. Providing employment that best fits each individual will result in success in the job or career that each disabled person is employed.

The companies that have found success use flexible job assignments, which match the individual's strengths with the job. Also, a team-based approach with input from both the employer and the employees could be effective. These companies implement diversity of thought and are open to innovative ideas; also the companies provide advancement opportunities to the employees with disabilities. They provide financial reward and a worry-free environment where the disabled individuals know they can succeed and are expected to succeed. Some physical environment improvements are minimizing transportation barriers by employing the disabled person near where they reside, providing flexible work schedules, and being committed to diversity of the employees. Disability progressive companies aggressively recruit, train, and promote people with disabilities that provide a positive opportunity for both employer and employee. These companies provide technology and accessibility within the workplace for success of people with disabilities (Riley II 2006).

Again, the three biggest barriers of hiring these individuals are all based on fear. These fears are the perceived costs for the company, misunderstanding of the legal responsibility, and training for these individuals, just a lack of knowledge about employment support and resources available. Educating the companies on these things will go a long way in providing a more inclusive and diverse environment.

7.7 Socioeconomic Status as an Environmental Barrier

Most countries including the United States have large gaps in help needed for people with disabilities. Influencing these gaps is very dependent on the socioeconomic status of the family and friends of the individuals with disabilities. This is very stressful for both the caretakers and the people with disabilities. Getting help is often complicated and typically ranges from informal care provided by the families and friends to formal services provided by the government, nonprofit organizations, and for-profit sector. The out-of-pocket payment to private providers is costly. There are definitely disparities seen in high-income countries compared to low-income countries. In higher-income countries, families usually provide around 80% of the support especially to older adults (McKee et al. 2003). Adults with developmental disabilities primarily live at home (approximately 75 percent), and more than 25% of the caregivers are over the age of 60 (Braddock et al. 2008). This aging population taking care of aging disabled people is going to continue growing.

Personal support workers such as home health aides play an important role in helping caregivers, but unfortunately there is a shortage of these workers and high demand for their services. In the United States, the demand for these workers is expected to increase by 41% between 2016 and 2026 (Occupational employment and wages 2016). In the United States, the home health aides do not need formal qualifications and are poorly paid. This results in a high turnover and could also result in substandard care of the disabled individuals.

There are sometimes community living environments available to people with disabilities, but this also results in some environmental problems. Oftentimes, the person does not have a choice or control over the support in these homes. These community environments may fail to provide entry into employment to the disabled individuals, thus resulting in lower satisfaction and less meaningful activities (Kozma et al. 2009; Perrins and Tarr 1998).

7.8 The Human Rights Approach

The human rights approach to people with disabilities includes four principles. The first principle is awareness. Assessing how the built environment affects the people is of the greatest importance. The best way to accomplish this is through community outreach, census information, or surveys. Once the number of people with disabilities is assessed, the next step is to see how this population is affected. The environmental design in both rural and urban environments needs to be assessed to see what changes need to be made for people with disabilities as well as for the families of disabled people. Along with environmental design, environmental issues that affect the population include climate-related changes, food accessibility, safe drinking water, etc.

Once awareness has been established, engaging and interacting with the people these design changes will impact are crucial. The disabled persons and their families need to be included and empowered concerning their rights. Participation is of utmost importance. This is best established by inclusion in the planning and development of the environment in which they live. The person living with the disability as well as their caregivers and/or family are most knowledgeable of the requisite needs to maintain or improve quality of life of these individuals. By including these people, you utilize their level of expertise, and this will help enact or implement environmental changes that will benefit the disabled. Any time inclusion and decision-making are put in the hands of the impacted population; the outcome will result in the necessary changes to improve the quality of life of this population.

The next principle is comprehensive accessibility. This includes physical, communication, policy, and attitudinal access for people with disabilities. Awareness and participation have been implemented, but other barriers are excluding the population from participation. These barriers may include attitudes and perceptions from within the community. It's imperative that the community talk to the disabled person to see how they want to communicate. The person may prefer communication by email or via focus groups. Although disability is more inclusive than being deaf and blind, it is important to understand that not all people who are deaf know sign language and not all people who are blind have learned Braille. Communication breakdowns may be a major breakdown in being able to adequately implement positive change into the environment. It's also important to address safe access to facilities. What type of changes may aide in the access to facilities? Also, what about access to environmental opportunities such as shelter from impending weather or natural disasters, working in the community garden, etc.? In case of severe weather events, there may need to be reconstruction in buildings or change in the universal design in order to facilitate protection of people of disabilities. As far as community engagement, changes may be made so everyone has the ability to access the recreational activities.

The last inclusion requirement is referred to as twin track. Twin track refers to the full inclusion through mainstream access and working with disability-specific supports. Mainstream access refers to the inclusion of all people with disabilities related to environmental policies, whereas disability-specific access would insure that the environmental funds affect at least 15% of the disabled population. A mainstream policy would be to provide programs about the environment to people with disabilities and their family members. The disability-specific policy would include assistive devices and specialized training for this participation. Also mainstream would be to educate everyone including people with disabilities into environmental programs. Disability specific would be to document what lessons are learned via this community inclusion and changes enacted. Both policies work together to provide participation and equality. Mainstream services are more inclusive by providing specific activities such as rehabilitation, assistive devices, training in sign language for staff/community but exclusions still occur because there may not be services available for everyone. It is important to provide training and education to family and the community as well as to the disabled people. Since each disability is specific to the individual, a disability-specific approach would use lessons learned during community inclusion and work to enact changes that would provide the participation and equality to all disabled people.

7.9 Environment Affects Disability Paradigm

The new paradigm that the environment is actually equally a factor contributing to disability has really increased the scope of the scientific research. This includes assessment of the disability and the social and environmental factors that affect the disabled person (Hahn 1985; Mace et al. 1991; Law et al. 1996). This information resulted in the WHO including these environmental factors. It's also imperative that the people with disabilities actually meet with the environment professionals in focus groups so the buildings provide the broad spectrum of needs to meet this heterogeneous group. The buildings must also meet the mandates from the government and be economical. It's also important for the architects and engineers to have creative license to design these spaces.

7.10 Conclusion

This new universal design can be used by everyone. Environmental accessibility is the principal theme of the World Programme of Action concerning Disabled Persons. This environmental accessibility is inclusive of transportation, social and health services, educational and work opportunities, and cultural and social life. All the barriers and obstacles to accessibility must be eliminated in order to achieve this. Providing accessibility will benefit everyone in the community and is important within the United States and globally. This is done by enacting policy, design, planning, and development in all environments to be inclusive of all people. This is an important movement from legislative compliance to a holistic and public good initiative.

References

Atijosan, O., Simms, V., Kuper, H., Rischewski, D., and Lavy, C. (2009). The orthopaedic needs of children in Rwanda: Results from a national survey and orthopaedic service implications. Journal of Pediatric Orthopaedics, 29(8): 948–951.

Australian Bureau of Statistics. (2009). *National health survey 2007–2008: Summary of results*. Canberra: Australian Bureau of Statistics.

Barnes, C. (1991). *Disabled people in Britain and discrimination*. London: Hurst.

Beresford, B. & Rhodes, D. (2008). Housing and disabled children. York, Joseph Rowntree Foundation.

Braddock, D., Hemp, R., & Rizzolo, M. (2008). *The state of the states in developmental disabilities* (7th ed.). Washington, DC: American Association on Intellectual and Developmental Disabilities.

Brooke, V., Green, H., O'Brien, D., White, B. and Armstrong, A. (2000). Supported employment: It's working in Alabama [electronic version]. Journal of Vocational Rehabilitation, 14 (3), 163–171. Retrieved 18 Aug 2007, from http://search.ebscohost.com

Callahan, D. (1973). The WHO definition of 'health.' The Hastings Center Studies, 1(3): 77–87.

Caulfield, L. E., Richard, S. A., Rivera, J. A., Musgrove, P., & Black, R. E. (2006). Stunting, wasting, and micronutrient deficiency disorders. In D. T. Jamison, J. G. Breman, A. R. Measham, & G. Alleyne (Eds.), *Disease control priorities in developing countries* (pp. 551–567). Washington, DC: Oxford University Press/World Bank.

Eide, A., & Loeb, M. (2006). *Living conditions among people with activity limitations in Zambia: A national representative study*. Oslo: SINTEF.

Eide A.H. and Jele, B. (2011). Living conditions among people with disabilities in Swaziland: A national representative study. SINTEF report no. A, 20047.

Gilbride, D., Stensrud, R., Vandergoot, D., & Golden, K. (2003). Identification of the characteristics of work environments and employers open to hiring and accommodating people with disabilities. *Rehabilitation Counseling Bulletin, 46*(3), 130–137.

Hahn, H. (1985). Changing perceptions of disability and the future of rehabilitation. In L. G. Perlman & G. F. Austin (Eds.), *Societal influences in rehabilitation planning: A blueprint for the 21st century, A report of the ninth Mary E. Switzer seminar* (pp. 53–64). Alexandria: National Rehabilitation Association.

Jackson, M.A. (2018). Models of disability and human rights: Informing the improvement of built environment accessibility for people with disability at neighborhood scale? Laws, 7(1): 10.

Kozma, A., Mansell, J., & Beadle-Brown, J. (2009). Outcomes in different residential settings for people with intellectual disability: A systematic review. *American Journal on Intellectual and Developmental Disabilities, 114*, 193–222.

Krane, D., & Hanson, K. W. (2004) 2004 N.O.D./Harris survey of Americans with disabilities. National Organization of Disability (U.S.) Harris Interactive, New York, NY.

Law, M., Cooper, B., Strong, S., Stewart, D., Rigby, P., & Letts, L. (1996). The person-environment-occupation model: A transactive approach to occupational performance. *Canadian Journal of Occupational Therapy, 63*(1), 9–23.

Leonardi, M., Bickenbach, J., Ustun, T. B., Kostanjsek, N., & Chatterji, S. (2006). MHADIE consortium the definition of disability: What is in a name? *Lancet, 368*, 1219–1221.

Loeb, M., & Eide, H. (2004). *Living conditions among people with activity limitations in Malawi: A national representative study*. Oslo: ISNTEF.

Maart, S., & Jelsma, J. (2010). The sexual behavior of physically disabled adolescents. *Disability and Rehabilitation, 32*, 438–443.

Mace, R., Hardie, G., & Plaice, J. (1991). Accessible environments: Toward universal design. In W. F. E. Preiser, J. C. Vischer, & E. T. White (Eds.), *Design interventions: Toward a more humane architecture* (p. 156). New York: Van Nostrand Reinhold.

McCary, K. (2005). The disability twist in diversity: Best practices for integrating people with disabilities into the workforce [electronic version]. *Diversity Factor, 13*(3), 16–22.

McConachie, H., Colver, A. F., Forsyth, R. J., Jarvis, S. N., & Parkinson, K. N. (2006). Participation of disabled children: How should it be characterized and measured? *Disability and Rehabilitation, 28*, 1157–1164.

McIlfatric, S., Taggart, L., & Truesdale-Kennedy, M. (2011). Supporting women with intellectual disabilities to access breast cancer screening: A healthcare professional perspective. *European Journal of Cancer Care, 20*, 412–420.

McKee, K. J., Philp, I., Lamura, G., Prouskas, C., Oberg, B., Krevers, B., Spazzafumo, L., Bieri, B., Parker, C., Nolan, M. R., Szczerbinka, K., & COPE Partnership. (2003). The COPE index-a first stage assessment of negative impact, positive value, and quality of support of caregiving in informal careers of older people. *Aging & Mental Health, 7*, 39–52.

Miller, P., Parker, S., & Gillinson, S. (2004). *Disablism: How to tackle the last prejudice*. London: Demos.

Mitra, S., Palmer, M., Kim, H., Mont, D., & Grace, N. (2017). Extra costs of living with a disability: A review and agenda for research. *Disability and Health Journal, 10*, 475–484.

Nankervis, K. (2006). Conceptions of disability. In I. Dempsey & K. Nankervis (Eds.), *Community disability services: An evidence-based approach to practice* (pp. 3–26). Sydney: UNSW Press.

Nirje, B. (1994). The normalization principle and its human management implications*. *SRV-VRS: The International Social Role Valorization Journal, 1*, 2. First published 1969.

Norwegian Ministry of Children, Equality and Social Inclusion. (2016). *The government's action plan for universal design 2015–2019*. Oslo: NMCE and SI.

Oliver, M. (1983). *Social work with disabled people*. Basingstoke: Macmillan.

Oliver, M. (1990). *The politics of disablement*. Basingstoke: Macmillan/St Martin's Press.

Oliver, M. (1998). Theories in health care and research: Theories of disability in health practice and research. *British Medical Journal, 317*, 1446–1449.

Oliver, M. (2013). The social model of disability: Thirty years on. *Disability and Society, 28*, 1024–1026.

Park, A., Curtice, J., & Thomson, K. (2007). *British social attitudes survey 23rd report*. London: Sage.

Perrins, K., & Tarr, J. (1998). The quality of day care provision to encourage the transition to adulthood for young women with learning difficulties. *Research in Post-Compulsory Education, 3*, 93–109.

Quinn, G., Degener, T., Bruce, A., Burke, C., Castellino, J., Kenna, P., Kilkelly, U., & Quinlivan, S. (2002). *Human rights and disability the current use and future potential of United Nations human rights instruments in the context of disability. Report, to the United Nations*. New York/Geneva: United Nations.

Riley, C. A., II. (2006). *Disability and business: Best practices and strategies for inclusion*. New Hampshire: University Press of New England.

Scotch, R. K. (2000). Models of disability and the Americans with disabilities act. *Berkeley Journal of Employment & Labor Law, 21*, 213–222.

Scotch, R. K., & Shriner, K. (1997). Disability as human variation: Implications for policy. *The Annals of the American Academy of Political and Social Science, 549*, 148–159.

Siperstein, G. N., Norins, J., Corbin, S., & Shriver, T. (2003). *Multinational study of attitudes towards individuals with intellectual disabilities*. Special Olympics Inc: Washington, DC.

Smith, R. D. (2000) Promoting the health of people with physical disabilities: a discussion of the financing and organization of public health services in Australia. *Health Promotion International, 15*, 79–86.

Smith, K., Webber, L., Graffam, J., & Wilson, C. (2004). Employer satisfaction with employees with a disability: Comparisons with other employees. *Journal of Vocational Rehabilitation, 21*, 61–69.

Soder, M. (2009). Tensions, perspectives and themes in disability studies. *Scandinavian Journal of Disability Research, 11*, 67–81.

Thornicroft, G., Rose, D., & Kassam, A. (2007). Discrimination in health care against people with mental illness. *International Review of Psychiatry (Abingdon, England), 19*, 113–122.

Barriers to inclusive education. (2008). Policy Guidelines on Inclusion in Education. United Nations Educational Scientific and Cultural Organization (UNESCO). Paris, France.

United States Bureau of Labor Statistics. (2016). *Occupational employment and wages*. Washington, DC: United States Bureau of Labor Statistics.

Visagie, S., Eide, A.H., Dyrstad, K., Mannan, H., Swartz, L., Schneider, M., Miji, G., Munthali, A., Khogali, M. van Rooy, G., Hem, K.G., MacLachlan, M. (2017). Factors related to environmental bariers experienced by persons with and without disabilities in diverse African settings. PLOS ONE https://doi.org/10.1371/journal.pone.0186342.

Whiteneck, G.G., Meade, M.A., Dijkers, M., Tate, D.G., Bushnik, T., and Forchheimer, M.B. (2004) Environmental factors and their role in participation and life satisfaction after spinal cord injury. Archieves of Physical Medicine and Rehabilitation, 85: 1793–1803.

Wolfensberger, W. (1969). The origin and nature of our institutional models. In changing patterns in residential Services for the Mentally Retarded. Washington, DC: President's Committee on Mental Retardation. Available online: http://www.disabilitymuseum.org/dhm/lib/detail.html?id=1909&page=all

Chapter 8
On the Economic Impact of Innovation and Technological Transformation for People with Mobility Limitations

Nur M. Onvural

Acronyms

AT	Assistive technology
AP	Assistive product
BCIs	brain computer interfaces
DFID	Department of International Development
GDP	Gross domestic product
ICT	Information and communication technology
IoT	Internet of Things
ISO	International Standard Organization
OECD	Organization of Economic Development
WHO	World Health Organization

8.1 Introduction

People with disabilities represent the world's largest minority group. There are nearly a billion people with disabilities, in the world. In the USA, there are 56.7 million people with disabilities (World Health Organization 2011). They are often unemployed or in a job with less earnings than people without disabilities. As a matter of fact, in October 2017, the US Department of Labor (https://www.dol.gov/odep/) indicated that the unemployment rate for people with disabilities was at 7.6%, compared to 3.7% for people without disabilities. This statistic implies that people with disabilities are almost twice as likely as non-disabled people to be unemployed. Additionally, the labor force participation in the USA is only 21% for people with disabilities, compared to 68.3% for people without disabilities.

N. M. Onvural (✉)
Pfeiffer University, Morrisville, NC, USA
e-mail: Nur.Onvural@pfeiffer.edu

D. Hollar (ed.), *Advances in Exercise and Health for People With Mobility Limitations*, https://doi.org/10.1007/978-3-319-98452-0_8

Unfortunately, this statistics about labor force participation is more severe than the unemployment percentages in terms of magnitude. Moreover, globally, 50–90% of people with disabilities are unemployed, according to the United Nations. Hence, any advancement in the health of people with mobility disabilities to improve their employability and earnings would be valuable.

The innovation begins with improving their environment. People with disabilities have a definite need for clear information, communications that work best for them, buildings and services they can get into and utilize to the best of their abilities, health care in places near where they live, more choices and control over their health care, as well as money to help pay for these services (WHO 2011). The health-care expenditures for this group of population are clearly very high. In fact, although individuals with special/supportive care needs constitute less than 20% of the US population, they account for more – perhaps far more – than 35% of the total annual national health expenditures (over $800 billion, including more than $450 billion for nonmedical services) (Carter et al. 2016). That's where technology comes in play. Technology has always provided tools for people with disabilities or disorders to help them improve their environment and employability. There are several apps and gadgets that can help ease the difficulties people with disability face on a daily basis. These tools could be anything from a low-tech device, such as a magnifying glass, to a high-tech device, such as a computer that talks and helps someone communicate.

In this chapter, we focused on the economic impact of assistive technologies (AT), information and communication technology (ICT), progress of brain computer interfaces (BCI), the Internet of Things (IoT), and significance of connectivity for people with mobility disabilities. Ideally, these would be disruptive and help them contribute to the economy in the form of independent living and employment and hence earnings. However, initial cost and access to these innovations prevent these populations from utilizing all these tools and applications. In many cases, there is a need to provide these tools and devices through governmental organizations and volunteers, which limits the exposure and reduces the potential to reach full capacity.

The expected outcome of utilizing these innovations would be disruptive and positive; however that needs to be justified with research and accurate analysis. Regrettably, although approximately one billion people in the world live with physical disabilities, there is a lack of rigorous research on the economic impacts of providing assistive devices for persons with disabilities (Grider and Wydick 2016). Connectivity, on the other hand, or connection of all devices that disabled people are using, is a significantly new interference that will enhance the quality of life for disabled. Similarly, detailed research and analysis should be done in this area to understand economic impacts on the health, lifestyle improvements, employability, and earnings of these populations.

The chapter first summarizes employment and earnings for people with disabilities as reported in the 2016 Disability Report in the USA and briefly discusses global situations. It reviews definitions of innovations and technology and examines assistive technology tools. It, then, examines the role of assistive technologies in increasing independence and extending the participation of people with disabilities in society. Next, it highlights how these connected devices can improve independence and community participation through the information and communication technology, the progress of brain computer interfaces (BCI), and the Internet of Things. Finally, the chapter briefly discusses obstacles and challenges on the development of these networks. It concludes with recommendations.

8.2 Employment and Earnings for People With and Without Disabilities

The employment rates of persons with disabilities are a third to half of the rates for persons without disabilities, with unemployment rates as high as 80–90% in some countries (including developed and developing economies) (Mizunoya and Mitra 2012). A high unemployment rate for persons with disabilities increases a country's expenditure on welfare, which is in fact counterproductive to their social inclusion and economic self-sufficiency (Burkhauser and Daly 2011; Etherington and Ingold 2012; OECD 2010). As such, any developments to improve the employability of disabled people would add value to any country in the world.

According to Kraus (2017) in the USA in 2015, the difference between the employment percentage for people with disabilities (34.9%) and people without disabilities (76.0%) was 41.1 percentage points. For people with disabilities, employment rates ranged from a high of 57.1% (Wyoming) to a low of 25.4% (West Virginia). For those without disabilities, the employment ranged from 70.1% (Mississippi) to 83.8% (Minnesota). States with the highest gap were concentrated from the Atlantic Coast to Missouri and Arkansas. In 30 states, the employment percentage gap was 40 percentage points or greater. The highest gap was found in Maine (50.1%), Kentucky (47.4%), and the District of Columbia (46.1%). In only three states was the gap less than 33.3% – Wyoming (22.0%), South Dakota (30.9%), and Utah (32.5%). Even incremental changes in these gaps utilizing information, technology, and connectivity would bring progresses for people with disabilities.

Approximately 80% of the world's disabled people live in a developing country, while 80–90% of disabled people of working age are unemployed, and one-third of school-age children do not receive education because they are disabled or because they are caring for a disabled family member (World Bank 2013). People with disabilities are more likely to be unemployed and are generally paid less when they are employed. The global employment rates for men with disabilities (53%) and women with disabilities (20%) are lower than men (65%) and women (30%) without disabilities (WHO 2011).

Similarly, the earnings for disabled vs. non-disabled differ widely. In 2015, according to Kraus (2017), the median earnings of people with disabilities ages 16 and over in the USA were $21,572, about two-thirds of the median earnings of people without disabilities, $31,874. This disparity of over $10,000 in median earnings between those with and without disabilities continues a trend, which has existed since at least 2008 and has increased in magnitude since 2013. The range of median earnings in states for people with disabilities in 2015 was $15,938 in Idaho to $30,268 in Alaska. In six states (Alaska, Maryland, Hawaii, Nevada, New Jersey, and District of Columbia), the median earnings for people with disabilities were over $25,000, while fourteen (14) states had median disability earnings lower than $20,000 (Kraus 2017). In comparison, the median earnings for people without disabilities ages 16 ranged from $25,680 in Idaho to $49,891 in the District of Columbia in 2015. States varied widely in earnings gap (the difference between the median earnings for those with and without disabilities) – from a low of $4490 in Nevada to a high of $24,073 in the District of Columbia. Generally, states in the northern USA had a higher earnings gap; states in the southern USA had a lower earnings gap.

In the rest of the world, specifically, in developing countries, disabled people are more likely to be among the poor, as exclusion from economic, education, and health-care opportunities due to difficulties in traveling around often prevents them from breaking out of poverty (Disability and Development, World Bank 2013). In fact, the relationship of disability being both a cause and a consequence is described as a vicious circle in the following Fig. 8.1, poverty leading to disability and disability worsening poverty (DFID 2000).

The World Bank estimated the global gross domestic product (GDP) loss due to disability to be between $1.71 trillion and $2.23 trillion annually (Table 8.1) which amounts to be between 5.35% and 6.97% of the global GDP (Metts 2004).

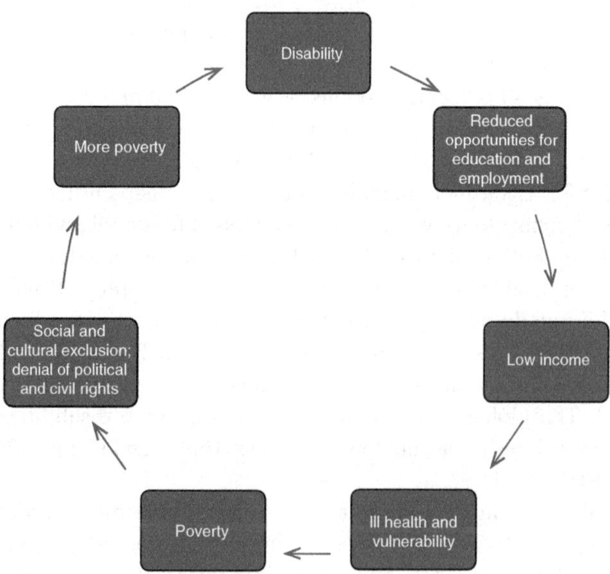

Fig. 8.1 This diagram represents the negative cycle linking disability, poverty, and vulnerability. (Adapted from DFID (2000), p. 4)

Table 8.1 GDP lost due to disability (Metts 2004)

Value of GDP lost (US$)	Low estimate	High estimate
High-income countries	1,224,014,055,600	1,594,439,361,900
Medium-income countries	377,700,686,120	492,004,841,130
Low-income countries	110,495,236,440	143,934,584,310
Total	1,712,209,978,160	2,230,378,787,340

Additionally, between 12% and 20% of the populations of developing countries were considered to be nonproductive due to disability (Social Analysis and Disability 2007). The Asian Development Bank maintains that while there are costs associated with including people with disabilities, these are far outweighed by the long-term financial benefits to individuals, families, and society (Asian Development Bank, Disability Brief 2005).

From an economic point of view, an individual experiences a doubling of the cost of disability: firstly, there are direct costs for treatment or rehabilitation, including user fees and transport costs; secondly, income is foregone – potentially both for the person with a disability and their assistants or families (World Report on Disability 2011). The amount by which economic output is reduced in this way constitutes the net economic cost of disability (Metts 2004).

Consequently, there is a constant push to generate positive changes to reduce the net economic cost of disability and to improve the employment percentages and earnings for people with disabilities in the USA and globally to create economic improvements in the lifestyles and environments for these populations. Even incremental changes would contribute to GDP, to consumption and investment, and to access to health insurance and medical care to result in decreases in health-care expenses. These are unquestionably areas to research understanding their economic impacts. However, first we will focus on what might lead to these improvements by discussing innovations and technology that have been creating advances in the lives and environments of people with disabilities.

8.3 Innovations and Technology

There are several tools, gadgets, applications, and innovative ways technology can assist people with disabilities. Utilization of these tools results in more involvement of people with limited mobility in society and further enhances the quality of life of people with disabilities. Such environments can foster the participation and inclusion of disabled individuals in social, economic, political, and cultural life (WHO 2011).

In this section, we briefly discuss areas of assistive technologies (ATs), the value of information and communication technologies (ICT), the progress of brain computer interfaces (BCI), and then the Internet of Things (IoT). We address barriers and challenges related to these technologies and provide recommendations on the economic impacts to generate value for the communities.

8.4 Assistive Technologies (ATs)

Assistive technologies (ATs) are devices or equipment that can be used to help a person with a disability to fully engage in life activities. According to the international standard ISO 9999:2011, an assistive product is "any product (including devices, equipment, instruments, and software), especially produced or generally available, used by or for persons with disability: for participation; to protect, support, train, measure or substitute for body functions/structures and activities; or to prevent impairments, activity limitations, or participation restrictions."

ATs can help enhance functional independence and make daily living tasks easier through the use of aids that help a person travel, communicate with others, learn, work, and participate in social and recreational activities. Canes and walkers help infirm elderly stay out of nursing homes; walk-in showers and grab bars prevent hip fractures and allow those who have had a fracture to live independently; microwave ovens make it easier for the frail elderly to cook; and telephones with larger keypads enable the visually impaired to communicate (Cutler 2001).

AT encompasses an enormous range of devices, including mobility aids (wheelchairs, canes, and walkers), augmentative communication devices (voice synthesizers and communication boards), prosthetic and orthotic devices, and a myriad of adaptive computer equipment. AT can be "low-tech" (a cup holder for a wheelchair tray) or "high-tech" (brain computer interfaces for communication and environmental control) (Li and Sellers 2009). Other examples of accessible technology solutions for disabled are voice recognition systems, adapted and virtual keyboards, joysticks and adapted mouse, the use of eye gaze and gestures to control devices, and remote and online access to work, education, and other services (Raja 2016). Also, smartphones have greatly expanded the availability and accessibility of assistive technology for people. In addition, education regarding the availability of assistive products and technologies and knowledge and training that empower users to self-advocate or have a significant other (e.g., family member, friend, or professional) advocate for them are important elements in achieving successful access to appropriate assistive products and technologies and related services (National Academies of Sciences, Engineering, and Medicine 2017).

Despite staggering progress in AT, there are still a large number of people with severe motor disabilities who cannot fully benefit from AT due to their limited access to current assistive products (APs) (Millán et al. 2010). Accordingly, the lack of support services can make handicapped people overly dependent on their families, which prevents them from being economically active and socially included (Domingo 2012). Also, new assistive devices and technologies are advancing faster than reimbursement systems and clinician education, which may limit access to these devices and training in their use (National Academies of Sciences, Engineering, and Medicine 2017).

Furthermore, there are numerous barriers in using assistive technology by individuals with lower limb disabilities worldwide, and they appear to be of high intensity in low-income countries (WHO 2011). According to Raja (2016) for people with physical disabilities (loss of mobility, dexterity, and control over some body functions), examples of barriers in social, economic, and community participation are entering, navigating, and using buildings, classrooms, and other physical spaces as well as using writing tools such as pens and pencils, keyboards, and mouse.

One then wonders the following question: What would be the economic impact of utilizing these devices on the employability and earnings of disabled people? A number of studies have been exploring that potential.

Specifically, in the book *The Promise of Assistive Technologies to Enhance Activity and Work Participation* (2017), the authors indicate that a number of assistive products and technologies (wheelchairs and other seated mobility devices, upper-limb prostheses, and hearing and speech assistive technologies) were examined to assess the extent to which people have access to and use these devices, as well as the extent to which the devices support occupational success. The findings indicate that data on the prevalence of use of assistive products and technologies and the extent to which they mitigate impairments are fragmented and limited, making it difficult to quantify their impact on employability. Assistive products and technologies have the potential to partially or completely mitigate the impacts of some impairments, provided the appropriate products and technologies are available, properly prescribed, and fitted; the user receives training in their use and appropriate follow-up; and societal and environmental barriers are limited. However, access to assistive devices and to qualified providers who can properly evaluate, fit, and train people in their use is frequently limited and varies significantly among individuals by state, geographic area (urban to rural and frontier areas), and funding source, the report says. Furthermore, personal factors – for example, the person's age and previous work experience – and social and environmental factors, such as workplace attitudes and the physical workspace, can pose barriers to employment. An evaluation of a person's functioning ideally would include the assistive products and technologies he or she normally uses, but professionals involved in disability determinations cannot assume that such devices necessarily enable the person to work. Environmental, societal, and personal factors also need to be taken into account (National Academies of Science, Engineering, and Medicine 2017).

Although academic research has been shown to successfully advance the technical capabilities of AT, it is worth noting that its usefulness in improving AT economics may be limited by an important caveat: the ownership of intellectual property and the eventual affordability of developed devices (Li and Sellers 2009). Additional research is needed to understand how the specifications for and use of assistive technologies and products and related services impact inclusion in society and work participation for individuals with disabilities (National Academies of Science, Engineering, and Medicine 2017).

MacDonald and Clayton (2013) explored how disabled people engage with digital and assistive technologies in order to overcome disabling barriers and social exclusion. Unfortunately, they found no evidence that digital and assistive technologies had any impact on reducing social exclusion for disabled people, and further their research discovered that these technologies seemed to construct new forms of disabling barriers as a consequence of the digital divide. OECD (2001) defines the digital divide as "the gap between individuals, households, businesses and geographic areas at different socio-economic levels with regard both to their opportunities to access information and communication technologies (ICTs) and to their use of the Internet for a wide variety of activities."

There is definitely a need for more research to enhance knowledge on the economics of these devices and eventually produce better assessments of resource allocation as well as cost benefit analyses for the use of these devices and related services.

8.5 Information and Communication Technology

Information and communication technology (ICT) is an umbrella term, which includes any information and communication device or application and its content. Such a definition encompasses a wide range of access technologies, such as radio, television, satellites, mobile phones, fixed lines, computers, and network hardware and software. Among these services, the Internet presents a myriad of opportunities for individuals with physical disabilities to increase quality of life and well-being, including access to vital health information, social networking, education, and accessible employment (Cheatham 2012). The importance of ICT lies in their ability to open up a wide range of services, transform existing services, and create greater demand for access to information and knowledge, particularly in underserved and excluded populations, such as persons with disabilities (The ICT Opportunity 2013).

ICT has changed how people build their skills, how they search for work, how they do their work, how they interact with coworkers and clients, and how they receive and use benefits in the workplace (Raja et al. 2013). ICT is increasingly enabling people with disabilities to level the playing field in access to lifelong education, skills development, and employment (Broadband Commission for Digital Development et al. 2013). Although positive relationships are detected between the Internet and well-being within samples of individuals with physical disabilities, however, further attention of researchers is needed for studies employing heightened methodological rigor (Cheatham 2012).

Manzoor and Vimarlund (2017) examined the contribution of e-services in terms of how they diminish barriers and constraints on social inclusion by reviewing the period between 2010 and 2016 (6 years) – only including studies that discussed the social inclusion of people with disabilities or presented prototype solutions to this problem. Their findings indicate that there is a lack of theoretical framework, which can be used to measure the effectiveness of the e-services or innovations in the area of e-services in the contexts that were examined. They argue that existing research studies are normally generic and do not discuss whether the requirements that are imposed on a particular e-service differ depending on (i) the type of disability, (ii) the ICT maturity or skill of the end user, or (iii) the context in which the e-service is used.

Nam and Park (2017) investigated the effects of the smart environment on the information divide experienced by people with disabilities regarding three aspects: access, skill, and competence. The access rate was higher for the general group than for that of those with disabilities, and this difference appeared to be greater in the smart environment. These results provide evidence that the smart environment further creates the information divide for people with disabilities. They recommend that strategies should be formed to reduce this divide, particularly within smart environments.

Hence, there is a vast void to fill in order to determine how ICT-based innovations would facilitate the social integration of people with disabilities and eventually improve the employability of these populations to bring economic benefits to the communities they live.

8.6 Brain computer interfaces (BCIs)

Brain computer interfaces (BCIs) are collaborations between a brain and a device that allow signals from the brain to direct some external activity, such as control of a prosthetic limb. The advances of brain computer interfaces (BCIs) made possible the development of prototype such as brain-controlled prosthetic devices, wheelchairs, keyboards, and computer games (Millán et al. 2010). BCI systems could eventually provide an important new communication and control option for those with motor disabilities and might also give those without disabilities a supplementary control channel or a control channel useful in special circumstances (Wolpaw et al. 2002). As a matter of fact, Leeb et al. (2013) shared the lessons they learned through transferring BCI technologies from the lab to the user's home or clinics. They trained 24 motor-disabled participants, without BCI experts present where 50% of the participants achieved good BCI performance and could successfully control the applications (tele-presence robot and text entry system).

The brain-controlled interface facilitates a direct communications pathway between the brain and the object to be controlled. Neurophysiological signals (electroencephalogram, EEG) originating from the brain are used to control external devices (e.g., TV, phone, computer, bed) (Millán et al. 2010). BCIs are not yet ready for independent home use; to establish BCIs as AT in the end user's home, three gaps need to be bridged: (1) the usability, (2) the reliability, and (3) the translational gap (Rudiger 2014). Millan et al. suggest that, eventually, BCI technologies will be brought out of the lab and transform into real-world applications.

Disabled people will benefit from the advancements in BCI technology combined with assistive technologies in four basic application areas (Millán et al. 2010): communication and control (Internet browsing, e-mails), motor substitution (in particular grasping and assistive mobility), entertainment (gaming, music browsing, photo browsing, and virtual reality), and motor recovery. With continued development and clinical implementation, BCIs could substantially improve the lives of those with severe disabilities (Wolpaw 2013).

8.7 Internet of Things (IoT) for People with Mobility Disabilities

The Internet of Things can offer people with disabilities the assistance and support they need to achieve a good quality of life and allow them to participate in the social and economic life (Domingo 2012). Recent developments in both networks and devices are enabling a much greater range of connected devices and the Internet of Things (IoT) functionalities; the phrase "Internet of Things" refers to the world of smart connected objects and devices (White paper 2015). Smart device usage is rapidly growing in everyday life, so the ability to use a smart device is increasingly important, yet there is little data supporting increased digital inclusion of people with disabilities in mobile device use (Nam and Park 2017).

The IoT is recognized as one of the most important areas of future technology and is gaining vast attention from a wide range of industries (Lee and Lee 2015). These new IoT applications add convenience and a new level of importance when used by people with disabilities and older adults. The potential of the Internet of Things can aid as an enabler of assistive technologies and increase the accessibility support and services for people with disabilities in domains such as service provision, health care, job integration, education and learning, independent and assisted living, as well as navigation and mobility support in public spaces including public transport, cultural places, and shopping for goods (Eid 2015). For IoT applications to work, the sensors and the actuators must be able to communicate with the devices that inform their action, whether it is a smartphone or something as simple as a remote thermometer (White paper 2015). The IoT systems for the people with mobility disabilities need to collect, analyze, and apply recommendations autonomously and unobtrusively (Reis and Maximiano 2016).

The IoT creates enabling environments by offering people with disabilities assistance in building access, transportation, information, and communication (Domingo 2012). For example, for people with mobility-related disabilities, smart home technology holds the promise of allowing the user to control things in his or her home that may be physically difficult to reach, such as lights, door locks, or security systems (White paper 2015). Domingo (2012) envisions that the IoT for disabled people (especially physically disabled individuals) will evolve dramatically in the following years. The Internet of Things will mean more independent living, more personalized care, more flexibility and mobility, and better employment and education outcomes through wearable and mobile technologies (White paper 2015).

The concept of the smart home is a promising and cost-effective way of improving home care for the elderly and the disabled in a non-obtrusive way, allowing greater independence, maintaining good health, and preventing social isolation (Chan et al. 2009). Ali Hussein et al. (2014) presented a framework that would help disabled people to live life on their own through an adaptable home embedded with sensors and other devices. Health care and safety of the users inside the house are essential features in addition to automation and security; these tasks are, for example, accomplished using a fall detection mechanism, humidity sensors, oxygen sensors, and constant monitoring of vital signs and monitoring the user's daily activities for abnormal events such as lack of eating or slow movements. Figure 8.2 provides a depiction of smart home for the disabled population (White Paper 2015).

A regular feature in a smart home is automation, which allows controlling and monitoring of all devices in the house as well as security which is possible using access code on main doors and windows, motion sensors, smart cameras with face recognition to identify movement around the house, smart fire alarm, and a reliable connection with the police department (Ali Hussein et al. 2014).

A key challenge is customization of these devices for people with disabilities. Since handicapped people have special needs, the IoT should be adapted to their particular circumstances (Domingo 2012). The system in the smart home should monitor medical issues and alert for medication schedules with potential and reliable connections with the emergency personnel and the medical team. The activity of one feature could sometimes depend on another feature, which is why the smart house system should be fully connected through a backbone network so features can interact and exchange information for better decisions and cooperation (Ali Hussein et al. 2014).

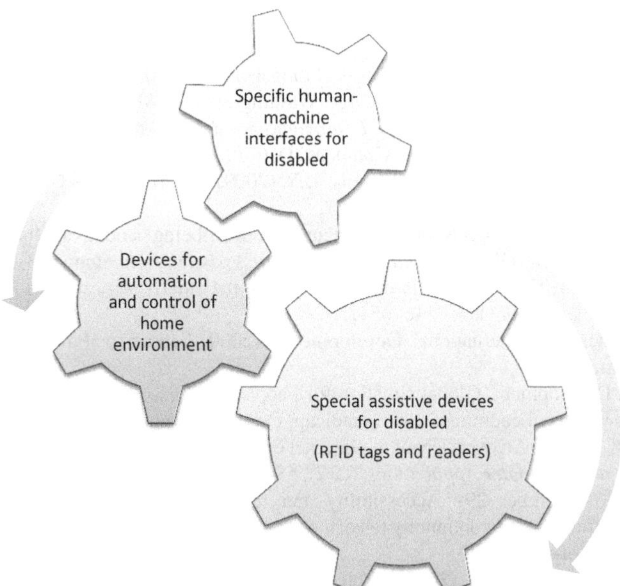

Fig. 8.2 A smart home depiction

8.8 Conclusions and Recommendations

We explored the economic impact of assistive technologies (ATs), as well as the significance of connectivity – the information and communication technology (ICT), the brain computer interfaces (BCI), and the Internet of Things (IoT) – for people with mobility disabilities. Certainly, there is evidence of encouraging outcomes of these devices on the lifestyle and environment of disabled people; however these devices and connections are still in their infancy phases yet slowly moving toward more daily implementations. The continuous progresses in these technologies and the promise to incorporate these in daily lives lead us to believe that with continuous utilization, the gaps in employment and earnings between people with and without disabilities will be decreased in the future. It is imperative that these technologies become increasingly adaptable and affordable. To expedite that, there has to be considerable collaboration and allocation of public and private resources and funds.

References

Asian Development Bank. (2005). *Disability brief: Identifying and addressing the needs of disabled people*. © Asian Development Bank. http://hdl.handle.net/11540/4878. License: CC BY 3.0 IGO.

Broadband Commission for Digital Development, G3ict, IDA, ITU, Microsoft, The Telecentre.org Foundation, and UNESCO. (2013). The ICT opportunity for a disability-inclusive development framework. http://g3ict.org/resource_center/publications_and_reports/p/productCategory_whitepapers/id_297

Burkhauser, R. V., & Daly, M. C. (2011). *The declining work and welfare of people with disabilities: What went wrong and a strategy for change*. Washington, DC: AEI Press.

Carter, K., Lewis, R., & Ward, T. (2016). *Improving care delivery to individuals with special or supportive care needs*. McKinsey & Company. Detroit, Michigan

Chan, M., Campo, E., Estève, D., & Fourniols, J. Y. (2009). Smart homes – Current features and future perspectives. *Maturitas, 64*(2), 90–97.

Cheatham, L. P. (2012). Effects of Internet use on well-being among adults with physical disabilities: A review. *Disability and Rehabilitation: Assistive Technology, 7*(3), 181–188.

Cutler, D. M. (2001). The reduction in disability among the elderly. *Proceedings of the National Academy of Sciences, 98*(12), 6546–6547.

DFID (Department for International Development). (2000, February). Poverty, disability and development, p. 4.

Disability and Development. Global situation for people with disabilities. Retrieved from http://www.hiproweb.org/fileadmin/cdroms/Handicap_Developpement/www/en_page22.html

Domingo, M. C. (2012). An overview of the Internet of Things for people with disabilities. *Journal of Network and Computer Applications, 35*(2), 584–596.

Eid, N. (2015, November 29). Accessibility and future of Internet of Things. *Blog Post*. Retrieved from http://community.telecentre.org/profiles/blogs/accessibility-and-the-future-of-the-internet-of-things

Etherington, D., & Ingold, J. (2012). Welfare to work and the inclusive labour market: A comparative study of activation policies for disability and long-term sickness benefit claimants in the UK and Denmark. *Journal of European Social Policy, 22*, 30–44.

Grider, J., & Wydick, B. (2016). Wheels of fortune: The economic impacts of wheelchair provision in Ethiopia. *Journal of Development Effectiveness, 8*(1), 44–66.

Grübler, G., & Hildt, E. (Eds.). (2014). Brain-computer interfaces in their ethical, social and cultural contexts. *The International Library of Ethics, Law and Technology, 12*. https://doi.org/10.1007/978-94-017-8996-7_2, © Springer Science+Business Media Dordrecht.

Hussein, A., Adda, M., Atieh, M., & Fahs, W. (2014). Smart home design for disabled people based on neural networks. The 5th international conference on emerging ubiquitous systems and pervasive networks (EUSP N-2014). *Procedia Computer Science, 37*, 117–126.

Krahn, G. L., Walker, D. K., & Correa-De-Araujo, R. (2015). Persons with disabilities as an unrecognized health disparity population. *American Journal of Public Health, 105*(S2), S198–S206.

Kraus, L. (2017). *2016 disability statistics annual report*. Durham: University of New Hampshire.

Lee, I., & Lee, K. (2015). The Internet of Things (IoT): Applications, investments, and challenges for enterprises. *Business Horizons, 58*(4), 431–440.

Leeb, R., Perdikis, S., Tonin, L., Biasiucci, A., Tavella, M., Creatura, M., Molina, A., Al-Khodairy, A., Carison, T., & Millán, J. D. (2013). Transferring brain-controlled computer interface beyond the laboratory: Successful application control for motor-disabled users. *Artificial Intelligence in Medicine, 59*(2), 121–132.

Li, W., & Sellers, C. (2009). *Improving assistive technology economics for people with disabilities: Harnessing the voluntary and education sectors*. Science and technology for humanity (TIC-STH), 2009 IEEE Toronto international conference, pp. 789–794. © Copyright 2010 IEEE.

Macdonald, S. J., & Clayton, J. (2013). Back to the future, disability and the digital divide. *Disability & Society, 28*(5), 702–718.

Manzoor, M., & Vimarlund, V. (2017). E-services for the social inclusion of people with disabilities: A literature review. *Technology and Disability, 29*(1–2), 15–33.

Metts, R. (2004). Disability and development, background paper for the World Bank, *Banque Mondiale*, p. 32. http://siteresources.worldbank.org/DISABILITY/Resources/280658-1172606907476/mettsBGpaper.pdf

Millán, J. d. R., Rupp, R., Müller-Putz, G. R., Murray-Smith, R., Giugliemma, C., Tangermann, M., et al. (2010). Combining brain–computer interfaces and assistive technologies: State-of-the-art and challenges. *Frontiers in Neuroscience, 4*, 161. https://doi.org/10.3389/fnins.2010.00161.

Mizunoya, S., & Mitra, S. (2012, May). Is there a disability gap in employment rates in developing countries? *Social Science Research Network*. http://papers.ssrn.com/sol3/papers.cfm?abstract_id=2127568

Nam, S.-J., & Park, E.-Y. (2017). The effects of the smart environment on the information divide experienced by people with disabilities. *Disability and Health Journal, 10*(2), 257–263.

National Academies of Sciences, Engineering, and Medicine. (2017). *The promise of assistive technology to enhance activity and work participation*. Washington, DC: The National Academies Press. https://doi.org/10.17226/24740.

OECD. (2001). *Understanding the digital divide*. OECD.

OECD (Organization for Economic Co-operation and Development). (2010). Sickness, disability and work: Breaking the barriers. A synthesis of findings across OECD countries. Retrieved from http://www.oecd-ilibrary.org/social-issues-migration-health/sickness-disability-and-work-breaking-the-barriers_9789264088856-en

Raja, D. S. (2016). Bridging the disability divide through digital technologies. *Background paper for the World Development report*.

Raja, S., Imaizumi, S., Kelly, T., Narimatsu, J., & Paradi-Guilford, C. (2013). *How information and communication technologies could help expand employment opportunities*. Washington, DC: World Bank https://openknowledge.worldbank.org/bitstream/handle/10986/16243/809770WP0Conne00Box379814B00PUBLIC0.pdf?sequence=1.

Reis, C. I., & Maximiano, M. d. S. (2016). *Internet of Things and advanced application in healthcare*. IGI Global

Rupp, R., Kleih, S. C., Leeb, R., Millan, J. d. R., Kübler, A., & Müller-Putz, G. R. (n.d.) *Brain–computer interfaces and assistive technology*.

Rupp R., Kleih S.C., Leeb R., del R. Millan J., Kübler A., Müller-Putz G.R. (2014) Brain–Computer Interfaces and Assistive Technology. In: Grübler G., Hildt E. (eds) Brain-Computer-Interfaces in their ethical, social and cultural contexts. The International Library of Ethics, Law and Technology, vol 12. Springer, Dordrecht.

Social Analysis and Disability, A Guidance Note, Banque Mondiale, 2007, p. 1. http://siteresources.worldbank.org/EXTSOCIALDEV/Resources/3177394-1175102311639/3615048-1175607868848/SocialAnalysis&Disability-Full.pdf

The ICT Opportunity for a Disability_Inclusive Development. (2013, September). Retrieved from the ICT opportunity for a disability-inclusive development … – ITU.

White Paper. (2015, July). Internet of Things: New promises for persons with disabilities a G3ict business case white paper series researched in cooperation with AT&T.

WHO Report. (2011). World report on disability. Retrieved from https://www.unicef.org/protection/World_report_on_disability_eng.pdf

Wolpaw, J. R. (2013). Chapter 6 – Brain-computer interfaces. *Handbook of Clinical Neurology, 110*, 67–74.

Wolpaw, J. R., Birbaumer, N., McFarland, D. J., Pfurtscheller, G., & Vaughan, T. M. (2002). Brain–computer interfaces for communication and control. *Clinical Neurophysiology, 113*(6), 767–791.

World Bank. (2013). *Improving accessibility to transport for People with Limited Mobility (PLM): A practical guidance note*. Washington, DC: World Bank Group http://documents.worldbank.org/curated/en/575221468278939280/Improving-accessibility-to-transport-for-People-with-Limited-Mobility-PLM-a-practical-guidance-note.

Chapter 9
Medical Imaging for Persons with Mobility Limitations

Meredith Gammons

Abbreviations

ACR	American College of Radiology
ADA	Americans with Disabilities Act
CT	Computed tomography
DXA	Dual-energy x-ray absorptiometry
FDG	Fluorodeoxyglucose radioactive marker for PET
IV	Intravenous
MQSA	Mammography Quality Standards Act of 1992
MRI	Magnetic resonance imaging
PET	Positron emission tomography
PICC	Peripherally inserted central catheter
TMJ	Temporomandibular joint

9.1 Introduction

For nearly 56.7 million people in the United States with disabilities, a medical imaging exam is something they will experience as part of their medical journey (United States Census Bureau 2012). Medical imaging can be used not only to diagnose but to assess treatment progress. Statistics from 2010 indicate that "roughly 30.6 million (people in the United States) had difficulty walking or climbing stairs, or used a wheelchair, cane, crutches, or walker" (United States Census Bureau 2012). For some, such as Paul Martino, a mobility disability might lead to concerns about employment opportunity limitations. In 2018 he shared, "I moved to New Mexico, from New York, in 1998 to attend the University of New Mexico. In 2001, I applied for a job at a local company. I got the job and worked in the office for about six years. I was diagnosed with Becker muscular dystrophy when I was a teenager.

M. Gammons (✉)
Novant Health, Winston-Salem, NC, USA
e-mail: mlgammons@novanthealth.org

D. Hollar (ed.), *Advances in Exercise and Health for People With Mobility Limitations*, https://doi.org/10.1007/978-3-319-98452-0_9

About 10 years ago, I started having more issues with mobility and was not steady on my feet. At that time, I was not ready to use a wheelchair full time. I mentioned to the director of my division at the time, that with my mobility issues I might have to stop working within a few months. He suggested that, if I would like to continue working for the company, I might consider a move to another division and transition to working from home. I agreed and, within a year, had to transition to a wheelchair full time, so this job opportunity could not have come at a better time. I worked in the new-to-me division full time from home for about five years and came to the office a few times a month for meetings and training. I was then promoted to a senior role in the department and took on more job responsibilities. I stayed with the division for another five years. I have been with the company for about 16 years in total. A couple months ago a new job opportunity was offered to me in another department, which I accepted. Everyone in this department has been great with the transition and I am very appreciative of all the help. It has been a long journey and I am grateful for everything the company does for their long-term, valuable employees. Many other organizations could learn a lot from my company" (Martino 2018). Paul's employer worked with him to ease the anxiety surrounding his employment status. Concerns with how to manage everyday life with a mobility disability can mount up. One such anxious moment might stem from the thought of having a radiology imaging test.

Mobility disabilities may be permanent, temporary, or relieved with therapy or medication. They can range from a spinal cord injury, amputation, back disorder, cerebral palsy, or neuromuscular disorder to multiple sclerosis, arthritis, and fibromyalgia. Many disabilities lead to the use of mobility devices (i.e., canes, crutches, walkers, wheelchairs, motorized aids, and stretchers). The use of these devices also logistically increases with age from about 5% of those age 65 to over 15% by age 75 to over 40% by age 85 (Kaye et al. 2000). Subsequently, the risk of falling also increases with a mobility disability. All these conditions and concerns can lead to a need for imaging.

9.2 Medical Imaging Modalities

On November 8, 1895, Wilhelm Conrad Roentgen discovered an unknown type of rays that provided a noninvasive way to see inside the body. A mere 50 days after his initially reported observation, he published an article entitled "On a New Kind of Ray, A Preliminary Communication" in the Wurzburg Physico-Medical Society Journal (Roentgen 1896). This new kind of ray – called "X" for "unknown" – led to the development of radiology, the branch of medicine that utilizes ionizing radiation (including x-rays and radiations emitted by radioactive materials) for the diagnosis and treatment of disease. Before widespread use of x-ray imaging, medical practitioners could only hypothesize what was going on inside their patients. While radiology today still involves the same fundamental physics concepts Roentgen realized, the science boasts many advances beyond what he could have dreamed. And the progress continues.

The purpose for all medical imaging procedures is to improve patient outcomes. Most imaging examinations are performed in a radiology department. Full-service radiology departments can be found in major medical centers and for-profit and nonprofit hospitals. Medical imaging can also occur outside a hospital setting in free-standing imaging centers, urgent care settings, physician's offices, and rehabilitation centers and with mobile units.

Overall, the act of medical imaging is noninvasive. However, procedures such as intravenous (IV) or other catheter placements, drains, or biopsies that are performed in the imaging room are invasive. Common features for any imaging room, in very basic terms, include a source of radiation, a patient table, a radiation detector or image receptor, a control panel, a power supply or generator, and display monitors. Depending upon the type of healthcare facility, these components often must be able to accommodate a range of patient needs as many radiology departments serve people from formation in the womb until after death in postmortem. For example, the radiology equipment must be able to care for a 3-pound neonate, a 400-pound 30-year-old, and a 115-pound 85-year-old. These very different patient body types are a technical challenge for manufacturers and purchasers of equipment. Not only are the technical components a design challenge but also the physical aspect of the imaging equipment. The imaging table needs to support the patients of various body types and size and be able to move for the examination. But it must also allow for easy, independent transfer and lift compatibility for patients with mobility disabilities (Federal Register 2017).

Imaging modalities include radiography and fluoroscopy (commonly referred to as "x-ray"), computed tomography (CT), magnetic resonance imaging (MRI), mammography, bone densitometry (sometimes called dual-energy x-ray absorption or DXA), sonography (ultrasound), nuclear medicine, and positron emission tomography (PET). (Nuclear medicine and PET may also be referred to collectively as molecular imaging.) Each of these modalities is unique in the way it portrays the body's anatomy and physiology and the environment in which the imaging takes place.

X-ray images are made by detecting the x-rays transmitted through a part of the body when it is exposed to the radiation. An x-ray room consists of a table upon which the patient may lay for the examination and an x-ray source (tube) mounted on a ceiling track to facilitate positioning of the tube over the body part to be imaged. While the table holds the radiation detector (called an "image receptor") that captures the image, many x-ray rooms also contain an upright image receptor used for exams that require the patient to remain upright (such as a chest x-ray) or if the patient's condition prohibits or limits the ability to lie down.

Radiography provides static (still) images as shown in Fig. 9.1. Images captured by the detector are digitally transmitted to a computer monitor beside the control panel where they are reviewed for quality control purposes. The quality image is then sent electronically to an image interpreter (radiologist) who reviews the image for pathology and creates a report for the referring provider (primary care physician,

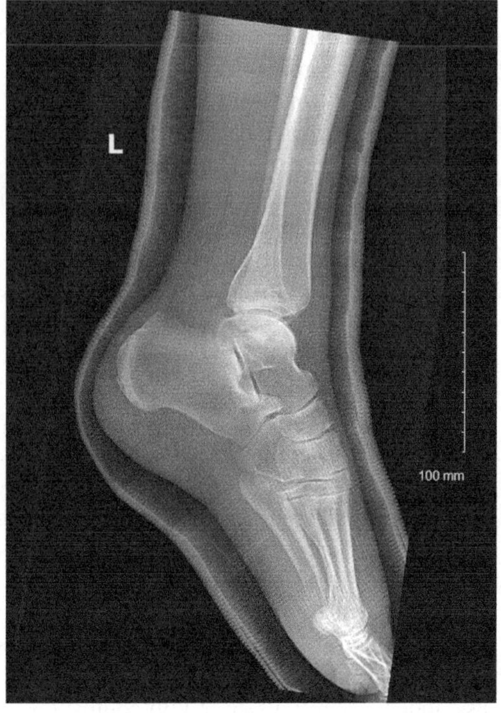

Fig. 9.1 A lateral radiography projection of the left ankle/foot. This image is unique in that the patient is also wearing a cast. (Image provided with permission from Novant Health)

nurse practitioner, or physician assistant) who ordered the procedure. Radiology exams should be interpreted only by physicians with appropriate training and experience and who are certified by an appropriate medical specialty board such as the American Board of Radiology.

An example of unique radiography equipment is the Panorex machine. This machine is designed for dental, mandible, and temporomandibular joint (TMJ) imaging which is helpful in emergent situations. The machine can accommodate the standing or sitting patient.

While the majority of imaging equipment is fixed or stationary, when it is impractical for medical reasons to move the patient to fixed radiographic equipment for an imaging procedure, a mobile radiography unit may be deployed so that the exam may be completed at the patient's bedside (Fig. 9.2). Such mobile equipment is commonly utilized in intensive care units (where critical, constant patient monitoring is required), in the operating room (where sterile field must be maintained), and in the emergency department (where the condition of trauma patients might be worsened if they are moved).

Another type of x-ray technology is fluoroscopy, which shows continuous x-ray images, much like a movie clip. This modality affords dynamic (moving) imaging, thus enabling the visualization of the esophagus as the patient swallows or the movement of a joint in real time. Fluoroscopy can be used for guidance for the placement of lines, catheters, and drains. Figure 9.3 shows fluoroscopy's use for

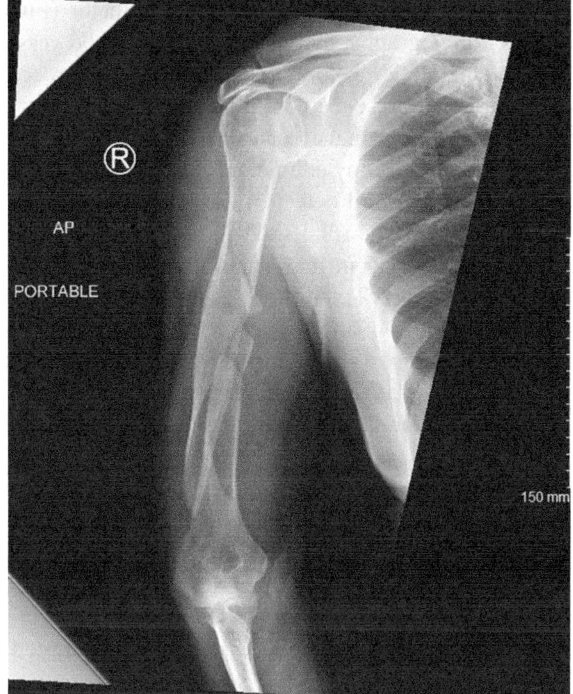

Fig. 9.2 Anteroposterior (AP) view of the right humerus with an oblique-comminuted fracture of the right humeral shaft – acquired with mobile radiography. (Image provided with permission from Novant Health)

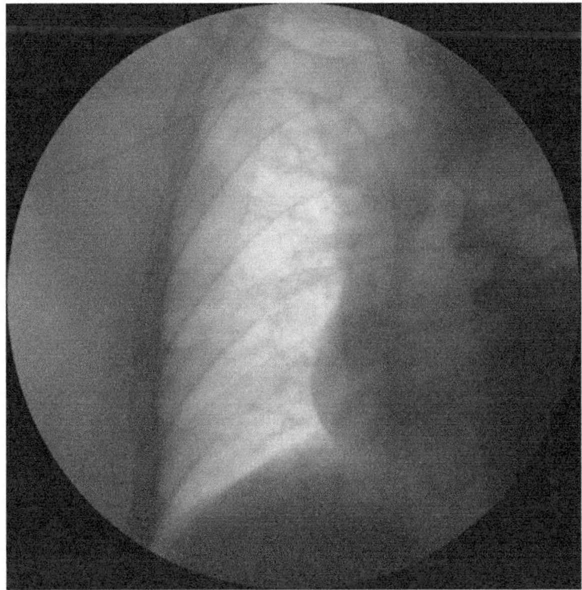

Fig. 9.3 Fluoroscopy image used for a peripherally inserted central catheter (PICC) line placement in interventional radiology. (Image provided with permission from Novant Health)

placing a peripherally inserted central catheter (PICC) line. Fluoroscopy is also used for angiography, the visualization of blood vessels, which is prevalent in cardiac catheterization laboratories. Angiographic procedures may be diagnostic (e.g., to confirm the presence of a blockage in a coronary artery) or interventional (to remove a blockage in a coronary artery).

Mobile fluoroscopy equipment (known as "C-arms" due to the configuration of the x-ray source and detector) are utilized primarily in operating and procedure room settings. Figure 9.4 shows an image of a patient's broken wrist taken with mobile fluoroscopy in the operating room after surgical hardware was placed to stabilize the wrist. The modalities of radiography and sonography (which will be discussed further in another section) are the top two mobile modalities and can be found in emergency and intensive care departments in this form in order to continue care urgently at bedside. Certain radiology exams may necessitate that they be performed in an emergency, operating, long-term care, or hospital room. However, not all imaging modalities allow for the portability of their equipment due to physical constraints.

Due to the specific physical requirements or the potential hazards of the imaging equipment, some modalities do not have mobile versions of their equipment and therefore cannot be performed at the patient's bedside. To date, these include mammography, bone densitometry, MRI, nuclear medicine, and PET. Several manufacturers now offer a mobile CT scanner with limited capabilities. Used for head imaging only, these mobile CT scanners are taken to patients in neurology intensive

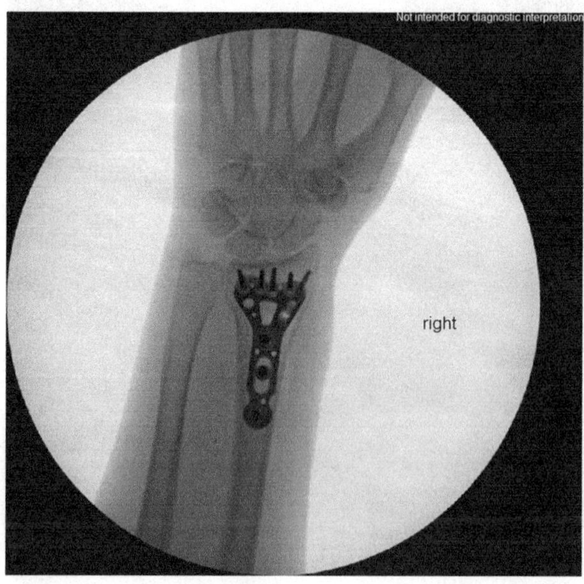

Fig. 9.4 Anteroposterior (AP) right wrist with hardware placement – acquired in the operating room during surgery. (Image provided with permission from Novant Health)

care units or utilized in ambulance vehicles primarily for time-sensitive stroke imaging (Wilson et al. 2015).

The concept of mobile imaging equipment utilized to perform exams at the patient's bedside must not be confused with imaging equipment installed on board a tractor trailer. For example, Fig. 9.5 shows a mobile PET-CT scanner housed in a tractor trailer, and a view from inside the trailer is seen in Fig. 9.6. The latter provides imaging procedures such as mammography, CT, MRI, or PET to communities where such imaging services are not available.

Some imaging requires contrast to enhance the appearance of organs or vessels as compared to surrounding tissues or certain pathologies. Radiography and fluoroscopy may use barium orally or rectally and if needed an IV contrast containing iodine (iodinated contrast). MRI uses IV gadolinium-based contrast and in some instances a barium-based oral contrast. Many contrast agents are eliminated by the body through the urinary and digestive systems. Persons with impaired functions of these systems, in some cases, may receive reduced contrast doses or may not be able to receive the contrast at all.

While radiography is used to image nearly the entirety of the human body, each modality of the radiologic sciences has a specialty. For each indication that a healthcare provider orders an exam, there is a modality that will be the best to discover that answer. The American College of Radiology (ACR) has developed appropriateness criteria, which can be accessed on their website, describing the use of medical imaging by body region and indication (ACR 2018). To date, the categories include breast, cardiac, gastrointestinal, musculoskeletal, neurologic, pediatric, thoracic, urologic, vascular, women, interventional, and radiation oncology. To further assist

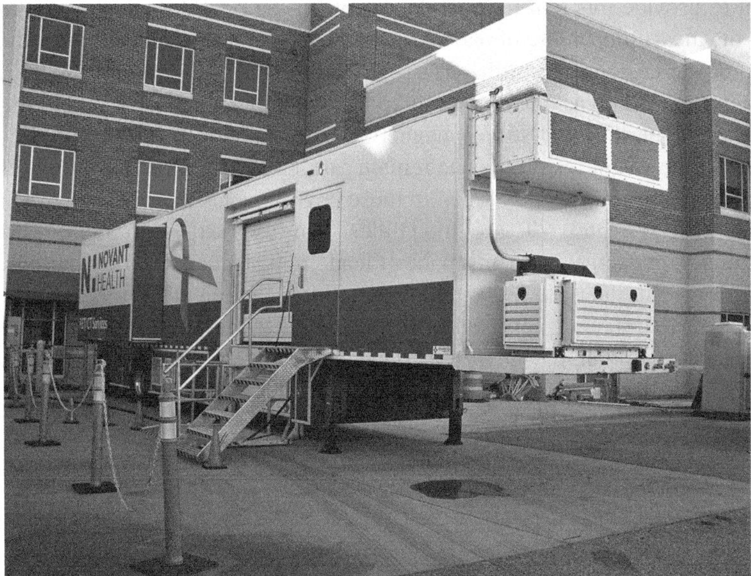

Fig. 9.5 A mobile PET-CT scanner is housed in this trailer. (Photograph by the author)

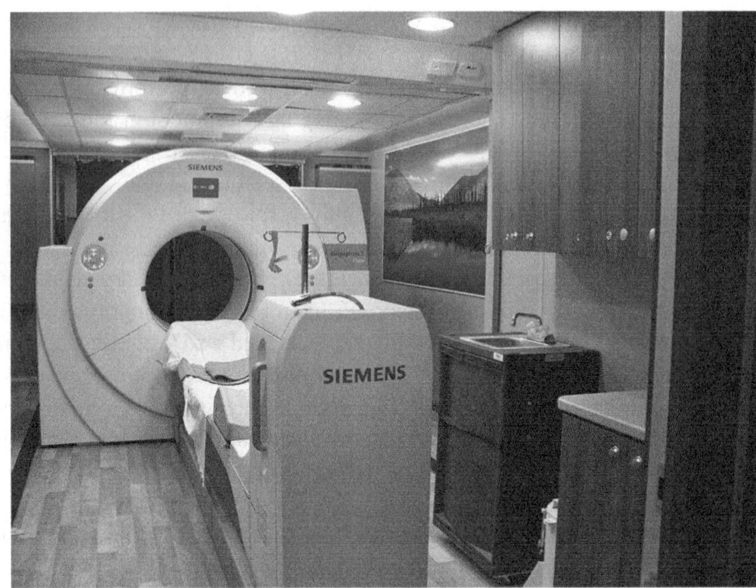

Fig. 9.6 Photograph from inside the mobile PET-CT scanner trailer. (Photograph by the author)

ordering providers in selecting the most appropriate exam, the ACR created ACR Select ™, an electronic clinical decision support database based on national standards with over 3000 clinical scenarios and 15,000 criteria (ACR 2018). ACR Select ™ is an algorithmic tool that can be embedded into an electronic medical record system to provide this real-time guidance. When the provider chooses the correct exam, the most efficient use of patient time and money along with facility, radiology team time, and resources is utilized.

Several hazard signs are seen in radiology relating to radiation (e.g., Fig. 9.7), radioactive materials, and strong magnetic fields. Patients should watch for these signs and follow staff instructions to remain safe. In each of these hazard situations, precautions may be necessary when in those environments. For example, radiography, fluoroscopy, and CT are modalities that use x-rays to obtain images. Accordingly, protective garments made of lead-equivalent material are worn by personnel to protect their radiosensitive organs, including blood forming organs and gonads. In MRI, the magnetic field is potentially harmful to a person with certain implanted devices that may be impacted mechanically, electrically, or magnetically. Another important sign in radiology instructs females to tell the technologist if they are or could be pregnant. This is important because non-emergent exams may be delayed until after the first trimester, the most sensitive stage of development to radiation exposure.

Artifacts, things not naturally present in the body, can occur on medical images as a consequence of patient motion, objects a person may be wearing or have ingested, along with implants, and equipment malfunctions. Technologists attempt to minimize artifacts as much as possible because artifacts can be detrimental to an

Fig. 9.7 Caution sign for healthcare workers and employees in imaging areas. (Photograph by the author)

exam. Artifacts can potentially obscure anatomy and pathology that is vital for correct interpretation by the radiologist.

The CT scanner is a doughnut-shaped machine that uses x-rays to create images. The patient lies on a table that moves in and out of the doughnut, called a gantry, while the x-ray source rotates around the patient. The scan itself is painless. A unique feature that CT shares with MRI is its ability to create cross-sectional images of the body. Sections of the body are virtually sliced as though they were sliced like a loaf of bread. Images may be acquired of nearly every body structure. An example of a CT exam is the cardiac (heart) calcium scoring seen in Fig. 9.8. In this procedure, no IV contrast is used. However, the images of the heart are acquired according to signal from an electrocardiogram (EKG). The coronary calcium is then quantified after the exam. This procedure is important because coronary calcifications correlate directly to the amount of coronary plaque and to the risk of future coronary disease. Early detection and modification of risk factors can slow the progression of coronary artery disease. A low score suggests a low likelihood of coronary artery disease but does not exclude the possibility of significant coronary artery narrowing.

MRI stands for magnetic resonance imaging. In this modality, the patient lies on a bed that is pushed into a large doughnut-shaped magnet, called the bore. The bore may be standard sized, large, or open. Some examples of MRI images are seen in Fig. 9.9, a sagittal image of the female pelvis, and Fig. 9.10, a coronal image of the

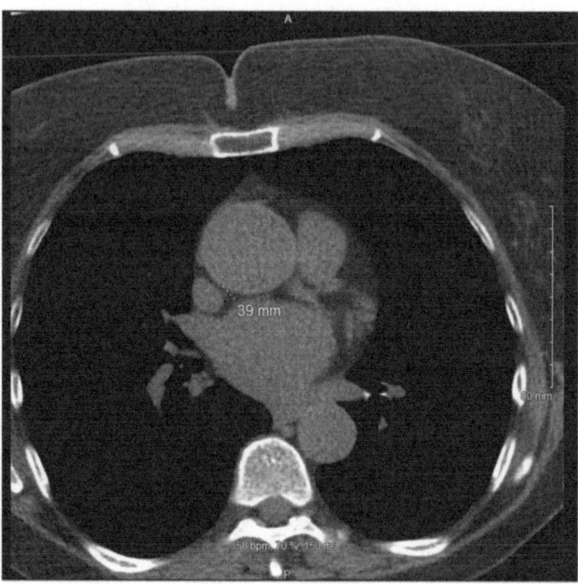

Fig. 9.8 Axial CT cardiac (heart) calcium scoring imaging of the chest. The dotted line and numbers indicate the measurement of the aorta at 39 mm. (Image provided with permission from Novant Health)

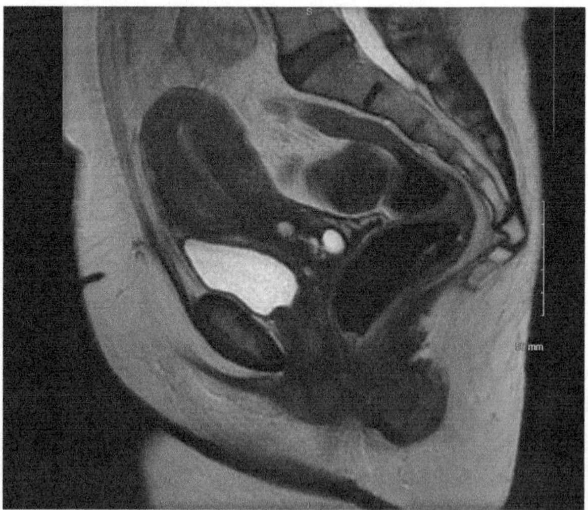

Fig. 9.9 Sagittal image of the pelvis (T2 propeller sequence). (Image provided with permission from Novant Health)

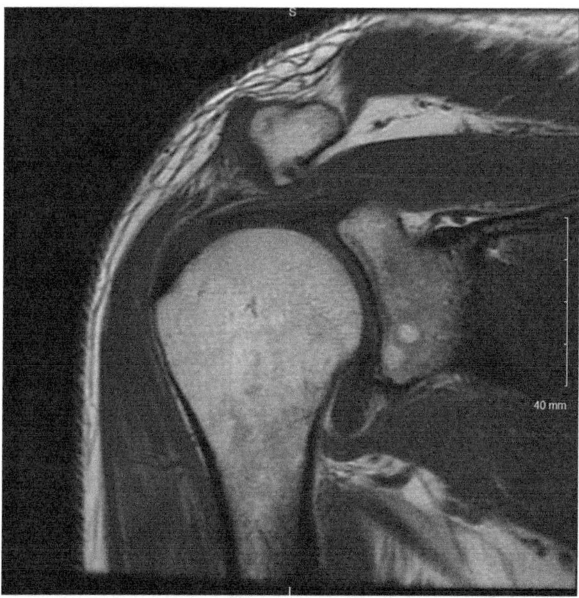

Fig. 9.10 Coronal T1-weighted image of the right shoulder. (Image provided with permission from Novant Health)

right shoulder. These terms refer to how the magnet is configured for patient comfort. After the patient is pushed into the bore, images are acquired by exposing the patient to radiofrequency radiation and gradient magnetic fields. The creation of these gradient magnetic fields results in distinctive and excessive noise. Hence, patients undergoing an MRI scan must wear hearing protection in the form of earplugs, earphones, or a combination of both. While imaging a patient, the MRI scanner sounds like a jackhammer, whereas the CT scanner sounds like an electric washing machine.

Because of their doughnut shape, CT and MR may be confused due to their similar physical appearance. However, MR presents significant danger due to the magnetic field. Accordingly, the MR department is sectioned into Zones 1–4 that reflect the potential risk. These zones indicate where certain persons may enter. Only persons who have been safety screened (interviewed to make certain they are free of unsafe items) by trained MRI personnel may enter Zone 4, the scanner room. All external metal objects must be removed from the patient before entering the scanner room. Depending upon the type of metal, such objects may become dangerous projectiles, torque, and heat and potentially cause burns. Creating the images involves the scanner, which contains the magnet and gradient and radiofrequency coils, an imaging bed with receiving coils, a computer, and generator system.

Although known primarily for women's health mammography is useful for both women and men. Used for early detection of breast pathology, it involves a radiation source (x-ray tube), compression paddle, and an image receptor placed under the

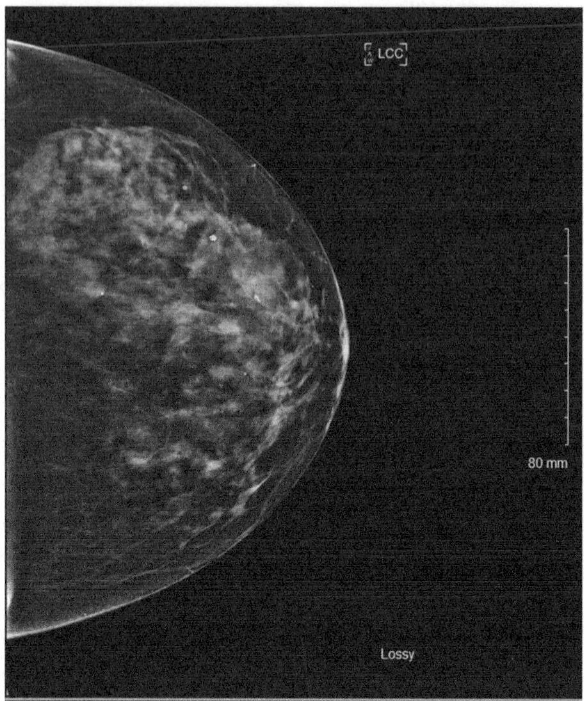

Fig. 9.11 Left craniocaudal (LCC) breast tomosynthesis view. (Image provided with permission from Novant Health)

patient's breast. Breast compression is needed to increase the image quality but may cause discomfort. Traditionally, mammography has been a two-dimensional tool, but now equipment is widely clinically available with three-dimensional capability. An example of a breast tomosynthesis (3D) image is seen in Fig. 9.11. Mammography is designed to be performed with the patient standing. However, a person can be imaged in the seated position.

Bone densitometry, sometimes called dual-energy x-ray absorptiometry (DEXA), involves an imaging table with a scanning arm that contains the radiation source and moves over the patient without touching them. The purpose of the exam is to determine bone density. Mild loss (osteopenia) or profound loss (osteoporosis) is diagnosed with this imaging tool. Low-dose ionizing radiation is used to scan the lumbar (lower) spine and hips. It is preferred that when comparing scans from visit to visit (to assess the rate of bone loss) they be performed on the same machine. Unlike other modalities, DXA tables do not raise and lower – they are only available in one standard height. Protocols exist for the imaging team to complete an assisted transfer to a bone densitometer using a stretcher. Utilizing a stretcher or bed that is able to equal the height of the fixed imaging table is important. Also important is to be able to bridge any gap between a stretcher and imaging table.

Ultrasound uses high-frequency sound waves to generate images. A probe (called a transducer) generates sound waves that are directed into the body and then detects the sound waves that are reflected back by structures (i.e., organs and tissues) in the body. This exam is generally painless except for the pressure that must be applied to the probe placed against or into the body so that the sound waves can reach the organs and other structures being examined. Sonography is probably most notable for imaging an embryo or fetus in utero, a common practice with expectant mothers. However, it is also useful to determine the condition of organs, bones, and vessels. Sonograms are usually performed as a person lies on a bed, not a special imaging table. Because the probe uses a coupling gel to assist in acquiring the images, a patient may be asked to change into a gown to free the body of layers of clothing and keep clothing from getting soiled by the gel.

In nuclear medicine, the patient is injected with a small quantity of a radiopharmaceutical that consists of a radioactive isotope attached to a chemical compound. The nuclear medicine camera (Fig. 9.12) detects the gamma rays emitted from the body, thus creating an image that represents the distribution of radioactivity throughout the body. Pathology is indicated by "hot spots" (i.e., areas of increased uptake of the radiopharmaceutical) or "cold spots" (i.e., areas of decreased uptake.) Unlike other radiology modalities that consider anatomy, nuclear medicine assesses organ function. The radiopharmaceutical used depends upon the type of examination performed. While different radioisotopes are utilized (including but not limited to thallium-201, xenon-133, gallium-67, and indium-111), the most common radioisotope is technetium-99 m. All radioisotopes used in nuclear medicine have short half-

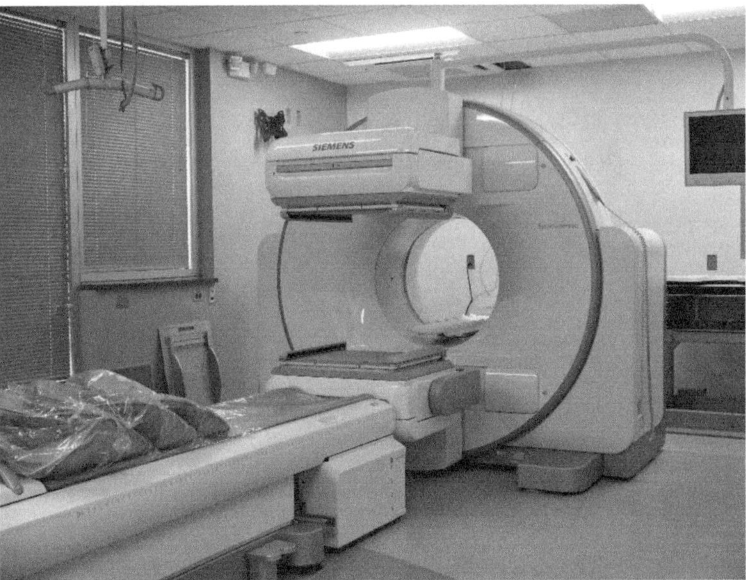

Fig. 9.12 Nuclear medicine SPECT-CT dual-head gamma camera. (Photograph by the author)

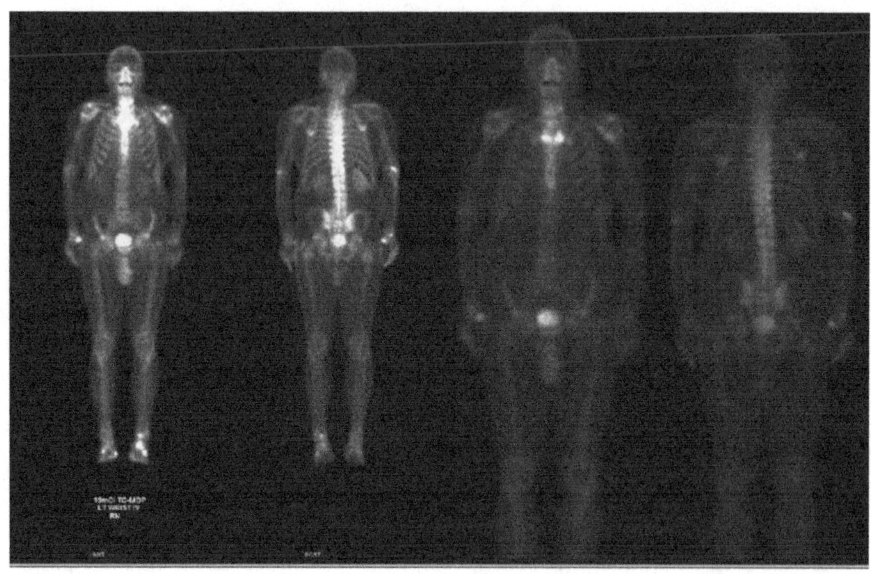

Fig. 9.13 Nuclear medicine bone scan images. (Images provided with permission from Novant Health)

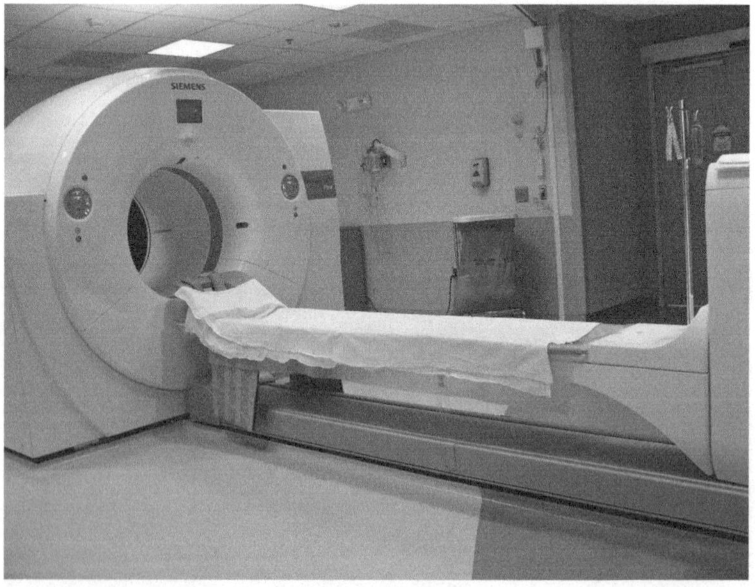

Fig. 9.14 PET-CT scanner. (Photograph by the author)

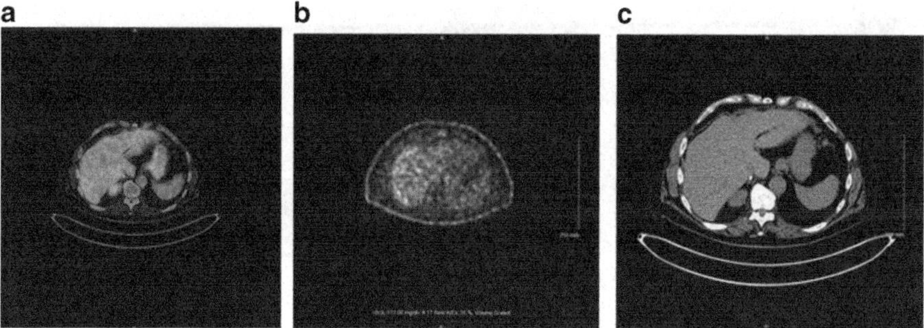

Fig. 9.15 Axial PET-CT fused image (**a**), PET alone image (**b**), and CT alone image (**c**)

lives – meaning they decay rapidly to stable isotopes. Nuclear medicine can also be used to treat disease. The most common therapy is the administration of radioactive iodine-131 to treat hyperthyroidism or, with larger quantities, thyroid cancer. Figure 9.13 shows a nuclear imaging whole body bone scan.

Hybrid imaging combines two modalities. For example, PET-CT (Fig. 9.14) and PET-MR are hybrid forms of imaging. PET stands for positron emission tomography and is a specialized type of nuclear medicine procedure. The most common PET radiopharmaceutical is ^{18}F-fluorodeoxyglucose (^{18}FDG) used for imaging cancer. The modalities of CT and MRI are now being combined with PET to create one image that fuses anatomic data (from the CT or MRI) with metabolic data (from PET). An example of a PET-CT fused image is seen in Fig. 9.15a along with the PET (Fig. 9.15b) and CT (Fig. 9.15c) images. Fusion imaging is important because it increases the sensitivity for detecting malignancy, tumor staging, and disease recurrence or metastasis (Chen et al. 2010).

9.3 Medical Imaging Personnel

Imaging technologists are professionals who are competent and skillful in radiologic sciences and who care for those they serve. They are dedicated to providing high-quality images and excellent patient care. Each imaging professional may have entered and remained in the profession for a different reason. Whether to sustain life, to increase status, and to find a lifelong career, or a higher calling, radiology team members are participants in improving the patient's health. They are human beings who aspire to not only make a living but to also make a difference.

As one would choose a medical doctor who is board certified as a medical practitioner and in a specialty (i.e., podiatry, orthopedics, gynecology, etc.), a medical imager should be credentialed in the specific work they are doing. When a board certifies medical practitioners, it is stating that the individual has completed structured education and been tested by their peers. To demonstrate the importance of appropriate training, Fig. 9.16 shows a radiography example. The image on the left

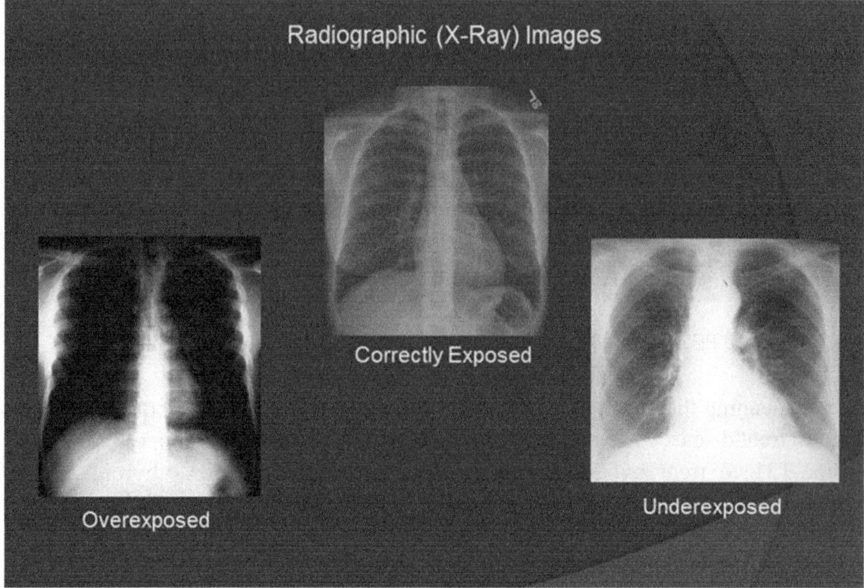

Fig. 9.16 Importance of quality radiographic (x-ray) images. (Images provided with permission from Novant Health)

shows an overexposed posterior-anterior (PA) chest x-ray, the center image is correctly exposed, and the image on the right is underexposed. In either the overexposed or underexposed image, finding an abnormality would indeed be challenging. Working together with the registered technologist, a board-certified radiologist would reject an improperly exposed image and request that the exam be repeated. This example indicates why educated and qualified technologists and radiologists are so important to patient care.

The largest credentialing organization for radiologic technologists is the American Registry of Radiologic Technologists (ARRT). This group registers and credentials qualified individuals in medical imaging, interventional procedures, and radiation therapy. With more than 330,000 registrants, the ARRT promotes high standards of patient care with each new credential awarded (Welcome To ARRT 2018).

Being appropriately educated and clinically competent is the aim of every ARRT registrant. This is accomplished through structured education, training on the ARRT Code of Ethics, and successful completion of a national examination. Registered radiologic technologists are educated in anatomy, patient positioning, examination techniques, equipment protocols, safety, protection, and patient care. Beyond the initial certification, registration is renewed annually via continued adherence to ethical practice and education with qualifications reviewed every 10 years. As of January 1, 2015, the minimum educational requirement to apply for primary examination certification with the ARRT is an associate's degree (Weening 2012). However, there is a trend indicating that an increasing number of RTs have baccalaureate degrees (Reid 2015).

9.4 Medical Imaging Challenges

The three main goals of modern US healthcare, as set forth in the Patient Protection and Affordable Care Act (PPACA) of 2010, are to improve access, cost, and quality. There seems to be a firm relationship between these outcomes. When access and quality are increased, so is cost. When cost is decreased, access and quality are reduced. Reflective of a means to thrive in the present healthcare economy, many mergers of healthcare entities are taking place. The merger trend to obtain improved bargaining power with insurers, although popular, does not improve quality of care, reduce the cost of care, or necessarily increase access to care (Roberts 2017). It seems that the healthcare environment is not sufficiently economically positioned to offer an environment of continued improvement in these categories.

Physical access to healthcare may be the first barrier a person with a mobility limitation faces. "Due to barriers, individuals with disabilities are less likely to get routine preventative medical care than people without disabilities" (U.S. Department of Health and Human Services 2012). An attempt to remedy this comes in the form of a federal civil rights law, the Americans with Disabilities Act of 1990 (ADA). The ADA prohibits discrimination against individuals with disabilities in everyday activities, including medical services. A part of this law established requirements for new facility construction and considerations for persons with mobility disabilities regarding existing facilities. Modifications to existing facilities must be made where "removal is readily achievable" (U.S. Department of Health and Human Services 2012). Because of this provision, there are some pre-regulation healthcare facilities that can pose physical access issues.

Obstacles to obtaining care, and radiology services, may include limitations in being able to access care services in one's local area, inclement weather, lack of reliable or limited transportation, and challenges with or lack of mobility aids. For ease of use, a medical center's imaging area should be on the street level or accessible by elevator. Doorways, including imaging room doorways, and hallways should be wide enough to accommodate the person and their mobility device. Accessible alternatives to stairs may be ramps or elevators. Automatic or easy-to-open doors and accessible or valet parking with safe drop-off sites are a plus for those with mobility disabilities. Restrooms should also be easily accessible for the person and their mobility device.

Imaging exams have historically been one of the most expensive items on a patient's medical bill. For example, while MRI provides great detail, a high sensitivity, and low specificity for various pathologies, it is an expensive test. Prices can range from $1000 to $5000 depending on the body part imaged and whether or not contrast is administered. In some care settings, there is also a separate fee from a radiologist for image interpretation. These prices vary per institution based on a variety of factors. Operating costs are high in medical imaging. The imaging facility must not only pay physical facility costs but also equipment purchases and system upgrades, personnel wages and benefits, supplies, and any specific items needed for certain exams. In the past, a fee-for-service environment existed in which the care facility was reimbursed by insurance, Medicare, or Medicaid at a contracted rate. In the hospital setting, a newer reimbursement trend involves a process called bundling. Mabotuwana et al. (2017) write that "Under bundled payment methods, radiology does not get reimbursed for each and every inpatient procedure, but rather, the hospital gets reimbursed for the entire hospital stay under an applicable diagnosis-related group code" (2017, p. 301). This new reimbursement model provides yet another challenge for radiology administrators to provide excellent care with potentially less financial support (Wadhera et al. 2018).

Quality and safety are often factors that are grouped together. For radiology, quality means consistently providing good images resulting in an accurate interpretation. Safety means that no undue harm comes to the patient because they had the exam. Medical imaging tests are often looked upon as being able to answer all of an ordering provider's questions; however, no medical test is flawless. There is never a perfect algorithm for imaging a particular condition or disease state. Sometimes there is no straightforward path to an answer for a medical question – leading to unfortunate outliers of a disease or condition algorithm. For example, the magnetic resonance cholangiopancreatography (MRCP) exam's purpose is to evaluate the liver, gallbladder, bile ducts, pancreas, and pancreatic duct for disease. Located in these organs can be stones. The composition, size of pathology, location, patient characteristics (i.e., body habitus), and ancillary findings play a role in whether or not a patient's condition is able to be imaged or found with the MRI. The composition of these stones, for example, if they were found in the gallbladder, may be primarily bile, calcium, bilirubin, or cholesterol. Their size can range from 0.5 cm to 5.0 cm. However, only the stones that are pigmented (contain metal ions) and are 2 cm or greater will be visualized with MRI (Tsai et al. 2004). The patient's anatomy may not be standard (i.e., tortuous cystic duct variation), or a greater health concern may be found that changes the scope of the exam (i.e., looking for gallstones and instead discover liver cancer). These peculiarities are not specific to MRI but to all medical imaging modalities. That is why exam selection for a particular patient is so important and why one test may not provide the answer and thus another test must be performed. Nonetheless, each test provides a piece of the puzzle leading to a diagnosis. The test results must be paired with the expert knowledge of the ordering provider to put everything into perspective.

Healthcare is an environment where safety is a top priority and radiology is no exception. Radiology's culture of safety and continuous improvement involves all aspects of safety surrounding the imaging exam, infection prevention, and critical test results. A safe department adheres to regulatory and accreditation requirements (Johnson et al. 2012). Beyond the regulatory requirements, many quality measurement programs are designed to insure a safety culture. A quality assurance (QA) program insures that a department addresses discrepancies, complications, incidents, equipment downtime, overall performance, compliance, and any other significant departmental occurrences. A quality control (QC) program involves the testing of the equipment to make certain that quality imaging is consistently produced. The QC program involves the cooperation of technologists, radiologists, and medical physicists. A quality improvement (QI) program improves image quality and reduces workflow inefficiencies (Glavis-Bloom et al. 2017). The QI initiative addresses issues found in the QA and QC programs by incorporating interventions. Each of these programs should allow a team member to report a problem or concern without fear of reprisal. This culture of safety looks beyond individual errors to identify processes and systems for lasting improvement (Johnson et al. 2012).

Deyle writes that ultimately the ordering provider is responsible for the exam ordering decision (2011). Once that decision is made, the technologist performs the exam and the interpreting physician creates a report. While in their care, the patient trusts that the professionals will do their best for them. Brusin wrote that "medical errors, even those that are relatively minor, can have serious consequences, such as misdiagnosis and longer and costlier hospital stays" (2014, p. 61). As with any medical care involving human beings, technology, and complex disease processes or injury, there is the potential for error; and radiology is no exception. Because of this potential for error, patients are encouraged to "feel empowered to participate in their own care" (Brusin 2014, p. 63). Good communication is needed between the patient, ordering provider, technologist, and radiologist to ensure that the correct exam is performed and without error. The patient may be asked to repeat statements made by the technologist simply to determine if the patient understands.

Another factor in attempting to receive medical care may be equipment usability. Older equipment that lacks the latest design features available can be a concern. Equipment dimensions of the appropriate height, width, and length may not be available in every setting to accommodate the person with a mobility limitation. Ideally, all medical equipment would be developed with the Principles of Universal Design (The Center for Universal Design 1997) in which the equipment would be usable for all persons regardless of abilities. In 2009, Story et al. reported in detail from work with focus groups the difficulties that persons with disabilities have in using medical equipment. This research noted that persons with disabilities had concerns about the exam table contact surfaces, height, and lack of positioning support.

The contact surfaces of exam tables were described as being too hard, uncomfortable, and too slippery for safe transfer. The effects of these contact surfaces can especially be a concern for those susceptible to pressure sores. There is concern that the tables do not lower in height, provide a step stool, or grab bars for safe, independent transfer resulting in a need for moving help. Once on the narrow table, participants noted they lacked the support to achieve and maintain body positions while on the equipment. In some cases, side railings and arm or leg support would help with contractures and joint discomfort. The proposed standards from the Medical Diagnostic Equipment (MDE) Advisory Committee recommends that "gripping surfaces be free of sharp or abrasive elements and have rounded edges" (Federal Register 2017).

Challenges may be considered barriers – or opportunities. Designing medical equipment can be likened to automobile design. Certain things must be placed on the auto because it works best when placed there. There are certain standards that are required by government regulation (they must be met), there are standards set by the industry (they must be met), there are things that make the car unique to the manufacturer (this must be met in order to establish the brand), there are things the consumer has come to expect (these will be next on the list to put on the car), and there are things the consumer would like to have on their car (these are add-on, additional purchasable features). In practice, the manufacturer has "X" amount of money to spend in producing a product for the marketplace. The manufacturer understands the price that facilities are willing to pay for their medical device. As many features as possible, within that price range, are placed on the equipment. In some cases, a mechanism that would aid the disabled person may not be included to allow for a technical component.

A patient's body habitus can make imaging challenging. The Centers for Disease Control (CDC) estimates that "obesity rates for adults with disabilities are 58% higher than for adults without disabilities" (CDC 2017). The morbidly obese or broad-shouldered persons, depending on the exam, may not be able to be accommodated by every scanner. A standard-sized bore is 50 cm. A large bore is 70 cm. MRI scanners that are often referred to as "open" (although all MR scanners manufactured today are not closed on one end) have room for a patient to be able to extend their arms away from their body; however the area from the surface of the body to the scanner components may be the same or less depending upon the manufacturer. The theory is that most are obese and if unable to help with movement will need additional facility staff to assist. Manufacturers publish weight limits that their tables will support. Sometimes those weight limits are what the table will physically support. However, with that amount of weight in place, and its distribution on the imaging table, the table's movement mechanisms may not function as needed.

The technologist or sonographer benefits from all knowledge they can obtain about the patient prior to the exam. For example, knowledge of special needs will aid the imager in requesting that scheduling staff block off extra time for the exam. This additional time for the exam will ensure that the current patient has their needs met, staff members do not feel rushed, and the next patient can maintain their scheduled appointment. Arranging for adequate transfer equipment's availability for the patient such as lift equipment, moving help, may all need to be arranged for in advance. Foreknowledge of how the patient prefers to be moved is also important. A patient may be able to move without assistance and therefore prefers to self-move. This means that staff can focus on other parts of the exam. Knowing what the patient can and cannot do or wants or does not want to do, their range of mobility, etc. is helpful to the imager. Knowing the patient's weight and distribution of that weight can be helpful in advance of an imaging exam. For example, if a person regularly utilizes a body sling with their lift equipment for transfers in and out of bed, perhaps leaving a sling under the patient will allow for a more comfortable experience at the imaging facility. Often a communication (phone call, text message, e-mail, online chart notification) will be sent to the patient or their caregiver prior to their exam appointment. This is the perfect opportunity to ask questions and ask to speak with a technologist that may perform the exam. Share with the technologist any special needs or considerations that could make a visit a smooth one for all involved.

Barriers exist at imaging facilities which may include a lack of compatible equipment, lack of accessory supplies for the equipment, or a lack of training with the equipment. In some cases, a facility may have equipment, but it may not be specifically what is needed for a particular situation. There is a variety of lifting, swiveling, and smooth transition equipment that may be available to imaging department staff for use with physical patient transfers. For all imaging exams, the patient is positioned in a certain manner to obtain a required view of the area of interest. Persons with disability may find holding that position to be a challenge. To meet this challenge, several positioning aids have been developed to assist. For example, the scoliosis chair is used in radiography to accomplish spine imaging for the cerebral palsy patient who is unable to remain in the upright position for the image. Radiographic stands may be used to steady someone when other types of upright imaging are needed. Also, a technologist may use positioning sponges, safety straps, medical tape, or various wraps that may be readily available and safely applied. Contacting the imaging department supervisor or manager before a scheduled exam can ensure that imaging staff will have the proper equipment and be prepared for specific needs associated with a disability. Patients should voice any concern, discomforts, or accommodation needs that they have, and the imaging team should identify best practices for obtaining the image with the least discomfort and inconvenience to the patient. In some situations, the patient has definite ideas about how imaging department staff can assist them when a transfer is needed. Team members can often comply with these methods but may have to wait for additional team members to assist.

Another challenge for the technologist or sonographer may be the actual operation of the equipment. The technologist or sonographer may have only had an initial training session when obtaining certification and in employee orientation. For some, using transfer equipment may be a concept that falls behind their priority of technical education. Adept clinical sites will have periodic reviews with team members on the proper operation of this equipment (U.S. Department of Health and Human Services 2012).

For the person with a mobility disability, each visit to a healthcare facility can provide challenges specific to that visit. However, allowing the patient to self-identify as having a mobility disability and explain their needs is important. This allows imaging personnel the opportunity to arrange for an accessible room, add extra exam time to the appointment, and make certain all supplies needed are available. Facility staff will maintain professionalism and not make the patient feel uncomfortable because additional alternative arrangements were made for their care. Sometimes the patient does not know, or is unable to communicate, the best way to accomplish the transfer. Perhaps, the patient or their caregiver has not been faced with the particular situation that an imaging room presents. Imaging team members are trained in safe, ergonomic moving techniques allowing them to use their professional knowledge to make the appropriate choice for transfer.

9.5 Accreditation and Regulation of Medical Imaging

There are voluntary accrediting opportunities for owners of medical imaging equipment through the American College of Radiology (ACR), Intersocietal Accreditation Commission (IAC), and The Joint Commission (TJC). Imaging equipment accreditation programs are available as a dedicated method to ensure quality patient care. "Effective January 1, 2012 all providers that bill for CT, MRI, breast MRI, nuclear medicine and PET under part B of the (U.S.) Medicare physician fee schedule must be accredited in order to receive reimbursement for the technical component from Medicare" (ACR 2018). The regulation that stipulates this reimbursement clause is the Medicare Improvements for Patients and Providers Act (MIPPA) of 2008. This multifaceted federal legislation applies exclusively to facilities applying for reimbursement for patients who use Medicare. MIPPA recognizes the accrediting bodies of ACR, IAC, and TJC (CMS 2008).

The ACR Accreditation is considered the gold standard in medical imaging and when awarded is valid for 3 years. The ACR provides accreditation programs for breast MRI, breast ultrasound, CT, mammography, MRI, nuclear medicine and PET, radiation oncology practice, stereotactic breast biopsy, and ultrasound. Upon achieving ACR Accreditation, a certificate and accreditation gold seal are awarded that can be displayed (ACR 2018). The IAC "provides accreditation programs for vascular testing, echocardiography, nuclear/PET, MRI, diagnostic CT, dental CT, carotid stenting, vein treatment and management, cardiac electrophysiology, and cardiovascular catheterization" (IAC 2018). Both the ACR and the IAC use peer reviews to make evaluations toward accreditation. The TJC provides an imaging center accreditation program rather than focusing on specific modalities or exam types. (This TJC accreditation of imaging equipment is not to be confused with the accreditation that an entire medical facility may receive from them.) The TJC does not use peer reviews in its evaluations but rather focuses on patient care and patient and staff safety. Each of these accreditation programs involves a fee paid to the accrediting organization by the facility seeking the accreditation.

Some states are non-licensure states. For example, in Missouri and North Carolina, there is no minimum requirement or standard for the training of the person performing the medical imaging. In states without licensure and regulation of who can perform an exam with ionizing radiation, anyone could be designated as a medical imager – regardless of educational preparedness or clinical competence. There is no minimum state-mandated education requirement for the lay person as an imager in a state devoid of such legislation. Licensure laws are generally a states' rights concern. However, for reimbursement purposes, many medical centers and imaging centers affiliated with medical centers, in non-licensure states, hire only credentialed persons to perform medical imaging exams.

Mammography is currently the only medical imaging modality specifically standardized by federal legislation, Mammography Quality Standards Act of 1992 (MQSA). The intent of MQSA is to "ensure that all women have access to quality mammography for the detection of breast cancer in its earliest, most treatable stages" (FDA 2017). The program associated with this Act is managed from the US Food and Drug Administration (FDA) within the Center for Devices and Radiological Health. Complying with this Act involves facility certification and inspection and through a new initiative called Enhancing Quality Using the Inspection Program (EQUIP), the inspection will focus on the quality assurance of images.

Equipment design and operation have not ever been federally regulated in regard to patient ease of use. However, "the PPACA of 2010 added an amendment to Section 510 of the Rehabilitation Act which authorized the U.S. Access Board to develop accessibility standards for medical diagnostic equipment in consultation with the Food and Drug Administration" (ADA 2014). These standards "establish minimum technical criteria that will allow patients with disabilities independent entry to, use of, and exit from medical diagnostic equipment to the maximum extent possible" (ADA 2014). For example, a wheelchair-bound person beside a standard-height examination table (32 inches) is better suited for a table of 17–19 inches which is correct for a lateral transfer. The standards also address diagnostic exam tables for use by a person in a supine, prone, or side-lying positioning. Likewise, a person with a mobility disability needs to be able to access the table or bed on the long side or short side of the surface.

9.6 Continued Advances

A concept gaining clinical acceptance, but one that is not available at all facilities, is the use of medical images for creating computer algorithms for three-dimensional printed models of anatomy and pathology (Trace et al. 2016). These 3D models are used in preparation for surgery, education (Bernhard et al. 2016), and for use in creating 3D-printed precise surgical implants. For example, CT images were used in combination with 3D printing to create "accurate, custom-designed prosthetic replacements for damaged parts of the middle ear" (Hirsch et al. 2017). Other examples include a total knee arthroplasty and acetabulum (hip) implants in which MRI images were used in combination with 3D printing to create a custom knee and acetabulum implant (Mok et al. 2016). Prior to the use of imaging in combination with 3D printing tools, some surgeries had a higher percentage of failure and patient dissatisfaction due to incorrectly sized implants. For example, in the past, total knee arthroplasty (TKA) implants were made in certain sizes with the hope that the surgeon would select a size close enough to the patient's knee size for replacement. Unfortunately, these "off-the-shelf" implants would fail to sufficiently restore a person's knee function. Custom-made knee replacements not only allow for a better prosthetic fit but also guide the surgeon with landmarks for placement (Insall and Scott 2018). Another concept utilizing medical imaging and surgery involves a 5D model (Gillaspie et al. 2016).

9.7 Conclusions

While persons with mobility limitations may find challenges in medical imaging, a team of dedicated professionals and their tools are able to assist in meeting those challenges. Although each imaging modality is unique, their unified goal is to improve healthcare results and provide a safe patient experience. From the radiologic sciences discovery in 1895 to the present, technological advances have helped improve quality of care and treatment for a variety of conditions.

References

ADA National Network. (2014). Accessible medical examination tables and chairs. https://adata.org/factsheet/accessible-medical-examination-tables-and-chairs

American College of Radiology (ACR). (2018). www.acr.org

Bernhard, J. C., Isotani, S., Matsugasumi, T., Duddalwar, V., Hung, A. J., Suer, E., et al. (2016). Personalized 3D printed model of kidney and tumor anatomy: A useful tool for patient education. *World Journal of Urology, 34*(3), 337–345.

Brusin, J. H. (2014). Reducing errors in radiology. *Radiologic Technology, 86*(1), 61–78.

Centers for Disease Control (CDC). Disability and Obesity. (2017, August 1). https://www.cdc.gov/ncbddd/disabilityandhealth/obesity.html

Centers for Medicare and Medicaid Services (CMS), HHS. (2008). Medicare program: Changes to the hospital inpatient prospective payment systems and fiscal year 2009 rates; payments for graduate medical education in certain emergency situations; changes to disclosure of physician ownership in hospitals and physician self-referral rules; updates to the long-term care prospective payment system; updates to certain IPPS-excluded hospitals; and collection of information regarding financial relationships between hospitals. Final rules. *Federal Register, 73*(161), 48433.

Chen, M. Y., Pope, T. L., & Ott, D. J. (2010). *Basic radiology*. McGraw Hill Professional.

Deyle, G. (2011). The role of MRI in musculoskeletal practice: A clinical perspective. *Journal of Manual & Manipulative Therapy, 19*(3), 152–161.

Federal Register. (2017, January 9). Standards for accessible medical diagnostic equipment. https://www.federalregister.gov/documents/2017/01/09/2016-31186/standards-for-accessible-medical-diagnostic-equipment

Gillaspie, E. A., Matsumoto, J. S., Morris, N. E., Downey, R. J., Shen, K. R., Allen, M. S., & Blackmon, S. H. (2016). From 3-dimensional printing to 5-dimensional printing: Enhancing thoracic surgical planning and resection of complex tumors. *The Annals of Thoracic Surgery, 101*(5), 1958–1962.

Glavis-Bloom, J., Rizzo, R., & Sura, A. (2017). Developing a technologist-focused quality improvement program. *Journal of the American College of Radiology, 14*(12), 1598–1602.

Hirsch, J. D., Vincent, R. L., & Eisenman, D. J. (2017). Surgical reconstruction of the ossicular chain with custom 3D printed ossicular prosthesis. *3D Printing in Medicine, 3*(1), 7.

Insall, J. N., & Scott, W. N. (2018). Surgery of the knee. In *Custom-Made Knee Replacements*. New York: Churchill Livingstone.

Intersocietal Accreditation Commission. (2018). https://www.intersocietal.org/

Johnson, C. D., Miranda, R., Osborn, H. H., Miller, J. M., Prescott, S. L., Aakre, K. T., et al. (2012). Designing a safer radiology department. *American Journal of Roentgenology, 198*(2), 398–404.

Kaye, H. S., Kang, T., & LaPlante, M. P. (2000). *Mobility device use in the United States* (Vol. 14). Washington, DC: National Institute on Disability and Rehabilitation Research, US Department of Education.

Mabotuwana, T., Hall, C. S., Flacke, S., Thomas, S., & Wald, C. (2017). Inpatient complexity in radiology – A practical application of the case mix index metric. *Journal of Digital Imaging, 30*(3), 301–308.

Martino, P. (2018, January 5). Personal conversation. Governance manager, American Society of Radiologic Technologists. *ASRT Leaders Connection*. Albuquerque: American Society of Radiologic Technologists.

Mok, S. W., Nizak, R., Fu, S. C., Ho, K. W. K., Qin, L., Saris, D. B., et al. (2016). From the printer: Potential of three-dimensional printing for orthopaedic applications. *Journal of Orthopaedic Translation, 6*, 42–49.

Patient Protection and Affordable Care Act., PUBLIC LAW 111–148—MAR. 23, 2010, United States Government.

Reid, J. (2015). Demographics of the profession. *Radiologic Technology, 86*(4), 449–451.

Roberts, D. (2017, December 31). 'Bigger is not better.' Experts warn patient costs could rise after NC hospital deal. The Charlotte Observer.

Roentgen, W. C. (1896). On a New Kind of Ray, A Preliminary C. Wurzburg Physico-Medical Society Journal.

Story, M. F., Schwier, E., & Kailes, J. I. (2009). Perspectives of patients with disabilities on the accessibility of medical equipment: Examination tables, imaging equipment, medical chairs, and weight scales. *Disability and Health Journal, 2*(4), 169–179.

The Center for Universal Design. (1997). *The principles of universal design, version 2.0*. Raleigh: North Carolina State University.

Trace, A. P., Ortiz, D., Deal, A., Retrouvey, M., Elzie, C., Goodmurphy, C., et al. (2016). Radiology's emerging role in 3-D printing applications in health care. *Journal of the American College of Radiology, 13*(7), 856–862.

Tsai, H. M., Lin, X. Z., Chen, C. Y., Lin, P. W., & Lin, J. C. (2004). MRI of gallstones with different compositions. *American Journal of Roentgenology, 182*(6), 1513–1519.

U.S. Food and Drug Administration (FDA). (2017, November 16). About the mammography program. https://www.fda.gov/Radiation-EmittingProducts/MammographyQualityStandardsActandProgram/AbouttheMammographyProgram/default.htm

U.S. Department of Health and Human Services. (2012). Americans with Disabilities Act: Access to medical care for individuals with mobility disabilities. https://www.ada.gov/medcare_mobility_ta/medcare_ta.htm

United States Census Bureau. (2012, July 25). Nearly 1 in 5 people have a disability in the U.S. https://www.census.gov/newsroom/releases/archives/miscellaneous/cb12-134.html

Wadhera, R. K., Yeh, R. W., & Maddox, K. E. J. (2018). The rise and fall of mandatory cardiac bundled payments. *Journal of the American Medical Association, 319*, 335.

Weening, R. H. (2012). Degree requirement & employment opportunity in radiologic science. *Radiologic Technology, 83*(6), 541–548.

"Welcome To ARRT." (2018) ARRT Certification & Registration, https://www.arrt.org/.

Wilson, M. H., Habig, K., Wright, C., Hughes, A., Davies, G., & Imray, C. H. (2015). Pre-hospital emergency medicine. *The Lancet, 386*(10012), 2526–2534.

Chapter 10
Understanding Barriers Preventing Those with Limited Mobility from Obtaining Equal Access and Opportunity to Exercise and Achieve Overall Health

Jennifer S. Lewis

Abbreviations

ADA	Americans with Disabilities Act
ADAAG	Americans with Disabilities Act Accessibility Guidelines
ADL	Activities of Daily Living
AIMFREE	Accessibility Instruments Measuring Fitness and Recreation Environments
CRPD	Convention on Rights of People with Disabilities
IADL	Instrumental Activities of Daily Living
ICF	International Classification of Functioning, Disability and Health
NHANES	National Health and Nutrition Examination Survey
WHO	World Health Organization

10.1 Introduction

This chapter examines the barriers that those with mobility limitations experience when attempting to engage in physical activities and the degree to which such inaccessibility may further adversely impact these individuals overall health. To obtain an understanding of the potential barriers preventing access to physical activity for those suffering from limited mobility, one must understand the nature of mobility, the regulatory requirements for providing accessible exercise facilities, the factors that influence if individuals engage in physical activity, and the nature of the secondary conditions that can deter participation in physical activity. Moreover, one also needs to understand the relationship between decreasing levels of physical

J. S. Lewis (✉)
The University of Southern Mississippi, Hattiesburg, MS, USA
e-mail: Jennifer.Lewis@usm.edu

D. Hollar (ed.), *Advances in Exercise and Health for People With Mobility Limitations*, https://doi.org/10.1007/978-3-319-98452-0_10

activity and increasing mobility limitations that culminate in the development major mobility limitations. Upon achieving a general understanding of mobility limitations and the effects incidental to letting such limitations continue to progress thereby becoming major mobility limitations resulting in disabililty, one can then examine the degree to which the barriers to physical activity affect individuals with mobility impairments thereby providing a means of determining if such individuals do in fact have the ability to engage in exercise and offset secondary conditions or if their opportunities remain limited as a result of ongoing barriers to equal access and opportunity.

A review of the literature provides an understanding of the barriers that have been examined as well as to what degree the examinations undertaken comprehensively address all the populations that are affected by mobility limitations. Moreover, the literature will also reveal to what degree barriers are being removed by comparing, when present, data from early 2000s with more current data, which can help us understand both how far we have come in removing such barriers as well as how far we have to go. If either the barriers exist to an increased degree or additional barriers exist, then those with mobility limitations are not able to obtain equal access and opportunity to health and exercise. Once we have achieved an understanding in terms of the degree to which such barriers exist, we can then examine the potential for decreasing the impact of mobility limitations through treatment or technology: both those that exist and those that are being researched for potential future use given the degrees of technological advancement in recent years, which represent an avenue for eliminating barriers to mobility overall. Identifying any barriers that those who have limited mobility face in seeking to access the opportunities to exercise allows subsequent researchers to examine how best to address such barriers with the short-term goal being to decrease the impact and the long-term goal being to remove the barrier entirely.

10.2 Mobility

Before examining what barriers exist as it pertains to mobility, we must first understand the importance of mobility, its definition, and the prevalence of mobility limitations. To complete the activities that one needs to perform on a daily basis (i.e., activities of daily living), it is vital that one be mobile (Telci et al. 2013). Essentially, mobility is necessary to remain active (Webber et al. 2010). For those aging, mobility represents a means of retaining the level of activity needed to allow them to remain independent and to continue being productive in their lives (World Health Organization 2007). In fact, achieving mobility leads to improved health as well as enhanced quality of life (Webber et al. 2010). Alternatively, losing the ability to be mobile due to "physical deconditioning" coincides with decreased social interaction and results in diminished health and decreased quality of life (Groessl et al. 2007; Metz 2000; Yeom et al. 2008). Ultimately, diminished mobility can be an early means of predicting physical disability (Hirvensalo et al. 2000).

Generally, mobility is defined as the ability to move around independently and to do so safely either by ambulating independently or using a device or transportation to assist with the goal being to access areas beyond one's home (Rantakokko et al. 2013; Webber et al. 2010). Specifically, mobility involves unassisted movement to perform "physical capabilities" such "as walking, climbing stairs, and standing" (Iezzoni et al. 2001). By definition, those with limited mobility are individuals who cannot walk "a quarter of a mile" at all or cannot do so without some degree of "difficulty" (Bolten et al. 2015). Hence, mobility limitations adversely affect the ability of individuals to engage in task or perform actions as part of activities thereby causing what is termed by the International Classification of Functioning, Disability and Health (ICF) activity limitations (World Health Organization 2008).

Within the overall population, mobility limitations represent "the most common disability" (Mottram et al. 2008). In fact, mobility represents the "most common limitation in older people" (Mottram et al. 2008, p. 529). In those who are older, mobility limitation is accompanied by pain (Mottram et al. 2008). Although, mobility diminishes with age (Rantakokko et al. 2013; Webber et al. 2010). Mobility limitations also occur among individuals irrespective of age (Iezzoni et al. 2001). Within the same 1990 Census, it was estimated that "13.2 million Americans," which translated into 70.5 per 1000 people as of the time the Census was taken, who were 16 or older had either a "mobility or ADL disability" (Guralnik et al. 1996, p. 27). Data for 2001 indicated that 19 million or 10.1% of the population experienced some degree of mobility issue (Iezzoni et al. 2001). As of 2012, the US Centers for Disease Control and Prevention data indicated that 7.3% of those individuals residing in the United States suffered from limited mobility (U.S. Department of Health and Human Services 2014).

Data from the 2014 American Community Service assessed the frequency of disabilities in those aged 18 and over, and this information was included within the *Healthy People 2020* progress report indicating that 10.4 million of individuals aged 65 and older experience ambulatory issues, which are defined as experiencing significant difficulties with walking or using the stairs (U.S. Department of Health and Human Services and Offices of Disease Prevention and Health Promotion n.d.). Given that a total of 20.6 million individuals suffer from ambulatory issues, data indicates that 10.2 million people age 18 and over experience ambulatory issues (U.S. Department of Health and Human Services, Office of Disease Prevention and Health Promotion n.d.). In 2016, the *American Community Survey 1-Year Estimate* indicated that of the 253,058,350 individuals aged 16 and over who were not institutionalized, 38,127,449 had a disability (United States Census Bureau 2016). Within the *American Community Survey 1-Year Estimate*, it was not indicated to what degree the disability was ambulatory in nature, and no data was collected in terms of those under 16 years of age (United States Census Bureau 2016).

Data from the National Health Survey conducted in 2015 indicates that those with limited mobility have increased to 7.0% of the population of the United States (United States Centers for Disease Control and Prevention 2015). However, it should be noted that both the 2012 and 2015 do not include any individuals under age 18 (United States Centers for Disease Control and Prevention 2015). Census data from 2008 to 2012 indicate that among individuals 65 or older almost 40% experienced one disability, which represents 15.7 million individuals. Of those 15.7 million individuals, 66.7% or 10,471,900 experienced issues that limit their ability to either walk or climb to some degree (United States Census Bureau 2014). Alternatively, 13% of individuals experience severe issues walking or standing (Courtney-Long et al. 2015).

10.3 Conditions Causing Limited Mobility

Many conditions can result in mobility limitations. In fact, medical conditions that manifest commonly often result in an individual developing mobility limitations in their lower extremities (Iezzoni et al. 2001). Moreover, studies have shown and continue to indicate that as individuals age they are likely to develop multiple conditions known as multimorbidity, and in low-level as well as mid-level income countries, individuals dealing with multiple morbidity, which are chronic in nature, decrease their physical activity (Vancampfort et al. 2017). To truly understand the impact of limited mobility on individuals, one needs to understand the impact of limited mobility.

10.4 Limited Mobility Represents a Disability

Disability is typically assessed based on the degree to which an individual can engage in certain activities (Guralnik et al. 1996). Some individuals cannot engage in activities known as those of daily living (ADLs) that include bathing, moving from their bed to a chair, using the restroom, and eating, which are those we would typically recognize as abilities in which a disabled person cannot engage (Guralnik et al. 1996). Disability can also exist in those who cannot perform what are known as "instrumental activities of daily living (IADLs)" that are defined as being of increased difficulty as compared to ADLs (Guralnik et al. 1996, p. 26). Among the activities that fall within IADLs are grocery shopping and taking transportation (Guralnik et al. 1996). In terms of mobility, it represents aspects of both ADLs and IADLs such as transfers, walking varying distances, and ascending as well as descending stairs (Guralnik et al. 1996). Indicative of the fact that mobility represents a disability, the 1990 Census specifically questioned the degree to which individuals were able to travel outside of their homes and qualified this as a "mobility disability" (Guralnik et al. 1996, p. 27).

10.5 Disability

Although disease and disability are often used interchangeable, they represent completely different concepts with disease sometimes exacerbating a disability (Iezzoni and O'Day 2006). Traditionally, a disability exists if an individual has "an impairment of one or more body functions or structures that interferes with activities" (Sharby et al. 2015). However, the 1990 Americans with Disabilities Act (ADA) (1991) broadened the definition by including both physical and mental issues that restrict at least one life activity and noting that these impact major activities of life (Iezzoni 2011; Rehabilitation Act of 1973, 1973). To put it simply, individuals with a disability face the challenge of navigating a world designed for those who are not disabled (Dunn 2016). As a resulting of having to navigate a world that is not designed for them, those with a disability experience many different types of challenges including "physically, socially, cognitively, and emotionally" (Dunn 2016, p. 255).

As noted in Chapter 126 entitled *Equal Opportunities for Individuals with Disabilities* as contained in Title XLII of the US Code, major life activities by definition include specific actions related to mobility such as walking, standing, and bending (1990). The World Health Organization's Convention on the Rights of People with Disabilities (CRPD) represents a policy document influenced by the ADA that adopts a much broader approach to disability (Sharby et al. 2015). Under the CRPD, the importance of the environment as it relates to those who are disabled is highlighted by stating that "disability results from the interaction between persons with impairments and attitudinal and environmental barriers that hinders full and effective participation in society on an equal basis with others" (Sharby et al. 2015).

According to the medical model, a disability represents a negative manifestation of health that typically requires medical assistance for prevention, treatment, or development of a cure as a means of eliminating the negative manifestation (Sharby et al. 2015). Given that the medical model of disability focuses on reducing the issue with the ultimate goal of elimination, some describe it as a "deficit model" (Sharby et al. 2015). In response, other models have evolved. One such model is the social model of disability which focuses on how attitudes of others including biases taint how those with a disability are treated, and as a result those individuals are not fully free to exercise their rights as well as the opportunities incidental thereto (Sharby et al. 2015). Additionally, the social model of disability focuses on the physical factors attributable to a disability (Sharby et al. 2015). Aptly named for the role of socialization within the model, the model highlights the importance of providing accommodations socially to make participation easier as well as providing access as a whole (Sharby et al. 2015). Not surprisingly, the social model focuses in on fixing what is inaccessible as a means of increasing avenues for socialization, rather than focusing in on the underlying medical issue (Sharby et al. 2015).

Because disability represents a complex concept, other models have been developed that focus on explaining disability from other perspectives. For instance, The World Health Organization (WHO) developed the International Classification of Functioning, Disability and Health (ICF) as a means of universally defining and monitoring disability (Sharby et al. 2015). As opposed to other models, the ICF represents an ecological model that considers all aspects that the individual interacts with as they affect the ability or lack thereof of an individual to engage in activities of importance to them (Sharby et al. 2015). Among such interactive factors are those relative to medical conditions the individual suffers from in terms of how those conditions impair the ability of an individual to engage in activities (Sharby et al. 2015). Notably under the ICF, environmental factors can be modified such as by using an accessibility aid, which serves as a "contextual factor," but doing so does not result in activity, just in participation (Sharby et al. 2015, p. 3304). Additionally, the ICF also considers the social network as well as "education, personality, age, motivation, and job skills" as personal factors that fall within the category of contextual factors that determine to what degree an individual can participate in activities (Sharby et al. 2015). Based on the comprehensive approach adopted by ICF, it is clear that interacting with the environment on a variety of levels affects the degree to which an individual becomes disabled and more physical activities that individuals engage in the healthier they are able to remain.

10.5.1 Importance of Physical Activity

Physical activity and exercise represent points on a continuum: the final or cumulative point represents achieving the level of physical activity that constitutes physical fitness (Caspersen et al. 1985). By definition, physical activity represents "any" movement of the body resulting from use of "skeletal muscles" that result in the use of energy measured in kilocalories (Caspersen et al. 1985). While physical activity can be grouped into a variety of activities ranging from sports to household activities, exercise represents a more specific group of activities that are scheduled, ongoing, and aimed at achieving a specific goal such as increasing one's physical fitness or maintaining physical fitness levels that have already been reached (Caspersen et al. 1985; World Health Organization 2017a, b, c). Meanwhile, physical fitness represents a group of characteristics related to well-being or obtaining a specific skillset typically associated with athleticism (Caspersen et al. 1985; World Health Organization 2017b). However, it is also important to understand that in addition to engaging in physical activity research has shown that individuals must avoid being sedentary for protracted periods of time due to the adverse effects that may result though specific "optimal levels of sedentary behavior" remain unknown (González et al. 2017; Katzmarzyk 2010).

Indicative of the impact of physical activity across all age groups and the importance of remaining physically active, the World Health Organization in 2010 developed age-based recommendations on what physical activity was needed (2017a). Within these recommendations, the World Health Organization noted that inactivity or lack of physical activity represents the fourth highest factor that increases the risk of death globally, which can be attributed to 6% of deaths on a global level (2017b). Generally, appropriate levels of physical activity achieved regularly actually have many health benefits including a decreased risk of developing many conditions such as hypertension, heart disease, heart attacks, diabetic conditions, cancers of the breast or the colon, depression, and falling (World Health Organization 2017b). In fact, adequate regular physical levels of activity increase bone density and overall health (World Health Organization 2017b). According to the US Department of Health and Human Services' *2008 Physical Activity Guidelines for Americans*, maximizing health benefits requires adults to engage in at least "150 minutes (2 hours and 30 minutes)" of exercise per week at a moderate level of intensity or "75 minutes (1 hour and 15 minutes)" per week at a vigorous level of intensity, which is also recommended by the World Health Organization (2010). However, a 2017 study conducted by González, Fuentes, and Márquez indicated that that minimum levels of activity as delineated within the guidelines for health were inadequate to decrease the risk of cardiovascular incidence. As further studies are conducted relative to the minimum level needed to offset chronic conditions, it may be that the levels needed to offset chronic conditions will need to be adjusted; and the adjustment may be due to other environmental factors that are diminishing the benefits of physical activity as a whole (González et al. 2017). However, additional research will be needed before a determination of that level can be made (González et al. 2017).

Despite what we do not know, we do know that those who engage in physical activity on a regular basis improve their personal fitness and in so doing achieve a multitude of health benefits (Eberhardt et al. 2001). Among the health benefits achieved are a reduced risk of "cardiovascular disease, diabetes, obesity, some cancers, musculoskeletal conditions," "reproductive diseases, diseases of the digestive tract, and pulmonary and kidney" disease (Eberhardt et al. 2001, p. 40; Booth et al. 2014, p. 1143). Notably, even activity of a physical nature engaged in that relates to one's employment, upkeep of their home or "transportation-related activities" can benefit a person's health (Eberhardt et al. 2001).

Given the correlation between physical activity and health benefits, there are multiple studies that delineate the positive correlation that exists between physical activity and health and impact that results on the quality of life overall (Leitzmann et al. 2007; US Department of Health and Human Services. Healthy People 2020 (2020). Specifically, engaging in physical activity has been shown to positively impact overall health including mental, physical, and intellectual aspects of health (United States Department of Health and Human Services 2008). In fact, physical activity can decrease pain (Fransen et al. 2015).

Moreover, engaging in physical activity can decrease depression (Kelley et al. 2015). Using meta-analysis to review data on 2449 individuals, Kelley et al. (2015) found that depression among individuals suffering from arthritis was reduced by engaging in physical activity. Though one might expect similar results for anxiety, fewer studies exist making the same assessment as to anxiety; this may be partially because most studies did not focus on recruiting individuals to participate who had high levels of anxiety (Stonerock, et al. 2015). Moreover, an assessment of those studies that do exist could not be used to show a causal relationship between increased exercise and decreased anxiety due to shortcomings in how those studies were performed (Stonerock et al. 2015).

For those with mobility limitations, being unable to engage in physical activity represents a critical concern because failing to engage in physical activity results in the development of secondary conditions as well as potentially leading a limited mobility issue to progress into a major mobility condition (Iezzoni et al. 2001). Among the secondary conditions that can develop are those that manifest physically and those that evolve into mental health concerns (Iezzoni et al. 2001). In 2001 when Iezzoni, McCarthy, Davis, and Siebens conducted their study, estimates indicated that 19 million individuals or 10.1% of the population exhibited mobility limitations. As of 2015, data indicates that of the 77 million adults 18 and older experienced at least one basic limitation or a more complex limitation: this translates into 32.2% of those 18 and older experiencing mobility limitations to one degree or another (National Center for Health Statistics 2016). Of those experiencing difficulty in physical functioning, 18.2 million of the individuals aged 18 and older are either incapable of walking or experience difficulties when attempting to walk; this translates into 7.5% of those in that age group (U.S. Department of Health and Human Services, Centers for Disease Control and Prevention, National Center for Health Statistics 2015).

One large scale study included 228,024 multinational participants in "low and middle-income countries", and the researchers found that chronic conditions typically resulted from decreased levels of physical activity among all individuals though to a more noticeable degree this occurred among older individuals (Vancampfort et al. 2017, p. 1). Another study indicated that although limited mobility appeared to result in the development of chronic conditions it may be that the chronic conditions contributed to the mobility issue; and the researchers recommended that future studies need to differentiate between the "specific chronic diseases" and mobility limitation to understand the degree of correlation to a more accurate degree (Kriegsman et al. 1997). However, other researchers continue to conclude that chronic disease is causally related to the lack of physical activity, including a multinational study of 228,024 individuals from 46 countries (Vancampfort et al. 2017).

10.5.2 Opportunities to Exercise

For those with mobility limitations, the opportunity to exercise requires a proactive approach to the creation of said opportunities: whether that be through their own efforts or those opportunities that result from the adherence to laws established to remove the barriers that impede the ability of those with mobility limitations to be able to exercise. To create such an opportunity requires planning to decrease the barriers that present themselves including those in the environment in which the individuals live, barriers related to socialization, and efforts focused on ensuring proactively that the limitations of those affected by mobility constraints are considered when developing opportunities for increased mobility (Rantanen 2013). However, removing the barriers to exercise in our society represents a social obligation that has been legislated by federal law. Gaining an overall understanding of what is possible as a result of the federal obligations that are in effect provides insight into the challenges that those with limited mobility experience when such regulations are correctly adhered to as opposed to when they are not because ultimately such regulations strive to provide equal access under the law.

Regulating Equal Access Equal access by definition represents a comparable in terms of the degree to which the population of those with mobility limitations may access exercise and achieve health as opposed to the overall population. As it pertains to disabilities, there are specific laws that require that access be provided. The primary law providing for access for those with disabilities both in terms of services as well as physical access is the Americans with Disabilities Act of 1990 also known as the ADA (U.S Department of Justice 2010). Within the 1973 Rehabilitation Act, Section 504 specifically prohibits discrimination against persons with disabilities (U.S. Department of Justice 2010). In fact, Title III requires privately owned businesses to comply with the requirement to make facilities accessible because they are considered places of *public* accommodation: places of *public* accommodation are defined as business establishments open for *public* access (United States Department of Justice Civil Rights Division n.d. a). Moreover, recreational facilities are one of the 12 categories of *public* accommodation specifically listed under Title III (United States Department of Justice Civil Rights Division n.d. a). In terms of enforcement of ADA requirements, it is important to note that specifications relative to "design and construction" are civil right law requirements; but they do not require an inspection and permit to confirm adherence (United States Access and Design Board n.d.). Rather, those businesses and organizations subject to the requirements are mandated to meet the requirements or risk having to respond to a complaint through a federal agency or by way of litigation (United States Access and Design Board n.d.). ADA compliance requires a review of 28 CFR Part 36 subpart D plus the 2004 ADAAG which is consolidated within the 2010 ADA Standards for Accessible Design; and together these regulations constitute an update to the 1991 standards (United States Department of Justice 2010; Americans with Disabilities n.d.).

Pursuant to the ADA, those individuals with disabilities cannot access facilities that have architectural barriers present thereby necessitating the removal of such barriers (Wiley and Rein 2010). Within the *2010 ADA Standards for Accessible Design*, which are applicable to any new construction or alterations on or after March 15, 2012, entities subject to Title III such as *public* exercise facilities are mandated to design accessible facilities by making at least a part of a facility accessible for those with disabilities (United States Department of Justice 2010). However, if an entity can show that making a facility accessible is not possible structurally such as when the area is configured in a way that makes implementing accessibility features impossible, then the entity will qualify for an exception to the requirement for accessible design (United States Department of Justice 2010). In addition to new construction, *public* entities under Title III must also perform alterations so that the facility or a part of a facility is accessible as to all such alterations performed after January 26, 1992; and any such alternation must be performed in such a way as to not obstruct the path that disabled individuals use to gain access to restrooms, phones, and water fountains including individuals using wheelchairs, except when the costs are proportionally higher than the costs of the overall alterations by 20% (United States Department of Justice 2010). In further detailing the term "path of travel," the 2010 guidelines include "sidewalks, curb ramps and other interior or exterior pedestrian ramps; clear floor paths through lobbies, corridors, rooms, and other improved areas; parking access aisles; elevators and lifts; or a combination" as "paths of travel" (United States Department of Justice para. 6). Moreover, a separate paragraph highlights the importance of curb ramps and notes that they must be provided for both new construction and alterations as a means of allowing entry from the street onto raised areas as a means of traversing the intersections between "streets, roads or highways" (United States Department of Justice 2010, para. 16). Among the other overall accommodations that need to be made are each of the following: an accessible means of entry and exit, accessible parking, water fountains, swimming pools, saunas/steam rooms, sinks, toilet and bathing facilities, and dressing rooms (United States Department of Justice 2010). Moreover, the standards also require a proportionally adequate number of accessible parking spaces compared to the overall number of parking spaces (Department of Justice 2010). In terms of specific components of an exercise facility, the 2010 standards require that basketball courts provide a connection between court sides, and exercise equipment shall be configured in a way as to ensure that it is located on a route that is accessible (United States Department of Justice 2010). Notably, the advisory text also indicates that having one type of machine that is accessible would be inadequate even if the one machine provides the same exercise function to a certain body part that the inaccessible machines do (United States Department of Justice 2010). In terms of specificity, the standards also detail specific accessibility requirements as to height and width: the width that must be clear for doorways, height of stairs, the width of toilets as well as showers, turning space in changing rooms, height for sinks, height along with the width for pool lifts, and the width for vehicle parking, which also provides different requirements for vehicles of different sizes (United States Department of Justice 2010). Additionally, the standards detail the degree of stability required of walking surfaces, knee and toe clearance, the area that must be free of obstructions, and the permissible level of slope (Department of Justice 2010). Despite the number of requirements, several exceptions present serious concern for those with mobility limitations (United States Department of Justice 2010). One such exception permits facilities to refrain from installing an accessible elevator if their size is less than 3000 square feet per floor or less than three floors as long as they do not contain a shopping center/mall, a healthcare provider's office, *public* transportation station, or an airport terminal (United States Department of Justice 2010). In addition to exceptions, the standards sometimes conflict (United States Department of Justice 2010). For instance, the clear space between exercise machines can overlap; although, this appears to present a challenge in design based on the advisory note detailing that this requires careful consideration (United States Department of Justice 2010).

In addition to the focus on physical barriers that need to be removed for accessibility to occur, the ADA also requires publicly accommodating locations/establishments to modify how services are provided to allow all individuals irrespective of their ability or disability to use the facility (Rashinaho et al. 2006; Wiley and Rein 2011). Moreover, Title III indicates that discrimination occurs if a place of public accommodation fails to reasonably modify their "policies, practices, and procedures" unless doing so is demonstrated to change the makeup of the goods and services offerred to a significant degree (Wiley and Rein 2011).

As is clearly illustrated, there are specific requirements in place to provide for accessibility most of which do apply to all *public* facilities such as exercise facilities, but given that the only checks and balances are by way of a complaint or litigation, the potential exists for lack of adherence with this requirements, which in and of itself represents a barrier to access for those with mobility limitations. A review of some of the settlements in which the Department of Justice has been involved relative to accessibility represents a means of determining to what degree such non-compliance exists thereby representing an ongoing barrier to access. When an ADA issue arises that needs to be handled through litigation, the United States through the Office of the Attorney often has to initiate an enforcement action. In fact, as recently as this past summer, there were four settlements entered into against different physical fitness facilities across the nation almost all of which were YMCAs. One case specifically related to a policy modification to allow an aide to assist a child who was using the YMCA facilities without said aide having to also hold a membership (United States Department of Justice Civil Rights Division n.d. b). As part of the settlement, the YMCA eliminated the requirement for the aide to hold a membership as a written modification to its policies across each of its branches and also provided for free months of membership to credit for the time since the suit was filed through the time of the settlement entry (United States Department of Justice Civil Rights Division n.d. b). Another case against Total Lifetime Care Health and Fitness Club also sought to provide access to an aide for a disabled adult who needed assistance to use the facilities but did not feel it fair that the aide pay for a membership in order to access the facilities solely to assist them (United States Department of Justice Civil Rights Division n.d. d). As part of the Total Lifetime Care settlement, the consent order sets forth that providing for an aide to access the facility without a membership represents a reasonable accommodation as long as the aide does not benefit themselves by using the facilities or the services provided by the club (United States Department of Justice Civil Rights Division n.d. d). Moreover, the Total Lifetime Care settlement also required the development of a request for accommodations, a complaint process, nondiscriminatory signage, and overall policy modifications to ensure reasonable accommodations in the future, establish ongoing mandatory training, and award fines in the amount of $15,000 divided between the United States and the complainants (United States Division of Justice Civil Rights Division n.d. d). Another recent YMCA case entitled United States of America vs Norwich Family YMCA involved a discriminatory environment and the discriminatory practices incidental thereto that imposed added criteria on the disabled individual as a result of "stereotypes and generalizations" thereby discriminating based on disability (United States Department of Justice Civil Rights Division n.d. c). In the settlement agreement, the YMCA eliminated the screening methodology that precluded individuals living at facilities that care for those with developmental disabilities from being approved as members at the Norwich YMCA and required the YMCA to rewrite their policies to provide for accommodations for the disabled, update their mission, provide mandatory training related to ADA for all staff, post nondiscriminatory signage, and update their website to reflect that discrimination would not be tolerated (United States Department of Justice Civil Rights Division n.d. c). Moreover, monetary damages were also part of the Norwich YMCA settlement both to the US government and to the complainant (United States Department of Justice Civil Rights Division n.d. c). One case in which the United States filed suit against The YMCA of Reading and Berks County even involved architectural barriers, which must be removed if doing so can be accomplished relatively easily and without undue cost (United States Department of Justice Civil Rights Division n.d. e). In the YMCA of Reading and Berks County case, the US Office of the Attorney issued a letter of finding indicated that there were several architectural barriers to accessibility including a family restroom built between 2006 and 2008, parking, signage at the entry, and the pool lift (United States Department of Civil Rights Division n.d. e). As part of the terms of the settlement, the YMCA of Reading and Berks County agreed to create a parking accessible space for a van, post signage at entrances that are inaccessible advising of the accessible location, post parking accessibility signage, post signage in bathroom areas indicating where accessible areas are located, install a lift compliant with ADA standards, and update the family restroom to make it accessible: accessibility of the family restroom will be achieved through placement of toilet, grab bars, non-twisting faucet hardware, placement of seat and grab bars in transfer show, and the addition of a shower hose in transfer shower (United States Department of Civil Rights Division n.d. e).

10.5.3 Barriers to Physical Exercise

There are several factors that represent barriers to health including poor-rated health, (Booth et al. 1997; Clark 1999; Grossman and Stewart 2003; Hirvensalo et al. 1998; McPherson and Yamaguchi 1995; O'Neill and Reid 1991; Satariano et al. 2000; Whaley and Ebbeck 1997), pain related to disease progression and fear of experiencing pain (Clark 1999; Hays and Clark 1999), lethargy (King et al. 2000), and safety of the surrounding environment (Garber and Blissmer 2002; Grossman and Stewart 2003; Katzmarzyk 2010; McPherson and Yamaguchi 1995; Whaley and Ebbeck 1997).

As is highlighted by the focus on removing environmental factors under the Americans with Disabilities Act and the inclusion of environmental factors as a component in the 2017 version of the International Classification of Functioning, Disability and Health (ICF), environmental factors can present barriers to mobility including among older individuals (World Health Organization 2017a; World Health Organization 2017b; World Health Organization 2017c). Using the aforementioned general factors, we will examine the specific ways in which such factors manifest themselves those who are affected by mobility limitations. Using this comparison contrast approach, a greater understanding will be achieved in terms of to what degree those with limited mobility are experiencing barriers to exercise that might improve their health in some form as opposed to those who do not have to overcome limited mobility before availing themselves of exercise opportunities.

10.5.4 Poor Health

Disability impacts "health outcomes" (Krahn et al. 2015). In fact, the *Healthy People 2020* progress review specifically notes that those with disabilities are at an increased risk of experiencing "poor health outcomes such as obesity, hypertension, falls-related injuries, and mood disorders such as depression" (U.S. Department of Health and Human Services, Office of Disease Prevention and Health Promotion n.d.). In fact, those with disabilities are "four times more likely" to experience health rated at fair or poor levels than those without disabilities, which translates into 40.3% versus 9.9% (Altman and Bernstein 2008). Even though not every condition that results in a disability manifests in poor health, the World Health Organization noted that those with disabilities sought healthcare to a greater degree as a whole and to a larger degree did not succeed in having their healthcare needs satisfied (2018). Moreover, mobility as a disability represents a causative factor in those who experience "falls" as shown in studies such as the one conducted in 2015 (Davis et al. 2015).

In one 2001 study, 38.4% of the 145,007 individuals aged 18 and older whose responses were examined self-assessed themselves as being in poor health as opposed to only 3.8% of those who had no mobility limitations (Iezzoni et al. 2001). Moreover, the 2015 Healthy People data indicates that there were significantly fewer individuals with disabilities able to achieve the required level of physical activity necessary to meet aerobic as well as "muscle strengthening objectives" within the 18 and over category (2015, para. 1).

Following the development of limited mobility, certain conditions typically develop as a result of lifestyle changes incidental to diminished mobility. These conditions are known as secondary conditions and present an added barrier preventing those with limited mobility from "engag[ing] in self-initiated health promotion practices" such as exercise (Rimmer and Rowland 2008, p. 409). Notably, the conditions that arise are often not directly related to the initial disability but develop as a result of the individual being limited in their ability to seek out the necessary level of activity needed to remain healthy (Rimmer and Rowland 2008).

To understand the types of conditions that may arise in those who are not able to seek out health through exercise, researchers have sought to identify conditions typically attributable to lack of physical activity. Globally, one study examined the connection between physical activity or lack thereof and chronic conditions such as "chronic back pain, angina, arthritis, asthma, diabetes, hearing problems, tuberculosis, visual impairment, and edentulism," which is also known as toothlessness (Vancampfort et al. 2017, p. 1). Another study found that those experiencing mobility constraints reported increased rates of "depression, fear, anxiety, confusion, obesity, poor vision, dizziness, imbalance, which caused individuals to steady themselves using walls" (Iezzoni et al. 2001, p. 239). Some of the diminished vision and lack of equilibrium represent factors that increase the potential for individuals to fall (i.e., become fall risks) (Iezzoni et al. 2001). Moreover, such falls can further impair mobility quickly depending on the severity of the fall and the injuries incidental to the fall (Rantanen 2013). Hence, if an individual with limited mobility has developed one of the aforementioned mental or physical conditions, they may be wary to engage in little more than limited movement thereby further decreasing the potential for them to improve their health through exercise.

10.5.5 Mental Health

To place mobility into perspective, it is important to understand the impact that mobility has on mental health. Mobility provides a means of accessing life whether that is within one's own home or out in the community at large (Iezzoni et al. 2001). Given the mobility provides the means of interacting with others; it represents an essential component of what is tantamount to the formula for quality of life. Hence, those with limited mobility often develop medical conditions as a result of being deprived of the ability to of their own free will exercise their ability to access the outside world and interact with others. In fact, the need to move physically represents an essential Maslovian need, which if unmet decreases the potential for satisfaction (Rantanen 2013). Not surprisingly, individuals who lack full mobility often suffer from "isolation, anxiety, and depression" (Iezzoni et al. 2001). In fact, depression affects those with major mobility concerns to a larger degree than the general population: 30.6% of those with mobility limitations experience disability as opposed to only 3.8% of individuals without mobility limitations (Iezzoni et al. 2001).

10.5.6 Obesity

Some studies indicated that those suffering from obesity experienced mobility limitations or vice versa. In Iezzoni et al.'s 2001 study, the researchers could not determine if obesity was caused by mobility limitations or if the obesity led to mobility limitations; the data showed that of those who reported mobility limitations, approximately 30% were obese (Iezzoni 2011). Among those without mobility limitation, only 15. 2% were obese (Iezzoni 2011). In one study, the researchers evaluated the impact of mobility impairment on healthcare concerns and found that those with the lowest level of obesity were those who were not disabled (Jones and Sinclair 2008). Moreover, the highest level of obesity was found among those individuals that had mobility limitations and those with mobility limitations as well as coming from minorities also had higher rates of obesity (Jones and Sinclair 2008).

10.5.7 Osteoporosis

By definition, osteoporosis represents the "low bone mass and microarchitectural deterioration of bone tissue, leading to enhanced bone fragility and a consequent increase in fracture risk" (Kanis et al. 1994, p. 1137). Once osteoporosis develops, the potential for fractures increases thereby adversely impacting the potential to engage in physical activity and limiting mobility (Kerr et al. 2017).

10.5.8 Cardiovascular and Breathing Issues

The Mayo Clinic defines acute cardiovascular disease as a series of conditions that constrict or completely block the vessels carrying blood to the heart thereby resulting in pain (angina): a cerebrovascular incident also known as a stroke or a myocardial infarction (MI)/attack to the heart represents an example of acute cardiovascular disease (Mayo Clinic 2018). Acute cardiovascular issues commonly cause disability related to mobility limitations (Iezzoni et al. 2001). Like acute cardiovascular disease, breathing issues include impairments that impact respiration through the reduction of "ventilator capacity" (Fragoso et al. 2014). When older individuals experience conditions that impair their ability to breathe, their ability to engage in physical activity is adversely impacted including their ability to ambulate or be mobile (Fragoso et al. 2014).

10.5.9 Lack of Motivation and Lethargy

Expecting positive outcomes and one's potential to complete a task can motivate individuals to participate in exercise (Grembowski et al. 1993; Resnick et al. 2000). Research has shown that receiving careful monitoring by a physician, receiving advice from a physician, and having exercise evaluated by a physician and high-quality instruction served as motivators for exercise (Cohen-Mansfield et al. 2004). Obtaining instruction from a physician and support from both peers and relatives also serves as motivation to engage in exercise (Damush et al. 2005). Being advised to exercise by a physician or other healthcare professional has also been found to be related to an increased level of engagement in physical exercises (Hirvensalo et al. 2003). Just as motivation can further or diminish activity levels, lethargy or fatigue can also affect the degree to which individuals engage in activity (Dean et al. 2006). By definition, fatigue represents the feeling of overall "tiredness or exhaustion" (Belza 1994). Ultimately, fatigue results when the level of actual or recognized strain in performing an action or engaging in an activity exceeds the "real or perceived difficulty of a task or exercise" (Abd-Elfattah et al. 2015, p. 351). Like lack of motivation, lethargy represents a barrier to exercise because the individual feels that they can not exert themselves to the degree necessary to engage in the activity (King et al. 2000). As both conditions illustrate, if an individual finds themselves feeling as if they cannot engage in exercise, then the individual will not engage in exercise without some external factor changing their perception of their limitations.

10.5.10 Pain

One aspect of the difficulty that those with limited mobility may experience is pain incidental to mobilizing themselves to whatever degree they are able to do so. Many chronic conditions result in incidental pain (Smith et al. 2010). However, independent of any chronic condition, pain in and of itself increases the probability of disability (Ling et al. 2003; Ling et al. 2006; Song et al. 2006; Adamson et al. 2003). Moreover, pain bars individuals from pursuing an active lifestyle (Vancampfort et al. 2017). If individuals engage in activities regardless of the pain which they experience, pain tends to dissipate, interferes less with their activities, and decreases in intensity (Jensen et al. 2016).

Generally pain symptoms accompany mobility limitations (Mottram et al. 2008). A significant number of studies have been conducted on mobility limitations and pain in those older than 50 including studies conducted overseas (Mottram et al. 2008; Stubbs et al. 2016). Among the findings observed relative to pain and mobility limitations were determined to occur to a higher degree in those who were older, as to females, and in those who were from "lower socio-economic groups" (Mottram et al. 2008). Not surprisingly, those who reported pain were more likely to report limited mobility (Mottram et al. 2008). Moreover, those aged 50–65 reported higher levels of pain than those who were older (Mottram et al. 2008). Overall, a higher number of individuals who were older experienced limited mobility as a result of pain thereby illustrating that the impact that pain has on mobility is increased based on the age of the individual (Mottram et al. 2008).

A variety of conditions can result in pain at a level that limits mobility including arthritis which is a commonly occurring condition that results in mobility limitations due to pain incidental to the inflammation of the joint (Iezzoni et al. 2000). Of the 100 types of arthritis, the most common two types of arthritis are osteoarthritis and rheumatoid arthritis (Mayo Clinic 2010). For those suffering from arthritis, what begins as joint pain increases in severity due to swelling and stiffness until function is lost (Mayo Clinic 2010). Several studies have indicated that those who suffer from arthritis develop mobility limitations incidental to the pain caused by arthritis and using excercise those suffering from arthritis are able to improve pain levels, increase mobility, and decrease disability (Vancampfort et al. 2017; Fransen et al. 2015; Veldhijzen van Zanten et al. 2015).

In their 2015 literature review, Fransen, McConnell, Harmer, Van der Esch, Simic, and Bennell reviewed 54 studies to determine the results of therapeutic exercises and found that in 44 studies the exercise reduced pain to a significant degree as well as improved physical function. Fransen et al. 2015 examined those who had developed osteoarthritis of the knee, which is incurable, and determined that with exercise therapy pain reduction occurred almost immediately by 12 points on a 100-point scale where most pain was noted to be approximately 44 points. Hence, Fransen, McConnell, Harmer, Van der Esch, Simic, Bennell's meta-analysis of the data demonstrated that a significant pain reduction occurred through exercise for a severe condition that affects the ability of individuals to ambulate (2015). Moreover, the results were comparable with those who undertook steroidal injections, and those undertaking the recommended exercises continued to benefit from the pain relief for a period of 2–6 months thereby demonstrating the impact having undertaken the exercises had on participants. Hence, though pain adversely impacts the ability to engage in exercise as well as overall mobility, exercise represents a means of pain relief that elicits results comparable to those obtained using anti-inflammatory intramuscular injections (Fransen et al. 2015).

10.5.11 Environment

Safety or lack thereof represents an environmental barrier especially for older individuals who have a mobility limitation as it pertains to "their outdoor environment," which those with mobility limitations likely need assistive devices to traverse (Rantanen 2013). In terms of safety, those with limited mobility need to be able to access areas without risking injury especially if they must travel via city streets. For those with limited mobility to safely surmount environmental barriers, such barriers need to be addressed thereby creating an accessible environment (Rantanen 2013). Moreover, removal of the environmental barriers that represent an impediment to the mobility of those with limited mobility represents a means of stalling further declines to mobility by supporting appropriate levels of physical activity (Rantanen 2013). In addition to the aforementioned environmental barriers, other environmental barriers are specifically addressed in the 2017 version of the ICF as published by the World Health Organization (2017c). Moreover, it is important to consider the fact that environmental barriers can exist in terms of what is lacking (such as services) versus its existence (in terms of prejudices) (2017c). Even broader concerns such as poverty can present barriers to accessing physical activity if in fact opportunities to engage in physical activity require the expenditure of funds that do not exist (World Health Organization 2017c).

For those older individuals residing in residence communities who are experiencing mobility limitations, residing in a community where services are available to support their mobility can positively impact their long-term mobility (Rantanen 2013). Rantanen (2013) hypothesized that if medical professionals provided psychological interventions to those with limited mobility, then those individuals would independently augment their physical activity. In the quantitative study of 600 individuals with self-reported limited mobility who ranged from age 75 to 81 years in a residence community that Rantanen conducted, Rantanen found that those early on in their mobility decline who were provided a session with a physiotherapist and subsequent sessions via phone approximately every 4 months for a 2-year term exhibited decreased mobility limitation increase as compared to those who did not receive such medical services (2013).

For those using city streets, street maps lack the level of specificity for those with limited mobility to determine if they can safely negotiate a trip using city streets (Bolten et al. 2015). Among the considerations that must be undertaken are changes in altitude that must be negotiated, curb cuts, which are also known as curb ramps [and] "ramped passages, etc." (Bolten et al. 2015; Disability Rights Education and Defense Fund 2017). Despite the increasing number of individuals with limited mobility, the data detailing whether travel by city streets is safe for those with limited mobility continues to be difficult to obtain in a form that they can easily use (Bolten et al. 2015). Moreover, there are different considerations that must be undertaken when dealing with a motorized versus a wheelchair that is manual as well as preparing for concerns that arise relative to weather such as rain making the surface of a street slicker, which would represent a concern for both those in wheelchairs as well as those mobilizing themselves using a cane for assistance (Bolten et al. 2015).

Safety could also be represented based on the safety precautions available within a facility where an individual may seek to take part in exercise. In order for an individual with limited mobility to be able to actually use exercise facilities safely, said exercise facilities must be accessible. Accessibility requires that such a facility take certain action to make their otherwise inaccessible facilities accessible. A 2005 study examined the degree to which such measures were being taken by "health club and fitness facilities" using the Accessibility Instruments Measuring Fitness and Recreation Environments (AIMFREE) (Rimmer et al. 2005). The researchers reviewed 35 facilities using the aforementioned instrument which not only accessed the physical/structural features that needed to be present but also assessed the environment in terms of the existing policies as well as the behavior of the staff in terms of making those with mobility disabilities comfortable (Rimmer et al. 2005). Though the ADA addresses some important areas relative to accessibility, more than just what is covered within the ADA, requirements must be done to be truly accessible (North Carolina Office on Disability and The Center for Universal Design 2008). In fact, the *Removing Barriers to Health Clubs and Fitness Facilities* authors indicate that both "flexibility and receptiveness" are needed to facilitate the ability for those with a disability to engage in purposeful exercise (North Carolina Office on Disability and The Center for Universal Design 2008). Achieving such flexibility is predicated on adopting the principle of universal design thereby increasing usefulness and removing the barriers within the environment that literally adversely impact access (North Carolina Office on Disability and The Center for Universal Design 2008).

In one study focused on determining the accessibility of exercise facilities, the researchers conducted quantitative research and used the Accessibility Instruments Measuring Fitness and Recreation Environments (AIMFREE), which examines the level of accessibility based on six areas, including equipment, the policies of the facilities, as well as the behavior of the professional staff (Rimmer et al. 2005). To some degree, each facility had accessibility deficiencies, and some deficiencies rose to the level of being violations of the Americans with Disabilities Act specific to the building of the facility (Rimmer et al. 2005). In putting into context the importance of making such facilities accessible, Rimmer quotes the *Healthy People 2010* report indicated that 56% of those with disabilities engaged in no physical activities for leisure (2005). Moreover, data detailed within the *Healthy People 2010* chapter entitled *Disability and Secondary Conditions* seemed to indicate that the reason behind the low rate of activities resulted from not only barriers within the environment but also "organizational policies and practices, discrimination, and social attitudes" (Rimmer et al. 2005, p. 2022). Notably, the *Healthy People 2010* chapter indicated that more needed to be done to assist those for whom walking represented an issue as a result of "arthritis, extreme obesity, or balance impairments" (Rimmer et al. 2005, p. 2022).

In examining the data elicited from the 35 professionals from 9 of 10 regions of the country who participated in the convenience sample, the researchers found that more than 50% of the facilities had "slip-resistant flooring, adjustable lighting levels, hand-held shower heads" as well as "accessible routes from accessible parking spaces to the facility", "locker room dressing benches of suitable size", "grab bars in elevators and bathroom stalls, fold seats or shower benches in shower areas, and automatic entrance doors" (Rimmer et al. 2005). Moreover, the facilities studied typically had features consistent with the "ADA Accessibility Guidelines (ADAAG)" relative to "elevators, bathrooms, entrance doors, water fountains and parking areas" (Rimmer et al. 2005).

In a more recent study from 2012, Johnson, Stoelzle, Finco, Foss, Carstens examined the extent to which facilities in the western area of Wisconsin complied with Title III. The results of the research were compared with other data from four studies conducted in other areas of the nation (Johnson et al. 2012). After analyzing the data, the researchers found that facilities were highly compliant with Title III as to the customer service (84%) as well as to clearing the path individuals would travel within the facility (72%); yet, overall, the facilities were not entirely compliant (Johnson et al. 2012). Among the areas that were not to be severely non-compliant with the ADA were the locker rooms (32%) (Johnson et al. 2012). However, the biggest barrier and the one area in which no compliance with the law existed related to the lack of training fitness instructors received on how to safely train those with disabilities, including how to assist with transfers (Johnson et al. 2012). The researchers noted that only 2 of the facilities of the 16 evaluated included machines where either the seat or the bench could be removed in order to provide access for a wheelchair, which thereby resulted in 14 of the 16 facilities or 87.5% of the facilities being inaccesible to those in a wheelchairing (Johnson et al. 2012).

Although the earlier study indicated that the opportunity for accessibility had increased as a result of the accommodations made in terms of the environment at healthcare facilities, the later study indicated that there was still some significant levels of non-compliance. Such non-compliance occurred in areas that effectively would have barred individuals with mobility from potential using the health facilities in question due to environmental barriers. Such barriers create an environment that is on its face unwelcoming to those with physical limitations such as mobility limitations. Hence, those with mobility limitations faced with such obvious barriers to their use of exercise facilities are likely to find themselves feeling unwelcome based on the lack of effort made to provide accommodations consistent with the law much less as a means of providing customer service to those with disabilities.

10.5.12 Poverty

Poverty can represent an environmental barrier to opportunities, including those related to accessing overall health (Rimmer and Rowland 2008). Research indicated that those with mobility limitations, who typically had no more than a high school education, were more likely to be both unemployed and poor (Iezzoni et al. 2001). In Iezzoni et al.'s 2001 study, the data indicated that 25% of those with mobility issues had "household incomes below the poverty level compared to 8.7 percent of others" (p. 237). Using data from the American Community Survey, the Older Americans with a Disability 2008–2012 report indicated that among individuals with a disability, the rate of poverty was higher: 13% lived in poverty of those aged 65 and older which was almost twice the rate (i.e., 7%) of those who lived in poverty but did not experience a disabling condition (He and Larsen 2014). According to the 2018 poverty guidelines, in all states except Hawaii and Alaska, which have higher costs of living, a family of one individual who makes $12,140 or less is in poverty, and a family of four who make $25,100 would also be considered as living in poverty (U.S. Department of Health and Human Services 2017). Data from 2016 indicate that 40.6 million individuals were considered to be living in poverty (Semega et al. 2017). As of 2018, the Federal Poverty Level was defined as $12,140 for one person, $16,460 for a family comprised of two people, $20,780 for a family comprised of three individuals, and $25,100 for a household comprised of four people (Heathcare.gov 2018). Data suggests that those who live in poverty are likely to be sedentary as a result of barriers to health that result from their socioeconomic situation including lack of actual free resources ranging from local parts to centers for recreation (Estabrooks et al. 2003).

10.5.13 Rural

Research shows that those who live in rural areas develop chronic conditions to a higher degree than those who live in urban areas (Befort et al. 2012; Eberhardt et al. 2001; National Center for Health Statistics 2016). Declining rates of both heart disease and cancer in urban areas have increased the gap between mortality rates in urban versus rural areas (Cossman et al. 2010). Projections generated based on existing patterns of prevalence indicate that the trend of increased nonmorality occurring to a higher degree in rural areas represents one that will persist thereby culminating in 50% of deaths related to heart disease and cancer (Cossman et al. 2010). Researchers reviewing mortality prevalence patterns noted that this was a reversal of a previous "century-long" trend in which those in metropolitan areas developed chronic conditions and had higher rates of mortality (Cossman et al. 2010, p. 1419). Though Cossman et al. (2010) did not make any determinations as to why there was a higher incidence of chronic conditions and mortality in nonmetropolitan areas, they did note that one potential cause for such a prevalence may be related to "health behaviors" (p. 1419).

Such health behaviors could include lack of exercise and would to some degree manifest in development of among other things obesity, which occurs at an increased rate in rural communities as well as coinciding with a decreased rate of physical activity in these same communities (Seguin et al. 2014). Studies evaluating the prevalence of obesity in rural areas indicate that obesity occurs to a higher degree in rural areas (Befort et al. 2012). In fact, even youth are at risk of being so inactive in rural areas that they ultimately develop obesity (Yousefian et al. 2009). Due to differing methods of measuring physical activity across the different data sets evaluated (i.e., NHANES (National Health and Nutrition Examination Survey), BRFSS (Behavioral Risk Factor Surveillance System), and NHIS (National Health Interview Survey), Befort et al. (2012) were not able to determine to what degree lack of physical activity contributed to the escalated obesity rates was identified. However, Befort et al. (2012) noted that they had reviewed an earlier study conducted by Wilcox, Castro, King, Houseman, Brownson in 2000 and Parks, Housemann,

Brownson in 2003 that suggested the occurrence of lower levels of physical activity in rural areas.

In the Wilcox et al. (2000) study, the researchers examined the physical activity levels of older individuals from minority subsets of the population who resided in rural communities. In summarizing their findings, researchers concluded that women in rural areas appeared to experience higher levels of barriers to engage in physical activity and that the barriers that they had to surmount were very different than their urban counterparts (Wilcox et al. 2000). Moreover, the researchers found that in addition to their advanced age and lower educational level, rural women also experienced comparably less support for exercising, which all translated into a lower overall level of physical activity engaged in by rural women when compared with their urban counterparts (Wilcox et al. 2000). In 2001, data within the *Health, United States 2001 Urban and Rural Health Chartbook* indicated that those in rural areas exhibited decreased physical activity levels (Eberhardt et al. 2001). Following the study in 2000, Housemann and Brownson joined Parks in 2003 in further examining the physical activity level of adults (Parks et al. 2003). In the 2003 study, Parks, Housemann, and Brownson confirmed that those residing in rural areas were at a decreased potential for achieving the level of recommended physical activity and found that those in urban and/or more economically affluent areas were over two times as likely to attain the physical activity recommendations.

Among the reasons for decreased levels of physical activity in rural areas are the lack of activities available in the rural community (World Health Organization 2017c). When activities or facilities are available within rural communities, facilities may not be located in close proximity to their home, which is typically where individuals seek out such facilities (Sallis et al. 1990). Even if facilities are available to use within rural communities, the cost of using such facilities may place use of such facilities out of reach of individuals who cannot afford the costs (Seguin et al. 2014). Because not all physical activity has to be engaged in within a facility, some studies have examined the potential for those in rural communities exercising outdoors by engaging in activities such as cycling and walking, which can present viable options if doing so does not present a safety concern and that level of mobility is possible for the individual (Seguin et al. 2014). Yet, even if individuals want to engage in outdoor activities within their rural community, not only do the areas they do so have to be safe, they also have to be close to their home (Giles-Corti et al. 2008).

More recently, Frost et al. (2010) examined possible barriers to achieving increased physical activity by analyzing 20 studies to determine to what degree the built environment impacted levels of physical activity in rural communities. After reviewing the limited data specific to rural settings, which represented 17 of the 20 studies, Frost et al. (2010) determined that increased physical activity occurred in rural communities if people felt safe thereby not fearing crime, had recreational facilities, and could take advantage of trails, parks, or other destinations within walking distance. Frost et al. (2010) recommended further studies to evaluate if sidewalks, shoulders, traffic, and street lighting would consistently result in increased levels of physical activity in rural areas.

10.5.14 Social Capital

Though social capital initially represented an evolution of Marx's theories about monetary capital resulting from relationships, it has evolved (Lin et al. 2001). As currently used, those using the term social capital illustrates when an individual gains assistance with those that he or she has a social relationship (Rosso et al. 2014). According to the definition, Lin explained that social capital represent the resources ingrained within the relationships with others that are accessed purposefully (Lin 1982; 2001). One of the broader environmental concerns highlighted by the World Health Organization within the ICF (International Classification of Functioning, Disability and Health) was lack of social capital or relationship with other individuals as an indicator of poor health (2017c). Not surprisingly, research has shown that those with mobility limitations typically live alone (Iezzoni et al. 2001). Examinations of the effect of social capital on health have shown that those with social capital are healthier than those with low levels of social capital (Bolin et al. 2003). Moreover, as individuals age they achieve lower levels of social capital (Bolin et al. 2003). Although social capital positively impacts health, it does not have the same effect on mental health (Liu et al. 2016). Moreover, for adults aged 60 and over, social capital has a greater effect on their health than on those younger than 60 (Liu et al. 2016).

10.5.15 Cultural and/or Social Biases

Disability laws tends to focus on removing physical barriers and in so doing often fail to adequately highlight the impact of biases on creating barriers to assess, including, both cultural and social biases against those who are disabled that deter their ability to interact with others based on the negative ways in which others react to them either overtly or covertly (Wilson et al. 2000). Many individuals who are not limited in their abilities hold biases against those who they perceive as disabled (Employers Network for Equality and Inclusion 2014). Data indicates that bias against the disabled exist to a higher degree than biases based on race or gender (Employers Network for Equality and Inclusion 2014). In fact, 36% of those surveyed held the belief that the disabled were less productive than others (Employers Network for Equality and Inclusion 2014). Even as to employment, the biases against those who are disabled appear to be evident as data from 2015 indicates that 34.9% of those who are disabled aged 18–64 were employed as opposed to 76.0% of those who were not disabled (Lewis 2017). Not surprisingly, earnings disparities exist those who are disabled earn significantly less than those who are not disabled with median earnings of $10,000 less for those who were disabled as opposed to those who were not (Lewis 2017).

10.6 Critique and Further Discussions

10.6.1 Mobility Limitations in Younger Age Groups

Though it might be perceived otherwise, mobility issues represent a concern for far more than those individuals of advanced years (Iezzoni et al. 2001). One study specifically addressed the need to examine the impact and prevalence of mobility limitations on individuals "aged 18 and older" (Iezzoni et al. 2001, p. 235). In one study, researchers used data collected by the National Center for Health Statistics (NCHS) as part of their 1994–1995 National Health Interview Survey, Disability Supplement (NHIS-D): this represents the disability supplement focused at estimating the national rate of disability among all individuals irrespective of age who were not institutionalized (Iezzoni et al. 2001). In analyzing the data of the 145,007 individuals, which was comprised of individuals aged 18 and older, the researchers noted that they focused on those whose mobility was such that they could not transverse an area without assistance either of a person or a mechanical device in order to perform activities of daily living (Iezzoni et al. 2001). Of those aged 18–49, 4% reported mobility difficulties as opposed to 15.4% of those aged 50–69 (Iezzoni et al. 2001). However, 46% indicated that their mobility issues began before age 50 (Iezzoni et al. 2001). Data also illustrated some patterns in terms of gender and race: 3 more women than men exhibited mobility issues, and 15% of African Americans experienced higher levels of mobility, as opposed to 10% of those of white or Hispanic origin (Iezzoni et al. 2001).

Unlike their older counterparts who experienced limited mobility to a large degree as a result of age-related conditions such as chronic diseases, individuals younger than 50 experienced mobility limitations for different reasons (Iezzoni et al. 2001). A review of the data indicated that mobility issues affecting those 18–49 tended to be related to back pain likely caused by overuse or following an accident (Iezzoni et al. 2001). Moreover, among those 18–49, some individuals attributed their mobility limitation to a variety of conditions with 1.5% reporting multiple sclerosis, which is a "chronic inflammatory disease of the central nervous system" that tends to develop progressively over the life of the individual (Beiske et al. 2007) and 1.1% reporting "partial paralysis" (Iezzoni et al. 2001, p. 238). As this research illustrates, the conditions that affect those who are younger than 50 are much different than those affecting those over age 50. Though there is a significant degree of research conducted in terms of mobility limitations incidental to back pain and some research on barriers to exercise for those with multiple sclerosis, there were only a handful of studies on younger adults. To determine what barriers exist for the younger population, a greater understanding is needed in terms of how the conditions that affect them impact their mobility and their ability to engage in physical activity at the level necessary to achieve health benefits.

10.6.2 *Increased Biases Against Disabled Adversely Impacting Physical Activity*

Given that limitations related to mobility represent visible manifestations likely perceived as a disability, such biases need to be examined to determine to what degree they present a barrier preventing those with limited mobility from availing themselves of opportunities to exercise. Such biases may also affect whether or not individuals feel comfortable in using assistive devices as use of such devices represents a more visible indicator of disability. A greater understanding is needed of the impact of such implicit biases and how they affect the ability of those with mobility limitations for taking advantage of opportunities to exercise.

10.6.3 *Lack of Data Regarding Younger Demographic*

No research was identified detailing the percentage of those aged under 18 who suffer from mobility limitations. Though one could contend that this represents lack of prevalence in this age group, it seems unlikely that those under age 18 are not suffering from mobility limitations given that data on disabilities in general that includes those aged 16 through 18 indicates increased numbers and some of the conditions that this age group appear to be developing are associated with the development of mobility limitations. For instance, in the United States, we are experiencing an increased number of youth aged 2–19 years suffering from obesity: rates from 1999 to 2000 were 13.9% and have risen to 18.5% in 2015–2016 (United States Centers for Disease Control and Prevention 2016). According to the National Survey of Children's Health, 31.2% of those children aged 10–17 could be categorized as over their expected weight or obese (2016). Hence, one could infer that such an age group also has mobility limitations that they need to overcome. Interestingly, Healthy People examined obesity for this age group as a leading health indicator (Office of Disease Prevention and Health Promotion). Yet, unlike other health factors which were assessed as to disability and the potential that such a health indicator represented an increased likelihood of developing a disability, the data does not assess such a causal connection between obesity and disability in those aged 2–19 (Office of Disease Prevention and Health Promotion). In fact, one could logically hypothesize that some of the physical activities of this group such as engaging in gym as part of their education may be affected as a result of mobility limitations that would be unique as to this group. However, no research appears to have examined their experience in surmounting the barriers to physical exercise, including how this age group seeks out recreational exercise opportunities among their peers despite their limited mobility.

10.6.4 Lack of Strategic Mental Health Care

Offsetting the impact of mental health as a barrier requires a proactive approach to ongoing mental health assessment as well as a long-term view of treatment as a means of maintaining any gains achieved. Failing to establish a mental health support infrastructure risks losing any short-term gains and also represents a long-term means of allowing mental health conditions to deteriorate unmanaged. Unmanaged mental health results in those affected being unable to cope with daily challenges. Given that said individuals cannot cope with daily challenges, their focus is on trying to surmount those challenges and not on further taxing themselves by seeking to achieve health through exercise.

10.6.5 Lack of Data Pertaining to Mobility Limitations

There is a gap in the literature as it pertains to the extent of mobility limitations affecting the overall population, irrespective of age. Though there is extensive research on mobility in terms of access and opportunity to exercise in the aging population, scant research exists in terms of other age groups. What little does exist is limited to those experiencing long-term debilitating conditions, rather than an examination of those whose conditions are manageable, i.e., those with limited mobility. As to those who have treatable conditions, being left without the opportunity to exercise as a result of a mobility limitation adversely impacts their overall health. The adverse effect of failing to engage in physical activity is illustrated throughout the literature as a catalyst to fostering the development of secondary conditions. Moreover, the importance of creating an overall environment absent of barriers to mobility has been legislated through accessibility legislation. However, it is clear that we need to obtain a more concrete understanding of how to comprehensively address the needs of the growing population of individuals afflicted with limited mobility to prevent those who develop low mobility limitations from developing major mobility limitations. The literature also suggests that mobility limitations could be increasing overall based on the increasingly sedentary lifestyle that people are leading, and given that there is little understanding of optimal sedentary levels, recommendations relative to the degree to which a set number of sedentary hours should not be exceeded have yet to be made. However, before any such recommendations can be made, there has to be a greater understanding as to the impact that a sedentary lifestyle has on health so that both individuals and their medical providers can formulate practices aimed at avoiding reaching the sedentary level at which an adverse impact to health results.

References

42 U.S.C. 125 §12102. (1990). *Equality opportunity for individuals with disability*. Retrieved from https://www.law.cornell.edu/uscode/text/42/12102

Abd-Elfattah, H. M., Abdelazeim, F. H., & Elshennawy, S. (2015). Physical and cognitive consequences of fatigue: A review. *Journal of Advanced Research, 6*(3), 351–358. https://doi.org/10.1016/j.jare.2015.01.011.

Adamson, J., Hunt, K., & Ebrahim, S. (2003). Socioeconomic position, occupational exposures and gender: The relation with locomotor disability in early old age. *Journal of Epidemiology and Community Health, 57*, 453–455.

Altman, B. M., & Bernstein, A. (2008). *Disability and health in the United States, 2001–2005*. Retrieved from https://www.cdc.gov/nchs/data/misc/disability2001-2005.pdf

Americans with Disabilities. (n.d.). *ADA standards for accessible design*. Retrieved from https://www.ada.gov/2010ADAstandards_index.htm

Americans with Disabilities Act of 1990. (1991). Pub. L. No. 101–336, § 2, 104 Stat. 328.

Befort, C. A., Nazir, N., & Perri, M. G. (2012). Prevalence of obesity among adults from rural and urban areas of the United States: Findings from NHANES 2005–2008. *The Journal of Rural Health, 28*(4), 392–397. https://doi.org/10.1111/j.1748-0361.2012.00411.x.

Beiske, A. G., Naess, H., Aarseth, J. H., Andersen, O., Elovaaara, I., Farkkila, M., Hansen, H. H., Mellgren, S. I., Sandberg-Wollheim, M., Sorensen, P. S., & Myhr, K. M. (2007). Health-related quality of life in secondary progressive multiple sclerosis. *Multiple Sclerosis, 13*(3), 386–392. https://doi.org/10.1177/1352458507013003010l.

Belza, B. (1994). The impact of fatigue on exercise performance. *Arthritis Care and Research, 7*(4), 176–180.

Bolin, K., Lindgren, B., Lindstrom, M., & Nystedt, P. (2003). Investments in social capital- implications of social interactions for the production of health. *Social Science & Medicine, 56*(12), 2379–2390. https://doi.org/10.1016/S0277-9536(02)00242-3.

Bolten, N., Amini, A., Hao, Y., Ravichandran, V., Sephens, A., & Caspi, A. (2015). *Urban sidewalks: Visualization and routing for individuals with limited mobility. Urban GIS'15, Proceedings of the 1st International ACM SIGSPATIAL Workshop on Smart Cities and Urban Analytics* (pp. 122–125). Seattle: ACM Sigspatial International Conference on Advances in Geographic Information Systems (ACM Sigspatial 2015).

Booth, M. L., Bauman, A., Owen, N., & Gore, C. J. (1997). Physical activity preferences, preferred sources of assistance, and perceived barriers to increased activity among physical inactive Australians. *Preventive Medicine, 26*, 131–137.

Booth, F. W., Roberts, C. K., & Laye, M. J. (2014). Lack of exercise is a major cause of chronic disease. *Comprehensive Physiology, 2*(2), 1143–1211. https://doi.org/10.1002/cphy.c110025.

Caspersen, C. J., Powell, K. E., & Christenson, G. M. (1985). Physical activity, exercise, and physical fitness: Definitions and distinctions for health-related research. *public Health Reports, 100*(2), 126–131.

Clark, D. O. (1999). Identifying psychological, physiological and environmental barriers and facilitators to exercise among older low income adults. *Journal of Clinical Geropsychology, 5*, 51–62.

Cohen-Mansfield, J., Marx, M.S., Biddison, R., Curalnik J.M. (2004). Socio-environmental exercise preferences among older adults. *Prev Med, 38*(6), 804–811.

Cossman, J. S., James, W. L., Cosby, A. G., & Cossman, R. E. (2010). Underlying causes of the emerging nonmetropolitan mortality penalty. *American Journal of public Health, 100*(8), 1417–1419. https://doi.org/10.2105/AJPH.2009.174185.

Courtney-Long, E. A., Carroll, D. D., Zhang, Q., Stevens, A. C., Griffin-Blake, S., Armour, B. S., & Campbell, V. A. (2015). Prevalence of disability and disability type among adults, United States – 2013. *MMWR. Morbidity and Mortality Weekly Report, 64*, 777–783.

Davis, J. C., Best, J. R., Bryan, S., Li, L. C., Hsu, C. L., Gomez, C., Vertes, K., & Liu-Ambrose, T. (2015). Mobility is key predictor of change in well-being among older adults who experience falls: Evidence from the Vancouver Falls Prevention Clinic Cohort. *Archives of Physical Medicine and Rehabilitation, 96*(9), 1634–1640. https://doi.org/10.1016/apmr.201.02.033.

Damush, T.M., Perkins, S.M., Mikesky, A.E., Roberts, M., O'Dea, J. (2005). Motivational factors influencing older adults diagnoed with knee osteoarthiritis to join and maintain an exercise program. *J Aging Phys Act 13*(1), 45–60.

Dean, M., Harris, J. D., Regnard, C., & Hockley, J. (2006). Fatigue, drowsiness, lethargy and weakness. In *Symptom relief in palliative care* (pp. 101–108). Oxford: Radcliffe Publishing.

Disability Rights Education & Defense Fund. (2017). *Recreation and fitness centers*. Retrieved from https://dredf.org/legal-advocacy/laws/access-equals-opportunity/recreation-and-fitness-centers/

Dunn, D. S. (2016). Teaching about psychosocial aspects of disability: Emphasizing person–environment relations. *Teaching of Psychology, 43*(3), 255–262. https://doi.org/10.1177/0098628316649492.

Eberhardt, M. S., Ingraham D. D., Makuc D. M., Pamuk, E. R., Freid, V. M., Harper, S. B., Schoenbom, C. A., & Xia, H. (2001). *Health, United States, 2001 Urban and rural health chartbook. Health, United States, 2001 with rural and urban chartbook.* (NCHS Publication No. PHS 01–1232). Hyattsville: National Center for Health Statistics. Retrieved from https://www.cdc.gov/nchs/data/hus/hus01cht.pdf

Employers Network for Equality and Inclusion. (2014). *Disability: A research study on unconscious bias.* Retrieved from https://abilitymagazine.com/unconscious-bias-pwds-workplace/

Estabrooks, P. A., Lee, R. E., & Gyurcsik, N. C. (2003). Resources for physical activity participation: Does availability and accessibility differ by neighborhood socioeconomic status? *Annals of Behavioral Medicine, 25*(2), 100–104.

Fragoso, C. A., Beavers, D. P., Hankinson, J. L., Flynn, G., Berra, K., Kritchevsky, S. B., Liu, C. K., McDermott, M. M., Manini, T. M., Rejeski, W. J., & Gill, T. M. (2014). Respiratory impairment and dyspnea and their associations with physical inactivity and mobility in sedentary community-dwelling older persons. *Journal of American Geriatric Society, 62*(4), 622–628. https://doi.org/10.1111/jgs.12738.

Fransen, M., McConnell, S., Harmer, A. R., Van der Esch, M., Simic, M., & Bennell, K. L. (2015). Exercise for osteoarthritis of the knee: A Cochrane systematic review. *British Journal of Sports Medicine, 49*(24), 1554–1557. https://doi.org/10.1136/bjsports-2015-095424.

Frost, S. S., Goins, R. T., Hunter, R. H., Hooker, S. P., Bryant, L. L., Kruger, J., & Pluto, D. (2010). Effects of the built environment on physical activity of adults living in rural settings. *American Journal of Health Promotion, 24*(4), 267–283.

Garber, C. E., & Blissmer, B. J. (2002). The challenges of exercise in older adults. In P. M. Burban & D. Riebe (Eds.), *Promoting exercise and behavior change in older adults; Interventions with the transtheoretical model* (pp. 29–56). New York: Springer.

Giles-Corti, B., Knuiman, M., Timperio, A., Van Niel, K., Pikora, T. J., Bull, F. C., Shilton, T., & Bulsara, M. (2008). Evaluation of the implementation of a state government community design policy aimed at increasing local walking: Design issues and baseline results from RESIDE, Perth Western Australia. *Preventive Medicine, 46*(1), 46–54.

González, K., Fuentes, J., & Márquez, J. L. (2017). Physical inactivity, sedentary behavior and chronic diseases. *Korean Journal of Family Medicine, 38*(3), 11–115. https://doi.org/10.4082/kjfm.2017.38.3.111.

Grembowski, D., Patrick, D., Diehr, P., Durham, M., Beresford, S., Kay, E., & Hecht, J. (1993). Self-efficacy and health behavior among older adults. *Journal of Health and Social Behavior, 34*(2), 89–104.

Groessl, E. J., Kaplan, R. M., Rejeski, W. I., Katula, J. A., King, A. C., Frierson, G., Glynn, N. W., Hsu, F., Walkup, M., & Pahor, M. (2007). Health-related quality of life in older adults at risk for disability. *American Journal of Preventative Medicine, 33*, 214–218. https://doi.org/10.1016/j.amepre.2007.04.031.

Grossman, M. D., & Stewart, A. L. (2003). "You aren't going to get better by just sitting around". Physical activity perceptions, motivations and barriers in adults 75 years of age or older. *American Journal of Geriatric Cardiology, 12*, 33–37.

Guralnik, J. M., Fried, L. P., & Salive, M. E. (1996). Disability as a *public* health outcome in the aging population. *Annual Reviews public Health, 17*, 25–46.

Hays, L. M., & Clark, D. O. (1999). Correlates of physical activity in a sample of older adults with Type 2 diabetes. *Diabetes Care, 22*, 706–712.

He, W., & Larsen, L. J. (2014). *Older Americans with a disability: 2008–2012: American Community Survey reports*. Retrieved from https://www.census.gov/content/dam/Census/library/publications/2014/acs/acs-29.pdf

Healthcare.gov. (2018). *Federal poverty level (FPL)*. Retrieved from https://www.healthcare.gov/glossary/federal-poverty-level-FPL/

Hirvensalo, M., Lampinen, P., & Rantanen, T. (1998). Physical exercise in old age: An eight-year-follow-up study on involvement, motives, and obstacles among persons age 65–84. *Journal of Aging and Physical Activity, 6*, 157–168.

Hirvensalo, M., Rantanen, T., & Heikkinen, E. (2000). Mobility difficulties and physical activity as predictors of mortality and loss of independence in the community-living older population. *Journal of the American Geriatrics Society, 48*, 493–498.

Hirvensalo, M., Heikkinen, E., Lintunen, T., & Rantanen, T. (2003). The effect of advice by health care professionals on increasing physical activity of older people. *Scandinavian Journal of Medicine and Science in Sports, 13*, 231–236.

Iezzoni, L. I. (2011). Eliminating health and health care disparities among the growing population of people with disabilities. *Health Affair, 2011*(30), 1947–1956. https://doi.org/10.1377/hlthaff.2011.0613.

Iezzoni, L. I., & O'Day, B. L. (2006). *More than ramps. A guide to improving health care quality and access for people with disabilities*. New York: Oxford University Press.

Iezzoni, L. I., McCarthy, E. P., Davis, R. B., & Siebens, H. (2000). Mobility impairments and use of screening and preventive services. *American Journal of public Health, 90*(2000), 955–961.

Iezzoni, L. I., Mcarthy, E. P., Davis, R. B., & Siebens, H. (2001). Mobility difficulties are not only a problem of old age. *Journal of General Internal Medicine, 16*(4), 234–243. https://doi.org/10.1046/j.1525-1497.2001.016004235.x.

Jensen, M. P., Smith, A. E., Alschuler, K. N., Gillanders, D. T., Amtmann, D., & Molton, I. R. (2016). The role of pain acceptance on function in individuals with disabilities: A longitudinal study. *Pain, 157*(2016), 247–254.

Johnson, M. J., Stoelzle, H. Y., Finco, K. L., Foss, S. E., & Carstens, K. (2012). ADA compliance and accessibility of fitness facilities in Western Wisconsin. *Topics in Spinal Cord Injury Rehabilitation, 18*(40), 340–353. https://doi.org/10.1310/sci1804-340.

Jones, G. C., & Sinclair, L. B. (2008). Multiple health disparities among minority adults with mobility limitations: An application of the ICF framework and codes. *Disability & Rehabilitation, 30*, 901–915.

Kanis, J. A., Melton, J., Christiansen, C., Johnston, C. C., & Khaltaev, N. (1994). The diagnosis of osteoporosis. *Journal of Bone and Mineral Research, 9*(8), 1137–1141. https://doi.org/10.1002/jbmr.5650090802.

Katzmarzyk, P.T. (2010). Physical activity, sedentary behavior, and health: Paradigm paralysis or paradigm shift? *Diabetes, 59*(11), 2717–2725. https://doi.org/10.2337/db10-0822.

Kelley, G. A., Kelley, K. S., & Hootman, J. M. (2015). Effects of exercise on depression in adults with arthritis: A systematic review with meta-analysis of randomized controlled trials. *Arthritis Research & Therapy, 3*(17), 21. https://doi.org/10.1186/s13057-015-0533-5.

Kerr, C., Bottomley, C., Shingler, S., Giangregorio, L., de Freitas, H. M., Patel, C., Randall, S., & Gold, D. T. (2017). The importance of physical function to people with osteoporosis. *Osteoporos International, 28*(5), 1597–1607. https://doi.org/10.1007/s00198-017-3911-9.

King, A. C., Castro, C., Wilcox, S., Eyler, A. A., Sallis, J. F., & Brownson, R. C. (2000). Personal and environmental factors associated with physical inactivity among different racial-ethnic groups on U.S. middle-aged and older-aged women. *Health Psychology, 19*, 354–364.

Krahn, G.L., Walker, D.K, Correa-De-Araujo, R. (2015). Persons with disabilities as an unrecognized health disparity population. Am J Public Health, 105 Suppl2, 198–206. https://doi.org/10.2105/AJPH.2014.302182.

Kriegsman, D. M., Deeg, D. J., van Eijk, J. T., Penninx, B. W., & Boeke, A. J. (1997). Do disease specific characteristics add to the explanation of mobility limitations in patients with different chronic conditions? A study in The Netherlands. *Journal of Epidermiol Community Health, 51*(6), 676–685.

Leitzmann, M.F., Park, Y., Blair, A., Ballard-Barbash, R., Mouw, T., Hollenbeck, A.R. & Schatzkin, A. (2007). Physical activity recommendations and decreased risk of mortality. *Arch Intern Med. 167*(22), 2453–2460.

Lewis, K. (2017). *2016 disability statistics annual report*. Durham: University of New Hampshire. Retrieved from https://disabilitycompendium.org/sites/default/files/user-uploads/2016_AnnualReport.pdf

Lin, N. (1982). Social resources and instrumental action. In P. Marsden & N. Lin (Eds.), *Social structure and network analysis* (pp. 131–145). Beverly Hills: *Sage*.

Lin, N. (2001). *Social capital: A theory of social structure and action*. New York: Cambridge University Press.

Lin, N., Fu, Y., & Hsung, R. M. (2001). The position generator: Measurement techniques for investigations of social capital. In N. Lin, K. Cook, & R. S. Burt (Eds.), *Social capital: Theory and research* (pp. 57–81). New York: Walter de Gruyter.

Ling, S. M., Fried, L. P., Garrett, E. S., Fam, M. Y., Rantanen, T., & Bathon, J. M. (2003). Knee osteoarthritis compromise early mobility function: The Women's Health and Aging Study II. *Journal of Rheumatology, 30*, 114–120.

Ling, S. M., Xue, Q. L., Simonsick, E. M., Tian, J., Bandeen-Roche, K., Fried, L. P., & Bathon, J. M. (2006). Transitions to mobility difficulty associated with lower extremity osteoarthritis in high functioning older women: Longitudinal data from the Women's Health and Aging Study II. *Arthritis and Rheumatism, 55*, 248–255.

Liu, G. G., Xue, X., Yu, C., & Wang, Y. (2016). How does social capital matter to the health status of older adults? Evidence from the China Health and Retirement Longitudinal Survey. *Economics & Human Biology, 22*, 177–189. https://doi.org/10.1016/j.ehb.2016.04.003.

Mayo Clinic. (2010). *Arthritis*. Retrieved from https://healthletter.mayoclinic.com/secure/pdf/SRAR.pdf

Mayo Clinic. (2018). *Heart disease*. Retrieved from https://www.mayoclinic.org/diseases-conditions/heart-disease/symptoms-causes/syc-20353118

McPherson, B. D., & Yamaguchi, Y. (1995). Aging and active lifestyles: A cross-cultural analysis of factors influencing the participation of middle-aged and elderly cohorts. In S. Harris, E. Heikkinen, & W. S. Harris (Eds.), *Physical activity, aging and sports, Part 2: Psychology, motivation and programs* (Vol. IV, pp. 293–308). Albany: Center for the Study of Aging.

Metz, D. (2000). Mobility of older people and their quality of life. *Transport Policy, 7*, 149–152.

Mottram, S., Peat, G., Thomas, E., Wilkie, R., & Croft, P. (2008). Patterns of pain and mobility limitation in older people: Cross-sectional findings from a population survey of 18,497 adults aged 50 years and over. *Quality of Life Research, 17*(4), 529–539.

National Center for Health Statistics. (2016). *Health, United States, 2016: With chartbook on long-term trends in health.* Retrieved from https://www.cdc.gov/nchs/data/hus/hus16.pdf#042

North Carolina Office of Disability and Health & The Center for Universal Design. (2008). *Removing barriers to health clubs and fitness facilities: A guide to accommodating all members, including people with disabilities and older adults*. Retrieved from http://fpg.unc.edu/sites/fpg.unc.edu/files/resources/other-resources/NCODH_RemovingBarriersToHealthClubs.pdf

O'Neill, K., & Reid, G. (1991). Perceived barriers to physical activity by older adults. *Canadian Journal of public Health, 82*, 392–396.

Office of Disease Prevention and Health Promotion. (n.d.-a). *Health disparities*. Retrieved from https://www.healthypeople.gov/

Office of Disease Prevention and Health Promotion. (n.d.-b) *Viewing latest disparity data for: NWS-10.4 obesity among children and adolescents (percent, 2–19 years)*. Retrieved from https://www.healthypeople.gov/hdwidget/embed/disparaties?objid=4928

Parks, S., Housemann, R., & Brownson, R. (2003). Differential correlates of physical activity in urban and rural adults of various socioeconomic backgrounds in the United States. *Journal of Epidemiology & Community Health, 57*(1), 29–35. https://doi.org/10.1136/jech.57.1.29.

Rantakokko, M., Manty, M., & Rantanen, T. (2013). Mobility decline in old age. *Exercise and Sport Sciences Reviews, 41*, 19–25. https://doi.org/10.1097/JES.0b013e3182556f1e.

Rantanen, T. (2013). Promoting mobility in older people. *Journal of Preventive Medicine & public Health, 46*(Suppl 1), S50–S54. https://doi.org/10.3961/jpmph.2013.46.S.S50. https://www.ncbi.nlm.nih.gov/pmc/articles/PMC3567319/.

Rashinaho, M., Hirvensalo, M., Leinonen, R., Lintunen, T., & Rantanen, T. (2006). Motives for and barriers to physical activity among older adults with mobility limitations. *Journal of Aging and Physical Activity, 15*, 90–102.

Rehabilitation Act of 1973. (1973). 29 U.S.C. §701 et. seq.

Resnick, B., Zimmermann, S. I., Orwig, D., Furstenberg, A. L., & Magaziner, J. (2000). Outcome expectations for exercise scale: Utility and psychometrics. *Journals of Gerontology. Series B, Psychological Sciences and Social Sciences, 55*(6), S352–S356.

Rimmer, J. H., & Rowland, J. L. (2008). Health promotion for people with disabilities: Implications for empowering the person and promoting disability-friendly environments. *American Journal of Lifestyle Medicine, 2*(209), 409–420. https://doi.org/10.1177/1559827608317397.

Rimmer, J. H., Riley, B., Wang, E., & Rauworth, A. (2005). Accessibility of health clubs for people with mobility disabilities and visual impairments. *American Journal of public Health, 95*(11), 2022–2028. https://doi.org/10.2105/AJPH.2004.051870.

Rosso, A. L., Tabb, L. P., Grubesic, T. H., Taylor, J. A., & Michael, Y. L. (2014). Neighborhood social capital and achieved mobility of older adults. *Journal of Aging and Health, 26*(8), 1301–1319. https://doi.org/10.1177/0898264314523447.

Sallis, J. F., Hovell, M. F., Hofstetter, C. R., Elder, J. P., Hackley, M., Caspersen, C. J., & Powell, K. E. (1990). Distance between homes and exercise facilities related to frequency of exercise among San Diego residents. *public Health Reports, 105*(2), 179–185.

Satariano, W. A., Haight, T. J., & Tager, I. B. (2000). Reasons given by older people for limitations or avoidance of leisure time physical activity. *Journal of the American Geriatrics Society, 48*, 505–512.

Seguin, R., Connor, L., Nelson, M., LaCroix, A., & Elridge, G. (2014). Understanding barriers and facilitators to healthy eating and active living in rural communities. *Journal of Nutrition and Metabolism, 2014*, 1–8. https://doi.org/10.1155/2014/146502.

Semega, J. L., Fontenot, K. R., & Kollar, M. A. (2017). *Income and poverty in the United States: 2016*. Retrieved from https://www.census.gov/library/publications/2017/demo/p60-259.html

Sharby, N., Martire, K., & Iverson, M. D. (2015). Decreasing health disparities for people with disabilities through improved communication strategies and awareness. *International Journal of Environmental Research and Public Health, 12*(3), 3301–3316.

Smith, A. K., Cenzer, I. S., Knight, S. J., Puntillo, K. A., Widera, E., Williams, B. A., Boscardin, W. J., & Covinsky, K. E. (2010). The epidemiology of pain during the last two years of life. *Annals of Internal Medicine, 153*(9), 563–569.

Song, J., Chang, R. W., & Dunlop, D. D. (2006). Population impact of arthritis on disability in older adults. *Arthritis and Rheumatism, 55*, 248–255.

Stonerock, G. L., Hoffman, B. M., Smith, P. J., & Blumenthal, J. A. (2015). Exercise as a treatment for anxiety: Systematic review and analysis. *Annals of Behavioral Medicine, 49*(4), 542–556. https://doi.org/10.1007/s12160-014-9685-9.

Stubbs, B., Schofield, P., & Patchay, S. (2016). Mobility limitations and fall-related factors contributed to the reduced health-related quality of life in older adults with chronic musculoskeletal pain. *Pain Practice, 16*(1), 80–89. https://doi.org/10.1111/papr.12264.

Telci, E. A., Yagci, N., CAN, T., & Cavlak, U. (2013). The impact of chronic low back pain on physical performance, fear avoidance beliefs, and depressive symptoms: A comparative study on Turkish elderly population. *Pakistan Journal of Medical Sciences, 29*(2), 560–564.

U.S. Department of Health and Human Services, Centers for Disease Control and Prevention, National Center for Health Statistics. (2015). *Summary health statistics; National Health Initiative Survey, 2015- Table A-10a*. Retrieved from https://ftp.cdc.gov/pub/Health_Statistics/NCHS/NHIS/SHS/2015_SHS_Table_A-10.pdf

U.S. Department of Health and Human Services, Office of Disease Prevention and Health Promotion. (n.d.). *Healthy people 2020 progress review*. Retrieved from https://www.healthypeople.gov/sites/default/files/hp2020_dh_and_hrqol_wb_progress_review_presentation.pdf

United States Access and Design Board. (n.d.). *Chapter 1: Using the ADA standards*. Retrieved from https://www.access-board.gov/guidelines-and-standards/buildings-and-sites/about-the-ada-standards/guide-to-the-ada-standards/chapter-1-using-the-ada-standards#b

United States Census Bureau. (2014). *Percentage of County population age 65 and over with a disability: 2008–2012*. Retrieved from https://www.census.gov/content/dam/Census/newsroom/releases/2014/cb14-218_graphic.jpg

United States Census Bureau. (2016). *2016 American community survey 1-year estimates*. Retrieved from https://factfinder.census.gov/faces/tableservices/jsf/pages/productview.xhtml?src=bkmk

U.S. Department of Health and Human Services. (2014). Summary health statistics for U.S. adults: National Health Interview Survey, 2012. Retrieved from, https://www.cdc.gov/nchs/data/series/sr_10/sr10_260.pdf

United States Centers for Disease Control and Prevention. (2015). Summary health statistics: National health interview survey, 2015- Table A-10a. Age-adjusted percentages (with standard errors) of difficulties in physical functioning among adults aged 18 and over, by selected characteristics, United States, 2015. Retrieved from https://ftp.cdc.gov/pub/Health_Statistics/NCHS/NHIS/SHS/2015_SHS_Table_A-10.pdf

United States Centers for Disease Control and Prevention. (2016). *Figure 5-Ternds in obesity prevalence among adults aged 20 and over (age adjusted) and youth aged 2–19 years: United States, 1999–2000 through 2015–2016*. Retrieved from https://www.cdc.gov/nchs/data/databriefs/db288_table.pdf#5

United States Department of Health and Human Services. (2008). *Physical activity guidelines advisory committee: Physical activity guidelines advisory committee report*. Retrieved from https://health.gov/paguidelines/report/

United States Department of Health and Human Services. (2017). *U.S. Federal poverty guidelines used to determine financial eligibility for certain Federal programs*. Retrieved from https://aspe.hhs.gov/poverty-guidelines

United States Department of Justice. (2010). *2010 ADA standards for accessible design*. Retrieved from https://www.ada.gov/regs2010/2010ADAStandards/2010ADAstandards.htm

United States Department of Justice Civil Rights Division. (n.d.-a). *Public accommodations and commercial facilities (Title III)*. Retrieved from https://www.ada.gov/ada_title_III.htm

United States Department of Justice Civil Rights Division. (n.d.-b). *Settlement agreement between the United States of America and the family YMC of greater Augusta under the Americans with Disabilities Act*. Retrieved from https://www.ada.gov/ymca_augusta.html

United States Department of Justice Civil Rights Division. (n.d.-c). *Settlement agreement between the United States of America and the Norwich family YMCA, Norwich, New York under the Americans with Disabilities Act*. Retrieved from https://www.ada.gov/norwich_ymca_sa.html

United States Department of Justice Civil Rights Division. (n.d.-d). *United States of America v. Total Lifetime Care Health & Fitness Club, Inc.-Consent decree*. Retrieved from https://www.ada.gov/tlc-health-fitness.htm

United States Department of Justice Civil Rights Division. (n.d.-e). *Settlement agreement between The United States of America and The YMCA of Reading and Berks County*. Retrieved from https://www.ada.gov/reading_berks_ymca_sa.html

US Department of Health and Human Services. Healthy People 2020. (2020) Health-Related Quality of Life and Well Being. Available at: http://www.healthypeople.gov/2020/topics-objectives/topic/health-related-quality-of-life-wellbeing

Vancampfort, D., Koyanagi, A., Ward, P. B., Rosenbaum, S., Schuch, F. B., Mugisha, J., Richards, J., Firth, J., & Stubbs, B. (2017). Chronic physical conditions, multimorbidity and physical activity across 46 low- and middle-income countries. *International Journal of Behavioral Nutrition and Physical Activity, 14*(6), 1–13.

Veldhuijzen van Zanten, J.J., Rouse, P.C., Hale, E.D., Btoumanis, N., Metsios, G.S., Duda, J.L, & Kitas, G.D. (2015). Perceived barriers, facilitators and benefits for regular physical activity and exercise in patients with rheumatoid arthritis: A review of the literature. *Sports Med 45*(10), 1401–1412. doi: https://doi.org/10.1007/s40279-015-0362-2.

Webber, S. C., Porter, M. M., & Menec, V. H. (2010). Mobility in older adults: A comprehensive framework. *The Gerontologist, 50*(4), 443–450. https://doi.org/10.1093/geront/gnq013.

Whaley, D. E., & Ebbeck, V. (1997). Older adult's constraints to participation in structured exercise classes. *Journal of Aging and Physical Activity, 5*, 190–212.

Wilcox, S., Castro, C., King, A. C., Housemann, R., & Brownson, R. C. (2000). Determinants of leisure time physical activity in rural compared with urban older and ethnically diverse women in the United States. *Journal of Epidemiological Community Health, 54*, 667–672.

Wiley & Rein. (2010). *ADA and the ADA Standards for Accessible Design legal issues and liability reduction*. Retrieved from https://www.wileyrein.com/newsroom-articles-2111.html

Wiley & Rein, LLP (2011). ADA and the ADA Standards for Accessible Design legal issues and liability reduction. Retrieved from https://www.wileyrein.com/newsroom-articles-2111.html

Wilson, K., Getzel, E., & Brown, T. (2000). Enhancing the post-secondary campus climate for students with disabilities. *Journal of Vocational Rehabilitation, 14*(1), 37–50.

World Health Organization. (2007). *Global age-friendly cities: A guide*. Retrieved from http://www.who.int/ageing/publications/Global_age_friendly_cities_Guide_English.pdf

World Health Organization. (2008). *International classification of functioning, disability and health*. Retrieved from http://www.who.int/classifications/icf/site/index.cfm

World Health Organization. (2010). *Global recommendations on physical activity for health*. Retrieved from http://apps.who.int/iris/bitstream/handle/10665/44399/9789241599979_eng.pdf;jsessionid=4B3EFC7C77485A25C095F2CA04152FDA?sequence=1

World Health Organization. (2017a). *Global recommendations on physical activity for health*. Retrieved from http://www.who.int/dietphysicalactivity/publications/9789241599979/en/

World Health Organization. (2017b). *Physical activity*. Retrieved from http://www.who.int/dietphysicalactivity/pa/en/

World Health Organization. (2017c). *International classification of functioning, disability and health*. Retrieved from http://apps.who.int/classifications/icfbrowser/

World Health Organization. (2018). *Disability and health*. Retrieved from http://www.who.int/en/news-room/fact-sheets/detail/disability-and-health

Yeom, H. A., Fleury, J., & Keller, C. (2008). Risk factors for mobility limitation in community-dwelling older adults: A social ecological perspective. *Geriatric Nursing, 29*, 133–140.

Yousefian, A., Ziller, E., Swartz, J., & Hartley, D. (2009). Active living for rural youth: Addressing physical inactivity in rural communities. *Journal of Public Health Management and Practice, 15*(3), 223–231.

Chapter 11
A Model of Human Cognitive Biases and Complacency Toward Opportunities for the Disabled

David Hollar

Abbreviations

ADA	Americans with Disabilities Act
AIMFREE	Accessibility Instruments Measuring Fitness and Recreation Environments
AUC	Area under the curve
EDF	Électricité de France
GLO	Gulonolactone oxidase
IDEA	Individuals with Disabilities Education Act
IEP	Individualized Education Plan
NCHPAD	National Center on Health, Physical Activity, and Disability
NIDILRR	National Institute on Disability, Independent Living, and Rehabilitation Research
RERC	Rehabilitation Engineering Research Center
RRTC	Rehabilitation Research and Training Center
ROC	Receiver Operator Characteristic
SCI	Spinal cord injury
TBI	Traumatic brain injury
UD	Universal design
UDL	Universal Design for Learning

11.1 Introduction

In 2006, the French utility company EDF (Électricité de France) ran a *Diversité* commercial that simulated living in a world where every aspect of society was constructed around disability accommodations (e.g., a library with only Braille books). Similarly, the Taiwanese TC Bank in 2011 ran *Dream Rangers*, an inspiring

D. Hollar (✉)
Health Administration, Pfeiffer University, Misenheimer, NC, USA
e-mail: David.Hollar@pfeiffer.edu

D. Hollar (ed.), *Advances in Exercise and Health for People With Mobility Limitations*, https://doi.org/10.1007/978-3-319-98452-0_11

commercial about five older adult men with serious health issues who decided to live and circumnavigate their entire country by motorcycle. These efforts promote inclusion in society for people who often are stigmatized and marginalized, plus they demonstrate social responsibility and positive marketing strategies for the respective businesses.

Nevertheless, the move to promote full independence and social integration for people living with mobility and other disabilities is both sporadic and daunting. The reasons for this situation are myriad, but they ultimately involve individual and group psychological dynamics that tend to conceptually distance that which is different, it's somebody else's problem, or that we have made token efforts to adequately attack the problem. Dynamic behavioral change is difficult, requires substantial energy and commitment, and must be sustained (Hollar 2017a). Our continuing task is to promote health and opportunities for every person and their situation, including the removal of health, exercise, and nutrition barriers facing people who are living with mobility limitations and other disabilities.

For people living with disabilities, it is easy for public perception to falsely view their capabilities and ultimate outcomes as limited. There can be the tendency to feel sorry for them or, conversely, to view them as a burden upon society and its *apparent* limited resources. Such false presuppositions lie at the center of the self-worth movement in education and human development (Covington 1992). Most of us at some point in time encounter people in positions of authority who belittle our abilities and who attempt to limit our prospects. The situation is multiply compounded for people living with disabilities. Those of us who *currently* are not living with significant disabilities have the task of removing the conceptual barriers against disability and opening the possibilities for every person.

People tend to resist change unless it is captivating and involves compelling advantages to individual and group success or survival. We see the rapid, even addictive, expansion of smart telephone technologies to several billion people in less than 10 years because these companies have miniaturized the many technological components and maximized their capabilities across various life areas. Such creativity creates a dramatic force for public demand. The exponentiation of applications on these devices offers benefits for everyone, including people living with disabilities. However, from a physical perspective, this technology has limitations, and other technological areas and especially human institutions.

In an ideal world, everybody would stop to help any person who was suffering. Such actions involve the setting aside of continuous overlapping time and resources to affect a multitude of individual conditions and situations to the point of overwhelming our systems from performing their existing missions. We have established social support institutions to help people for various categories of events in their lives. Nevertheless, most of these events are acute in nature. We are much less prepared to deal with the diversity of health and other life conditions that are unique to each person and that often are chronic. Only recently have health-care systems moved to preventative care with the promotion of improved exercise and nutrition in populations, this being a reactionary response to the market forces of escalating health-care costs and prevalent unhealthy behaviors driven by individuals and other market forces that reinforce these behaviors.

Reaching the needs of every single person on earth is impossible from a practical perspective. However, maximizing opportunities and access for people with and without disabilities can be achieved when our institutions commit to change, innovation, and efficiency, but moreover engaging in systems-based thinking. A systems approach can accentuate such innovation and provide improved delivery systems worldwide. Such an approach would go far beyond the sporadic volunteer and other charitable work that exists today. Instead, it would be a naturally included component of the way that our institutions and systems function, not from more costs but from the synergy of individual supports within organizational/systemic functioning.

From a broader, evolutionary perspective, Wilson (1975, 1984, 2012) emphasized that 19 eusocial species exist, species that live together for multiple generations in organized communities, the young are protected, and labor is divided to promote reproductive success and survival. Sixteen of these species are insects, including the ants and honeybees, but the only eusocial primate is our own species. Nevertheless, Wilson (2012) argued that our own species' social systems are highly inefficient, even dysfunctional, compared to other eusocial species because our cognitive processes are wired for mistrust and conflict, our institutions are outmoded, and we have developed expanding technologies that are outpacing our decision-making processes and institutions to wisely use the technologies. For our perspective on exercise for people living with mobility limitations, we here highlight Wilson's observations with respect to our resistance to major systemic changes in our thinking and systems aimed to recognize the needs of this population.

11.2 Decision-Making Theories in Synopsis

Festinger (1957) demonstrated that people naturally engage in decision justification even when they make bad decisions, a phenomenon that he termed cognitive dissonance, a nonrational decision heuristic that relieves the mental conflict between actions and outcomes. We prefer to believe that a decision has been good even when the outcomes might be negative; therefore, we seek the positive aspects of the outcomes for highlights. Staw (1976; see also Hollar et al. 2000) showed that individuals and groups tend to invest and reinvest time, resources, and finances into losing outcomes, a phenomenon termed escalation behavior, also called the sunk-cost effect. Individuals and groups engage in group-think and self-justifying arguments to continue the negative course of action. Multiple social and environmental forces (e.g., saving face with respect to prevailing public opinion) can drive such behaviors (Hollar et al. 2000). Only gradually have organizational behaviorists started to stress the importance of allowing failure for innovation and culture changes to occur within organizations (Brown 2009; Drucker 1985; Kotter 1995; Kotter and Rathgeber 2005, 2016). Teamwork in health care has followed the same approach in response to the 2000 Institute of Medicine report on hospital deaths due to medical errors (Kohn et al. 2000), although medical errors appear to be increasing dramatically due to the related complexity of forces that are impacting health care (Makary and Daniel 2016). Newton et al. (2008) discovered that several large cohorts of medical students showed declining levels of empathy toward patients during their medical school training.

Both Janis and Mann (1977) and Dawes (1988) highlighted various types of such nonrational behaviors and offered various decision heuristics to improve individual and group decision-making processes. Whereas researchers such as Damasio (1994) correctly identified decision-making as a combined cognitive-emotional process, Hollar (2016) found that the emotional construct of empathy may be elusive and may act within a relative relatedness distance gradient, albeit with less empathy for related individuals then increasing and gradually declining for those who are relationally distance-removed from the decision-maker. This finding is consistent with Nowak et al. (2010) finding that altruism operates by complex social interaction patterns between members of a group rather than from genetic relatedness alone. The empathy component is critical from a decision-making/innovation viewpoint because we are cognitively overwhelmed with information and areas of concern such that we can lose focus on the needs of millions of Americans and hundreds of millions of people worldwide who could benefit from technology and improved health promotional facilities. Just in the United States alone, there are at least 1.7 million new incidences of traumatic brain injury (TBI) each year, with a long-term TBI disability prevalence rate of at least 3.2 million people (Ma et al. 2014; Waxweiler et al. 1995; Zaloshnja et al. 2008)

Assessments of human reasoning utilizing alternative decision scenarios show that most people have poor statistical reasoning skills, and they have difficulty choosing logical, beneficial choices, a phenomenon that occurs even among highly educated professionals (Kahneman 2011; Kahneman and Tversky 1979; Tversky and Kahneman 1974, 1981, 1986). Kahneman and Tversky (1979) showed that people tend to place greater value on potential losses than on potential gains, again irrespective of educational or social background. Kahneman (2003) distinguished perception/intuition (System 1 thinking), which is fast and effortless, versus reasoning (System 2 thinking), which is slow and rule-governed, as two principal types of reasoning. Education should focus on improving statistical reasoning involved in intuitive decision processes, although no educators or scientists have offered any effective curricula to improve human thinking (Nickerson 2004). This decision-making weakness is extremely applicable to moral reasoning, as most people fail to map out alternative consequences of their actions, a process that can be improved with careful reflection and a commitment to a higher cause (Graham 1965; Schaeffer 1968/1990; Solzhenitsyn 1973).

Likewise, philosophers for thousands of years since Aristotle (2012) have noted numerous arguments of reasoning (i.e., fallacies) that lead even highly educated people to erroneous decisions. Swets et al. (2000) developed a decision-making matrix, used in statistical analysis and Receiver Operator Characteristic (ROC) diagnostics, for testing decision tools and diagnostic approaches versus real outcomes. They found that triangulation of multiple decision tools leads to improved assessments of situations (i.e., improved prediction) on ROC curves.

Nevertheless, people lead complicated lives and are bombarded with many sources of information. Consequently, poor decision-making skills persist. Besides poor decision-making skills (Kahneman 2003), people across cultures tend to focus upon subtle aspects of social status differences. Lucas and Phelan (2012) found social distance effects for people with intellectual and physical disabilities that lead to stigmatization. The World Health Organization (2011) cited stigmatization as a continuing barrier to opportunities for people living with disabilities. Goffman (1959, 1963) outlined the effects of stigmatization upon individuals, with the results including long-term labeling and social ostracism for reduced life outcomes.

People living with disabilities are more highly concentrated in rural and low socioeconomic regions of the United States, areas many of which have been identified by the US Department of Health and Human Services to be Health Professional Shortage Areas (HPSAs) and Medically Underserved Areas (MUAs) (Hollar 2017b; Iezzoni et al. 2006; Mendoza-Vasconez et al. 2016). People living in rural areas have less access to primary and especially specialty physicians, accessible health-care facilities with updated equipment, accessible exercise facilities, and adequate nutrition as well as variety of dietary sources (e.g., food deserts). Such deprivation due to locality can lead to further stigmatization through the separation of "haves" from "have nots." The situation is very problematic in Third World Countries that have less transportation infrastructure and distributed/coordinated health-care systems. Even in other Western nations, lack of healthcare access for people with disabilities in rural and low socioeconomic areas represents a substantial health disparity problem (Popplewell et al. 2014). Myriad social and economic forces have produced this situation despite substantial federal efforts in the United States to promote increased health-care providers and facilities in rural areas. The reality exists that health providers gravitate to medical centers in major metropolitan areas that offer greater intellectual, leisure, and cultural benefits, along with infrastructure and population concentrations. Furthermore, exercise facilities and nutrition follow the same market forces that drive movements to cities. Rural areas are left with a poor business/industrial base that cannot provide a comparable infrastructure for transportation, rapid access and diagnosis of conditions, and other resources (e.g., exercise, nutrition) to rural residents. This creates less access for people living with mobility limitations and other disabilities, plus it increases the probability of increased acquired disabilities and secondary conditions due to greater epidemiological latency times from disease/condition occurrence to diagnosis and treatment.

Case and Deaton (2015) documented that between 1999 and 2013, the US Caucasian population experienced increased mortality for the first time in many decades, in contrast to other racial/ethnic groups. The largest increases in mortality occurred among less educated people across all race/ethnic groups, and the primary circumstances of death involved substance abuse-related conditions and/or suicide. The situation is much higher in rural areas, where Stein et al. (2017) demonstrated significantly higher mortality rates, especially by overdose, poisonings, and suicide, for younger (age 25–54) Caucasians from 1999 to 2015. Ivey-Stephenson et al.

(2017) corroborated the increased rural suicide rates across this same time period for both males and females across different race/ethnicities, although males experienced significantly higher rates compared to females, and both Native American and Caucasian rural populations experienced dramatic increases in suicide rates.

Whereas the interface between disability and these recently discovered trends in rural health has not been extensively explored, we do know that people living with multiple sclerosis and spinal cord injury have significantly higher suicide rates than the general population, possibly higher for people living with intellectual and developmental disabilities as well (Giannini et al. 2010). Furthermore, we do know that people with disabilities are more likely to live in rural and health underserved areas (Hollar 2017b). Krueger (2017) implicated long-term trends in the loss of manufacturing jobs, demographic changes, and the Great Recession of 2008 that have dramatically and negatively impacted the health of American workers, especially males in rural and other affected areas. These negative effects include the opioid crisis, and Krueger (2017) strongly recommended public health interventions to assist these affected populations. Bor (2017) cited these conditions and the declining health of rural US populations as a major factor that impacted the 2016 presidential election, as impacted populations voiced a need for support and change in their life conditions from the federal government.

Hollar (2013) and Hollar and Lewis (2015) demonstrated that people living with mobility limitations experienced significantly higher risks for obesity, allostatic load, and associated negative heart age differentials compared to people without disabilities. The most likely causes for these poor health outcomes include lack of access to exercise facilities and assistive exercise devices, lack of access to prompt health care, lack of access to good nutrition, lack of transportation, and lack of social/community supports, including employment and friendship (Hollar 2013; Hollar and Moore 2004; Nary 2004).

The problem of poor health outcomes exists not only among people living with cognitive disabilities, but with *people in general*. There has been extensive research on systems and devices to help people living with disabilities but little translation of such research into actual, affordable devices that dramatically improve significant aspects of these people's lives. We here suggest that it is humanity's decision-making limitations/disabilities as a whole that has resulted in a lack of proper attention to the needs of people living with mobility limitations and with other disabilities. As with three of Kotter's Eight Stages of Change model (Kotter 1995; Kotter and Rathgeber 2005), we must create a sense of *urgency* for the widespread need to help people living with disabilities. Likewise, we must build *buy-in* from leaders and policymakers as well as must be *relentless/persistent* with our efforts to innovate and to advance change. Maintaining the urgency probably is the most critical component, as our species' cognitive decision-making limitations (shall we call it a species' disability?) tend to prevent us from making the dramatic changes that can benefit so many people.

As an illustration on this point, *Homo sapiens* represents a relatively homogeneous species, although there is wide variation in numerous traits given a historical trend toward migration and admixture of populations. Williams (1956) calculated that for every 100 genes (and humans have at least 50,000 operational genes), the probability of having zero abnormal genes is 0.95^{100}, or less than 1%. Consequently, every person carries at least several abnormal genes, either relatively harmless in a homozygous incompletely penetrant state or masked in heterozygosity, and is therefore mutant (Eckhardt 2001). Additionally, all humans, many primates, and guinea pigs are homozygous for the lethal allele conferring gulonolactone oxidase (GLO) deficiency (Nishikimi et al. 1994), a condition easily treated by dietary intake of L-ascorbate (vitamin C). Variation is the rule, not the exception, and normative ideologies are fallacious in both ethical and evolutionary perspectives. Furthermore, the immediate ramifications of every person's uniqueness (i.e., mutantness) and, therefore, disability of one type or another leads to a clear solution for which we have the unique capability: we modify the environment of each person for their optimal success. Located at the core of modern human developmental psychophysiology (Covington 1992), this philosophy makes sense to most people, but we must promote the urgency to truly reach each individual's needs, some of whom have greater physical, environmental, and social barriers to overcome than do others. We are not talking about outlandish whims of some individuals that too often make the headline news and talk radio/television venues, but genuine physical, psychological, and other health needs that currently are only minimally met by our health systems.

We take for granted the occasional muscle tear, fracture, or nearsightedness that we experience in daily living. These are acute, temporary, or easily treated disabilities, just as with our dietary supplementation of vitamin C for our lethal gene mutation described above. It is a very different situation for someone living with a neural tube birth defect, spinal cord injury from an accident, stroke, or intellectual/developmental disability. These are chronic conditions that potentially can expand into further secondary conditions that reduce their quality of life. Nevertheless, we have the knowledge and resources to innovate with solutions that enable people with these conditions to perform optimally close to the performance of people who do not have these conditions. These more serious conditions could strike any of us at any time.

11.3 Overcoming the Cognitive Impasse

Alan Lightman and Owen Gingerich (1991, p. 690) defined a scientific anomaly as "an observed fact that is difficult to explain in terms of the existing conceptual framework," and they suggest the use of retrorecognition as a psychological tool to address unexplained facts/givens within new frameworks and to provide improved theories of knowledge. They cited several famous scientific examples, most notably Nicolaus Copernicus' correct conceptualization of the heliocentric solar system model by firmly addressing the problem of inner planetary retrograde motion that had been previously accepted as a curious but tolerable anomaly within the incorrect earth-centered model. From a decision-making perspective, this example illustrates the human tendency to accept situations as they are and that little can be done to change the situation (i.e., complacency).

Lightman and Gingerich's (1991) argument is further illustrated by Dyson's (2004) reminiscence of a research strategy change. Citing a meeting with Nobel Laureate Enrico Fermi, he stated that attempts to solve scientific problems require a clear model of the situation (i.e., reality) and a robust mathematical formalism to describe this model. This approach is consistent with our understanding of the predictive validity for models (Messick 1988) and deductive, experimental research designs (Charlton 1996; Popper 2002; Rothman and Greenland 1998).

Retrorecognition is a little used but System 2 thinking/reasoning tool that recasts accepted status quo concepts into new models for potential solutions. Universal access and assistive devices/technology across all levels of society represent structural and psychological changes that can be beneficial to everyone. It begins with the identification of functional issues and the interface of physical, biological, psychological, social, and environmental barriers to optimum functioning for any person. The mental shift is from the person with a disability accepting the way things exist to how we can change the situation and environment.

11.4 Universal Access

In the United States, the primary driving forces for full access and inclusion of people living with disabilities have been the Rehabilitation Act of 1973 and its amendments (29 U.S.C. § 701 et seq., Public Law 93–112, 87 Statute 355) and the Americans with Disabilities Act and its amendments (ADA; 42 U.S.C. § 12,101, Public Law 101–336). The Rehabilitation Act specifically charges federal government agencies to prohibit employment discrimination against people living with disabilities and to provide state grants to support vocational rehabilitation programs. The Rehabilitation Act affirms civil rights protections for this population, and it provides for research and training grants to improve health and access in society, education, and industry/business. With the civil rights provisions in Section 504, the act charges federal agencies to provide reasonable accommodations and access for people living with disabilities.

The 1990 ADA and its amendments placed disability on an even plane with race, religion, and other characteristics defined under the US Civil Rights Act of 1964 (Public Law 88–352; 78 Statute 241). The ADA specifically prohibits discrimination against people living with disabilities in all aspects of employment, and it requires public institutions and transportation to provide access and accommodations. Public and commercial facilities such as businesses and hotels must be accessible, and all new construction must be accessible, with some exceptions for historic sites. Despite its employment provisions, people living with disabilities remain significantly under- and unemployed compared to people without disabilities, at approximately a 2:7 ratio. As with age discrimination, some employers have been able to navigate the ADA in various aspects of hiring and changes in staffing for various positions, although some positions do justifiably prohibit certain disabilities due to safety issues and the physical nature of the work. Nevertheless, the ADA too often is viewed only as an accessibility issue, not the true spirit of inclusion for this population.

Therefore, these two laws demonstrate the legal requirement of accessibility to health and exercise for people living with mobility limitations and other disabilities. Over several decades since the enactments of this legislation, businesses and institutions have steadily worked to improve accessible options. However, many organizations lag behind in terms of full accessibility to facilities, often due to costs. Pharr (2013) surveyed 63 members of a medical management organization, finding that lack of knowledge of accessible equipment to meet patient needs was a primary factor in their clinics' lack of full compliance with the ADA.

For physical and recreational facilities, Rimmer et al. (2005) tested their AIMFREE (Accessibility Instruments Measuring Fitness and Recreation Environments) instrument on 35 exercise centers, finding that most facilities provided staff training and accessible print materials for people with varying disabilities. However, most centers did not have the full range of equipment spacing, adjustments, and accessibility; moreover, most centers did not have people with disabilities on their advisory boards. Arbour-Nicitopoulos and Martin Ginis (2011) also tested the AIMFREE with 44 Canadian exercise centers, finding that none of the facilities were fully accessible, and AIMFREE ratings for the centers ranged from a low of 31 to a maximum of 63 out of 100 total points.

These studies highlight the substantial need for improved accessibility to health and exercise facilities/equipment for this population. The barriers seem to primarily lie with knowledge of equipment, procedures, and legislation as well as cost barriers. Other studies address additional, significant extrinsic issues such as transportation, neighborhood safety, and social supports (Escobar-Viera et al. 2014; Levasseur et al. 2015; Rosenberg et al. 2011).

Principles of universal access for people living with mobility limitations and other disabilities are advocated by many organizations. These principles mirror architectural guidelines for universal design to access new construction. The Amputee Coalition (www.amputee-coalition.org) addresses universal access with respect to the Rehabilitation Act and the ADA through a factsheet of universal access guidelines. These recommendations include an individual contacting the health clinic or fitness center to discuss accessibility options and various accommodations that the clinic or center can provide. These options range from parking accessibility, adjustable examination tables or exercise devices, scales and examination diagnostic equipment that can accommodate wheelchairs, plenty of spaces for maneuvering, adequate time for facilities usage, and adequate staff training to provide appropriate assistance.

The 7 principles of universal design (UD; Carr et al. 2013; Imrie 2011; Story 1998; The Center for Universal Design 1997; see also https://www.cdc.gov/ncbddd/disabilityandhealth/disability-strategies.html) include the following central concepts (in addition to 29 supplementary tenets):

1. The design can be used by people with different types of abilities and disabilities (i.e., equitable).
2. The design broadly accommodates different disability needs (i.e., flexibility).
3. The design is simple for the user at first contact/use (i.e., simple).
4. The design can be identified immediately by different user perceptual capabilities (i.e., perceptible).
5. The design poses minimal physical risks to the user (i.e., tolerance for error).
6. The design requires minimal physical exertion (i.e., low physical effort).
7. The design is spatially adjustable for different user needs, including space for movement around the design (i.e., size and space for approach and use).

These principles drive not only accessibility for building construction but also for the design of medical/health facilities, exercise and recreational centers, and, most importantly, the equipment that is used by people living with and without disabilities.

The UD principles have gained traction in other areas of accessibility, including Universal Design for Learning (UDL; Center for Applied Special Technology 2011), which promotes "multiple means of representation, expression, and engagement." This work is an extension of the Rehabilitation Act, ADA, plus the Individuals with Disabilities Education Act (IDEA; Public Law 101–476, 104 Statute 1142). Like the Rehabilitation Act, the 1990 IDEA substantially updated and replaced previous legislation such that greater inclusion and individual rights are promoted. The IDEA promotes equal educational opportunities for children with disabilities, including close parent/guardian-teacher collaboration to develop Individualized Education Plans (IEPs) for students with disabilities. Furthermore, students with disabilities are to be taught in inclusive classrooms that contain students without disabilities, and schools must provide reasonable educational accommodations to students free of charge.

Often overlooked is the Assistive Technology Act of 2004 (Public Law 108–364), which updated previous, similar legislation that provided grant funding to state programs that researched and provided assistive devices and services to people living with disabilities. The 2004 law expanded these services to include assisting people with identifying and acquiring assistive device technologies. Operationally defined, an assistive technology device helps a person to achieve optimum functionality. According to the original Technology-Related Assistance for Individuals with Disabilities Act of 1988 (Public Law 100–407, 102 Statute 1044), "The term 'assistive technology device' means any item, piece of equipment, or product system, whether acquired commercially off the shelf, modified, or customized, that is used to increase, maintain, or improve functional capabilities of individuals with disabilities."

From a human rights perspective, Atlantis Community, Inc. in Denver, Colorado, is the first American independent living center. It arose as a self-advocacy movement among people living with severe disabilities in nursing homes during 1973–1974. With the assistance of Reverend Wade Blank and numerous advocates with and without disabilities, the first center was established in 1975, and it continues independent living advocacy and civil rights support across the United States (www.atlantiscommunity.org). This led to the creation of more independent living centers promoting inclusion for people with disabilities across the United States, a movement that continues to grow but still has much expansion and widespread acceptance to achieve. Prior to Atlantis, people living with disabilities in nursing and other institutional facilities often were not provided basic social and exercise needs. Such conditions still exist sporadically in the United States and globally.

Closed related and of high importance to the independent living movement was the June 22, 1999, US Supreme Court decision for the plaintiffs (L.C.) in Olmstead versus L.C. (527 US 581). The court ruled that segregation of people with disabilities was a violation of Section 2 of the ADA. Initially, two women living in a Georgia state institution sued the state for the right to live in the community. The court's ruling maintained that people with disabilities could live independently in the community and receive health insurance and other benefits for their care if they do not require continuous, 24-hour care and if they do not pose a danger to themselves or to others. The court further required states to develop plans for transitioning people with disabilities into communities, something that only a few states have done as of late 2017, 18 years following the court's ruling. The Olmstead decision and its aftermath illustrate the continued, determined drive by people living with disabilities and their advocates to achieve equitable treatment in health care and in all aspects of society.

In accordance with the Rehabilitation Act, the above cited court ruling and legislation, and additional policy/legal actions at the state and federal levels, the US National Institute on Disability, Independent Living, and Rehabilitation Research (NIDILRR) is charged with providing annual research funding through grant competitions to universities, advocacy organizations, businesses, and other qualified entities to advance the Rehabilitation Act and the rights of people living with disabilities. NIDILRR funds numerous specialty Rehabilitation Research and Training Centers (RRTCs) and Rehabilitation Engineering Research Centers (RERCs) across the United States as well as single and multiyear funding streams to support disability research to advance the science and rehabilitation programs to assist people living with disabilities (see www.narrtc.org).

With respect to exercise and health, two of the top traumatic brain injury (TBI) and spinal cord injury (SCI) hospitals in the United States are Shepherd Center in Atlanta, Georgia, and Craig Hospital in Denver, Colorado. Such hospitals provide an array of neuroscience, rehabilitation, assistive technology, exercise programs and sports, and community reintegration services to people living with TBI, SCI, and stroke. Computer, wheelchair, voice and visual technologies, and exoskeleton training/certification programs and equipment are made available to thousands of patient/customers each year. Modified, accessible weightlifting and most sports (e.g., rugby, SCUBA) are available to wheelchair and other customers. These hospital and TBI/SCI/stroke rehabilitation centers receive public donations and grant funding, including from NIDILRR. Unfortunately, there are not enough of these excellent centers to support the hundreds of thousands of TBI, SCI, and strokes that occur every year.

The National Center on Health, Physical Activity, and Disability (NCHPAD; www.nchpad.org), another NIDILRR-funded center, conducts research and service activities to make exercise technologies available to a large segment of the population for people living with mobility limitations. NCHPAD works with universities and organizations (e.g., Rehabilitation Institute of Chicago, Christopher & Dana Reeve Paralysis Resource Center, etc.) to distribute educational materials and programs for the promotion of physical activity for people living with disabilities. Many additional rehabilitation engineering and rehabilitation psychology programs advance the science of rehabilitation technology and other support mechanisms across the United States and internationally.

The expansion of these programs has substantially improved treatment, rehabilitation, and especially community integration and independent living. Still, the programs in the United States have limited reach across a vast country of 330 million people. As with most of health care, concentrations of medical centers, higher education, and innovation are concentrated in large, metropolitan areas, leaving thousands of health professional underserved areas in rural as well certain high poverty urban areas. Transportation and geographic provision of health services has been a chronic problem for decades, and little has been accomplished at taking health education services and technologies to these areas even with advances in telemedicine and the explosion of information technologies during the past 20 years. It still remains the responsibility of the person with disability and their families/friends to travel to the major centers in cities for receipt of services, not the other way around. This situation might be further compounded with the predicted growth of megacities, consolidation of health care and other business services, and the increased concentration of people in these large urban centers. Economic forces continue to drive the separation of populations, haves and "have nots," when we have the technologies, knowledge base for even newer technologies, and delivery systems. The remaining tasks are for us to develop our own societal wherewithal to promote innovation and outreach, goals that can be achieved at low expense. Until we make these species' cognitive changes, we will continue to miss people when there are readily available service systems, leaving alienated, unhealthy populations who may seek improper solutions from further unhealthy sources.

11.5 The Process of Selection

As illustrated in Kahneman's (2003) and Swets et al. (2000) works described above, individual decision-making processes, perceptions, and tools of measurement are not perfect, either due to lack of validity or due to individual bias in tool construction (deliberate or accidental). The goal of decision processes is to maximize true positives and true negatives when the evaluation tool is matched with reality. True positives are those decisions that some phenomenon is true when it is, in fact, true (Table 11.1). Likewise, true negatives are those decisions that some phenomenon is false when it is false in reality. False positives and negatives (Table 11.1) represent

Table 11.1 Sensitivity chart comparing reality versus evaluation/measurement by social judgment on the "other" (see Hollar 2017a; Swets et al. 2000)

	Social "reality" of the "other"		
		Ability	Disability
Social decision toward the "other"	Ability (Select)	True positive	False positive
	Disability	False negative	True negative

errors in decision-making processes when the decision does not match reality. High rates of false positives and negatives detract from objective measures of reality. Yet, this is the problem we face when the needs of individuals with disabilities are marginalized: they become false positives or negatives, depending on the orientation of the tool and group perceptions. What we are getting at here is a mapping of individual and group decision-making accuracy to identify critical needs that are pertinent to greater inclusion for people living with mobility and other disabilities, here especially with respect to exercise and health programs.

Swets et al. (2000) described the decision matrix (Table 11.1) in diagnostic assessments, concluding that triangulation of multiple evaluation tools can yield improved assessments. Such an approach can be achieved using Receiver Operator Characteristic (ROC) curve analysis, which compares the sensitivity of measurement tools to specificity (Rothman and Greenland 1998). Sensitivity and specificity of Table 11.1 decision matrix are defined as follows (Dawes 2000; Rothman and Greenland 1998; Swets et al. (2000):

$$\text{Sensitivity} = \text{True Positives} / (\text{True Positives} + \text{False Negatives}) \quad (11.1)$$

$$\text{Specificity} = \text{True Negatives} / (\text{True Negatives} + \text{False Positives}) \quad (11.2)$$

Here, we define for convenience "true positives" as individuals selected as having favored traits, in accordance with evolutionary selection models (Hartl 1980) discussed below but converse to disease epidemiological models (Rothman and Greenland 1998). For selection involving social and health disparities faced by people living with disabilities and other stigmatized populations, selection and judgments by raters sometimes will classify people with disabilities as a "negative" condition within traditional medical models (Allison 2010; Baker 2002), even though accommodations can improve levels of functioning to true positive levels. Hence, certain individuals in non-accommodating environments might be stigmatized and socially marginalized as "false negatives" to be denied full assistance and accommodations that would enable full inclusion and independent living (Allison 2010; Baker 2002; Black 2003; Wolbring 2003).

The objective of ROC analysis for diagnosis is to maximize sensitivity and specificity, thereby reducing the numbers of false positive and negative conditions. Therefore, for an ideal, socially inclusive selection model with no discrimination, every person would be selected positive for full inclusion in society, no person would be deselected for stigmatization (negative), and both sensitivity (1.0/1.0) and specificity (0.0/0.0) would approach unity (Fig. 11.1).

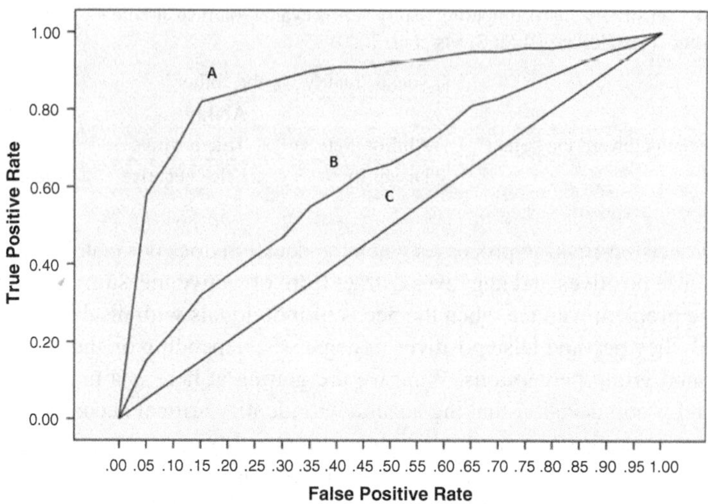

Fig. 11.1 Receiver operator characteristic curves. The true positive rate is sensitivity, whereas the false positive rate is (1 – specificity). See text plus Hollar (2017a) and Swets et al. (2000) for greater description

Wray et al. (2010) mathematically modeled the ROC area under the curve (AUC) parameter (Eq. 11.1; Fig. 11.1), finding that, for genetic studies, the AUC (plot of true positives versus false positives) can accurately relate heritability of genetic liability for disease. Dodd and Pepe (2003) determined that the AUC as a screening tool is proportional to the covariance and regression between predictors in disease diagnosis. In Fig. 11.1, Curve A (high sensitivity, low specificity) represents stronger predictability in distinguishing true positives from false positives, whereas Curve B represents weaker predictability, and diagonal Line C represents results no better than chance (50:50 probability of correct versus incorrect). Therefore, the limitation of the AUC is its capacity to maximize the curve (e.g., Curve A, Fig. 11.1) and the true positive rate while allowing false positives, the latter that should not exist (i.e., all persons are true positives) with a fully inclusive selection model. Hence,

$$\text{AUC} \sim cov\left(f,q\right) \sim B_{fq}\sigma_q^2 \tag{11.3}$$

where AUC represents the area integral under the ROC curve (Fig. 11.1) and B_{fq} represents the regression of fitness f on a given personal characteristic/trait q, a parameter dependent on the covariation between f and q.

Throughout these arguments, the emergent issues are the role and the validity of raters in establishing the threshold (if any) for selection and how it defines positive/negative situations. For a condition that can be lethal, such as cancer detection or machine structural anomalies (Dawes 2000; Swets et al. 2000), a test threshold logically should strictly identify safety marks for treatment or exclusion, respectively, although Swets et al. (2000) stressed the importance of triangulation in testing to correct for errors in sensitivity, specificity, and the AUC. For inclusion, situations that potentially could impact the civil rights of individuals and organizational cohesiveness, thresholds should be eliminated, for persons are not diseases or parasites despite what members of the in-group might fallaciously think. Consequently, decision-makers need to reject false or arbitrary dichotomous models in favor of a more realistic continuum of ability/disability diversity or arbitrary/invalid definitions of competence/incompetence. Our brief decision-making mathematical treatment below (and using Table 11.1) can serve as an applied tool (a type of Kahneman's (2003) System 2 reasoning heuristic) within organizations for identifying possible occurrences of false thresholds that marginalize persons who are "different" and who reflect "otherness."

11.5.1 Fitness, Environmental Selection, and Relational Systems Perspectives

The Price (1970) Eq. 11.4 as applied to nongenetic selection posits that the change in fitness (ΔQ) for a trait q equals the covariance between trait frequencies q and trait fitness f, with division by the arithmetic mean f_m of all trait fitness values:

$$\Delta Q = cov(f,q) / f_m \tag{11.4}$$

Since Cov(f, q) is equivalent to the product of the regression path β_{fq} of f on q and the variance of the trait frequency q (Price 1970),

$$cov(f,q) = B_{fq}\sigma_q^2 \sim \text{AUC} \tag{11.5}$$

Then (Price 1970):

$$\Delta Q = B_{fq}\sigma_q^2 / f_m \sim \text{AUC} / f_m \tag{11.6}$$

Therefore, if the slope of the regression line for fitness f (i.e., success) on trait prevalence is positive, then fitness increases, as does the AUC (Fig. 11.1). Similarly, if we substitute fitness with rater assessments of fitness and trait prevalence across levels of functioning (i.e., a measure of disability), then we can measure variations in these parameters for interacting groups using Eq. 11.4 above from Price's (1970) basic covariance model for nongenetic selection.

In Fig. 11.1, Curve A (high sensitivity, low specificity) represents stronger predictability in distinguishing true positives from false positives (Table 11.1), whereas Curve B represents weaker predictability, and diagonal Line C represents results no better than chance (50:50 probability of correct versus incorrect). Therefore, the limitation of the AUC is its capacity to maximize the curve (e.g., Curve A, Fig. 11.1) and the true positive rate while allowing false positives, the latter that should not exist (i.e., all persons are true positives) with a fully inclusive selection model. Dodd and Pepe (2003) determined that the AUC as a screening tool is proportional to the covariance and regression between predictors in disease diagnosis.

11.5.2 Truncation Selection and the Decision Matrix

A complementary approach to evaluating human selection in organizations, health care, and community facilities inclusion is the classic truncation selection model (Fig. 11.2; Hartl 1980; Lynch and Walsh 1998). Like contingency table analysis (Table 11.1 and Fig. 11.1), the truncation model assumes a normal distribution, and Eq. 11.7 relates distributions of a trait in selected and deselected populations (Hartl 1980; Lynch and Walsh 1998; Fig. 11.2):

$$\left(q'_{\text{sel}} - q'\right) / \sigma_q^2 = Z / \alpha \tag{11.7}$$

where q'_{sel} represents the mean of the selected sample group (e.g., "normal" in-group persons), q' represents the mean of the entire population, σ_q^2 represents the total population variance, Z represents the height of the normal distribution curve at the truncation/selection point T, and α represents the area under the selection curve $\int_0 f(x)dx$ (i.e., similar to the AUC, Fig. 11.1) for selected individuals to the right of the truncation point T (Fig. 11.2) (Hartl 1980). However, α ("presumptive positives") include both true and false positive individuals having the specified trait, whereas β represents "false negatives" deselected when they have a "preferred" trait, and $1 - \beta$ represents selected individuals with true "positive" traits (Fig. 11.2) (see also Table 11.1, Fig. 11.1).

Therefore, the classic selection model (Fig. 11.2) relates directly to nongenetic, contingency table decision-making processes (Table 11.1) and ROC analyses of

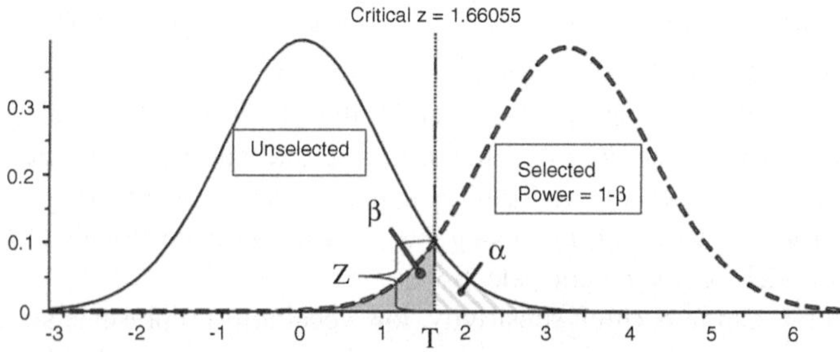

Fig. 11.2 Selection: two overlapping normal distributions for selection of individuals (dashed distribution) versus nonselected individuals (solid distribution), with T indicating the threshold truncation point (Hartl 1980). Graphic generated using G*Power (Faul et al. 2007)

these decisions (Fig. 11.1). This model (Fig. 11.2) applies to changes in group fitness due to environmental selection or human-controlled directional selection (Hartl 1980). In our organizational model, the selector represents an organizational dominant viewing the Gaussian curve of the group or even dominants within the group attempting to change the shape/position of their own distribution, even with other forces occurring.

For nongenetic selection processes, the decider/observer/rater(s) exercises the option of locating the truncation point T (e.g., who should pass or fail, included or excluded, etc.). The establishment of the truncation point can be impacted by a multitude of factors such as imperatives for treatment in cancer diagnoses, knowledge to perform specialized jobs that impact others to varying degrees, etc. (Dawes 2000; Swets et al. 2000). Consequently, the truncation point can slide to the left or right based upon the severity of the decision process and how it impacts overall social welfare. Continuing from Eq. 11.7, Hartl (1980) derived the t and standardized z statistics for the truncation point T and corresponding AUC ~ α:

$$t = \left(T - \left(\text{population mean}\right)\right) / \sigma = \alpha \sim \text{AUC} \tag{11.8}$$

$$z = \sigma Z \tag{11.9}$$

Furthermore, the intensity of selection i (i.e., how strong individuals or the environment is excluding others) is directly proportional to the z statistic (Eq. 11.9) and is inversely proportional to α (Eq. 11.10) (Hartl 1980):

$$i = z / \alpha = \sigma Z / \alpha \tag{11.10}$$

An important note is that we can also examine the two distributions (selected versus deselected) in Fig. 11.2 from a third temporal dimension perpendicular to the distributions, with changes in the distributions changing at recurrent periods (e.g., monthly, yearly). As a result, the two distributions can contract, expand, diverge, and merge, a measurable, time- and selection-dependent phenomenon pertinent to group and organizational dynamics that we will discuss below.

If almost every person is selected for inclusion, say 99% ($\alpha = 0.99$), then the intensity of selection will be very low ($i = 0.027$), and the truncation point will be far to the left in Fig. 11.2. In fact, there would be almost perfect overlap (i.e., merging) between the "unselected" and "selected" distributions such that they would become one distribution as the two groups became "inphase" with respect to group inclusion/qualification. From a conceptual viewpoint, the two distributions behave cyclically as waves of distributed individuals on a given characteristic, and the waves cycle or precess out-of-phase in real situations, but the waves or distributions overlap when they are identical. This "in−/out-phase" precessional wave relationship of the two distributions (e.g., as if they represented fluid flow hydrodynamic models) suggests a group decision-making solution to intragroup conflict, as described below.

Whereas reasonable decisions on work performance and company revenue decisions can justify truncation points in worker selection/deselection for promotion/retention/dismissal, truncation points can be misapplied to exclude/discriminate against persons based upon arbitrary traits/characteristics or upon legitimate work flows among group members that existed in the past but might be presently resolved. In other words, the decision is made and applied post hoc to convenient characteristics to exclude individuals, which is the case that occurs in mobbing events.

This 1% in an apparent low selection environment represents the central problem with the lack of distribution of resources to disadvantaged and disabled populations and possibly the poor job tenure of many persons with disabilities (Baker 2002; Hollar et al. 2008; Houtenville et al. 2013). Even in a "just" society and workplace, almost everybody will be accepted, but a few lone outliers can be targeted for deselection (Allen 2001; Allison 2010; Montagnon 2005). Therefore, intensity for selection will appear low and open when, in reality, individuals are targeted. Consequently, it is easy to mask discrimination with justified traits and rationalizations. Rarely does an organization have a profile such as Fig. 11.2 with clear groupings of individuals, even with stack rankings. In our low selection scenario, sensitivity will increase, whereas specificity will decrease, the latter weakening the corresponding AUC curve (Fig. 11.1) with higher numbers of false positives. Nevertheless, whereas this 99% scenario yields high overall social welfare from cost-benefit assessments (Adler and Posner 2006), 1% of individuals would be singled-out for deselection, both for justifiable and perhaps unjustifiable reasons.

Even if multiple raters decide on selection and enjoy high inter-rater agreements/reliability (Crocker and Algina 1986), the decision still can be invalid if relevant traits (i.e., overwhelming pertinence to the environmental situation) are not correctly chosen and if the raters fail to evaluate the full context of a person and their situation; the raters could become susceptible to "groupthink" (Janis 1972; Janis and Mann 1977). Furthermore, outliers should never be underestimated for potential value in preserving populations that crash into evolutionary bottlenecks (Eckhardt 2001). For example, an individual with an undervalued or overlooked skill might be terminated due to lack of need in a current market environment, even when contingency plans envision market changes that will demand that skill. Variation is valuable to all populations, so maximizing AUC ~ 1.0 by full inclusion of all individuals, both overtly and covertly within the organization's culture (Trice and Beyer 1984), can offer unknown potential future benefits to the organization.

It should be noted that Press and Dyson (2012) demonstrated that Markov iterated prisoner's dilemma scenarios are not necessarily egalitarian, even with short or long memory of opponent move contingencies. They showed that one player having knowledge of ultimatum strategies could establish the opponent's scores and extort a linear advantage over the opponent, to which the opponent's best response is to acquiesce to the extortion. Cropanzano et al. (2016) noted the importance of linking variations in managerial and employee neurological development and consequential ethical decision-making, including levels of empathy. These studies relate to degrees of empathy based upon individual relatedness or recognition

(Hollar 2016), organizational networking and altruism (Nowak et al. 2010), and the incompleteness of information associated with higher-level decision-making processes (Dawes 2000; Kahneman 2003).

Individuals and organizations can falsely rationalize poor decisions (Brockner et al. 1981; Festinger 1957, 1964). Arbitrary "evidence" is assembled, but as with criticisms of organizational stack rankings as well as related social comparisons in other venues (e.g., student performance in schools; Covington 1992), social evaluations too often focus on negatives, however minor, in spite of a plethora of positive performances. This raises the additional issue of validity (Arnesen and Norheim 2003; Messick 1988) for individual and organizational assessments/evaluations, an area that continues to be exceptionally weak given a variety of inconsistent and poorly studied approaches across organizations, including ineffective external audits that rarely address serious human resources problems.

11.6 Deselection and Opening Access

The primary approaches to promote inclusion in health, exercise, society, and employment should target organizational leadership, responsibility of leaders, improved intervention validities, and culture change (Kotter and Rathgeber 2006). Nevertheless, like many programs aimed at reducing recidivism into undesired behaviors, little evidence on long-term outcomes exists; when such evidence does exist, it consistently shows rapid declines to pretreatment levels without sustained personal supports and training. Consequently, there is a need for dramatic phase merging in organizational group behaviors that emphasize commonalities among individuals and the fact that the phenomenon of disability is within each of us.

With a phase merge approach, the objective, as outlined above, is to maximize the true positives and false positives, hence an AUC approaching 1.00 with full inclusion and the simultaneous reduction of selection intensity to 0, as shown in Eqs. 11.4, 11.7, and 11.10. This can be achieved by manipulating the truncation point (Fig. 11.2) to where individuals are evaluated on their commonalities for high covariance between individuals, genuinely important traits, and "fitness" while not measuring other job-irrelevant, unique features of individuals and even highlighting the values of these unique features.

We propose a nongenetic, methodological approach that merges the AUC and truncation selection approaches while recognizing:

$$\mathbf{Q}_{t+1} = \mathbf{F}_t \mathbf{Q}_t = \mathbf{Q}_t \tag{11.11}$$

where $\mathbf{Q}_t$ represents a matrix of all measured trait percentage values in a population/organization of interacting individuals at a given time t. $\mathbf{F}_t$ represents a unit matrix of one's perfect fitness matrix where there is zero selection against irrelevant traits/characteristics, therefore maximizing the AUC for epidemiological sensitivity and specificity and merging selected/"deselected" distributions on a given or multiple traits (i.e., merging the two distributions in Fig. 11.2). The ΔQ parameter is reduced to zero, and the two distribution means $\mu = \mu'$ when the overlapping/precessing distributions or waves are brought "into phase." That is, individuals separated by arbitrary characteristics are included under one commonality distribution.

11.7 Conclusion: Implications for Inclusion, Exercise, and Health

People living with mobility limitations and other disabilities face substantial social and environmental barriers, even with legislation, and attempt to demonstrate positive environments for this substantial population in all countries, communities, and regions. It has been demonstrated that lack of access plagues people living with disabilities as well as in lower socioeconomic regions. Lack of access to health and exercise has been associated with greater risk for obesity, allostatic load, and negative health outcomes.

Wilson (2012, 2017) correctly observed that much of human behavior is driven by dominance and visual displays. This sociobiological observation coincides with Kahneman's (2003) finding that humans over-rely on System 1 intuition – "first appearances" – that often leads to incorrect decisions (false positives and negatives, false selection, low AUC values in ROC curves). Due to this species' limitation, the appearance of disability can be viewed negatively, condescendingly as an object of pity, or not recognized at all, consciously or subconsciously. Instead of engaging in System 2 reasoning and identifying the social/environmental needs for people living with disabilities, we too often take the easy route and try to "fit" the individual into the existing system or structure instead of seeking novel, easy solutions to modify the system. As a result, people living with disabilities have fewer opportunities for participation in society, employment, exercise, and health, and these problems compound as time passes. Ablement and disablement depend on the environment, and we have the educational methods and technologies to adjust that environment.

Therefore, there is an urgency to change our cultures to truly promote community integration, especially with respect to exercise and health. The culture change requires a mental shift that is a species problem, in accordance with the neuroscience, decision-making, and evolutionary arguments here described. Such is a cognitive disability for our species, not to mention the physical and other disabilities that all of us will encounter at some point in our lives. Engaging in Kahneman's (2003) System 2 reasoning can lead to more thoughtful decisions in the way we provide access for people living with disabilities as well as to engage our best innovation for the urgency to improve access to improved technologies. Disability is not something that is referred to a specialist or counselor in Human Resources or Community Service departments of organizations. It is something that all of us must embrace with understanding and genuine empathy.

References

Adler, M. D., & Posner, E. A. (2006). *New foundations of cost-benefit analysis*. Cambridge, MA: Harvard University Press.

Allen, G. E. (2001). Essays on science and society: Is a new eugenics afoot? *Science, 294*, 59–61.

Allison, K. C. (2010). Public health, populations, and lethal ingestion. *Disability and Health Journal, 3*, 56–70.

Arbour-Nicitopoulos, K. P., & Martin Ginis, K. A. (2011). Universal accessibility of "accessible" fitness and recreational facilities for persons with mobility disabilities. *Adapted Physical Activity Quarterly, 28*(1), 1–15. https://doi.org/10.1123/apaq.28.1.1.

Aristotle. (2012). *Aristotle's Nicomachean ethics*. Bartlett, R.C. & Collins, S.D. (Trans). Chicago: University of Chicago Press.

Arnesen, T. M., & Norheim, O. F. (2003). Quantifying quality of life for economic analysis: Time out for time trade off. *Medical Humanities, 29*(2), 81–86.

Baker, B. (2002). The hunt for disability: The new eugenics and the normalization of school children. *Teachers College Record, 104*(4), 663–703.

Black, E. (2003). *War against the weak: Eugenics and America's campaign to create a master race*. New York: Thunder Mouth Press.

Bor, J. (2017). Diverging life expectancies and voting patterns in the 2016 US presidential election. *American Journal of Public Health, 107*, 1560–1562.

Brockner, J., Rubin, J. Z., & Lang, E. (1981). Face-saving and entrapment. *Journal of Experimental Social Psychology, 17*, 68–79.

Brown, T. (2009). *Change by design*. New York: HarperCollins.

Carr, K., Weir, P. L., Azar, D., & Azar, N. R. (2013). Universal design: A step toward successful aging. *Journal of Aging Research, 2013*, 324624. https://doi.org/10.1155/2013/324624.

Case, A., & Deaton, A. (2015). Rising morbidity and mortality in midlife among white non-Hispanic Americans in the 21st century. *Proceedings of the National Academy of Sciences USA, 112*(49), 15078–15083.

Center for Applied Special Technology. (2011). *Universal design for learning guidelines version 2.0*. Wakefield: Author.

Charlton, B. G. (1996). Attribution of causation in epidemiology: Chain or mosaic? *Clinical Epidemiology, 49*(1), 105–107.

Covington, M. V. (1992). *Making the grade: A self-worth perspective on motivation and school reform*. New York: Cambridge University Press.

Crocker, L., & Algina, J. (1986). *Introduction to classical and modern test theory*. Forth Worth: Harcourt Brace Jovanovich.

Cropanzano, R. S., Massaro, S., & Becker, W. J. (2016). Deontic justice and organizational neuroscience. *Journal of Business Ethics*. https://doi.org/10.1007/s10551-016-3056-3.

Damasio, A. R. (1994). *Descartes' error: Emotion, reason, and the human brain*. New York: Harper Perennial/Avon/Penguin.

Dawes, R. M. (1988). *Rational choice in an uncertain world*. San Diego: Harcourt Brace Jovanovich.

Dawes, R. M. (2000). A theory of irrationality as a 'reasonable' response to an incomplete specification. *Synthese, 122*, 133–163.

Dodd, L. E., & Pepe, M. S. (2003). Partial AUC estimation and regression. *Biometrics, 59*, 614–623.

Drucker, P. F. (1985). *Innovation and entrepreneurship*. New York: HarperBusiness.

Dyson, F. (2004). A meeting with Enrico Fermi. *Nature, 427*, 297.

Eckhardt, R. B. (2001). Genetic research and nutritional individuality. *Journal of Nutrition, 131*, 336S–339S.

Escobar-Viera, C. G., Jones, P. D., Schumacher, J. R., & Hall, A. G. (2014). Association between living alone and physical inactivity among people with and without disability, Florida Behavioral Risk Factor Surveillance System, 2009. *Preventing Chronic Disease: Public Health Research, Practice, and Policy, 11*, 140182. https://doi.org/10.5888/pcd11.140182.

Faul, F., Erdfelder, E., Lang, A. G., & Buchner, A. (2007). G*Power 3: A flexible statistical power analysis program for the social, behavioral, and biomedical sciences. *Behavior Research Methods, 39*, 175–191.

Festinger, L. (1957). *A theory of cognitive dissonance*. Stanford: Stanford University.

Festinger, L. (1964). *Conflict, decision, and dissonance*. Stanford: Stanford University Press.

Giannini, M. J., Bergmark, B., Kreshover, S., Elias, E., Plummer, C., & O'Keefe, E. (2010). Understanding suicide and disability through three major disabling conditions: Intellectual disability, spinal cord injury, and multiple sclerosis. *Disability and Health Journal, 3*(2), 74–78.

Goffman, E. (1959). *The presentation of self in everyday life*. Garden City: Anchor Books.

Goffman, E. (1963). *Stigma: Notes on the management of spoiled identity*. Englewood Cliffs: Prentice Hall.

Graham, B. (1965). *World aflame*. Charlotte: Billy Graham Evangelistic Association.

Hartl, D. L. (1980). *Principles of population genetics*. Sunderland: Sinauer Associates.

Hollar, D. (2013). Cross-sectional patterns of allostatic load among persons with varying disabilities, NHANES: 2001–2010. *Disability and Health Journal, 6*, 177–187.

Hollar, D. (2016). Validation of a new instrument to evaluate gradients of empathy. *Journal of Psychoeducational Assessment, 35*(4), 377–390. https://doi.org/10.1177/0734282915623882.

Hollar, D. (2017a). *Trajectory analysis in health care*. New York: Springer Nature http://www.springer.com/us/book/9783319596259.

Hollar, D. (2017b). Disability and health outcomes in geospatial analyses of Southeastern U.S. County Health Data. *Disability and Health Journal, 10*, 518–524.

Hollar, D., & Lewis, J. (2015). Heart age differentials and general cardiovascular risk profiles for persons with varying disabilities: NHANES 2001–2010. *Disability and Health Journal, 8*, 51–60.

Hollar, D., & Moore, D. (2004). Relationship of substance use by students with disabilities to long-term educational and social outcomes. *Substance Use & Misuse, 39*(6), 929–960.

Hollar, D. W., Hattie, J., Goldman, B., & Lancaster, J. (2000). Developing assessment procedures and assessing two models of escalation behavior among community college administrators. *Theory and Decision, 49*(1), 1–24.

Hollar, D., McAweeney, M., & Moore, D. (2008). The relationship between substance use disorders and unsuccessful case closures in vocational rehabilitation agencies. *Journal of Applied Rehabilitation Counseling, 39*(2), 25–29.

Houtenville, A., Brucker, D., Gould, P., Lauer, E., Santoro, J., Brennan-Curry, A., & Gianino, M. (2013). 2013 Annual Disability Statistics Compendium. Rehabilitation Research and Training Center on Disability Statistics and Demographics, University of New Hampshire, Durham, NH.

Iezzoni, L. I., Killeen, M. B., & O'Day, B. L. (2006). Rural residents with disabilities confront substantial barriers to obtaining primary care. *Health Services Research, 41*(4 Pt 1), 1258–1275.

Imrie, R. (2011). Universalism, universal design and equitable access to the built environment. *Journal of Disability and Rehabilitation, 34*(10), 873–882. https://doi.org/10.3109/09638288.2011.624250.

Ivey-Stephenson, A. Z., Crosby, A. E., Jack, S. P. D., Haileyesus, T., & Kresnow-Sedacca, M-J. (2017). Suicide trends among and within urbanization levels by sex, race/ethnicity, age group, and mechanism of death – United States, 2001–2015. *Morbidity and Mortality Weekly Report,* Surveillance Summaries *66*(18), 1–10.

Janis, I. (1972). *Victims of groupthink: A psychological study of foreign-policy decisions and fiascoes*. Boston: Houghton-Mifflin.

Janis, I., & Mann, L. (1977). *Decision making: A psychological analysis of conflict, choice, and commitment*. New York: The Free Press.

Kahneman, D. (2003). Maps of bounded rationality: Psychology for behavioral economics. *The American Economic Review, 93*(5), 1449–1475.

Kahneman, D. (2011). *Thinking, fast and slow*. New York: Farrar, Straus and Giroux.

Kahneman, D., & Tversky, A. (1979). Prospect theory: An analysis of decisions under risk. *Econometrica, 47*, 313–327.

Kohn, L. T., Corrigan, J. M., & Donaldson, M. S. (Eds.). (2000). *To err is human: Building a safer health system*. Washington, DC: National Academies Press.

Kotter, J. P. (1995). Leading change: Why transformation efforts fail. *Harvard Business Review* OnPoint 4231, reprint 95204, March–April, 1995.

Kotter, J., & Rathgeber, H. (2005). *Our iceberg is melting: Changing and succeeding under any conditions*. New York: St. Martin's Press.

Kotter, J., & Rathgeber, H. (2006). *Our iceberg is melting: Changing and succeeding under any conditions*. New York: St. Martin's Press.

Kotter, J., & Rathgeber, H. (2016). *That's not how we do it here! A story about how organizations rise and fall – and can rise again*. New York: Portfolio/Penguin.

Krueger, A. B. (2017). Where have all the workers gone? An inquiry into the decline of the U.S. labor force participation rate. *Brookings Papers on Economic Activity, BPEA Conference Drafts,* September 7–8, 2017. Washington, DC: Brookings Institute.

Levasseur, M., Généreux, M., Bruneau, J.-F., Vanasse, A., Chabot, É., Beaulac, C., & Bédard, M.-M. (2015). Importance of proximity to resources, social support, transportation and neighborhood security for mobility and social participation in older adults: Results from a scoping study. *BMC Public Health, 15*, 503. https://doi.org/10.1186/s12889-015-1824-0.

Lightman, A., & Gingerich, O. (1991). When do anomalies begin? *Science, 255*, 690–695.

Lucas, J. W., & Phelan, J. C. (2012). Stigma and status: The interrelation of two theoretical perspectives. *Social Psychology Quarterly, 75*(4), 310–333.

Lynch, M., & Walsh, B. (1998). *Genetics and analysis of quantitative traits*. Sunderland: Sinauer Associates.

Ma, V. Y., Chan, L., & Carruthers, K. J. (2014). The incidence, prevalence, costs and impact on disability of common conditions requiring rehabilitation in the US: Stroke, spinal cord injury, traumatic brain injury, multiple sclerosis, osteoarthritis, rheumatoid arthritis, limb loss, and back pain. *Archives of Physical Medicine and Rehabilitation, 95*(5), 986–995., e1. https://doi.org/10.1016/j.apmr.2013.10.032.

Makary, M. A., & Daniel, M. (2016). Medical error – the third leading cause of death in the US. *BMJ, 353*, i2139. https://doi.org/10.1136/bmj.i2139.

Mendoza-Vasconez, A. S., Linke, S., Muñoz, M., Pekmezi, D., Ainsworth, C., Cano, M., Williams, V., Marcus, B. H., & Larsen, B. A. (2016). Promoting physical activity among underserved populations. *Current Sports Medicine Reports, 15*(4), 290–297.

Messick, S. (1988). Validity. In R. L. Linn (Ed.), *Educational measurement* (3rd ed.). New York: American Council on Education, Macmillan.

Montagnon, R. G. (2005). Do be my enemy for friendship's sake: (Blake). *Journal of Analytical Psychology, 50*(1), 27–34.

Nary, D. (2004). Employment opportunities for persons with disabilities. Proceedings of the 2nd Conference of the National Center for Birth Defects and Developmental Disabilities, Washington, DC, July.

Newton, B. W., Barber, L., Clardy, J., Cleveland, E., & O'Sullivan, P. (2008). Is there hardening of the heart during medical school? *Academic Medicine, 83*(3), 244–249.

Nickerson, R. S. (2004). *Cognition and chance: The psychology of probabilistic reasoning*. Mahwah: Lawrence Erlbaum.

Nishikimi, M., Fukuyama, R., Minoshima, S., Shimizu, N., & Yagi, K. (1994). Cloning and chromosomal mapping of the human nonfunctional gene for L-Gulono-y-lactone Oxidase, the enzyme for L-ascorbic acid biosynthesis missing in man. *The Journal of Biological Chemistry, 269*(18), 13685–13688.

Nowak, M. A., Tarnita, C. E., & Wilson, E. O. (2010). The evolution of eusociality. *Nature, 466*, 1057–1062.

Pharr, J. (2013). Accessible medical equipment for patients with disabilities in primary care clinics: Why is it lacking? *Disability and Health Journal, 6*(2), 124–132.

Popper, K. (2002). *The logic of scientific discovery*. New York: Routledge.

Popplewell, N. T., Rechel, B. P., & Abel, G. A. (2014). How do adults with physical disability experience primary care? A nationwide cross-sectional survey of access among patients in England. *BMJ Open, 4*(8), e004714. https://doi.org/10.1136/bmjopen-2013-004714.

Press, W. H., & Dyson, F. J. (2012). Iterated Prisoner's Dilemma contains strategies that dominate any evolutionary opponent. *Proceedings of the National Academy of Sciences of the United States of America, 109*(26), 10409–10413.

Price, G. R. (1970). Selection and covariance. *Nature, 227*, 520–521.

Rimmer, J. H., Riley, B., Wang, E., & Rauworth, A. (2005). Accessibility of health clubs for people with mobility disabilities and visual impairments. *American Journal of Public Health, 95*(11), 2022–2028.

Rosenberg, D. E., Bombardier, C. H., Hoffman, J. M., & Belza, B. (2011). Physical activity among persons aging with mobility disabilities: Shaping a research agenda. *Journal of Aging Research, 2011*, 708510. https://doi.org/10.4061/2011/708510.

Rothman, K. J., & Greenland, S. (1998). *Modern epidemiology* (2nd ed.). Philadelphia: Lippincott-Raven.

Schaeffer, F. A. (1968/1990). The god who is there. In F. A. Schaeffer (Ed.), *Francis A. Schaeffer trilogy*. Wheaton: Crossway.

Solzhenitsyn, A. I. (1973). *The Gulag Archipelago: An experiment in literary investigation, I-II*. New York: Harper & Row.

Staw, B. M. (1976). Knee deep in the big Muddy: A study of escalating commitment to a chosen course of action. *Organizational Behavior and Human Performance, 16*, 27–44.

Stein, E. M., Gennuso, K. P., Ugboaja, D. C., & Remington, P. L. (2017). The epidemic of despair among white Americans: Trends in the leading causes of premature death, 1999–2015. *American Journal of Public Health, 107*, 1541–1547.

Story, M. F. (1998). Maximizing usability: The principles of universal design. *Assistive Technology, 10*(1), 4–12.

Swets, J. A., Dawes, R. M., & Monahan, J. (2000). Better decisions through science. *Scientific American, 283*(4), 70–75.

The Center for Universal Design. (1997). *The principles of universal design, version 2.0*. Raleigh: North Carolina State University.

Trice, H. M., & Beyer, J. M. (1984). Studying organizational cultures through rites and ceremonials. *Academy of Management Review, 9*(4), 653–669.

Tversky, A., & Kahneman, D. (1974). Judgment under uncertainty: heuristics and biases. *Science, 185*(4157), 1124–1131.

Tversky, A., & Kahneman, D. (1981). The framing of decisions and the psychology of choice. *Science, 211*(4481), 453–458.

Tversky, A., & Kahneman, D. (1986). Rational choice and the framing of decisions. *The Journal of Business, 59*, S251–S278.

Waxweiler, R. J., Thurman, D., Sniezek, J., Sosin, D., & O'Neil, J. (1995). Monitoring the impact of Traumatic Brain injury – a review and update. *Journal of Neurotrauma, 12*(4), 509–516.

Williams, R. J. (1956). *Biochemical individuality*. New York: John Wiley & Sons.

Wilson, E. O. (1975). *Sociobiology: The new synthesis*. Cambridge, MA: Belknap/Harvard University Press.

Wilson, E. O. (1984). *Biophilia*. Cambridge, MA: Belknap/Harvard University Press.

Wilson, E. O. (2012). *The social conquest of earth*. New York: W.W. Norton & Company.

Wilson, E. O. (2017). *The origins of creativity*. New York: Liveright/W.W. Norton & Company.

Wolbring, G. (2003). Disability rights approach toward bioethics? *Journal of Disability Policy Studies, 14*, 174–180.

World Health Organization. (2011). *World report on disability*. Geneva: Author.

Wray, N. R., Yang, J., Goddard, M. E., & Visscher, P. M. (2010). The genetic interpretation of area under the ROC curve in genomic profiling. *PLoS Genetics, 6*(2), e1000864. https://doi.org/10.1371/journal.pgen.1000864.

Zaloshnja, E., Miller, T., Langlois, J. A., & Selassie, A. W. (2008). Prevalence of long-term disability from traumatic brain injury in the civilian population of the United States, 2005. *Journal of Head Trauma & Rehabilitation, 23*(6), 394–400.

Chapter 12
Physical Activity, Chronic Conditions, and Disabilities Across the US Population: Comprehensive Assessment of Current Patterns and Two-Decade Time Trends

Katerina Ivanov

Abbreviations

ACS	American Community Survey
ADA	Americans with Disabilities Act
BRFSS	Behavioral Risk Factor Surveillance Survey
CDC	Centers for Disease Control and Prevention

12.1 Introduction

The goals of national health promotion and disease prevention include decrease of premature mortality, disease prevention, and improvement of health quality for the US population (US Department of Health and Human Services 1996). It has been widely recognized that regular physical activity reduces the risk of premature death and disability from a variety of conditions including cardiovascular disease, diabetes, osteoarthritis, and osteoporosis and cancer, as well as contributes to improved mental health, physical functioning, and weight control (Blair and Wei 2000). Regardless, a series of studies in line with Hootman et al. (2003) show that in early 2000s, US adults continued to get insufficient physical activity. In fact, physical inactivity was felt to be such a large public health problem that in 1996, the US surgeon general released the landmark report *Physical Activity and Health: A Report of the Surgeon General* (US Department of Health and Human Services 1996) which provides recommendations to all US adults to participate in regular, moderate-intensity, leisure-time physical activity (Hootman et al. 2003). Such activities will decrease the prevalence of chronic diseases that, in turn, are the

K. Ivanov (✉)
Pfeiffer University, Charlotte, NC, USA
e-mail: Katerina.Ivanov@pfeiffer.edu

D. Hollar (ed.), *Advances in Exercise and Health for People With Mobility Limitations*, https://doi.org/10.1007/978-3-319-98452-0_12

leading causes of death and disability in the United States (Schiller et al. 2012; Xu et al. 2016). Numerous studies have demonstrated the importance of physical activity to promote public health. According to Chowdhury (2016), "engaging in healthy behaviors (e.g., being more physically active, wearing seat belts, getting sufficient sleep, reducing alcohol consumption, quitting smoking, and eating a nutritious diet) and using preventive services (e.g., routine medical checkup, blood pressure and cholesterol screening, cancer screening, and recommended vaccinations) can reduce morbidity and premature mortality from these chronic diseases." Overall, the importance of monitoring health-risk behaviors, chronic conditions, and the use of preventive services to help identify high-risk groups can hardly be overestimated and remains a significant step in preventing morbidity (including some disabilities) and mortality.

According to the Americans with Disabilities Act (ADA), "an individual with a disability has a physical or mental impairment that substantially limits one or more major life activities" (Perritt and Perritt 2003). Adults with disabilities are more likely to suffer from chronic conditions than adults with no limitations. Thus this vulnerable population with disabilities should be targeted for health promotion efforts (Doughan 2014; Talbot et al. 2003; Centers for Disease Control and Prevention (CDC) 2001; Pate et al. 1995), and the issue has been addressed by Healthy People 2020 (Dixon-Ibarra and Horner-Johnson 2014). At the same time, despite the increasing population with disabilities in the United States, there is little known about the causal relationship of physical activity and chronic health conditions such as obesity, myocardial infarction, stroke, and diabetes for people with disabilities. According to Doughan (2014), disability can impact healthy eating habits and physical activity; thus this group of population has higher chances to be exposed to risk of becoming overweight or obese and developing a variety of chronic conditions. Therefore, this paper merges two important strands of previous research and contributes to the literature by the following means. First, the study provides a comprehensive analysis of current patterns and long-term trends (20 years' time span) related to chronic conditions, self-perception of health status, healthcare coverage, disabilities, and a variety of socioeconomic characteristics of respondents who have participated in some physical activities or exercises such as running, calisthenics, golf, gardening, or walking for exercise during the past month. I compare the aforementioned outcomes for 1996, 2006, and 2016. Second, the paper identifies the causal effect of the physical activity as well as the wide range of socioeconomic factors on coronary heart disease, stroke, and diabetes among people with disabilities based on 2016 data.

The paper proceeds as follows. In Sect. 12.2, I present a data collection process. In Sect. 12.3, I discuss the methodology and provide theoretical background behind empirical analysis. Sect. 12.4 delivers the results of the empirical tests, while Sect. 12.5 focuses on implications, limitations, and further extensions. Concluding remarks are provided in Sect. 12.6.

12.2 Data Collection

This paper employs the BRFSS, which is "a state-based landline and cellular telephone survey conducted by state health departments with assistance from CDC" (US Department of Health and Human Services 1996). Since 1984, BRFSS has been a unique source of data for health-risk behaviors, chronic diseases or conditions, healthcare access, and the use of preventive health services for states/territories (Caspersen and Merritt 1995). BRFSS data are frequently used to set health goals as well as to monitor progress of public health programs and policy implementation at national, state, and local levels (Caspersen et al. 1985). According to Brownson et al. (2005), the BRFSS is generally representative of the overall US population, although it underrepresents non-Whites, persons with less than a high school education, and those with lower incomes. For example, 2016 BRFSS includes 70.82% of White, 7.8% of people who did not graduate high school, and 8.57% of respondents with annual household income less than $15,000. To account for these disparities and provide more accurate national estimates, BRFSS data were weighted according to the age, sex, and racial distributions of the United States.

To explore the population-wide profile of people who perform exercise activities, I employ a diverse range of variables for the years of 1996, 2006, and 2016. Table 12.1 provides definitions of the variables being utilized for the analysis. In total there are 14 variables to reflect health status of respondents, chronic conditions, and disabilities, 6 variables to explore the health coverage status of respondents, and 7 variables to identify their socioeconomic standing (Table 12.1).

12.3 Methodology

The methodology of this study incorporates the following two steps. The first step is to explore current patterns and two-decade time trends of (1) socioeconomic status, (2) health coverage, and (3) health status, chronic conditions, and disabilities of people who participate in some physical activities or exercises during the past month. The initial sample varies from 122,645 respondents in 1996 to 355,710 in 2006 and in 486,297 in 2016. In this paper physical activity index is based on a BRFSS question, which asks "During the past month, did you participate in any physical activities such as running, calisthenics, golf, gardening, or walking for exercise?" (the methodology is similar to Caspersen and Merritt 1995). Since the first step in this paper focuses on physically active population, I eliminate respondents who did not participate in any physical activities during the past month. Thus the final sample for the first step consists of 85,705 respondents in 1996, 263,968 and 361,649 respondents in years 2006 and 2016, respectively.

Table 12.1 Variables definitions based on BRFSS data

Variable name	Questions
Health status, chronic conditions, and disabilities	
EXERANY	During the past month, other than your regular job, did you participate in any physical activities or exercises such as running, calisthenics, golf, gardening, or walking for exercise?
GENHLTH	Would you say that in general your health is:
PHYSHLTH	Now thinking about your physical health, which includes physical illness and injury, for how many days during the past 30 days was your physical health not good?
MENTHLTH	Now thinking about your mental health, which includes stress, depression, and problems with emotions, for how many days during the past 30 days was your mental health not good?
DIABETES	(ever told) you have diabetes
HAVARTH	(ever told) you have some form of arthritis, rheumatoid arthritis, gout, lupus, or fibromyalgia? (arthritis diagnoses include rheumatism, polymyalgia rheumatica; osteoarthritis (not osteoporosis); tendonitis, bursitis, bunion, tennis elbow; carpal tunnel syndrome, tarsal tunnel syndrome; joint infection, etc.)
CVDINFAR	(ever told) you had a heart attack, also called a myocardial infarction?
CVDCORHD	(ever told) you had angina or coronary heart disease?
CVDSTROK	(ever told) you had a stroke
SMOKEDAY	Do you now smoke cigarettes every day, some days, or not at all?
DRNKANY	During the past month, have you had at least one drink of any alcoholic beverage such as beer, wine, wine coolers, or liquor?
RFWHBMI	Adults who have a body mass index (BMI) greater than 25.00 (overweight or obese)
ASTHMA	(ever told) you had asthma
QLACTLM	Are you limited in any way in any activities because of physical, mental, or emotional problems?
USEEQUIP	Do you now have any health problem that requires you to use special equipment, such as a cane, a wheelchair, a special bed, or a special telephone? (include occasional use or use in certain circumstances.)
Healthcare coverage	
HLTHPLAN	Do you have any kind of healthcare coverage, including health insurance, prepaid plans such as HMOs, or government plans such as Medicare, or Indian Health Service?
MEDICARE	Do you have Medicare?
TYPCOVR	What is the primary source of your healthcare coverage?
MEDCOST	Was there a time in the past 12 months when you needed to see a doctor but could not because of cost?
CHECKUP	About how long has it been since you last visited a doctor for a routine checkup?
RATECARE	How would you rate your satisfaction with your overall healthcare?
Socioeconomic status	
SEX	Indicate sex of respondent
RACE	Race/ethnicity categories
AGE	Two-level age category

(continued)

Table 12.1 (continued)

Variable name	Questions
MARITAL	Are you: (marital status)
EDUCA	What is the highest grade or year of school you completed?
EMPLOY	Are you currently…?
INCOME	Is your annual household income from all sources:

The second step is to estimate the causal effects of exercise activities on chronic conditions (in particular, on coronary heart disease, stroke, and diabetes) for population with disabilities.[1] Disability sample is extracted based on the following question in the BRFSS: "Are you limited in any way in any activities because of physical, mental, or emotional problems?" The analysis is performed for 2016 to reflect the most recent patterns, and the final sample for this step includes 27,246 respondents. I run three multinomial logistic regression models summarized in Eqs. (12.1, 12.2, and 12.3) below.[2] The dependent variable is an indicator variable, which equals 1 if a respondent has a particular chronic condition and 0, otherwise. All independent variables are nominal with two or more levels as well. The definitions of variables can be located in Table 12.1 above.

$$\begin{aligned} CVDCORHD_i = \beta_0 + \beta_1 EXERANY_i + \beta_2 PHYSHLTH_i + \beta_3 MENTHLTH_i + \\ \beta_4 SMOKEDAY_i + \beta_5 DRNKANY_i + \beta_6 MARITAL_i + \\ \beta_7 EDUCA_i + \beta_8 EMPLOY_i + \beta_9 SEX_i + \beta_{10} RACE_i + \\ \beta_{11} AGE_i + \beta_{12} INCOME_i + \beta_{13} RFWHBMI_i, \quad i = 1\ldots 27{,}246 \end{aligned} \tag{12.1}$$

$$\begin{aligned} CVDSTROK_i = \beta_0 + \beta_1 EXERANY_i + \beta_2 PHYSHLTH_i + \beta_3 MENTHLTH_i + \\ \beta_4 SMOKEDAY_i + \beta_5 DRNKANY_i + \beta_6 MARITAL_i + \\ \beta_7 EDUCA_i + \beta_8 EMPLOY_i + \beta_9 SEX_i + \beta_{10} RACE_i + \\ \beta_{11} AGE_i + \beta_{12} INCOME_i + \beta_{13} RFWHBMI_i, \quad i = 1\ldots 27{,}246 \end{aligned} \tag{12.2}$$

$$\begin{aligned} DIABETES_i = \beta_0 + \beta_1 EXERANY_i + \beta_2 PHYSHLTH_i + \beta_3 MENTHLTH_i + \\ \beta_4 SMOKEDAY_i + \beta_5 DRNKANY_i + \beta_6 MARITAL_i + \\ \beta_7 EDUCA_i + \beta_8 EMPLOY_i + \beta_9 SEX_i + \beta_{10} RACE_i + \\ \beta_{11} AGE_i + \beta_{12} INCOME_i + \beta_{13} RFWHBMI_i, \quad i = 1\ldots 27{,}246 \end{aligned} \tag{12.3}$$

[1] Disabilities include a wide range of physical, mental, and emotional problems for respondents 18 years old and more.

[2] Multinomial logistic regression is the linear regression analysis to conduct when either dependent or independents variables are nominal with more than two levels.

12.4 Results: Current Pattern and Long–Term Trends

12.4.1 Socioeconomic Status

According to BRFSS data, 70.22% of US adults were engaged in various levels of physical activity during recreational pursuits in 1996 vs 75.76% in 2006 and 75.48% in 2016. Women consistently are more physically active than men with the strongest variation being in 2006: 60.61% of female vs 39.39% of male among people who participate in physical activities. Among ethnic groups, White non-Hispanics are most likely to participate in physical activity; however, this group of people exhibit a declining trend within the past 20 years (82.90% in 1996 vs 80.06% in 2006 vs 77.05% in 2016). Around 55%–57% of respondents who exercise are married with little variations in this parameter across two decades. Data over time show a slight decline of 1.76% in physical activity for persons with 1–3 years of college education, compared with a significant increase of 10.64% for people with a college education of 4 years and more. About 10.72% of physically active respondents earned $75,000[3] and more in 1996 vs 30.94% in 2016, while people whose annual household income from all sources is less than $49,999 demonstrate a declining pattern in exercise activity during the last 20 years.[4] Remarkably, 64.38% of physically active respondents were employed in 1996 with the decline down to 59.49% in 2006 and even further decline during the last decade down to 53.18% in 2016. Considerable age variation for exercise activities occurs within the United States across time as well. In 1996 only 16.69% of senior people (age of 65 and more) were engaged in leisure exercise, while this number has almost doubled up to 32.40% in 2016. Abundant amount of studies[5] have demonstrated that participation in a regular exercise program is an effective modality to reduce a number of functional declines associated with aging. Reductions in risk factors associated with disease states improve overall health status and contribute to an increase in life expectancy (Arriaza Jones et al. 1998). In addition, "strength training helps offset the loss in muscle mass and strength typically associated with normal aging" (Cavanagh et al. 1998). Together, these training adaptations greatly improve the functional capacity of older people, in that way improving the quality of life in this population. To summarize, the socioeconomic profile of physically active people is quite different in 2016 compared to 20 years ago. The results presented in this section contribute to a set of literature that has shown that socioeconomic characteristics should be viewed as an important determinant of health and physical activity in adults and are related to a variety of chronic diseases and mortality (e.g., Borrell et al. 2004; Pollitt et al. 2007; Drenowatz et al. 2010; Gould et al. 2006). At the same time, one should keep in mind that trying to quantify the relationship between socioeconomic

[3] It refers to annual household income from all sources.

[4] Since income brackets in BRFSS have not been subject to changes to reflect inflation, one should be cautious with interpreting these numbers.

[5] Among them there are Carroll et al. (1995), Guralnik et al. (1993), Hubley-Kozey et al. (1995), McAuley (1994), and Oddis (1996).

Table 12.2 Socioeconomic status of physically active respondents based on BRFSS data

Variable name	Value label	1996, %	2006, %	2016, %
SEX	Male	41.17	39.39	45.00
	Female	58.83	60.61	54.99
RACE	White non-Hispanic	82.90	80.06	77.05
	Black non-Hispanic	7.16	7.14	7.47
	White Hispanic	5.96	3.10	8.07
	Asian/Pacific islander	2.03	0.62	2.29
	American Indian/Alaska native	1.02	1.74	1.39
	Other non-Hispanics	0.59	6.35	0.44
AGE	18–64	82.95	77.28	66.17
	65+	16.68	20.72	32.40
MARITAL	Married	55.78	57.99	54.78
EDUCA	College 1 to 3 years	29.36	27.10	27.60
	College 4 years or more	31.08	37.78	41.72
EMPLOY	Employed (including self-employed)	64.38	59.49	53.18
INCOME	Less than $10,000	5.22	3.67	3.15
	$10,000 to $14,999	5.52	4.09	3.48
	$15,000 to $19,999	7.66	5.61	5.26
	$20,000 to $24,999	10.02	7.36	6.83
	$25,000 to $34,999	16.09	10.88	8.52
	$35,000 to $49,999	18.03	14.74	12.16
	$50,000 to $74,999	14.24	16.11	14.55
	$75,000 or more	10.72	24.39	30.94
	Don't know/not sure	5.28	5.28	6.29
	Refused	7.23	7.87	8.84

characteristics and physical activity is not an easy exercise since physical activity levels are assessed by self-report (Raudsepp and Viira 2008) and, therefore, are biased indicators (Table 12.2).

12.4.2 *Health Coverage*

As it is presented in Table 12.2, according to 1996 BRFSS data, 88% of respondents who have been engaged in physical activity during the past month have some kind of healthcare coverage, and this percentage steadily increases throughout the past 20 years reaching 93% in 2016. These results are in support of Sommers et al. (2015) who estimate national changes in self-reported coverage and access to care during the ACA's first two open enrollment periods. The authors employ a different data set, the Gallup-Healthways Well-Being Index,[6] and conclude that the

[6] Gallup-Healthways Well-Being Index is a continuously fielded daily telephone survey of US adults that includes cell phone and landline users in all 50 states and Washington, DC.

Table 12.3 Healthcare coverage status of physically active respondents based on BRFSS data

Variable name	Value label	1996, %	2006, %	2016, %
HLTHPLAN	Yes	88.12	89.24	93.15
	No	11.61	10.51	6.49
	Refused to answer	0.03	0.08	0.15
MEDICARE	Yes	20.38	n/a	37.92
TYPCOVR1	Someone else's employer	20.29	n/a	48.37
	A plan that you or someone else buys on your own	9.45	n/a	11.10
	Medicare	4.28	n/a	25.49
	Medicaid or medical assistance	4.28	n/a	7.32
	The military, CHAMPUS, or the VA	2.40	n/a	2.84
	The Indian Health Service	0.19	n/a	0.51
MEDCOST	Yes	9.97	10.26	9.05
CHECKUP	Within the past year	69.07	69.64	74.41
RATECARE	Excellent	27.51	n/a	n/a
	Very good	33.29	n/a	n/a
	Good	25.45	n/a	n/a
	Fair	6.81	n/a	n/a
	Poor	1.88	n/a	n/a

ACA enrollment is associated with significantly improved trends in self-reported coverage, access to primary care, medications, and affordability. Table 12.3 shows that 37.92% of respondents engaged in physical activity had Medicare in 2016, which is by 17.54% more than in 1996. These results are consistent with aforementioned observation on increased participation in physical activity among older men and women. Almost half of physically active population received insurance through employer in 2016 vs only 20.29% in the same category in 1996. Two decades ago 9.97% of respondents reported that there was at least one time in the past 12 months when they needed to see a doctor but could not do it because of cost; with slight variations across the last 20 years, this number went down to 9.05% in 2016. This position along with healthcare expenditures per capita and healthcare access parameter can serve as a proxy indicator to assess empirically the current patterns and long-time trends in affordability of healthcare services in the United States. While the ACA has been largely defined by its coverage expansions, its authors recognized the need to include mechanisms to slow the growth of healthcare costs (Weiner et al. 2017). According to Table 12.3, the positive impact of improved healthcare accessibility is reflected in the increasing number of people who have visited a doctor for a routine checkup within the past year: 74% in 2016 which is about 4% higher than a decade ago. Overall, the abovementioned analysis supports the set of studies which document an improved access to healthcare coverage: because of the coverage expansions enacted in the ACA, an estimated 20 million adults have gained health insurance coverage as of early 2016 (Simon et al. 2017).

12.4.3 Health Status, Chronic Conditions, and Disabilities

As it is demonstrated by CDC (2011), chronic diseases and conditions – such as heart disease, stroke, cancer, type 2 diabetes, obesity, and arthritis – are among the most common, costly, and preventable of all health problems (Barbour et al. 2017; CDC 2007). The data analysis of health status, chronic conditions, and disabilities among physically active US population reveals the following current patterns and long-term trends. Remarkably, there is a relative decline in self-perception of health status: in 1996 more than 27.15% of respondents report their health status being excellent as opposed to only 20.20% in 2016. At the same time, the percent of people who report that their physical (mental) health being not good during the past month remains just about unchanged and displays little variations around 30%. Over the past 20 years, the prevalence of chronic conditions in adults has been steadily increasing, particularly, for diabetes and arthritis. "Diabetes is the leading cause of kidney failure, lower-limb amputations other than those caused by injury, and new cases of blindness among adults" (Barbour et al. 2017; Van Cleave et al. 2010; CDC 2007). Rates of diabetes among people who perform exercise activities have been altered with the upper shift by 6.9% over the last two decades reaching out almost 10.85% in 2016. At the same time, the rate of increase is the most pronounced during the 1996–2006 time period with the growth from 3.95% to 8.16%.

Arthritis is the most common cause of disability. In their study, Barbour et al. (2017) have shown that out of the 54 million adults with doctor-diagnosed arthritis, more than 23 million say they have trouble with their usual activities because of arthritis. According to summary statistics displayed in Table 12.4, the frequency of arthritis among physically active population has jumped from 22.96% in 1996 to 34.92% in 2016. The prevalence of myocardial infarction, coronary heart disease, and stroke has been steadily increasing as well. As of 2016, 4.78% of respondents have ever had a heart attack, 4.97% have ever had angina or coronary heart disease, and 3.25% had a stroke.

Obesity is another serious health concern. According to Ogden et al. (2015), during 2011–2014 more than one-third of adults (36%), or about 84 million people, were obese.[7] The same authors also show empirically that about one in six youths (17%) aged 2 to 19 years was obese.[8] BRFSS 1996–2016 summary statistics reveal that there was a solid growth of obesity rates even among physically active population from 1996 to 2006 (26.09% and 37.87%, respectively), following the decline during the past decade down to 32.96%. The only chronic condition examined in this study, the frequency of which remained nearly unchanged during the past decade, is asthma with the rate of about 12% among people who exercise.

According to CDC (2007), health-risk behaviors such as lack of exercise or physical activity, poor nutrition, drinking too much alcohol, and tobacco use cause

[7] Defined as BMI is greater than or equal to 30 kg/m^2.

[8] Defined as BMI is greater than or equal 95th percentile.

Table 12.4 Health status, chronic conditions, and disabilities of physically active respondents based on BRFSS data

Variable name	Value label	1996, %	2006, %	2016, %
GENHLTH	Excellent	27.15	22.16	20.20
	Very good	36.32	35.57	36.50
	Good	26.12	29.03	30.13
	Fair	8.18	9.96	10.24
	Poor	2.08	2.98	2.71
PHYSHLTH	30 days	30.22	31.91	31.63
MENTHLTH	30 days	30.43	31.32	30.29
DIABETES	Yes	3.95	8.16	10.85
HAVARTH	Yes	22.96	n/a	34.92
CVDINFAR	Yes	3.85	4.51	4.78
CVDCORHD	Yes	3.90	4.86	4.97
CVDSTROK	Yes	1.85	2.79	3.25
ASTHMA	Yes	n/a	12.00	12.57
SMOKEDAY	Smoke every day or some days	45.73	36.72	30.84
RFWHBMI	Overweight and obese	26.09	37.87	32.96
QLACTLM2	Yes	n/a	19.52	19.76
USEEQUIP	Yes	n/a	5.90	8.10

much of the illness and early death related to chronic conditions. An estimated 36.5 million adults in the United States (15.1%) said they smoked cigarettes in 2015 (Agaku et al. 2014). BRFSS data reveals a significant decrease of smokers among physically active people from 45.73% in 1996 down to 30.84% in 2016.

The American Community Survey (ACS) estimates the overall rate of people with disabilities in the US population in 2015 was 12.6% (Kraus 2017). Table 12.4 shows that 19.76% of respondents who perform physical activity are limited in some way in some activities because of physical, mental, or emotional problems (versus 19.52% of respondents 10 years ago). The percent of people who exercise and also have health problems that require the use of special equipment, such as a cane, a wheelchair, a special bed, or a special telephone,[9] has upshifted from 6% in 2006 to 8.1% in 2016. In addition, one should remember that the percent of people with disabilities varies greatly by state, as do levels of people with disabilities in employment, poverty, earnings, and health behaviors. However, the details of such analysis are beyond the scope of this paper.

To summarize, the prevalence of chronic conditions among physically active population has increased considerably over the past 20 years. Multiple studies have proven empirically that chronic disease is a burden not only for the patients but also for the healthcare system overall. Those with chronic conditions, in particular with multiple diseases, have poorer health, use more health services, and spend more on healthcare (Buttorff et al., 2017).

[9] Includes occasional use or use in certain circumstances.

12.4.4 Regression Analysis

Although much physical activity research has focused on older adults who are free of disability and illness, the need still exists for a healthy aging research agenda specific to older adults with disability for prevention purposes (CDC 2016; Rosenberg et al. 2011). Promoting healthy aging among people who already have mobility disabilities has been subject to little attention. This section assesses the impact of a variety of socioeconomic and health risk factors such as lack of exercise activities, smoking, and obesity on certain chronic diseases: coronary heart disease, stroke, and diabetes. For this purpose, I utilize multinomial regression model to test Eqs. (12.1, 12.2, and 12.3) given in Sect. 12.3. The primary regressor variable is EXERANY to estimate the relationship between adults' physical activity and chronic conditions, while other independent variables are employed as controls. I begin with extracting a subsample, which reflects respondents who reported to be limited in some way in some activities because of physical, mental, or emotional problems. The analysis is performed for 2016 with the final number of observations being 27,246. The results of calibrated models specified in Eqs. (12.1, 12.2, and 12.3) are summarized in Tables 12.5, 12.6, and 12.7.

Table 12.5 contains the estimated coefficients of multinomial logistic regression analysis of exercise activities, socioeconomic factors, and obesity on coronary heart disease. A negative statistically significant effect of physical activity on coronary heart disease supports the conclusions of several papers that regular physical activity decreases the incidence of cardiovascular disease. This study makes one step further

Table 12.5 Multinomial logit regression assessment of physical activities on coronary heart disease. Dependent variable: CVDCORHD

Independent variables	Coefficient	Std. err	P-value	95% Conf. interval	
EXERANY	−0.1107	0.0404	0.0060	−0.1899	−0.0316
PHYSHLTH	0.0009	0.0022	0.6840	0.0034	0.0051
MENTHLTH	−0.0000	0.0019	0.9860	−0.0037	0.0037
SMOKEDAY	0.1207	0.0230	0.0000	0.0757	0.1658
DRNKANY	0.1488	0.0417	0.0000	0.0671	0.2305
MARITAL	−0.1182	0.0145	0.0000	−0.1465	−0.0899
EDUCA	0.0339	0.0198	0.0870	−0.0050	0.0728
EMPLOY	0.0955	0.0091	0.0000	0.0778	0.1133
SEX	−0.4452	0.0389	0.0000	−0.5215	−0.3689
RACE	−0.0277	0.0104	0.0070	−0.0480	−0.0074
AGE	0.7595	0.0417	0.0000	0.6777	0.8412
INCOME	−0.0474	0.0105	0.0000	−0.0679	−0.0269
RFWHBMI	0.2880	0.0447	0.0000	0.2004	0.3756
_CONS	−5.8656	0.2054	0.0000	−6.2683	−5.4630

Number of obs = 27,246
Prob > chi2 = 0.0000
Pseudo R2 = 0.1101

Table 12.6 Multinomial logit regression assessment of physical activities on stroke. Dependent variable: CVDSTROK

Independent variables	Coefficient	Std. err	P-value	95% Conf. interval	
EXERANY	0.0539	0.0442	0.2230	−0.0328	0.1406
PHYSHLTH	−0.0008	0.0024	0.7290	−0.0055	0.0038
MENTHLTH	0.0034	0.0021	0.0990	−0.0006	0.0074
SMOKEDAY	0.0339	0.0245	0.0000	0.0819	0.0141
DRNKANY	0.1976	0.0462	0.0000	0.1072	0.2881
MARITAL	−0.0639	0.0153	0.0000	−0.0939	−0.0339
EDUCA	−0.0269	0.0215	0.2110	−0.0691	0.0153
EMPLOY	0.1334	0.0103	0.0000	0.1133	0.1536
SEX	−0.1808	0.0430	0.0000	−0.2651	−0.0965
RACE	0.0110	0.0106	0.3000	−0.0098	0.0319
AGE	0.4468	0.0466	0.0000	0.3555	0.5380
INCOME	−0.0581	0.0115	0.0000	−0.0807	−0.0356
RFWHBMI	0.1154	0.0460	0.0120	0.2056	0.0253
_CONS	−4.6035	0.2189	0.0000	−5.0325	−4.1745

Number of obs = 27,246
Prob > chi2 = 0.0000
Pseudo R2 = 0.0769

Table 12.7 Multinomial logit regression assessment of physical activities on diabetes. Dependent variable: Diabetes

Independent variables	Coefficient	Std. err	P-value	95% Conf. interval	
EXERANY	−0.1349	0.0334	0.0000	−0.2005	−0.0694
PHYSHLTH	−0.0025	0.0018	0.1490	−0.0060	0.0009
MENTHLTH	−0.0067	0.0016	0.0000	−0.0097	−0.0036
SMOKEDAY	0.4836	0.0346	0.0000	0.4158	0.5515
DRNKANY	0.1278	0.0188	0.0000	0.0909	0.1646
MARITAL	−0.0410	0.0112	0.0000	−0.0628	−0.0191
EDUCA	−0.0102	0.0166	0.5370	−0.0427	0.0223
EMPLOY	0.0778	0.0069	0.0000	0.0642	0.0913
SEX	−0.0912	0.0326	0.0050	−0.1551	−0.0272
RACE	0.0353	0.0078	0.0000	0.0199	0.0506
AGE	0.4528	0.0362	0.0000	0.3819	0.5237
INCOME	−0.0255	0.0086	0.0030	−0.0424	−0.0086
RFWHBMI	1.2001	0.0422	0.0000	1.1175	1.2827
_CONS	−6.9553	0.1757	0.0000	−7.2996	−6.6110

Number of obs = 27,246
Prob > chi2 = 0.0000
Pseudo R2 = 0.1039

and provides empirical evidence focusing on population with disabilities. In particular, "negative relationship between exercise activities and coronary heart disease is attributed to higher expression and phosphorylation of the endothelial isoform of NO synthase, which results in a more effective radical scavenger system, a rejuvenation of the endothelium by circulating progenitor cells, and growth of preexisting coronary vessels by angiogenesis" (Linke et al. 2008; Brown 2003). The results of multinomial regression assessment are summarized in Table 12.5 below. Remarkably, self-reported physical health status does not contribute to statistically significant determinants of coronary heart chronic condition – this, in turn, goes back to Raudsepp (2008) point and questions the accuracy of self-reported data in BRFSS. On the other hand, as expected, both smoking and drinking habits are associated with increased rate of coronary heart disease prevalence. Among individuals with disabilities, female, low income, and obese people have higher chance to get exposed to chronic heart conditions as reflected by CVDCORHD indicator based on BRFSS survey data.

Moving to the discussion of the effect of exercise on stroke prevention, hypertension is recognized as the most important modifiable risk factor for both ischemic and hemorrhagic stroke (Lawes et al. 2004). A strong and well-recognized relationship exists between blood pressure and stroke risk (Collins et al. 1990). Going further, numerous studies including Paffenbarger et al. (1983), Blair et al. (1984), Pescatello et al. (1991), Gallanagh et al. (2011), Rosenberg et al. (2011), and Borrell et al. (2004) claim that physical activity is associated with reductions in blood pressure and thus is expected to positively alter a major contributor to stroke risk. Nonetheless, according to 2016 BRFSS survey data, there is no empirical proof to demonstrate statistically significant relationship between the exercise activities and a probability to have a stroke among population with disabilities. Results are summarized in Table 12.6.

The literature has shown the efficiency of exercise in the control of type 2 diabetes, being suggested as one of the best kinds of non-pharmacological treatments for its population (Asano et al. 2014). Thus Table 12.7 confirms the statistically significant negative impact of leisure-time exercise activities on the probability to be diagnosed with diabetes for individuals with both mental and physical disabilities.

Regression models summarized in Eqs. (12.1, 12.2, and 12.3) are significant at 1% significance level (Prob > chi2 = 0.0000) with pseudo R-squared being less than 12%. However, one should remember that an equivalent statistic to R-squared does not exist for logistic regression since the model estimates from a logistic regression are maximum likelihood estimates arrived at through an iterative process and thus should be interpreted with caution (Long and Freese 2006; Long 1997). To summarize, physical activity can help reduce the impact of diabetes and coronary heart decease for people with disabilities, yet according to BRFSS data as of 2016, nearly half of all adults with disabilities get no leisure-time physical activity.

12.5 Discussions, Limitations, and Further Extensions

Planning for the care of people with chronic conditions and disabilities is on the top of the research agenda as well as governmental regulations as baby boomers become eligible for Medicare. Given the growth of prevalence of chronic conditions among

US adult population demonstrated by several studies and the importance of physical activities for overall health, it becomes an interesting exercise to analyze the current patterns and long-term trends of socioeconomic, overall health status, and prevalence of chronic conditions and disabilities among physically active population. Two-decade trends presented in this study reveal the growth of chronic conditions among US adult population. Diabetes rate has more than doubled; arthritis rate has increased by 12%. There is also an increase in major chronic heart diseases, such as myocardial infarction, coronary heart disease, and stroke. Overweight and obesity rates jumped expressively over the past 20 years, although displaying a declining trend over the last decade.

For further extensions in this area, it is important to examine the aforementioned health characteristics for different levels of exercise activities. While this study focuses on population who reported in BRFSS to participate in some physical activities or exercises during the past month, "recommended activity requires meeting the CDC and the American College of Sports Medicine 1993 Physical Activity Recommendation, which states every U.S. adult should accumulate 30 min or more of moderate-intensity physical activity on most, preferably all, days of the week" (CDC 2011). Therefore, focusing on population who meet physical activity recommendations by CDC and American College of Sports, exploring the trends in the socioeconomic and overall health status as well as chronic diseases and disabilities of this population, and then comparing the results to the control group who participate in exercise activities but do not meet physical activity recommendations will serve as a valuable extension to the existing research.

Previous literature including but not limited to Wolff et al. (2005), Wolff et al. (2002), and Buttorff et al. (2017) has shown that people with multiple chronic conditions face more financial responsibilities and functional restrictions and often have worse health outcomes (Blumberg et al. 2014; Caswell et al. 2013; Paez et al. 2009). Basu et al. (2016) and Buttorff et al. (2017) have shown that people with multiple chronic conditions have higher hospital readmission rates and considerably higher healthcare expenses. Thus another extension for future agenda is to consider population with multiple chronic conditions: with this regard there might be several alternatives to approach the research question. One of them would be to extract the sample of respondents who are limited in some way and to empirically assess the impact of recommended level of physical activity on the prevalence of multiple chronic illnesses among population with disabilities. Finally, given that BRFSS is based on self-reported records, utilizing alternative data set such as Medicare population from data tables of chronic conditions for fee-for-service beneficiaries from the Centers for Medicare & Medicaid Services (CMS) and the National Health Interview Survey (NHIS) will serve to confirm the robustness of the results.

This study has several limitations that should be taken into account when using tables from this publication. Because BRFSS is a survey that relies on respondents to report on their own health, the data may be biased, i.e., underrepresent the actual prevalence of chronic condition if individuals are unaware that they have the disease. As it has been previously recognized in this paper, BRFSS underestimates non-Whites, population with less than a high school education, and those with lower income. Despite these limitations, BRFSS is a large and representative sample, which allows to estimate physical activity for subgroups, access to care, insurance coverage, and demographic information.

12.6 Concluding Remarks

In this paper, I start with examining the socioeconomic and health standings as well as prevalence of chronic conditions among physically active population within the 20 years' time span. Then I estimate the impact of exercise activities on chronic diseases among population with disabilities focusing on the most recent data available (2016). By exploring the BRFSS, this study provides a formal estimate on the impacts of 13 different characteristics factors on three chronic conditions, i.e., coronary heart disease, stroke, and diabetes. In particular, I apply a multinomial logistic regression approach to empirically test the aforementioned relationships, and the results can be summarized as follows. (1) There is 5% increase in physical activity rates among US population from 1996 to 2006 followed by stable rates around 76% over the past decade. (2) Higher number of physically active respondents have health coverage in 2016 compared to 1996. (3) There is significant decline in the number of smokers but significant increase in overweight and obese people among those who participate in exercises. (4) Rates of physically active population with some forms of disabilities remain moderately unaffected, while chronic conditions exhibit an expressive growth over the past 20 years. Overall, exercise activities have statistically significant negative impact on prevalence of coronary heart disease and diabetes.

References

Agaku, I. T., King, B. A., & Dube, S. R. (2014). Current cigarette smoking among adults-United States, 2005–2012. *Morbidity and Mortality Weekly Report, 63*(2), 29–34.

Arriaza Jones, D., Ainsworth, B. E., Croft, J. B., Macera, C. A., Lloyd, E. E., & Yusuf, H. R. (1998). Moderate leisure-time physical activity: Who is meeting the public health recommendations? A national cross-sectional study. *Archives of Family Medicine, 7*(3), 285.

Asano, R. Y., Sales, M. M., Browne, R. A. V., Moraes, J. F. V. N., Júnior, H. J. C., Moraes, M. R., & Simões, H. G. (2014). Acute effects of physical exercise in type 2 diabetes: A review. *World Journal of Diabetes, 5*(5), 659.

Barbour, K. E., Helmick, C. G., Boring, M., & Brady, T. J. (2017). Vital signs: Prevalence of doctor-diagnosed arthritis and arthritis-attributable activity limitation-United States, 2013–2015. *MMWR. Morbidity and Mortality Weekly Report, 66*(9), 246–253.

Basu, J., Avila, R., & Ricciardi, R. (2016). Hospital readmission rates in US states: Are readmissions higher where more patients with multiple chronic conditions cluster? *Health Services Research, 51*(3), 1135–1151.

Blair, S. N., & Wei, M. (2000). Sedentary habits, health, and function in older women and men. *American Journal of Health Promotion, 15*(1), 1–8.

Blair, S. N., Goodyear, N. N., Gibbons, L. W., & Cooper, K. H. (1984). Physical fitness and incidence of hypertension in healthy normotensive men and women. *JAMA, 252*(4), 487–490.

Blumberg, L. J., Waidmann, T. A., Blavin, F., & Roth, J. (2014). Trends in health care financial burdens, 2001 to 2009. *The Milbank Quarterly, 92*(1), 88–113.

Borrell, L. N., Diez Roux, A. V., Rose, K., Catellier, D., & Clark, B. L. (2004). Neighbourhood characteristics and mortality in the atherosclerosis risk in communities study. *International Journal of Epidemiology, 33*(2), 398–407.

Brown, M. D. (2003). Exercise and coronary vascular remodelling in the healthy heart. *Experimental Physiology, 88*(5), 645–658.

Brownson, R. C., Boehmer, T. K., & Luke, D. A. (2005). Declining rates of physical activity in the United States: What are the contributors? *Annual Review of Public Health, 26*, 421–443.

Buttorff, C., Ruder, T., & Bauman, M. (2017). Multiple chronic conditions in the United States. *Rand Corporation*: Santa Monica, CA, USA. Available online: https://www.rand.org/content/dam/rand/pubs/tools/TL200/TL221/RAND_TL221.pdf (accessed on 11 April 2018)

Carroll, J. F., Convertino, V. A., Wood, C. E., Graves, J. E., Lowenthal, D. T., & Pollock, M. L. (1995). Effect of training on blood volume and plasma hormone concentrations in the elderly. *Medicine and Science in Sports and Exercise, 27*(1), 79–84.

Caspersen, C. J., & Merritt, R. K. (1995). Physical activity trends among 26 states, 1986–1990. *Medicine and Science in Sports and Exercise, 27*(5), 713–720.

Caspersen, C. J., Powell, K. E., & Christenson, G. M. (1985). Physical activity, exercise, and physical fitness: Definitions and distinctions for health-related research. *Public Health Reports, 100*(2), 126.

Caswell, K. J., Waidmann, T., & Blumberg, L. J. (2013). Financial burden of medical out-of-pocket spending by state and the implications of the 2014 Medicaid expansions. *INQUIRY: The Journal of Health Care Organization, Provision, and Financing, 50*(3), 177–201.

Cavanagh, P., Evans, J., Fiatarone, M., Hagberg, J., McAuley, E., & Startzell, J. (1998). Exercise and physical activity for older adults. *Medicine and Science in Sports and Exercise, 30*, 1–29.

Centers for Disease Control and Prevention. (2001). Physical activity trends–United States, 1990–1998. *MMWR. Morbidity and Mortality Weekly Report, 50*(9), 166.

Centers for Disease Control and Prevention. (2011). National diabetes fact sheet: National estimates and general information on diabetes and prediabetes in the United States, 2010. https://www.cdc.gov/diabetes/pubs/pdf/ndfs_2011.pdf

Centers for Disease Control and Prevention. (2016). Increasing physical activity among adults with disabilities. *Disability and Health*. https://www.cdc.gov/ncbddd/disabilityandhealth/pa.html

Chowdhury, P. P. (2016). Surveillance for certain health behaviors, chronic diseases, and conditions, access to health care, and use of preventive health services among states and selected local areas—Behavioral Risk Factor Surveillance System, United States, 2012. *MMWR. Surveillance Summaries, 65*.

Collins, R., Peto, R., MacMahon, S., Godwin, J., Qizilbash, N., Hebert, P., et al. (1990). Blood pressure, stroke, and coronary heart disease: Part 2, short-term reductions in blood pressure: Overview of randomised drug trials in their epidemiological context. *The Lancet, 335*(8693), 827–838.

Dixon-Ibarra, A., & Horner-Johnson, W. (2014). Peer reviewed: Disability status as an antecedent to chronic conditions: *National health interview survey*, 2006–2012. Preventing Chronic Disease, 11.

Doughan, R. (2014). *Developmental disabilities and chronic diseases: An evaluation of an existing health promotion program in Atlanta, GA*.

Drenowatz, C., Eisenmann, J. C., Pfeiffer, K. A., Welk, G., Heelan, K., Gentile, D., & Walsh, D. (2010). Influence of socio-economic status on habitual physical activity and sedentary behavior in 8-to 11-year old children. *BMC Public Health, 10*(1), 214.

Gallanagh, S., Quinn, T. J., Alexander, J., & Walters, M. R. (2011). Physical activity in the prevention and treatment of stroke. *ISRN neurology, 2011, 1*.

Gould, E., Smeeding, T., & Wolfe, B. (2006). Trends in the health of the poor and near poor: Have the poor and near poor been catching up to the non poor in the last 25 years. In *Economics of Population Health: Inaugural Conference of the American Society of Health Economists*, Madison, WI.

Guralnik, J. M., LaCroix, A. Z., Abbott, R. D., Berkman, L. F., Satterfield, S., Evans, D. A., & Wallace, R. B. (1993). Maintaining mobility in late life. I. Demographic characteristics and chronic conditions. *American Journal of Epidemiology, 137*(8), 845–857.

Hootman, J. M., Macera, C. A., Ham, S. A., Helmick, C. G., & Sniezek, J. (2003). Physical activity levels among the general US adult population and in adults with and without arthritis. *Arthritis Care & Research, 49*(1), 129–135.

Hubley-Kozey, C. L., Wall, J. C., & Hogan, D. B. (1995). Effects of a general exercise program on passive hip, knee, and ankle range of motion of older women. *Topics in Geriatric Rehabilitation, 10*(3), 33–44.

Kraus, L. (2017). *2016 disability statistics annual report*. Durham, NH: University of New Hampshire.

Lawes, C. M., Bennett, D. A., Feigin, V. L., & Rodgers, A. (2004). Blood pressure and stroke: An overview of published reviews. *Stroke, 35*(4), 1024–1033.

Linke, A., Erbs, S., & Hambrecht, R. (2008). Effects of exercise training upon endothelial function in patients with cardiovascular disease. *Frontiers in Bioscience: a Journal and Virtual Library, 13*, 424–432.

Long J. S. (1997) Regression Models for Categorical and Limited Dependent Variables. Thousand Oaks, Calif: Sage Publications.

Long, J. S., & Freese, J. (2006). *Regression models for categorical dependent variables using Stata*. Stata Press, College Station: TX, USA.

McAuley, E. (1994). Physical activity and psychosocial outcomes. In C. Bouchard, R. J. Shephard, & T. Stephens (Eds.), *Physical activity, fitness, and health: The consensus knowledge* (pp. 551–568). Champaign: Human Kinetics.

Oddis, C. V. (1996). New perspectives on osteoarthritis. *The American Journal of Medicine, 100*(2), 10S–15S.

Ogden, C. L., Carroll, M. D., Fryar, C. D., & Flegal, K. M. (2015). *Prevalence of obesity among adults and youth: United States, 2011–2014* (pp. 1–8). Washington, DC: US Department of Health and Human Services, Centers for Disease Control and Prevention, National Center for Health Statistics.

Paez, K. A., Zhao, L., & Hwang, W. (2009). Rising out-of-pocket spending for chronic conditions: A ten-year trend. *Health Affairs, 28*(1), 15–25.

Paffenbarger, R. S., Jr., Wing, A. L., Hyde, R. T., & Jung, D. L. (1983). Physical activity and incidence of hypertension in college alumni. *American Journal of Epidemiology, 117*(3), 245–257.

Pate, R. R., Pratt, M., Blair, S. N., Haskell, W. L., Macera, C. A., Bouchard, C., & Kriska, A. (1995). Physical activity and public health: A recommendation from the Centers for Disease Control and Prevention and the American College of Sports Medicine. *JAMA, 273*(5), 402–407.

Perritt, H. H., & Perritt, H. H. (2003). *Americans with disabilities act handbook* (p. 22). New York: Aspen Publishers.

Pescatello, L. S., Fargo, A. E., Leach, C. N., & Scherzer, H. H. (1991). Short-term effect of dynamic exercise on arterial blood pressure. *Circulation, 83*(5), 1557–1561.

Pollitt, R. A., Kaufman, J. S., Rose, K. M., Diez-Roux, A. V., Zeng, D., & Heiss, G. (2007). Early-life and adult socio-economic status and inflammatory risk markers in adulthood. *European Journal of Epidemiology, 22*(1), 55–66.

Raudsepp, L., & Viira, R. (2008). Changes in physical activity in adolescent girls: A latent growth modelling approach. *Acta Paediatrica, 97*(5), 647–652.

Rosenberg, D. E., Bombardier, C. H., Hoffman, J. M., & Belza, B. (2011). Physical activity among persons aging with mobility disabilities: Shaping a research agenda. *Journal of aging research, 2011, 1.*

Schiller, J. S., Lucas, J. W., & Peregoy, J. A. (2012). Summary health statistics for US adults: National health interview survey, 2011.

Simon, K., Soni, A., & Cawley, J. (2017). The impact of health insurance on preventive care and health behaviors: Evidence from the first two years of the ACA Medicaid expansions. *Journal of Policy Analysis and Management, 36*(2), 390–417.

Sommers, B. D., Gunja, M. Z., Finegold, K., & Musco, T. (2015). Changes in self-reported insurance coverage, access to care, and health under the affordable care act. *JAMA, 314*(4), 366–374.

Talbot, L. A., Fleg, J. L., & Metter, E. J. (2003). Secular trends in leisure-time physical activity in men and women across four decades. *Preventive Medicine, 37*(1), 52–60.

US Department of Health and Human Services. (1996). Physical activity and health: A report of the Surgeon General. https://www.cdc.gov/nccdphp/sgr/index.htm

Van Cleave, J., Gortmaker, S. L., & Perrin, J. M. (2010). Dynamics of obesity and chronic health conditions among children and youth. *JAMA, 303*(7), 623–630.

Weiner, J., Marks, C., & Pauly, M. (2017). Effects of the ACA on health care cost containment. *LDI Issue Brief, 24*(4), 1–7.

Wolff, J. L., Starfield, B., & Anderson, G. (2002). Prevalence, expenditures, and complications of multiple chronic conditions in the elderly.

Wolff, J. L., Boult, C., Boyd, C., & Anderson, G. (2005). Newly reported chronic conditions and onset of functional dependency. *Journal of the American Geriatrics Society, 53*(5), 851–855.

Xu, J., Murphy, S. L., Kochanek, K. D., & Arias, E. (2016). *Mortality in the United States*, 2015.

Chapter 13
Exercise, Opportunity, and the Self-Fulfilling Prophecy

David Hollar

Abbreviations

ADA	Americans with Disabilities Act
CDC	Centers for Disease Control and Prevention
DHDS	Disability and Health Data System (CDC)
ICF	International Classification of Functioning, Disability and Health
IEP	Individualized Education Plan
NCHPAD	National Center on Health, Physical Activity, and Disability
NIDILRR	National Institute on Disability, Independent Living, and Rehabilitation Research
UD	Universal Design
UDE	Universal Design for Exercise
UDL	Universal Design for Learning

13.1 Disability and the Self-Fulfilling Prophecy

The International Classification of Functioning, Disability, and Health (ICF; WHO 2001) emphasizes the biopsychosocial interplay between body structures; body functions; the ability to participate in social activities, work, and community life based upon conditions and functioning; and the personal, social, and other environmental factors that help or hinder optimal functioning and the realization and full social integration within accepting, modifiable groups and environments. Groce (2018; Chap. 1 in this volume) stressed the insensitivity of negative social attitudes toward and stigmatization of people with disabilities, such as when people unconscionably tell someone to "just live with it." Similarly, as a volunteer disaster chaplain with the Billy Graham Evangelistic Association, I have been taught to avoid many similar stereotypical off-the-cuff statements such as "you will get over it"

D. Hollar (✉)
Health Administration, Pfeiffer University, Misenheimer, NC, USA
e-mail: David.Hollar@pfeiffer.edu

D. Hollar (ed.), *Advances in Exercise and Health for People With Mobility Limitations*, https://doi.org/10.1007/978-3-319-98452-0_13

(i.e., a traumatic event). It should be obvious to most people that the opposite is true: "No, you will not get over it." Instead, those of us who currently have minimal or no disabilities should develop a certain amount of perspective on the experiences of disability, set aside false assumptions, and take just a little extra time to make a social encounter, physical environment, or other situation less complicated and more accessible for people with disabilities.

Both Covington (1992) and Stipek (1993) discussed the problem of the self-fulfilling prophecy in educational environments, a phenomenon in which an authority figure such as a teacher develops a positive or negative opinion, justified or not, of a student based upon false preconceptions or from a limited, initial encounter/observation. In research, the same situation can arise from anecdotal observations, hence the need for random sampling and repeated measures in studies. The self-fulfilling prophecy leads to continued positive or negative evaluations even in the face of contradictory evidence (i.e., facts). The prophecy even can be based upon hearsay evidence from others to form the false impression in the decision-makers mind. Covington (1992) described strategies for avoiding this fallacy, the most important of which include the objective assessment of individual situations and the use of teams to avoid individual biases. None of these approaches are foolproof, but the decision-maker must realize their own limitations. For disabilities, this means the avoidance of false assumptions about individual capabilities. It also means the engagement of people with disabilities in equivalent sports and exercise activities that are inclusive and fair.

13.2 Disability and Related Factors: A US Southeast Regional Comparison

Approximately 57 million Americans have at least one disability (McNeil 2001; Cornell University 2013). Houtenville et al. (2013) estimated 38.4 million (12.3%) of American citizens have at least one disability and are living in the community. For most of the Pfeiffer University undergraduate recruitment demographic area, the CDC Disability and Health Data System (DHDS; http://dhds.cdc.gov/dataviews/) reports 24.2% of the population with disabilities in North Carolina, 25.7% in South Carolina, and 22.8% in Virginia. Similarly, the DHDS reports 26.6% of North Carolina, 28.1% of South Carolina, and 22.2% of Virginia veterans with disabilities. Houtenville et al. (2013) reported lower but significant percentages, 13.0%, 14.0%, and 10.8% of persons with disabilities in North Carolina, South Carolina, and Virginia, respectively. These statistical discrepancies for the numbers of persons with disabilities exist across federal databases and have been targeted for further study (Burkhauser et al. 2012).

Houtenville et al. (2013) reported an employment rate of 32.7% for all Americans with disabilities living in the community (aged 18–64), whereas the employment rate for persons without disabilities was 73.6%. For North Carolina, South Carolina, and Virginia, respectively, the rates were 30.2% versus 72.2%, 27.0% versus 71.4%, and 36.3% versus 76.5% for persons with and without disabilities. Houtenville et al. (2013) cited an employment gap of 40.8% for the United States, 42.0% for North Carolina, 44.1% for South Carolina, and 40.1% for Virginia. 2011–2012 experienced slight gap increases for the United States and South Carolina. Examining only full-time employment statistics, full-time 2012 employment for persons with and without disabilities was 19.0% versus 50.0% for the United States, 18.5% versus 49.7% for North Carolina, 16.9% versus 49.0% for South Carolina, and 20.9% versus 55.0% for Virginia. Poverty rates were more than double for persons with disabilities in each comparison (Houtenville et al. 2013).

Despite the Rehabilitation Act of 1973 (Public Law 93–111, 87 Stat. 355, H.R. 8070), Americans with Disabilities Act of 1990 (Public Law 101–336, 104 Stat. 327), Individuals with Disabilities Education Act (Public Law 101–476, 104 Stat. 1142), amendments, and related legislation, persons with disabilities experience significantly higher rates of unemployment or underemployment compared to persons without disabilities. This disparity remains the case for persons with disabilities who have advanced college degrees (Gray 2002; Hollar and Moore 2004; Hollar et al. 2008; Jones 1997; Jones and Stone 1995; Houtenville et al. 2013; U.S. Department of Labor 2007, 2008).

Disparity also prevails for veterans with disabilities. Collins et al. (2012, p. 3) studied the US Bureau of Labor Statistics employment trends for veterans and nonveterans during the 16 quarters between late 2008 and 2012. The post-9/11 veterans of Operation Enduring Freedom (Afghanistan) and Iraqi Freedom experienced 10.7% unemployment rates compared to pre-9/11 veterans (7.4%) and nonveterans aged 18 years and older (8.7%). Sixty-three percent of post-9/11 veterans were under age 35, compared to 37% of working nonveterans, and 31% of post-9/11 veterans have college degrees, compared to 36% of nonveterans (Collins et al. 2012, p. 2). The Institute for Veterans and Military Families (2013) reported comparable unemployment rates for post-9/11 veterans, with the highest unemployment rates occurring for female veterans. Lower veteran participation in higher education occurred despite expanded veterans assistance under the traditional GI Bill, Transition Assistance Program, Transition Goals Plans Success, Veterans Retraining Assistance Program, and Federal Hiring Preferences programs (Collins et al. 2012). Employment disparities remained persistent despite various Work Opportunity Tax Credits, including $4800–$9600 for employers hiring a veteran with VA disability compensation, depending on the veterans' length of unemployment (Collins et al. 2012).

Collins et al. (2012, p. 2) reported 14% of all veterans and 26% of post 9/11 veterans with disabilities. Erickson, Lee, and von Schrader (2013) analyzed 2011 American Community Survey data to obtain estimates of veteran service-connected disability, aged 21–64 years (http://www.disabilitystatistics.org/reports/acs.cfm?statistic=10). From a total US ACS sample size of 121,711 respondents and a base population of 12,049,300 veterans nationwide, they estimated that 19.1 +/− 0.32% of non-institutionalized US civilian veterans in this age range had service-connected disabilities (Erickson et al. 2013). For Pfeiffer University's North Carolina and South Carolina proximal service areas, the percentages were

21.3 +/− 1.40 (sample 4417, base 448,000) and 20.2 +/− 1.87 (sample 2408, base 243,200), respectively (Erickson et al. 2013).

Houtenville et al. (2013, p. 59) estimated 1,990,509 American civilian veterans with disabilities in 2012, 17.8% of whom lived in poverty, compared to only 7.4% poverty for 9,547,760 civilian veterans without disabilities. Civilian veterans with and without disabilities living in poverty were 17.6% versus 7.8% for North Carolina, 15.4% versus 8.5% for South Carolina, and 15.7% versus 4.7% for Virginia.

These results are similar across other US regions, although the prevalence of disabilities is highest in the Southeast, possibly due to multiple contributing factors of lower socioeconomic conditions and lower access to healthcare. These factors plus the high rates of injuries to soldiers returning from foreign conflicts illustrate the increased need for assistive devices, accessible healthcare, and accommodating exercise alternatives to benefit these populations. We can extrapolate that these needs are pervasive across all nations and cultures given the high rates of disability globally.

13.3 Bringing More Representativeness and Diversity into Health and Exercise Facilities

There are documented needs for health professionals with disabilities, including veterans with disabilities (Gray 2002; Luecking 2008; Madaus 2009), to promote life satisfaction and to reduce suicide rates for veterans and other persons with disabilities (Kaplan et al. 2009, 2012; McFarland et al. 2010; Roller 2002). The success of people with disabilities across many professions has been clearly demonstrated. Nevertheless, public and professional attitudes continue to negatively view the existence of disability as a false limitation to success in a given field. Despite attempts not to do so, the Individualized Educational Plans for students with disabilities in schools and colleges can be stigmatizing at later stages in college and career development.

Furthermore, social safety net programs to promote education and employment for people with disabilities have shown minimal long-term successes. The important linkage of education, career success, health, and exercise cannot be underestimated. Successful case closures from Vocational Rehabilitation Services programs have short job tenure (i.e., less than 6 months), with barriers to competitive employment including receipt of SSI/SSDI, mental illness, age, minority race, low education, and low self-esteem (Hayward and Schmidt-Davis 2005; Hollar et al. 2008). Furthermore, misconceptions exist in society and among university faculty on the capabilities of persons with disabilities to succeed in higher education and leadership (Beauchamp-Pryor 2012; Dowrick et al. 2005; Interagency Committee on Disability Research 2007a, b).

Weaver, Moses, and Snyder (2016) performed a controlled experiment to demonstrate the pervasiveness of the self-fulfilling prophecy. Using a basketball shooting exercise involving 127 university students, female and male, in coaching and player roles, participant coaches gave more shot attempts and higher ratings to participant players who had higher manipulated skill ratings, even when they had little or no previous basketball experience. Furthermore, higher ratings positively contributed to player performance and self-ratings. Covington (1992) and Stipek (1993) had observed these phenomena and strongly argued that proper use in human development could substantially enhance student long-term self-concepts and performance, findings that have been repeatedly replicated (Hattie 1992; Marsh et al. 2008). Furthermore, Martin (2012) provided strong evidence that these motivational strategies can be effective for youth with attention deficit hyperactivity disorder (ADHD) and with other disabilities.

Based upon these findings, there is a clear need to advance higher education, leadership, and sustained employment outcomes for persons with broad-spectrum disabilities, including the many talented injured veterans (i.e., Wounded Warriors) with service-related disabilities. Removing self-fulfilling prophecies in these public venues might be the key to broad expansion of social disability inclusion, ultimately translating to life success and positive health outcomes.

13.4 The Rehabilitation Act

The Rehabilitation Act of 1973 (Public Law 93–111, 87 Stat. 355, H.R. 8070) and its amendments advocate policy, programs, and research "to empower individuals with disabilities to maximize employment, economic self-sufficiency, independence, and inclusion and integration into society." Furthermore, the Act emphasizes "respect for individual dignity, personal responsibility, self-determination, and pursuit of meaningful careers based on informed choice; .... inclusion, integration, and full participation of the individuals; .... and support for individual and systemic advocacy and community involvement." The Rehabilitation Act promotes opportunities for people with physical, sensory, and psychological disabilities, providing them with resources, long-term assistance and resources, and peer supports to achieve and maintain careers in healthcare leadership, thereby serving as advocates and individual models of self-determination and community participation/leadership for the disability community.

The three focal domains of employment, community living and participation, and health and function were central to the 2013–2017 National Institute on Disability, Independent Living, and Rehabilitation Research (NIDILRR) Long-Range Plan (U.S. Department of Education 2013, p. 20301) Goals 1, 2, and 3:

- Goal 1: "Create a portfolio of research, development, and other activities that balances domains, populations of focus…." and "establish a balanced distribution of priorities focused on improved outcomes in the domains of employment, community living and participation, and health and function….establish a balanced distribution of priorities to address the needs of individuals with different disabilities, personal characteristics, and social circumstances….expand field-initiated research and development opportunities to support innovation." As modeled with other educational enrichment programs (e.g., STEM – Science, Technology, Engineering, and Mathematics), we need pipeline program to channel injured veterans and other persons with disabilities in community colleges and undergraduate colleges toward professional degree programs that involve them with peer supports and internship opportunities to encourage enrollment in graduate health programs and long-term supports for employment and careers in leadership positions.

- Goal 2: "Support centers and projects" that "provide for the training of emerging talent and leadership in research and development."
- Goal 3: "Promote the effective use of knowledge in areas of importance to individuals with disabilities and their families,….establish priorities that inform systems and policy development, as well as interventions and inventions, to improve individual outcomes,….support research and development activities of relevance that cut across disability categories and NIDILRR's three domains." Again, these systems can integrate previous NIDILRR center research on the employment and advancement of persons with disabilities and combine facilitators (e.g., peer mentoring, sustained long-term supports, educational training, and opportunities) to improve employment, community living, and social participation/leadership opportunities for persons with disabilities.

These priorities have been continued with the current 2018–2023 NIDILRR Long-Range Plan (draft plan available at https://www.acl.gov/sites/default/files/news%202017-05/NIDILRR-Long-Range-Plan-DRAFT.pdf). These three domains and associated goals parallel the contextual, biopsychosocial domains of the International Classification of Functioning, Disability and Health (ICF; WHO 2001), including activities and participation factors "Higher Education" (d830), "Apprenticeship" (d840), "Acquiring, Keeping, and Leaving a Job in an Appropriate Manner" (d845), "*Remunerative Employment*" (d850), "Complex Economic Transactions" (d865), "Economic Self-Sufficiency" (d870), and "Political Life and Citizenship" (d950) and environmental factors "Individual Attitudes of Acquaintances, Peers, Colleagues, Neighbors and Community Partners" (e425), "Individual Attitudes of People in Positions of Authority" (e430), "Individual Attitudes of People in Subordinate Positions" (e435), "Education and Training Services, Systems, and Policies" (e585), and "Labor and Employment Services, Systems and Policies" (e590) (WHO 2001).

Beginning with Healthy People 2010, the US Department of Health and Human Services (2000) Healthy People 2010 and Disability and Secondary Conditions Objectives 6.4 ("Increase the proportion of adults with disabilities who participate in social activities"), 6.6 ("Increase the proportion of adults with disabilities reporting satisfaction with life"), and 6.8 ("Eliminate disparities in employment rates between working-aged adults with and without disabilities") parallel the

Rehabilitation Act, NIDILRR Long-Range Plan, and ICF goals for increased employment and participation in society, including leadership roles, for persons with disabilities (Gray 2002, p. 17). Further supporting these goals were HP2010 goals for emotional support (Roller 2002, p. 71): Objectives 6.3 ("Reduce the proportion of adults with disabilities who report feelings such as sadness, unhappiness, or depression that prevent them from being active"), 6.5 ("Increase the proportion of adults with disabilities reporting sufficient emotional support"), and 6.6 ("Increase the proportion of adults with disabilities reporting satisfaction with life").

Pursuant to the current Healthy People 2020 objectives (U.S. Department of Health and Human Services 2010), objectives applicable to this effort specifically include DH-3 ("Increase the proportion of Master of Public Health" (MPH)) programs that offer graduate-level courses in disability and health. Additional applicable Healthy People 2020 objectives include DH-15 ("Reduce unemployment among people with disabilities"), DH-16 ("Increase employment of people with disabilities"), and DH-16 ("Increase the proportion of adults with disabilities who report sufficient social and emotional support"). These latter points remain to be realized: we must open the doors to people with disabilities across our institutions, businesses, and organizations so that they can take advantage of the increased health, insurance, promotion, and career development and exercise opportunities that many people without disabilities enjoy.

13.5 The Balance Between Economics, Geospatial Underserved Populations, and Despair

Recent decades have seen considerable legal and policy advances (e.g., Rehabilitation Act, ADA, IDEA, Olmstead decision) to promote the rights of people with disabilities. We still have the barrier of getting these concepts into the thoughts and practice of leaders within our political and social institutions, indeed in society as a whole given the pervasiveness of disability and every person's vulnerability to acute, temporary, or permanent disability at any point of the life journey.

Stein et al. (2017) analyzed American mortality rates by causes over the period from 1999 to 2015. Their study found dramatic and significant overdose, poisonings, and suicide increases, especially for younger cohorts (age 25–54) as well as Caucasians. In a similar study, Ivey-Stephenson et al. (2017) identified these large increases in both urban and rural economically depressed regions, but there were noticeably higher rural suicide rates across this same time period for both males and females across different race/ethnicities. Males had significantly higher rates compared to females, and Caucasian rural populations experienced dramatic increases in suicide rates (Ivey-Stephenson et al. 2017). In June 2018, the US Centers for Disease Control and Prevention presented statistics (https://www.cdc.gov/media/releases/2018/p0607-suicide-prevention.html) showing that suicide rates had increased for almost all US states and with rates increasing over 30% from 1999 to 2016 for one-half of the states.

The reasons for these increases include socioeconomic and geographic changes in populations that are negatively impacting individuals and families. The increased use of opioids and the widespread abuse of illegal, synthetic drugs to manage pain within this context represent further compounding problems. Stein et al. (2017) and Ivey-Stephenson et al. (2017) refer to this situation as an "epidemic of despair."

Changing environments have continuously impacted human populations. Many organizational leaders, including Fukuyama (1999) and Blackaby and Blackaby (2011) cite increased globalization, technology, demographic changes, socioeconomics, and cultural changes as principal drivers of these disruptions, and many people are having difficulty coping with such far-reaching changes in our societies. Whereas technology has produced many benefits, it has produced stress as well as market forces that overwhelmingly tend to favor certain groups of people over others. In this context, people with disabilities are likely to be left out of the advances, or they must wait until technologies obtain more widespread use (if at all) with lowered prices for availability. Furthermore, there is a tendency in academia for research projects to expand knowledge but not be applied to the marketplace and needy populations; this approach must change. Blackaby and Blackaby (2011) cite the need for organizational leaders with vision and compassion to reach the needs of people who are suffering. These leaders can be anyone, with or without a disability.

13.6 Implications

Title III of the Americans with Disabilities Act (ADA, Public Law 101–336, 104 Stat. 327) states that "public accommodations and commercial facilities must offer equal access and treatment, effective communication and removal of existing barriers for people with disabilities." This requirement extends to access to healthcare facilities and treatment within these facilities. Nevertheless, numerous studies have documented substantial noncompliance with ADA requirements by many healthcare facilities (Field and Jette 2007; Mudrick and Schwartz 2010).

Field and Jette (2007, p. 166) operationally defined "physical access" within the context of healthcare, citing three wheelchair consumer perspectives on accessibility barriers to ambulatory care centers, clinic examination tables, etc. Mudrick and Schwartz (2010) cited greater negative healthcare experiences among persons with basic and complex activity limitations compared to persons without limitations. Furthermore, they identify 186 ADA healthcare compliance complaints involving interior and exterior barriers to access.

Field and Jette (2007) identified several universal design features, based upon recommendations from the North Carolina Office on Disability and Health, for healthcare facilities, including power doors at interior and exterior entrances; wheelchair weight scales; seated mammography machines; alternate-handed, accessible restrooms and dressing rooms; and motorized, adjustable examination tables and chairs.

Despite these ongoing recommendations, Kersten et al. (2000) noted conflicting perceptions of consumer needs between rehabilitation patients and professionals, a phenomenon also observed by Hollar, McAweeney, and Moore (2008). In neurorehabilitation settings, Joines (2009) provided recommendations for clinician recognition of universal design in clinical settings.

More than 90% of dental practices report willingness to serve persons with disabilities (Edwards and Merry 2002), although dentists report time, equipment limitations, and physical access as principal barriers to providing adequate treatment. In a study of Canadian physician practices, McMillan et al. (2015) reported lack of training and low volume of patients with mobility limitations as barriers to acquiring accessible equipment and physical access.

Based upon these findings, there is a clear need to advance physical access to healthcare for persons with mobility limitations. There needs to be an affordable, wheelchair accessible examination table in accordance with Field and Jette's (2007, p. 167) universal design in healthcare recommendations.

In 2010, the Patient Protection and Affordable Care Act (Public Law 111–148, 42 USC 18001, 124 Statute 119, H.R. 3590) extended the provision of healthcare in the United States. The law includes a provision to amend the Rehabilitation Act to address access to medical diagnostic equipment, including examination tables and chairs, weight scales, x-ray machines and other radiological equipment, and mammography equipment. Under this amendment, the Board is authorized to develop access standards for medical diagnostic equipment in consultation with the Food and Drug Administration. The standards are to address independent access to, and use of, equipment by people with disabilities to the maximum extent possible. The Board is also responsible for periodically reviewing and updating the standards.

Specifically, the text of Section 510 of the Rehabilitation Act of 1973 as amended (29 U.S.C. §794f – Establishment of Standards for Accessible Medical Diagnostic Equipment) reads:

> (a) Standards – "Not later than 24 months after the date of enactment of the Affordable Health Choices Act, the Architectural and Transportation Barriers Compliance Board shall, in consultation with the Commissioner of the Food and Drug Administration, promulgate regulatory standards in accordance with the Administrative Procedure Act setting forth the minimum technical criteria for medical diagnostic equipment used in (or in conjunction with) physician's offices, clinics, emergency rooms, hospitals, and other medical settings. The standards shall ensure that such equipment is accessible to, and usable by individuals with accessibility needs, and shall allow independent entry to, use of, and exit from the equipment by such individuals to the maximum extent possible."
>
> (b) "Medical Diagnostic Equipment Covered – The standards issued under subsection (a) for medical diagnostic equipment shall apply to equipment that includes examination tables, examination chairs (including chairs used for eye examinations or procedures, and dental examinations or procedures), weight scales, mammography equipment, x-ray machines, and other radiological equipment commonly used for diagnostic purposes by health professionals."
>
> (c) Review and Amendment – "The Architectural and Transportation Barriers Compliance Board, in consultation with the Commissioner of the Food and Drug Administration, shall periodically review and, as appropriate, amend the standards in accordance with the Administrative Procedure Act."

Additionally, a previous NIDILRR Long-Range Plan (1999–2003) specifically stated the importance of healthcare and community access:

> "Universal design principles can be applied to the built environment, information technology, and telecommunications, transportation, and consumer products. These technological systems are basic to community integration, education, employment, health, and economic development. The application of universal design principles during the research and development stage would incorporate the widest range of human performance into technological systems. Universal design (UD) applications may result in the avoidance of costly retrofitting of systems in use and the possible reduction in the need to develop orphan products." (NIDILRR Long-Range Plan 1999–2003, pg. 53)

Such efforts will address contextual, biopsychosocial domains of the International Classification of Functioning, Disability and Health (ICF; WHO 2001), including Environmental factors "Individual Attitudes of Acquaintances, Peers, Colleagues, Neighbors and Community Partners" (e425), "Individual Attitudes of People in Positions of Authority" (e430), "Individual Attitudes of People in Subordinate Positions" (e435), "Education and Training Services, Systems, and Policies" (e585), and "Labor and Employment Services, Systems and Policies" (e590) (WHO 2001).

Further supporting these goals were HP2010 goals for emotional support (Roller 2002, p. 71): Objectives 6.3 ("Reduce the proportion of adults with disabilities who report feelings such as sadness, unhappiness, or depression that prevent them from being active"), 6.5 ("Increase the proportion of adults with disabilities reporting sufficient emotional support"), and 6.6 ("Increase the proportion of adults with disabilities reporting satisfaction with life").

13.7 Conclusion: Laws Versus Action

Despite these policies and laws, action is required. The unfortunate reality is that few of the technological advances to help people with disabilities are reaching people with major disabilities such as mobility limitations. Like the "War on Cancer," substantial resources are being provided to study particular problems related to disability. Still, what are needed are coordinated efforts, focused studies, a fast track to implementation, and social buy-in to the idea of disability inclusiveness for all activities.

Calder, Sole, and Mulligan (2018, in press) found that access to fitness centers in the United States remains poor due to a variety of factors, most notably the lack of universal design (UD) principles in these centers. Certainly many centers would welcome people with disabilities. The perception of increased costs that impact the fitness center business might be a substantial barrier for the owners of these facilities. If this is the case, then innovation and teamwork across businesses and regulatory bodies can occur to enact policy but at the same time get people to consensus for realistic solutions to the varied factors that are preventing organizations from adopting UD principles and making their facilities more accessible at both the physical as well as social/environmental levels.

Therefore, the problem ultimately falls on people working together to make great things happen: get past the regulatory hurdles, real and perceived, and move to accommodations and services that promote the health and exercise fitness of all people given each person's unique needs, promote innovation, and advocate with businesses and other institutions from a positive, not restrictive viewpoint, to make these facilities and human relationship successes possible (Blackaby and Blackaby 2011). Moreover, people with disabilities need family, peer, and social supports that genuinely motivate them to succeed in all areas of life. Hollar (2017) argued that there are only two ways to generate change, both requiring energy/resources: (a) jumping the system to a new state and (b) resonating the system with an external driving force (e.g., longitudinal supports). Therefore, let's jump and maintain help for those around us!

References

Beauchamp-Pryor, K. (2012). From absent to active voices: Securing disability equality within higher education. *International Journal of Inclusive Education, 16*(3), 283–295.

Blackaby, H., & Blackaby, R. (2011). *Spiritual leadership*. Nashville: B&H Publishing Group.

Burkhauser, R. V., Houtenville, A. J., & Tennant, J. R. (2012). Capturing the elusive working-age population with disabilities: reconciling conflicting social success estimates from the Current Population Survey and American Community Survey. *Journal of Disability Policy Studies, 24*(4), 195–205.

Calder, A., Sole, G., & Mulligan, H. (2018, in press). The accessibility of fitness centers for people with disabilities: a systematic review. *Disability and Health Journal*. https://doi.org/10.1016/j.dhjo.2018.04.002.

Collins, B., Bradley, D. H., Dortch, C., Kapp, L., & Scott, C. (2012). *Employment for veterans: Trends and programs*. Washington, DC: Congressional Research Service, Report 7-5700.

Cornell University Employment and Disability Institute. (2013). Disability Statistics. Accessed January 28, 2014 from http://www.disabilitystatistics.org.

Covington, M. V. (1992). *Making the grade: A self-worth perspective on motivation and school reform*. New York: Cambridge University Press.

Dowrick, P. W., Anderson, J., Heyer, K., & Acosta, J. (2005). Postsecondary education across the USA: Experiences of adults with disabilities. *Journal of Vocational Rehabilitation, 22*(1), 41–47.

Edwards, D.M., Merry, A.J. (2002). Disability Part 2: access to dental services for disabled people. A questionnaire survey of dental practices in Merceyside. *British Dental Journal, 193*(5), 253–255.

Erickson, W., Lee, C., & von Schrader, S. (2013). *Disability statistics from the 2011 American Community Survey (ACS)*. Ithaca: Cornell University Employment and Disability Institute (EDI) Retrieved 23 Jan 2014 from www.disabilitystatistics.org.

Field, M. J., & Jette, A. M. (2007). *The future of disability in America*. Washington, DC: National Academies Press.

Fukuyama, F. (1999). *The great disruption: Human nature and the reconstitution of social order*. New York: The Free Press.

Gray, D. B. (2002, September 20–21). Paper on social participation and employment of adults with disabilities. In U.S. Department of Health and Human Services Centers for Disease Control, U.S. Department of Education National Institute on Disability and Rehabilitation Research (Ed.), *Disability and secondary conditions, focus area 6, reports and proceedings, implementing the vision forum, Atlanta, Georgia* (pp. 17–27). Washington, DC: U.S. Department of Health and Human Services, U.S. Department of Education.

Groce, L. (2018). A testimony. In Hollar, D. (Ed.), *Advances in exercise and health for people with mobility limitations,* Chapter 1. New York: Springer.

Hattie, J. (1992). *Self concept*. Upper Saddle River: Lawrence Erlbaum.

Hayward, B. J., & Schmidt-Davis, H. (2005). *Longitudinal study of the Vocational Rehabilitation (VR) services program, third final report: The context of VR services*. Research Triangle Park: Research Triangle Institute (RTI).

Hollar, D. (2017). *Trajectory analysis in health care*. New York: Springer.

Hollar, D., & Moore, D. (2004). Relationship of substance use by students with disabilities to long-term educational and social outcomes. *Substance Use & Misuse, 39*(6), 929–960.

Hollar, D., McAweeney, M., & Moore, D. (2008). The relationship between substance use disorders and unsuccessful case closures in Vocational Rehabilitation Agencies. *Journal of Applied Rehabilitation Counseling, 39*(2), 25–29.

Houtenville, A., Brucker, D., Gould, P., Lauer, E., Santoro, J., Brennan-Curry, A., & Gianino, M. (2013). *2013 Annual Disability Statistics Compendium*. Durham: Rehabilitation Research and Training Center on Disability Statistics and Demographics, University of New Hampshire.

Interagency Committee on Disability Research. (2007a). *The Interagency Committee on Disability Research 2004–06 Report to the President and Congress*. Washington, DC: U.S. Department of Education.

Interagency Committee on Disability Research (2007b, September 19–20). *Employer perspectives on workers with disabilities: A national summit to develop a research agenda.* Washington, DC: U.S. Department of Labor.

Ivey-Stephenson, A. Z., Crosby, A. E., Jack, S. P. D., Haileyesus, T., & Kresnow-Sedacca, M.-J. (2017). Suicide trends among and within urbanization levels by sex, race/ethnicity, age group, and mechanism of death – United States, 2001–2015. *Morbidity and Mortality Weekly Report, Surveillance Summaries, 66*(18), 1–10.

Jones, G. E. (1997). Advancement opportunity issues for persons with disabilities. *Human Resource Management Review, 7*(1), 55–76.

Jones, G. E., & Stone, D. L. (1995). Perceived discomfort associated with working with persons with varying disabilities. *Perceptual and Motor Skills, 81*(3), 911–919.

Kaplan, M. S., McFarland, B. H., & Huguet, N. (2009). Firearm suicide among veterans in the general population: Findings from the National Violent Death Reporting System. *Journal of Trauma, 67*, 503–507.

Kaplan, M., McFarland, B. H., Huguet, N., & Valenstein, M. (2012). Suicide risk and precipitating circumstances among young, middle-aged, and older male veterans. *American Journal of Public Health, 102*(91), 9131–9137.

Kersten, P., George, S., McLellan, L., Smith, J. A. E., & Mullee, M. A. (2000). Disabled people and professionals differ in their perceptions of rehabilitation needs. *Journal of Public Health Medicine, 22*(3), 393–399.

Luecking, R. G. (2008). Emerging employer views of people with disabilities and the future of job development. *Journal of Vocational Rehabilitation, 29*, 3–13.

Madaus, J. W. (2009). JPED – Special issue: Veterans with disabilities. *Journal of Postsecondary Education and Disability, 22*(1), 1–2.

Marsh, H., Cheng, J., & Martin, A. J. (2008). How we judge ourselves from different perspectives: Contextual influences on self-concept formation. In M. Maehr, T. Urdan, & S. Karabenick (Eds.), *Advances in motivation and achievement* (Vol. 15, pp. 315–356). New York: Elsevier.

Martin, A. J. (2012). Attention Deficit Hyperactivity Disorder (ADHD), perceived competence, and self-worth: Evidence and implications for students and practitioners. In D. Hollar (Ed.), *Handbook on children with special health care needs* (pp. 47–72). New York: Springer.

McFarland, B. H., Kaplan, M. S., & Huguet, N. (2010). Self-inflicted deaths among women with United States military service: A hidden epidemic? *Psychiatric Services, 61*(12), 1177.

McMillan, C., Lee, J., Milligan, J., Hillier, L.M., Bauman, C. (2015). Physician perspectives on care of individuals with severe mobility impairments in primary care in Southwestern Ontario, Canada. Health Social Care Community (in press): doi:https://doi.org/10.1111/hsc.12228

McNeil, J. (2001). Americans with disabilities. Current population reports: Household studies, no. 1997. https://www.census.gov/prod/2001pubs/p70-73.pdf. Accessed 11 June 2018.

Mudrick, N. R., & Schwartz, M. A. (2010). Health care under the ADA: a vision or a mirage? *Disability and Health Journal, 3*, 233–239.

Roller, S. (2002, September 20-21). Paper on emotional support: people need people. In U.S. Department of Health and Human Services Centers for Disease Control, U.S. Department of Education National Institute on Disability and Rehabilitation Research. In *Disability and secondary conditions, focus area 6, reports and proceedings, implementing the vision forum*, Atlanta, Georgia (pp. 71–82). Washington, DC: U.S. Department of Health and Human Services, U.S. Department of Education.

Stein, E. M., Gennuso, K. P., Ugboaja, D. C., & Remington, P. L. (2017). The epidemic of despair among white Americans: trends in the leading causes of premature death, 1999-2015. *American Journal of Public Health, 107*, 1541–1547.

Stipek, D. J. (1993). *Motivation to learn: from theory to practice*. Needham Heights: Allyn & Bacon.

U.S. Department of Education. (2013). *NIDRR Long-Range Plan, 2013–2017*. Washington, DC: Author.

U.S. Department of Health and Human Services. (2000). *Healthy people 2010*. Washington, DC: Author. www.healthypeople.gov/2010/document/html/volume1/toc.htm Accessed 08.02.12.

U.S. Department of Health and Human Services. (2010). *Healthy people 2020*. Washington, DC: Author. http://Healthypeople.gov/2020/topicsobjectives2020/pdfs/HP2020objectives.pdf Accessed 08.02.12.

U.S. Department of Labor, Interagency Committee on Disability Research. (2007, September). Employer perspectives on workers with disabilities: A national summit to develop a research agenda (September 19–20, 2006). Washington, DC: Author. www.icdr.us.

U.S. Department of Labor, Interagency Committee on Disability Research (2008, June). Strengthening the intersection of demand-side and supply-side disability employment research: Toward a coordinated federal research agenda. Washington, DC: Author. www.icdr.us.

Weaver, J., Moses, J. F., & Synder, M. (2016). Self-fulfilling prophecies in ability settings. *The Journal of Social Psychology, 156*(2), 179–189.

WHO. (2001). *International Classification of Functioning, Disability and Health*. Geneva: World Health Organization.

Chapter 14
Moving Forward with Disability Health Education Innovation

David Hollar

Abbreviations

ADA	Americans with Disabilities Act
CDT	Cognitive development theory
ECAC	Eastern College Athletic Conference
ICF	International Classification of Functioning, Disability and Health
IDEA	Individuals with Disabilities Education Act
IEP	Individualized Education Program
MLB	Major League Baseball
NCAA	National Collegiate Athletic Association
NCHPAD	National Center on Health, Physical Activity, and Disability
NFL	National Football League
NIDILRR	National Institute on Disability, Independent Living, and Rehabilitation Research
UD	Universal design
UDE	Universal Design for Exercise
UDL	Universal Design for Learning

14.1 Introduction

The current situation in American K-12 education is a hypervigilant focus on standardized test performance in specific academic areas (e.g., mathematics, reading, science). Schools and teachers are rewarded and promoted based upon students' test performances. This focus has been maintained for over a decade, often at the expense of lower priority programs such as foreign language and physical education. It is falsely assumed that students will have ample time for exercise and outdoor activities following school hours, although evidence is showing that increased

D. Hollar (✉)
Health Administration, Pfeiffer University, Misenheimer, NC, USA
e-mail: David.Hollar@pfeiffer.edu

D. Hollar (ed.), *Advances in Exercise and Health for People With Mobility Limitations*, https://doi.org/10.1007/978-3-319-98452-0_14

quantities of homework, lack of parks and physical activity areas plus equipment in urban areas and especially for poverty areas, greater societal concerns for child safety and supervision outdoors, competition of television, computer games, and social media against active participation in sports, competition between fast foods and healthy food choices, and additional social pressures have strong negative impacts for physical activity in general. Consequently, the United States and many nations, both developed and developing, have experienced a significant obesity epidemic in their populations, especially school-age children with and without disabilities, since 2000.

Furthermore, students with disabilities are provided with disability-specific educational accommodations in accordance with the Americans with Disabilities Act (ADA) and the Individuals with Disabilities Education Act (IDEA) within inclusive classrooms, but they are rarely provided disability-specific exercise equipment and the opportunities to participate in intramural and extramural school team sports. We often see the news stories of a student with a disability who is elected to a school honor or position, but the vast majority of students with disabilities do not receive the school recognition or have the same college recruitment opportunities, academically or sports-related, as people without disabilities. For academics alone, people with disabilities complete high school at about the same rate as people without disabilities, but the college attendance and completion by people with disabilities are dramatically lower (Hollar and Moore 2004). For career training, another false assumption/fallacy is that people with disabilities are suitable only for low skill or vocational education programs, not business, healthcare, scientific, and professional education tracks, even when there are ample cases of people with disabilities who have excelled in these latter fields. The situation is even worse with respect to physical activity and sports, where the collegiate and overall societal/economic pressures are for high-performance athletics rather than across-the-board physical performance for entire populations.

In academics, physical activity, and social interaction in general, emphases are placed upon competition to be the best in order to achieve employment, friends, mates, promotions, and overall societal recognition. The presence of even slight disabilities (e.g., speech stutter) can become a severe negative for a job candidate facing an employment interview committee whose cognitive biases are often tuned toward any reason to reject. As Hollar (2018) outlined in Chap. 11, social selection is pervasive and works strongly against people with disabilities. Much of this problem lies in the broad human cognitive limitation of System 1 thinking (see Kahneman 2003), where even highly educated people have the tendency to rely on quick, associative reasoning with respect to past experiences instead of carefully studying with greater care detailed facts. Furthermore, body language and facial expressions, often falsely associated with lying and underlying psychological problems, may be more present with physical, developmental, and emotional disabilities, even though Ekman et al. (1999) point out that even highly trained observers can evaluate facial expressions and mannerisms only about 60–70% of the time.

Therefore, our continuing task is to promote health and opportunities for every person and their situation, including the removal of health, exercise, and nutrition barriers facing people who are living with mobility limitations and other disabilities (see Chap. 11, this volume). This process involves the exposure of fallacious reasoning and social inequalities in facilities and in sports beyond current institutional structures. Whereas a school might have only one child who uses a wheelchair or a child on occasion who requires a breathing apparatus and an assistant, school teachers and administrators can work with regional physical therapists, disability advocates, and other exercise professionals to creatively invent new sports that are inclusive, accommodate the disability, promote exercise for multiple body regions, and are fun for everyone to participate. Creativity and innovation are the answer.

It is easy for public perception to falsely view individual capabilities to be limited, not understanding that people develop at different rates and that human potential often depends upon the contexts of their environments and dynamically changing situations. Teachers can have false preconceptions of student capabilities (Stipek 1993). There can be the tendency to feel sorry for such students. Covington (1992) likewise discussed how student outcomes can be optimized for every individual situation. He also illustrated how people in general too often concentrate in groups and exclude those who are different. Such situations extend into the workplace and social environments, including exercise, where people with disabilities can be excluded either consciously or unconsciously. Like Kahneman (2003, 2011), both Goffman (1963) and Festinger (1957) outlined the respective ease of stigmatization of people based upon differences and the justification of such bad/fallacious decisions. These psychological tendencies constantly have to be countered by the social environments, activities, and facilities that we construct and maintain for our citizens.

14.2 Exercise and Universal Design

Principles of universal access for people living with mobility limitations have been published for over 20 years, yet architects have been slow to apply these principles to many facilities. Universal Design (UD) principles in healthcare and health education should emphasize adjustable exercise devices, facilities that can accommodate wheelchairs, room for physical or assistive device maneuvering, extended time for facilities usage, and adequate staff training to provide appropriate assistance. Within the educational environment, teachers should be trained on UD principles to engage students with mobility limitations into class exercise and sports activities.

The seven principles of universal design (UD; Carr et al. 2013; Story 1998; The Center for Universal Design 1997; see also https://www.cdc.gov/ncbddd/disabilityandhealth/disability-strategies.html) include the following central concepts (see also Chap. 11):

1. The design can be used by people with different types of abilities and disabilities (i.e., Equitable).
2. The design broadly accommodates different disability needs (i.e., flexibility).
3. The design is simple for the user at first contact/use (i.e., simple).

4. The design can be identified immediately by different user perceptual capabilities (i.e., perceptible).
5. The design poses minimal physical risks to the user (i.e., tolerance for error).
6. The design requires minimal physical exertion (i.e., low physical effort).
7. The design is spatially adjustable for different user needs, including space for movement around the design (i.e., size and space for approach and use).

These principles go beyond just the design and access to equipment. The Shepherd Center in Atlanta, Georgia, offers people with mobility limitations who are undergoing rehabilitation sports activities that include modified wheelchairs that are specific to each sport. Therefore, the educational environment can include alternative sports that involve all students regardless of physical functioning.

Universal Design for Learning (UDL; Center for Applied Special Technology 2011) promotes "multiple means of representation, expression, and engagement." UDL is geared more toward academics. However, its central principle of engagement directly leads to physical education activities. What is needed is a Universal Design for Exercise (UDE), perhaps modeled after the International Classification of Functioning, Disability and Health (ICF), that could be applied based upon levels of functioning to the exercise needs of anyone, regardless of disability status. Harvard University Medical Center physician and American College of Sports Medicine member Cheri Blauwet (2018) has advocated for UD in sports and exercise. Such a concept has not been clearly defined nor developed into components, but it likely would parallel the UD and UDL principles. Example priorities for UDE might include:

1. The design can be used interchangeably and smoothly through direct interaction between people with different types of abilities and disabilities.
2. The design is simple to use and to understand by the independent user.
3. The design has no more physical risks to the user than would be encountered during normal, everyday living.
4. The design readily engages all users and proportionately benefits each user regardless of ability or disability.
5. The design promotes physical activity, endurance, emotional Well-being, cooperativity, and participation for all users.
6. The design has potential for widespread adoption and interest by many different users.

These are mere suggestions for a start. Many disability and disability advocacy groups already have engaged in disruptive innovation (Drucker 1985) thinking to develop approaches that move people with even severe disabilities into many sports and exercise programs that one would not think to be modifiable. Just as one example, Corina Gutierrez uses a powered wheelchair, but she has modified Zumba exercise dancing for other wheelchair users and people with mobility limitations; she now teaches a class for people with and without disabilities (https://www.abilities.com/community/inclusive-dance-zumba.html). Just a little imagination, willpower, and community commitment to such slight changes can make exercise education and other health activities much more inclusive.

The National Center on Health, Physical Activity, and Disability (NCHPAD; https://www.aahd.us/initiatives/nchpad/) provides numerous educational, health, and exercise resources for people living with various mobility limitations, whether the condition involves spinal cord injury or birth defects. NCHPAD researchers modify routine physical activity routines to each type of disability. For instance, NCHPAD has published a series of flip chart guides such as "Exercise Guide for Persons with Limb Loss" that illustrate and concisely describe seated and other support activities for exercising various muscle groups.

Nevertheless, with any UDE model, it looks great as a set of principles but is meaningless without community buy-in and genuine implementation. As with any product, developers need to promote their produce, thereby demonstrating its value to users both with and without disabilities. It is difficult to determine how a new idea may or may not be captured by the population, even if the idea is superior to what already is available. Additionally, the constant action pace of sports is part of the attraction, and some observers might push back against the incorporation of adjustments that allow people with mobility limitations to play. The human factors elements of people's attitudes toward disability and preferences represent substantial hurdles to overcome. Still, the examination of the evolution of any sports (e.g., American football) shows substantial changes to various rules, protections, and conduct of sport over even a few decades until the sport becomes established.

14.3 Moving to an Meaningful, Alternative Sports Model

Collegiate sports, and even some high school sports, have devolved into outright businesses that involve vast associations of educational institutions, student-athletes, coaches, instructors, exercise physiologists and trainers, oversight organizations such as the National Collegiate Athletic Association (NCAA), attorneys, sports marketers, sports media, recruiters, professional sports franchises, and, unfortunately, the gambling industry. The complexity of these interactions, the exclusive nature of high athletic performance, hyper-elevated personas, the aura of great sports teams and institutions that house these teams, public demand and rational/nonrational allegiance toward teams, and obsession with "championships" can drive the focus on sports winning at all costs, even with the occasional token recognition of athletic achievements by people with disabilities. As a society, we have come a long way from 1873, when then Cornell University President Andrew White prohibited the football team from traveling and playing Michigan, stating, "I will not permit thirty men to travel 400 miles merely to agitate a bag of wind" (Shapiro 2006, p. 812). The numerous athletic scandals at higher education institutions indicate that these systems can spiral out of control due to human behavior and ethical weak links in these varied programs. They also illustrate the public preoccupation and the need to refocus on the diversity of human excellence in its infinite forms, including arbitrary definitions of disablement.

Special Olympics and the Paralympics, as embodiments of the Olympic Games, represented a start for promoting athletic achievement among people living with disabilities. These sporting events enable people living with intellectual and developmental disabilities plus people living with broad-spectrum disabilities, respectively, to engage in competitive sports and to be recognized for their efforts. These sports bring attention to the barriers faced by people living with disabilities and engage communities to encourage activities and participation by everyone, regardless of ability.

Even the college and professional sports have provided excellent examples of inclusion for people with disabilities. In 2018, the National Football League (NFL) Seattle Seahawks drafted Shaquem Griffin, who with only one hand has excelled as a linebacker and student-athlete for the undefeated University of Central Florida football team (Middlehurst-Schwartz 2018). Another notable NFL player, Tom Dempsey, kicked the longest field goal in league history in 1970 while wearing a special shoe that accommodated his birth with no toes; the record was recognized in the *Guinness Book of World Records* (McWhirter and McWhirter 1971, p. 484) and lasted for 43 years. In professional Major League Baseball, outfielder Pete Gray and pitcher Jim Abbott both were successful even when missing an arm and a hand, respectively. Several current American secondary school and college baseball players with disabilities, including catcher Luke Terry in Tennessee, are gaining recognition for their skill (Feinsand 2017).

In mountain climbing, American adventurer Erik Weihenmayer became the first blind person to successfully climb Mt. Everest in 2001. In 2006, New Zealand scientist and Paralympics champion Mark Inglis became the first double-leg amputee to successfully climb Mt. Everest. Inglis' achievement was followed by 69-year-old Chinese adventurer and cancer survivor Xia Boyu successfully climbing Mt. Everest in 2018. Boyu's achievement followed the removal of a 2017 Nepalese government safety ban on climbers who were blind or had amputations (Safi 2017, 2018). Other mountain climbers with varying disabilities have also climbed Mt. Everest and other tall peaks worldwide. Despite the difficulties involved in this and other sports, even for people without disabilities, the use of assistive devices (guides, prosthetic limbs) by these explorers with disabilities demonstrates how improved, accessible protocols and technologies can enable anyone to participate in sports. Also, note that these individuals refer to themselves as explorers and adventurers, thus demonstrating a personal drive to achieve excellence despite barriers in their social and physical environments. These are but a few examples of the growing number of courageous athletes with disabilities who have competed in the Paralympics and have successfully crossed over to Olympic and other highly competitive sports. We need more such stories to motivate people with and without disabilities to strive for their full potentials. Certainly, we see advertisements involving these and other high achievers, but our social and educational institutions need to genuinely create accessible environments that do not just make situations easier but that provide supports that motivate and guide people with disabilities to success in "abled" environments.

A number of collegiate sports programs have made accommodations for student-athletes with disabilities. Colleges such as the University of Alabama, Auburn University, Wright State University, Ohio State University, Arizona State University, University of Texas at Arlington, UCLA, Oregon State University, Edinboro University, and many others offer intramural sports in areas such as wheelchair basketball, tennis, baseball, soccer, and volleyball for students with mobility limitations and other disabilities (https://ablethrive.com/activities/21-colleges-adapted-sports-programs). Whereas such programs remain at the intramural realm, as is the case for most university students, the programs do offer the potential for individualized training, exercise, and inclusion for anyone and even preparation for more advanced sports performance such as the Paralympics. It remains to be seen if enough public awareness and interest could be generated to see the development of actual sports leagues that include both athletes with and without disabilities. The situation remains akin to the popularity of certain sports over others as well as the societal prioritization of male over female sports, etc.

Therefore, there is no certain starting point in elementary school, high school, and college environments to start or to expand more inclusive sports and exercise programs. It is probable that an earlier start in elementary schools would be best to encourage students to include peers of varying abilities and to address the need for exercise and activity as part of physical growth during this important developmental period. Still, such approaches need to be implemented at all educational levels. Pushback will come from supporters of the competitive nature of sports, but such opposition would need to be addressed by consensus agreements on rules that fairly balance each individual's needs to participate within a sport with reasonable accommodations.

Inclusive sports programs and activities must overcome both social and physical barriers as a result. The social component may be more daunting, as the human psychology and cultural aspects of behavior predominantly favor normalized situations to which most people are familiar. When dealing with the issue of disability, too many of our institutions follow a procedural viewpoint of physical access with respect to the legal letter of the law found in the Americans with Disabilities Act (ADA). Instead, what is needed is the development of, for example, inclusive basketball, where people with and without disabilities could play together, perhaps with one designated position per team for the accommodation that could be occupied by a person with or without disability who uses the accommodation. Rules could be modified accordingly. This is just an idea. Certainly efforts are being made for such inclusion across other sociocultural criteria, so why not disability?

At the minimum, we can envision sports leagues for wheelchair users or even exoskeleton sports that are fine-tuned for reasonable speed and exertion restraints. The issue of inclusion remains in such scenarios. Furthermore, many schools will face the issue of having enough players with specific disabilities to field teams. Therefore, having inclusive teams with modified sport themes and/or rules is the best solution. Costs of equipment could be minimal, even with sports-specific wheelchairs or other accommodating equipment. When we mention sport themes, imagination is required. This concept does not involve popular alternative sports (e.g., Frisbee golf) but genuine, competitive sports that can involve excitement and activity among all participating players, with and without disabilities.

The evolution of any new project, business, scientific endeavor, or sport takes time. It involves careful planning and development, building a guiding team, generating interest by players and the public, and relentless marketing at local, state, national, and international levels (Kotter 1995; Ginter et al. 2018).

Most sports follow a common arrangement of field (varying sizes), surface, two opposite goals, external and internal boundaries with time limits, rules for passing some type of "ball," rules for interactions between players and appropriate scoring, etc. The design of any sport can utilize this format and unique incorporate aspects of disability that can add to the experience and exercise/athleticism involved with the sport. Audible cues in the competition could be introduced that can involve a blind participant; conversely, visual aspects of the field can enable participation by an athlete with a hearing disability. As with ice skates in hockey for a frozen surface, fields that involve wheeled devices for participants could benefit players with mobility limitations. Sport analysis can identify features that can lead to the development of new, inclusive sports that eliminate the barriers to people living with mobility limitations and other disabilities.

The NCAA (2014) has included efforts at diversity and inclusion in its mission and strategic objectives. These efforts do mention disability, but disability has been subsumed under other inclusivity priorities and represents a long-term planning goal within these overall efforts at the organization's more recent meetings. However, at the April 26, 2016, Eastern College Athletic Conference (ECAC)/NCAA Inclusion forum, Paul Ackerman of the United States Olympic Committee Paralympic Program and Dr. Ted Fay of SUNY Cortland described several bold moves for that conference's sports programs (Ackerman and Fay 2016). Of note, they described a survey of 112 Paralympians, of whom only 14% under the age of 19 years participated in secondary school sports similarly only 14% aging 19–25 years who participated in college sports. The lateness of entry into sports programs immediately stimulated a priority on promoting and contacting secondary school coaches and administrators to involve student-athletes with disabilities as part of equal education opportunity efforts. Ackerman and Fay (2016) also cited four inclusion principles for disability in sports, including accommodations, incorporation of Paralympic events in collegiate competition and championships, and the creation of new leagues that involve student-athletes with and without disabilities in Paralympic sports. Their "Gateway to Gold" strategy seeks to identify youth with disabilities early in their schooling and to promote their athletic development (Ackerman and Fay 2016).

It probably will take some time for the ECAC and other such disability inclusion programs to reach school systems across many states and nationally. Of course, the school awareness and infrastructure supports need to be developed, and even with their implementation, the time frame of seeing more collegiate sports involvement by student-athletes with disabilities might be gradual for the next decade.

Moreover, our emphasis is not merely to reach a point where there is more recognition of disability athletic excellence but the involvement of all children, youth, and adults with disabilities in exercise, play, and sports activities at all levels. The Ackerman and Fay (2016) model might better promote this discussion between colleges, secondary and middle schools to achieve urgent action for promoting the health of people with and without disabilities.

14.4 The Human Development Component and Authority Preconceptions

The research literature clearly documents that people develop uniquely at different rates. Whereas much of psychological and physical development can be normalized along a standard curve that is fairly consistent across race, culture, and nation, the fact that outliers exist means that we address their needs as well, not that we discard them as a statistical anomaly or inconvenience. Despite research supporting several general child, adolescent, and adult developmental theories since the 1970s, educational programs have been slow in implementing these theories to assist people with their academic and athletic development. With respect to people living with disabilities, too much of the prevailing administrative and educator wisdom is that nothing can be done, they need to "just live with it" (see Chap. 1 of this volume), and that they automatically have limited life outcomes. The tendency toward normative educational programs has a long history, and even recent efforts at inclusion with the Individuals with Disabilities Education Act (IDEA) and its Individualized Education Programs (IEPs) for students have been too programmatic and lacking in innovation, often due to poor training and awareness for teachers and administrators, lack of sufficient funding, and preoccupation with school pressure groups for a bewildering array of other "inclusive" programs. As such, many educational systems have lost sight or motivation to diligently work with each student's unique needs to reach their true potential.

A variety of psychological developmental theories exist that generally describe stages of child cognitive development from initial sensory stages to socialization, moral/ethical decision making processes, and overall integration into society (Piaget 1954; Kohlberg 1973; Knefelkamp et al., 1978; Loevinger 1976; Erickson 1997; Haber 1997; Miller 1993). The stages follow age periods that coincide with milestones in cognitive development, some of which might be delayed for some children due to unique genetic/environmental interactions, specific upbringing, multiple factors contributing to developmental delay, psychological trauma, brain injury, etc. (see Hollar 2012). The general consensus among experts is that most children and youth successfully proceed through these stages and integrate into society by early adulthood. Piaget's (1954) model stresses early sensorimotor activities that are essential for both cognitive and physical activity, while all models stress human interaction, cooperativity, a sense of self, and a balance between individual motivation and cooperation with others (Miller 1993). Similarly,

Vygotsky's (1978) environmental/contextual model of development stresses the importance of social interactions, language, and the use of tools (e.g., sports, devices, etc.) for successful psychosocial development. With rapidly changing global societies, social stress, peer pressures, and technology have increasingly become areas of concern that might impact normal development for many children and youth who are exposed to these changing environments. Furthermore, the linkages between cognitive, psychosocial development and exercise/sports have been only superficially explored from a research perspective.

Marsh et al. (2007) demonstrated that the sport self-concept of middle school students had a significant, positive effect upon their later athletic performance. Jekauc et al. (2017) used a self-assessment instrument on physical self-concept and measures of motor ability and physical activity on nearly 700 German youth and adolescents. They found that motor ability significantly and indirectly affects physical activity, and vice versa, and that physical self-concept mediates both sets of interactions across several domains, including coordination and flexibility in both directions, strength on the former, and endurance on the latter direction.

Using data on over 900 children participating in the longitudinal Childhood and Beyond study, Slutzky and Simpkins (2009) found that participation in team sports, regardless of gender or ability, significantly contributed to individual positive sports self-concepts and overall self-esteem. Furthermore, Nippert and Smith (2008) found that individual characteristics, life event stressors, self-esteem, and social supports can impact how well individuals recover from athletic injuries. The authors suggest that positive supports are highly important for athletic performance as well as for continued high performance following injuries. This latter study is further supported by the strong correlations between allostatic load (e.g., stress), poor cardiovascular health, low social supports, and obesity that have been found among people living with mobility limitations (Hollar 2013; Hollar and Lewis 2015).

Given that sport self-concept and esteem are clearly important for developing children and adolescents, with lasting effects into adulthood, the importance likely is even greater for children and adolescents with disabilities. A considerable body of research also shows the importance of academic self-concepts for school success. It is very likely that the development of sport self-concept is equally critical for improved health and functioning, an issue of concern for people with disabilities due to their greater susceptibility to secondary conditions that exacerbate disability and poor health outcomes. Educators and school administrators should place greater emphasis on building positive self-concepts among students with disabilities, even as they develop into young adulthood and beyond. Unfortunately, there are many academicians and school/college programs that either ignore or blatantly maintain outmoded performance measures and assistive programs that do more than just tokenly offer basic services but that longitudinally monitor and work with students to achieve their academic and physical fitness goals.

The applications of sport self-concept naturally build upon several decades of academic self-concept research (Byrne 1996; Hattie 1992; Marsh and Craven 2006; Marsh et al. 2006; Marsh and O'Mara 2008; Shavelson et al. 1976). It is clear that the careful, positive development of student attitudes and feelings of self-concept and competence toward reading, science, mathematics, and exercise/sports work together for their overall cognitive, psychosocial, and physical development that mutually interact in one's development. It is the responsibility of educational systems to innovate away from outmoded, test-based memorization structures that detract from individualized development, the true mission of schools. Currently, the incremental, programmatic nature of educational systems fails to meet these motivational needs for people with and without disabilities, a fact that Covington (1992) voiced concern for 26 years ago.

Of additional concern is adult cognitive and psychosocial development that equivalently is related to exercise and physical activity. Albert Bandura's (1977) social learning theory is a lifelong development model that is similar to the earlier described child and adolescent developmental theories. Bandura's (1977) model likewise addresses the individual's cognitive development across attention, retention, production, and motivational processes (see also Miller 1993). Chickering's (1993) seven-stage theory of young adult development mirrors the other stage theorists (e.g., Piaget, Erickson, Loevinger) by emphasizing cognitive development, self, and social relationships. One of the most applied adult developmental theories is Robert Kegan's (1982) Constructive Development Theory (CDT) that emphasizes lifelong cognitive changes that drive development as the individual interacts with changing environments and interacts with new interpersonal relationships throughout life. Kegan's (1982) theory is of great interest because an enormous body of clinical neuroscience research clearly demonstrates that the mind and patterns of thinking change with age, learning, and life experiences, contrary to a false popular view that the brain is fully developed and static after the early 20s (Girgis et al. 2018). For educational systems from kindergarten through higher education, nontraditional education, and health behavior change education, we need to incorporate these improved theories to optimize the educational and exercise training and opportunities that can benefit people with and without disabilities across the life span.

Theories of adult development have been applied less, and higher education has a poor record of providing genuine accommodations in educational and professional development as well as for sport and exercise to people living with disabilities. A number of scientific and professional disciplines have been slow to incorporate a stronger developmental approach for the accommodation and success of students with disabilities. In both sports and academia, the emphasis remains on intensive competition within given rule boundaries, many archaic and arbitrary, when many people with "disabilities" have strong academic and even sport skills when the environment is adjusted to balance opportunity for all.

14.5 The UN Convention on the Rights of People with Disabilities

The United Nations Convention on the Rights of People with Disabilities was established in 2007–2008 and currently has been signed by over 160 nations. The convention affirms the rights of people with disabilities and their families to full participation and equal access in societies, following central principles of autonomy, dignity, independence, nondiscrimination, full participation and inclusion, respect, equality, and accessibility (United Nations 2007). Of particular note is Article 3(h) on "…evolving capacities of children with disabilities…" (United Nations 2007, p. 5). Kiuppis (2018) argues that the language of the UN Convention opens up the possibility of inclusive sport across many levels. Kiuppis (2018) differentiated inclusive education from inclusive sport given that the latter is an individual choice of participation. However, the argument identified several competing modalities for consideration, including separate and parallel activities for people with disabilities, disability sports, open inclusion, and modified activities. Kiuppis (2018) suggests the "Space, Task, Equipment, People (STEP)" approach to modifying exercise and sport activities to promote inclusion; the "people" component includes matching teams based upon similar ability at positions.

In the same volume dedicated to inclusive sports, Giese and Ruin (2018) discussed the conceptual barriers faced by people with disabilities and the structure of our social systems to identify issues of ableism and working toward greater participation. Similarly, Wickman et al. (2018) studied sport self-efficacy among children with disabilities, further supporting earlier described research showing the role of self-concepts in motivating exercise and sport inclusion for people living with disabilities.

Finally, Grenier and Kearns (2013) presented a model for incorporating disability sports in school physical education programs. The program involved revising the physical education curriculum to include disability-modified sports for full inclusion with the simultaneous education and input of students to improve attitudes toward fellow students with disabilities. The curriculum was tested with over 400 middle school students in southern New England. The results appeared to be positive as an approach to create alternative sports with a supporting goal-specific curriculum.

14.6 Summary

Over 25 years following the implementation of the Americans with Disabilities Act (ADA) and 10 years following the UN Convention on the Rights of Persons with Disabilities, people with disabilities have made steady but slow gains in reaching their dreams of full participation and recognition for sports and exercise excellence in their own, unique ways. Multiple barriers remain, particularly at the systemic level and with human behavioral preconceptions/misconceptions toward the capabilities of people living with mobility limitations and other disabilities. Efforts toward promoting physical activity and sports that are inclusive for people with and without disabilities have been planned, but moving the plans to action still encounters substantial systemic hurdles in our educational and political systems. The research evidence clearly demonstrates that the encouragement and development of academic plus sport self-concepts represent critical strategic goals for kindergarten through college education and even for lifelong education to promote physical activity, health, and exercise for people with and without disabilities of all ages. The next step involves greater action to implement innovative, inclusive sports and exercise programs in our communities, schools, colleges, and professional sports.

References

Ackerman, P., & Fay, T. (2016, April 26). *Creating new high performance opportunities for inclusive sport for athletes with Paralympic-eligible disabilities*. Indianapolis: NCAA Inclusion Forum. https://www.ncaa.org/sites/default/files/2016_Inclusion_Forum_Creating_New_Inclusive_20160426.pdf. Accessed 20 May 2018.

Bandura, A. (1977). *Social learning theory*. Englewood Cliffs: Prentice-Hall.

Blauwet, C. (2018, January 23). *Ensuring universal design in sports and exercise: A call to action*. Indianapolis: American College of Sports Medicine. http://www.acsm.org/public-information/acsm-blog/2018/01/23/ensuring-universal-design-sports-exercise. Accessed 10 May 2018.

Byrne, B. (1996). *Measuring self-concept across the lifespan: Issues and instrumentation*. Washington, DC: American Psychological Association.

Carr, K., Weir, P. L., Azar, D., & Azar, N. R. (2013). Universal design: A step toward successful aging. *Journal of Aging Research, 2013*, 324624. https://doi.org/10.1155/2013/324624.

Center for Applied Special Technology. (2011). *Universal design for learning guidelines version 2.0*. Wakefield: Author.

Chickering, A. W. (1993). *Education and identity*. San Francisco: Jossey-Bass.

Covington, M. V. (1992). *Making the grade: A self-worth perspective on motivation and school reform*. New York: Cambridge University Press.

Drucker, P. (1985). *Innovation and entrepreneurship*. New York: HarperCollins.

Ekman, P., O'Sullivan, M., & Frank, M. G. (1999). A few can catch a liar. *Psychological Science, 10*(3), 263–266.

Erikson, E. H. (1997). *The life cycle completed*. New York: W.W. Norton.

Feinsand, M. (2017, May 4). *Middle schooler catches Abbott's attention: Former Major-Leaguer calls one-armed 14-year-old's will to succeed 'fantastic'*. New York: Major League Baseball. https://www.mlb.com/news/luke-terry-catches-jim-abbotts-attention/c-228328858. Accessed 18 May 2018 .

Festinger, L. (1957). *A theory of cognitive dissonance*. Stanford: Stanford University.

Giese, M., & Ruin, S. (2018). Forgotten bodies – An examination of physical education from the perspective of ableism. *Sport in Society, 21*(1), 152–165.

Ginter, P. M., Duncan, W. J., & Swayne, L. E. (2018). *Strategic management of health care organizations* (8th ed.). San Francisco: Jossey-Bass/John Wiley.

Girgis, F., Lee, D. J., Goodarzi, A., & Ditterich, J. (2018). Toward a neuroscience of adult cognitive developmental theory. *Frontiers in Neuroscience, 12*, 4. https://doi.org/10.3389/fnins.2018.00004.

Goffman, E. (1963). *Stigma: Notes on the management of spoiled identity*. Englewood Cliffs: Prentice Hall.

Grenier, M., & Kearns, C. (2013). The benefits of implementing disability sports in physical education: A model for success. *Physical Education, Recreation & Dance, 83*(4), 23–27.

Haber, J. (1997). Understanding people across the life cycle. In Haber, J., Krainovitch-Miller, B., McMahon, A. L., & Price-Hoskins, P. (Eds.), *Comprehensive psychiatric nursing*, 5th ed. (Chapter 7, pp. 91–120). St. Louis: Mosby.

Hattie, J. (1992). *Self-concept*. Hillsdale: Lawrence Erlbaum Associates.

Hollar, D. (2012). Development from conception through adolescence: Physiological and psychosocial factors impacting children with special health care needs. In D. Hollar (Ed.), *Handbook on children with special health care needs,* chapter 15. New York: Springer.

Hollar, D. (2013). Cross-sectional patterns of allostatic load among persons with varying disabilities, NHANES: 2001–2010. *Disability and Health Journal, 6*, 177–187.

Hollar, D. (2018). A Model of Human Cognitive Biases and Complacency towards Opportunities for the dis-Abled. Chapter 11, this volume.

Hollar, D., & Lewis, J. (2015). Heart age differentials and general cardiovascular risk profiles for persons with varying disabilities: NHANES 2001–2010. *Disability and Health Journal, 8*, 51–60.

Hollar, D., & Moore, D. (2004). Relationship of substance use by students with disabilities to long-term educational and social outcomes. *Substance Use & Misuse, 39*(6), 929–960.

Jekauc, D., Wagner, M. O., Herrmann, C., Hegazy, K., & Wolf, A. (2017). Does physical self-concept mediate the relationship between motor abilities and physical activity in adolescents and young adults? *PLoS One, 12*(1), e0168539. https://doi.org/10.1371/journal.pone.0168539.

Kahneman, D. (2003). Maps of bounded rationality: Psychology for behavioral economics. *The American Economic Review, 93*(5), 1449–1475.

Kahneman, D. (2011). *Thinking, fast and slow*. New York: Farrar, Straus and Giroux.

Kegan, R. (1982). *The evolving self.* Cambridge, MA: Harvard University Press.

Kiuppis, F. (2018). Inclusion in sport: Disability and participation. *Sport in Society, 21*(1), 4–21.

Knefelkamp, L., Widick, C., & Parker, C. A. (Eds.). (1978). *Applying new developmental findings (new directions for student services, number 4)*. San Francisco: Jossey-Bass.

Kohlberg, L. (1973). The claim to moral adequacy of a highest stage of moral judgment. *Journal of Philosophy, 70*(18), 630–646.

Kotter, J. P. (1995, March–April). Leading change: Why transformation efforts fail. *Harvard Business Review.* OnPoint 4231, reprint 95204.

Loevinger, J. (1976). *Ego development: Conceptions and theories*. San Francisco: Jossey-Bass.

Marsh, H. W., & Craven, R. G. (2006). Reciprocal effects of self-concept and performance from a multidimensional perspective: Beyond seductive pleasure and unidimensional perspectives. *Perspectives in Psychological Science, 1*, 133–163.

Marsh, H. W., & O'Mara, A. (2008). Reciprocal effects between academic self-concept, self-esteem, achievement, and attainment over seven adolescent years: Unidimensional and multidimensional perspectives of self-concept. *Personality and Social Psychology Bulletin, 34*(4), 542–552.

Marsh, H. W., Craven, R. G., & Martin, A. (2006). What is the nature of self-esteem? Unidimensional and multidimensional perspectives. In M. Kernis (Ed.), *Self-esteem: Issues and answers* (pp. 16–25). New York: Psychology Press.

Marsh, H. W., Gerlach, E., Trautwein, U., Lüdtke, O., & Brettschneider, W. D. (2007). Longitudinal study of preadolescent sport self-concept and performance: Reciprocal effects and causal ordering. *Child Development, 78*(6), 1640–1656.

McWhirter, N., & McWhirter, R. (1971). *Guinness book of world records* (10th ed.). New York: Bantam.

Middlehurst-Schwartz, M. (2018, April 28). Shaquem Griffin drafted by Seahawks, becomes first one-handed player picked in NFL draft modern era. *USA Today*. https://www.usatoday.com/story/sports/nfl/draft/2018/04/28/shaquem-griffin-seattle-seahawks-nfl-draft-pick-history-hand/558751002/. Accessed 18 May 2018.

Miller, P. H. (1993). *Theories of developmental psychology* (3rd ed.). New York: W.H. Freeman.

NCAA (2014, May 5). *Inclusion of student-athletes with disabilities*. Indianapolis: Author. http://www.ncaa.org/sites/default/files/Inclusion%20of%20Student-Athletes%20with%20Disabilities.pdf. Accessed 20 May 2018.

Nippert, A. H., & Smith, A. M. (2008). Psychological stress related to injury and impact on sport performance. *Physical Medicine and Rehabilitation Clinics of North America, 19*(2), 399–418.

Piaget, J. (1954). *The construction of reality in the child*. New York: Basic Books.

Safi, M. (2017, December 30). Nepal bans blind people and double amputees from climbing Everest. *The Guardian*. https://www.theguardian.com/world/2017/dec/30/mount-everest-nepal-ban-blind-people-and-disabled. Accessed 18 May 2018.

Safi, M. (2018, May 15). Chinese double amputee conquers Everest on fifth attempt. *The Guardian*. https://www.theguardian.com/world/2018/may/15/chinese-double-amputee-conquers-everest-on-fifth-attempt. Accessed 18 May 2018.

Shapiro, F. R. (Ed.). (2006). *The Yale book of quotations.* Foreword by Epstein, J. New Haven: Yale University Press.

Shavelson, R. J., Hubner, J. J., & Stanton, G. C. (1976). Self-concept: Validation of construct interpretations. *Review of Educational Research, 46*, 407–441.

Slutzky, C. B., & Simpkins, S. D. (2009). The link between children's sport participation and self-esteem: Exploring the mediating role of sport self-concept. *Psychology of Sport and Exercise, 10*(3), 381–389.

Stipek, D. J. (1993). *Motivation to learn: From theory to practice*. Needham Heights: Allyn & Bacon.

Story, M. F. (1998). Maximizing usability: The principles of universal design. *Assistive Technology, 10*(1), 4–12.

The Center for Universal Design. (1997). *The principles of universal design, version 2.0*. Raleigh: North Carolina State University.

United Nations. (2007). *Convention on the rights of persons with disabilities*. New York: United Nations. http://www.un.org/disabilities/documents/convention/convoptprot-e.pdf.

Vygotsky, L. S. (1978). *Mind and society: The development of higher mental processes*. Cambridge, MA: Harvard University Press.

Wickman, K., Nordlund, M., & Holm, C. (2018). The relationship between physical activity and self-efficacy in children with disabilities. *Sport in Society, 21*(1), 50–63.

Index

D. Hollar (ed.), *Advances in Exercise and Health for People With Mobility Limitations*, https://doi.org/10.1007/978-3-319-98452-0

I

L

M

Printed in the United States
By Bookmasters